# Contents

Preface ........................................................ vii
1. A Contradictory Land ............................. 1
2. A Contradictory Man ............................. 5
3. Legend, Facts, and History ...................... 11
4. Before Spain ...................................... 21
5. Emergence of Spain .............................. 35
6. Bloody Years ..................................... 49
7. The Republic Revisited .......................... 65
8. Laws and Realities ............................... 73
9. Two Years to the Left ........................... 81
10. Two Years to the Right ......................... 89
11. The Plot .......................................... 105
12. Fear and Hope ................................... 115
13. Everything is Possible .......................... 123
14. Ten Months of Creativity ...................... 133
15. Two Years of Despair ........................... 147
16. Twenty-Five Million Pawns .................... 161
17. Franco's "New State" ........................... 171
18. A Paralyzed Country ........................... 189
19. Obsession with the Future ..................... 207
20. A Long Deathwatch ............................. 233
21. A King Again .................................... 251
22. The Future Is Now .............................. 285
Bibliography .................................................. 301
Index ........................................................ 313

# *Preface*

Since the death of Ferdinand VII, the last absolute monarch of Spain, in 1833, up until the death of the last (as of this writing) dictator of Spain, Francisco Franco, in 1975, 142 years had passed. During this period there were thirteen changes in political regimes, three dethroned monarchs, two exiled regents, four assassination attempts on the lives of kings, two republics, nine constitutions, five heads of state assassinated, and four civil wars—one lasting six years, another three years, the third nine months, and the fourth three years. This same period witnessed 127 governments: 109 of them within a period of 103 years, and 18 of them during the 39-year rule of Franco.

Seen from this statistical vantage point, Spaniards might appear to be sadomasochists who delight in torturing each other, creating conditions of uncertainty and anguish, and killing each other off. Yet anyone who knows Spain realizes that Spaniards are a people like any other—neither more cruel nor more irresponsible nor more ungovernable than the people of any other country.

To understand why Spain has had such a tumultuous history with so much political instability, one has to be aware of the historical conditions which have made this instability inevitable. And to understand what the Franco regime was all about, one has to know its origins. Likewise, to foresee what the future may be, one must have an idea of the forces at work present and past.

From Spain came Don Juan, Don Quixote, Goya and his *Caprichos*, Gaudí with his cathedral, Unamuno with his fear of death, Buñuel with the cruelty of his movies, and Picasso with his untiring experiments. Everything Spanish seems different. Even the Tourist Bureau coined the slogan "Spain is different" a few years ago.

But is it really? Or is it that the difference is just the product of peculiar social conditions? In this case, of course, the difference will persist until the social conditions change. This book attempts to provide the background to answer this question. It is written with the hope that soon the question will be unnecessary because the answer will have been found in the facts.

*Barcelona and Kent, Ohio, 1975-1977*

# TRANSITION
# IN SPAIN

# 1

# A Contradictory Land

It is said that the map of Spain reminds one of a bull's hide. I doubt that many readers have seen the hide of this animal. Looking at the map the Iberian Peninsula makes me think rather of an open hand, the wrist being the Pyrenees, and the five fingers, the five mountain ranges which cross the country from east to west, separating the four major rivers of the Peninsula.

If the mountains could be flattened, the surface of the country would be much greater than its actual 194,000 square miles; that is, a bit less than France, twice the United Kingdom, a fourth of Mexico, and a fifth of the United States. To go to the center, from any point on the coast, one must climb more than 3,000 feet and then descend the 1,800 feet which the Central Plateau averages. This plateau, which occupies nearly a fourth of the Peninsula, is divided into two parts by the central mountain range, and is completely different in terms of climate, landscape, and even the color of the sky, from the surrounding areas and the mountainous zones.

Looking at the map, one gets the impression that the Iberian Peninsula forms a coherent whole, a geographic unity. But in reality, it is very diverse. In climate: two-fifths of the area, to the north, is temperate, while the rest is semitropical, with very hot summers and fairly cold winters; two-thirds of the country is dry and one-third humid, with the disadvantage that the greatest humidity is in the mountainous, noncultivable regions. In landscape: the Mediterranean, with its coasts reminding one of those of Greece, gay and slow; the Cantabrian region, sad, green, Celtic; the Andalusian landscape, spectacular and bright; the plateau, arid and harsh. Next to the intimacy of the Catalan landscape, all in minor tones, is the asperity of the Aragonese and the asceticism of the Castilian landscapes. Jumps from one landscape to another are easy, because distances are short. There is no place in the country which is more than 450 miles from Madrid the capital, which is near the geographic center of Spain. There are but 660 miles from east to west, between the points farthest removed from each other. From the French frontier to Gibraltar the distance is the same; and Gibraltar is separated from Africa only by the eight miles of the furious waters of the strait.

The quadrilateral which roughly forms the Peninsula, has 1,022 miles of land frontiers and 1,954 miles of coasts. The strong Arabic influence of the Balearic Islands and the African influence of the Canary Islands increase the diversity and remind one of separate springboards, one toward the eastern Mediterranean, the other toward the western Atlantic.

A traveler, arriving by way of Cádiz, in the south, coming by ship from the other side of the Atlantic, would think that he is in a blooming country, with a warm and bright sky, and friendly and laughing people. If he arrived directly to Madrid by plane, he would think he had landed in a dry country, with great, open, naked landscapes, and austere and silent people; this, of course, outside of the capital where every human type can be found. If he arrived through Vigo, in the north, he might think that he was disembarking in Ireland, with its frequent drizzle, green hills, and sentimental people. If he set foot in Bilbao, he would suspect that he had arrived at an English port. Only if he arrived in Valencia or Barcelona would he feel as if he were where the map indicates, in a Mediterranean city such as Marseilles, Genoa, or Athens, with industry, well cared-for orchards, hurried people, kind but not cordial, and a temperate climate.

All this has contributed to there being in Spain, not only physical diversity in landscapes and climate but also great human diversity, in language, habits, political and social institutions, and even in their understanding of religion and life. There is much more difference between a Catalonian and a Galician, an Andalusian and a Basque, than between a Californian and a New Yorker, someone from Normandy and someone from Provence, or someone from Bavaria and someone from Hamburg.

The distribution of natural riches lends visibility to these human differences. Spain is not, nor has it ever been, rich. Taking advantage of water and transporting merchandise is expensive, due to the rugged terrain. A proverb says that the Catalans get bread from stones. This could be applied to all the inhabitants of Spain, as agriculture is poor. Out of 124 million acres only 52 million are arable; and due to the structure of agrarian property less than half of that is taken advantage of. There is an abundance of hunting grounds and pastures for fighting bulls.

The scarcity and irregularity of rain is the worst obstacle to a high agricultural yield. There are but 28.8 million cubic yards of water in dams (only 5.2 million forty years ago). Five million acres are irrigated and the rest are dedicated to cultivation of dry land products. The principal agricultural products of the country—exported to a great extent—are olives and oil in Andalusia and Catalonia; rice and oranges in Levanta; sugar (mainly from beets) in Aragon; also the wheat of Castile; Canarian bananas and tobacco; and wines from almost all regions (although the most famous are from Jerez and Rioja). Cattle raising is not remarkable either (except for the economically useless fighting bulls), and it does not add to exports. Fishing, on the other hand, is abundant.

In ancient times the mines of the Peninsula attracted many people; but today, with a larger population and modern industrial requirements, Spain is poor in minerals. There is coal in the north and in Andalusia, but of poor quality; iron in the outskirts of Bilbao and other places; copper and mercury in Andalusia; also potassium, silver, lead, gold, wolfram, tin, uranium, and some semiprecious stones, all in relatively small quantities. All this production of minerals is insufficient to support prosperous heavy industry. Mining companies are for the most part small and their installations antiquated.

Existing steel furnaces (in Bilbao and Sagunto) need state protection. Electricity is expensive; some 30 million kilowatt-hours are produced yearly, that is, less than 1,000 kilowatt-hours per year per inhabitant. Five million tons of iron and 14.5 million tons of carbon are extracted yearly. Petroleum production is negligible, and that of natural gas is still small.

The scarcity of electricity and coal determine part of the high industrial costs. The large company, with several hundred workers (there are only a dozen or so that employ thousands of workers), coexists with the artisan workshop and the family business. The corporation has only recently come into existence, since until a short time ago the family-owned company—passed from parents to children—predominated.

In the past few years light industries proper to a consumer society—although Spain is that only in the big cities—have increased rapidly. Cars and trucks, televisions, refrigerators, and all kinds of household appliances and plastic items are produced. Thus the proliferation of small and medium industry: there are over half a million private industries, of which one-third employ fewer than six workers and another third from seven to one hundred.

Commerce is old fashioned, and only now is it beginning to modernize in the wealthy urban neighborhoods. Spain has had a persistently deficient balance of payments, which in recent years has been compensated by foreign investments—mainly from the United States and West Germany—and above all by tourism. Every year 2.5 million tourists visit the country, that is, one tourist for every adult Spaniard.

Above industry and agriculture there is banking; it is the most powerful economic element of the country. Concentrated in a few financial institutions, it controls all industry and foreign trade by means of credit facilities and investments. This being the situation, it is no surprise that Spain has one of the lowest annual incomes in Europe: roughly 2,000 dollars per capita (in 1976). It is slowly increasing, but its distribution has never stopped being highly unequal.

Spain is not a typical underdeveloped country, nor is it an industrialized one. From an economic point of view, it is more backward than Italy, which in many ways was similar to it before 1945. It is slightly more advanced than Portugal and Greece—the two most backward countries in Europe. Argentina and Venezuela are, in terms of living conditions, closer to our times than Spain, and the great Latin American cities are more modern and prosperous than the Spanish ones.

This backwardness, disguised and forgotten under the dazzle of a golden imperial history and a great past culture, cannot be explained away merely by the mention of the poverty of soil and subsoil. It is a phenomenon with very deep social roots.

The outstretched hand that is Spain on the map, has been at times a hand that demanded, at others a beating hand, and still at others a hand groping for its way; and each Spaniard reads the lines of that hand in his own way.

# 2

# *A Contradictory Man*

Bujaraloz is a town lost in a dry, secluded, and scarce region. Its only intense moment of life came during the Civil War when an anarchist column occupied it as a center of operations. At the foot of the town belfry one finds a plaque: "After seven years of terrifying drought, which desolated these fields and ruined our estates, we inaugurate this reconstructed tower, as a firm testimony of faith in Divine Providence and of the irrevocable resolution to remain until death upon this eternally thirsty land of our elders." This inscription is perhaps the best description of the Spaniard. In it everything is included: obstinacy, arrogance, traditionalism, mystical faith, and skepticism.

Miguel de Unamuno, the Basque philosopher and one of those who has possibly best understood his compatriots, spoke of the arrogance of Spaniards. John Dos Passos and many other visitors to Spain emphasize the dignity with which the most impoverished Spaniard knows how to wear his poverty. But beside this dignity one finds an envy which leads to take sides against rather than in favor of something or someone. Possible manifestations of envy may well be the sense of possession and the veneration of virginity which characterize the relationships between the sexes. These may be summarized in the desire that no one else have what one has, that no one else be able to enjoy what one enjoys.

A survey made in Barcelona, the city of Spain with the most modern spirit, describes the personality of the present-day Spaniard in the following way: He is a Catholic, but does not practice his religion; he had his first sexual experience between the ages of thirteen and twenty with a prostitute (despite the fact that prostitution is illegal); he does not feel any obligation toward a woman with whom he has had sexual relations; he considers it very important to marry a virgin; he considers a woman who has had premarital sexual experiences as indecent; he does not place much importance on the economic factor in his selection of a wife; he believes that what bothers a woman most is lack of consideration; he prefers spiritual qualities in a woman and would not be pleased with a wife employed outside the home; he does not think that work outside the home is compatible with the functions of wife and mother, but he is in favor of divorce (which does not exist in Spain).[1] In all probability, if women were asked the same questions, the answers would be very similar. The very fact that a survey was not made among them is an indication of the persistence of the double standard which still characterizes Spanish society.

One-third of Spanish women work, but the majority of these are found in activities which require no specialization and always with less pay than men. In the entire country there are only nine women who are managers of businesses of any importance. In a country of 17 million women, there are 26,700 with a university degree (and only half of these work) and 270,000 with a high school diploma (including innumerable elementary teachers).[2] In spite of these mental attitudes, the birth rate has declined since the turn of the century from 35 to 21 per 1,000 inhabitants. Spain is a Catholic state, yet it is one of the few countries where contraceptives are sold without prescription in pharmacies.

The character of the Spaniard is as contradictory as his society and history. Thus it becomes increasingly difficult not only to classify but even to describe. There is something very hard to define which prevents the Spaniard from being considered a wretched being, despite the wretchedness so common in his life. Perhaps it is the arrogance which makes him consider himself his own judge.

> To the king, possessions and life
> one has to give, but not honor,
> which is the heritage of the soul,
> and the soul belongs only to God,

says a commoner in one of the works of Pedro Calderón de la Barca.

But while the Spaniard does not accept being judged by anyone under God, and does things "because he has the 'royal' desire to" (*porque me da la real gana*, as he says), he submits with ease, even with pleasure, to society's norms, regardless of how conventional and anachronistic they may be. There are some thirty thousand proverbs which enrich the language and impoverish the initiative of the inhabitants. For every situation and for every decision, there is a proverb to be found to justify one's behavior.

Another characteristic of the Spaniard is his desire to further humiliate the defeated. He conquers in order to annoy the one who loses more than to see his own ideas realized. He fights in elections, in civil wars, even in soccer games to prevent the triumph of his opponent more than to triumph himself. This is incorporated into the fanaticism of Spaniards, independent of their ideology. Fanaticism leads very easily to cruelty, with which the history of Spain is filled. This is especially true in its civil wars. This intolerance has led to startling extremes: when the parliament of the republic separated church and state, the head of the government announced: "Spain has ceased being Catholic"; and, thirty years later, when a publisher complained to the director of the censorship bureau that the suppression of all of his books was ruining him, the latter replied: "My friend, I prefer to see you ruined than to see you lose your soul because of my negligence."

Perhaps this fanaticism explains the surprising tenacity of Spaniards when faced with fighting or suffering. The civil wars have been long, hard, and implacable. Yet there is a realism, a type of pragmatism, which has produced, for example, this couplet of fierce skepticism:

> *The Saracens came,*
> *and crushed us with clubs,*
> *since God helps the bad*
> *when they number more than the good.*

Contradictions such as these are found in all levels of personality. It is said that the Spaniard is a mystic, but his art is implacably realistic. Honor is the theme of hundreds of works, yet it was Spain that gave birth to the picaresque novel.

The impression that the Spaniard produces at first glance does not seem so contradictory. In general, it commands respect. Stendhal said that "the Spanish character presents a complete antithesis to the French intelligence: hard, crude, inelegant, filled with savage pride, without giving the slightest importance to others' opinions." Some twenty years later, around 1850, the Englishman George Henry Borrow traveled throughout the country, distributing Protestant Bibles and winning the friendship of the gypsies. In his book *The Bible in Spain* he describes the Spaniards as he found them: "In their social relationships no other people of the world exhibits a more just sentiment of what corresponds to the dignity of human nature, nor a better comprehension of the attitude that a man should adopt toward his fellow man. It is one of the few countries of Europe where poverty is not treated with disdain nor wealth blindly worshipped." Yet for two centuries Spain has been a country where work, be it physical or intellectual, is not respected. It has been a country where to work for a living offers neither prestige nor honor despite the fact that the poor man, in order to live in Spanish poverty, has had to work extremely hard.

"When a Spaniard appears before a powerful individual, he does not bend like a rush in the wind, nor does he stammer and quake; he greets him and then comforts himself as if before a peer," wrote the Italian Pecchio. Nevertheless, in few places has there been—or is there now—so much respect for ceremonial form, so many quarrels over questions of precedence, or so much covetousness for titles and hierarchical positions.

At about the same time as Borrow, another Englishman, John Crocker, visited Spain. The latter discovered in Spaniards "an extremely surprising sobriety. I have never seen a drunken Spaniard. The lower class limits its ordinary meal to a piece of bread with an onion, an apple, or a pomegranate." Yet as soon as a Spaniard becomes a man of means, he eats with exuberance. As Crocker goes on to state: "Spain is the strangest country under the sun, since the intellectual life does not predominate in it." However, few peoples of the world have a greater capacity for abstract notions and absolute ideas.

The paradoxes do not end there. The Spaniard is religious to the point of mysticism and anticlerical to the point that for the last two centuries there has been no riot that has not been illuminated by burning churches. He is both skeptical and superstitious. He is violent in public matters, but Spain has one of the lowest rates of violent crime. He is called a passionate lover, yet Spanish women actually tend to be cold in bed, although very ardent in their possessiveness of their husbands and in the display of their jealousy. The Spaniard is called a Don Juan, but he is a rather meek husband, obedient, faithful, and resigned. He has lived most of his history under one form of censorship or another, yet the best of his literature and art is fundamentally sarcasm and social criticism.

Spanish passion manifests itself primarily in politics, with explosions that alternate with long periods of passivity and indifference. Spanish lifestyles are both very democratic, since, as a proverb says, each Spaniard carries a king within his person, and very feudal, since he always seeks to intercalate himself between a superior and several underlings. He has a profound sense of death. He knows how to die with elegance. And he makes brave, incredible efforts to survive under impossible conditions, such as the usual conditions of his country and, for example, those of the conquest of America. He is an ardent fan of both the bullfight, which is total individualism, and soccer, which is total team spirit. And thus ad infinitum.

Perhaps the clue to the Spanish character is in the fact that within the Spaniard virtues are carried to the extreme and thus converted into faults: personal worth becomes boastfulness, conviction turns to obstinacy, sobriety to paucity, pride to arrogance. These faults seem to have been more efficacious for him than the virtues in his march through history. And it is a long, dramatic history, filled with surprises, that has produced this contradictory man.

The first and most lasting of these surprises is the Spaniard himself. The Spaniard who, while being the author of history in a most pertinacious way, gives so great a sensation of being an anachronistic being, of living outside of time, of not pertaining to the period in which he lives. The Spaniard of the feudal period seems modern due to his egalitarian aspirations and democratic institutions. The Spaniard that conquered America appears Roman in his way of stating his mission. The Spaniard of today, when he speaks, and reacts, resembles more a man who, at the end of the past century, would have been considered outdated.

## NOTES

1. "Encuesta sobre el sexo masculino," *Indice*, nos. 214-15, pp. 22-25, Madrid, 1966.

2. Enrique Sopena, "La mujer en la sociedad española," *La Vanguardia Española*, Barcelona, June 21, 1969.

# 3

# *Legend, Facts, and History*

"Here lies one half of Spain; the other half murdered it." Thus Mariano Larra, a Spanish humorist at the middle of the past century, summarized the condition of his country. But it could easily have been that of any other era. Because all of Spain's history is, in certain measure, a constant struggle between one half of the country and the other, a kind of mute, intermittent, underground civil war. From time to time this internal strife emerges to the surface and reverts to a declared, dramatic, and overwhelming civil war.

In every age there has been one part of the country wanting to put it in harmony with the world, to keep pace with historical movement. Yet the other part has insisted on keeping it at the margin of history, to protect it against change. This need of one half of Spain for synchronization with the rest of the world, indicates one of the constants in the country's history, the wish to overcome its anachronism with the Western world, of which, both geographically and culturally, Spain is a part. This lack of synchronization with the remaining Western or Christian countries is apparent in every period.

Spain has always progressed either at an accelerated or a backward pace with respect to the rest of the world. For example, feudalism prospered in Spain when it was already declining in Europe, that is, in the thirteenth century, when the Christian Reconquest of the country was almost at an end. During the seven centuries of the Reconquest, the prevailing system was not feudal. Rather it was characterized by institutions that today would be called popular or democratic. In other countries these began to germinate just as Spanish feudalism emerged.

In Spain the Renaissance was prior to that of Italy, the classical heritage having been imparted by the Arabs and Jews, at the time when scholasticism dominated Europe. In the same way, the Reformation appeared in Spain before it had in Europe, with certain peculiarities. When it became generalized into its Lutheran and Calvinist forms, the Counterreformation triumphed in Spain. The heterodox Spaniards, about whom very little is ever mentioned, precisely because of the success of the Counterreformation, had similar ideas concerning the Church as did Luther, only earlier. Colonial imperialism lived in Spain prior to its appearance in England and France. Spain already possessed colonies two centuries before either of these countries.

When Europe found itself submitted to the influence of the French Revolution, Spain began a period of retrogression. When the European peoples bowed before Napoleon, looking to him as a promise of change, those who aspired to modernize Spain lined up against him. As France and England conquered their colonial empires, Spain was losing hers. When the Holy Alliance dominated Europe, the Spanish liberals held the reins in their country. But when the liberals predominated in France and England, the traditionalists fought the liberals in Spain. As the revolution in 1848 shook Europe, the conservatives held Spain in check. When Napoleon III reigned in France, the Spanish liberals ruled in Madrid, eventually overthrowing the monarchy. While Bismarck's influence was felt in Europe, left-wing Republicans governed Spain. The French Third Republic and the English liberals introduced the first steps of social progress into their countries, while Spain lived through the so-called foolish years of immobility.

The dictatorship of 1923-30 was Spain's answer to the English Labor governments and the French Cartel of the Left (and also Mussolini's Fascism). The Second Republic triumphed in a period of conservative predominance in Europe. The Civil War of 1936-39 carried the nation to an attempt at social revolution while fascism was on the ascent in the world, democracy in retrocession, and Communism in ideological decomposition under Stalin.

As the world marched toward a moderate Left after World War II, Spain stagnated under an authoritarian and antidemocratic regime. And as this regime, beginning in 1960, became more "liberal," and the country, very slowly, more radical, the world initiated a period of generalized conservatism and technocracy.

Spain, then, has never corresponded to its time. Its historical clock
has either run too fast or too slow. One of the fundamental characteristics of Spanish history, and possibly that which has most systematically gone unnoticed, is related to this permanent anachronism, that is, that Spain is the only country in modern history
that deserves the title of civilizer.

This needs to be explained. Rome conquered one-half of the
known world of its era. When the Roman Empire disintegrated, its
provinces—Gaul, Hispania, Dacia, etc.—were at the same level of
well-being, culture, technical knowledge, social structure, and institutions as Rome. Rome had civilized the territories it had conquered. It did not simply give them a few technical methods but also
a civilization, and with it, a language, a religion, and similar values.
Spain was the first country, since Rome, that possessed an empire
many times greater than its own territory. When it lost its American
colonies, these were at the same level of well-being, culture, technical knowledge, and institutions as Spain. They also had the same
social structure, language, religion, and values. Spain had civilized
its colonies at the same time that it had exploited and dominated
them.

Since Rome, there has been no other civilizing nation in the West
outside of Spain. When France and England left their colonies—
whose original population was as distinct and as backward as that of
America—the colonies were not at the same level of civilization as
their respective colonizers. But the Spanish colonies in America
were. Whether this level was a high or a low one has no importance
in classifying a nation as a civilizing one.

Why is it that Spain has been a civilizing nation while no other
modern countries have been? No satisfying answer to this question
has been found, but one might suspect that the search for it should
begin in Spain's lack of synchronization with the rest of the world.
Perhaps being a civilizer belongs to other historical periods, when
there still existed peoples that were permeable to a civilizing influence (and not merely a technical one). And Spain still pertained to
that period at the time of the conquest of America. But this may
possibly be reaching too far for an explanation.

It is easy to overlook—and it has been done often—another important characteristic of the country: the fact that the Spaniard is fundamentally a hybrid. Spain has been invaded, occupied, and civilized by a good number of peoples: Iberians, Celts, Africans, Phoenicians, Carthaginians, Greeks, Romans, Germanics, Arabs, and received many Jews. These peoples did not limit themselves to merely

passing through the country. They lived there, organized their own administration, they intermarried with the inhabitants they found, and influenced their language and beliefs.

This is true integration. The Spaniard is, then, a mestizo. Perhaps this contributes to the explanation of Spain's civilizing role, especially if one remembers that this was accomplished with people who were physically very distinct from the Spaniards. The half-breed intermingles very easily. He has a more direct and simple communication with different peoples than the man who believes he belongs to a "pure" race. To civilize, after all, is to integrate. Thus Spanish arrogance would also explain this civilizing gift of Spain. One does not integrate if he fears seeing himself absorbed. But one does integrate if he is proud enough to be sure of absorbing.

Little does the visitor, smitten with the bullfight, flamenco, and paella, realize that the image of Spain that he carries away with him is offensive to the Spaniard. Films, Goya's *Maja*, Hemingway's novels, Don Juan, the Inquisition, Carmen, and even the Civil War have contributed to making Spain a legend. Spain is just a country like any other, with one slight difference: this already-mentioned lack of synchronization with the rest of the world. This lack gives it an exotic tone that so greatly delights tourists and that today helps put a little more substance into its stewpan. But behind the legend, this mask that Spain wears, there is a country with its social structure, its problems. And in this country there are men with their daily lives, their hopes, and their frustrations.

Because of the civilizing character of Spain, knowledge of Latin American society aids a great deal in understanding Spanish society, and vice versa. In Spain, as in the majority of Spanish American countries (Spaniards do not like the adjective *Latin American*, which seems to eliminate them), one is faced with a large, submerged mass of country peasants and those uprooted from the countryside. These compose a proportion of the population that, although becoming smaller, still comprises approximately 60 percent of the Spaniards. One must add to this group the small businessmen, bureaucrats, small farmowners, and industrial day laborers. This latter group is as voluntarily submerged as is the former involuntarily, and it includes some 20 percent of the population.

Above this group, scarcely afloat, one finds a group which at times has been that of public opinion—intellectuals, professionals, the urban bureaucracy, industrialists, the church, the army, the industrial working class, and students. This group is especially concentrated in provincial capitals and several industrial zones (Catalonia, the Basque country, Valencia). These regions have traditionally been the seat of every social, political, and cultural battle of the country. The group itself comprises 18 percent of the population.

At the top lies a thin layer (2 percent of the population) of large property owners—the traditional aristocracy—the upper bourgeoisie, especially financiers, plus the top of the ecclesiastic and military hierarchies. That is, an oligarchy that controls political power and has controlled it, except for brief intervals, for the last four centuries. Spanish society is oligarchic in that political power is held in the hands of a few. Up until a few decades ago, it was linked to the possession of land. Since then, the Civil War and its aftermath has forced other oligarchic elements to emerge. But present-day Spain has been molded by this long history of aristocratic-landowning oligarchy.

In recent years, influenced by what is happening in the world, the agrarian structure has been changing to a certain degree. In spite of this, it still reminds one of the majority of Latin-American countries: of the little more than 5.9 million people who live in the countryside, 3.1 million own less than 2.5 acres (that is, less than what is necessary to sustain a family); 2.3 million possess from 2.5 to 25 acres; 450,000, from 25 to 250 acres (which is the area sufficient to support a family and produce surplus for the market); finally, 51,000 people own more than 250 acres each. In other terms: 5.4 million landowners work 40 million acres, 450,000 landowners have 31 million acres, and 51,000 own 33 million acres.[1] The proportions were even more heavily in favor of the large landed estate system prior to 1931 when the Republic was proclaimed. In recent years the growth of industry has induced many large landowners to sell their lands and devote themselves to industry and especially to banking.

Most of the cultivated land, about 96 percent, is arid. Only a small portion of it is irrigated. There is one tractor per every 500 acres of tilled land (in Italy there is one per every 175 acres). Most of the large estates are concentrated in Andalusia, Estremadura, and Castile. Small and medium-sized property holdings prevail in the periphery of the country.

All social groups depend upon this agrarian system. The degree of dependence and awareness of it vary according to the group and historical period. But any time that one or several of these groups has tried to free itself from this dependence, serious upheavals have occurred in the country, and not because of the desire for self-liberation, but rather because of strong opposition to such liberation. Spain's modern history is one of opposition to attempts to change the social structure and modernize the country.

The different degrees of success of these endeavors, added to geographic and historical differences, explain the diversity of situations and peoples in Spain: the submerged Spain, alternately submissive and rebellious, and the oligarchic Spain, alternately proudly complacent and frightened, the agricultural Spain and the industrial one, the traditional Spain and the modernizing one, the Spain of the interior and that of the periphery.

Beside these diversities, which might be called vertical, there are the horizontal ones. In the northwest is Celtic Galicia, with its own language, quite similar to Portuguese. It has its own culture and an emerging national sentiment. Next to the French border, along the Cantabrian Sea and heading southerly inward, like a wedge, is the Basque country or Euzkadi, an industrial region revolving around Bilbao, with the remaining agricultural and fishing areas. The Basques speak their own language, Euskaro, whose origin is as ancient as it is indefinite. They have a fierce national sentiment. In the northwest corner of the Peninsula, next to the French border, is Catalonia, mainly industrial, with small farms. Catalonia has a history as a small medieval Mediterranean empire, with its own language, culture, and a persistent national sentiment. In Valencia and the Balearic Islands Catalan is also spoken. Summarizing, two-fifths of the population of Spain speak, as a mother tongue, a language other than the official Spanish (or Castilian) and have more or less definite sentiments of local nationalism. Although not reaching this level of collective differentiation, other areas of the Peninsula have very pronounced characteristics. Andalusia is extremely different from Asturias, for example. One must not forget that for eighty years, in the sixteenth and seventeenth centuries, Portugal was also a part of Spain.

Spain has not absorbed these distinct nationalities, but has merely achieved their inclusion within the state. That is, in the Peninsula, Spain has not executed the same function as civilizer it had in America. The persistence of these diversities can only be explained by the difference between the social structure in the bulk of the country (Castile and Andalusia) and that of the peripheral regions with national consciousness. The Basque country lived a rural existence until the eighteenth century; at that time the industrialization process began. Since there are iron mines in this region, with coal deposits not far from it, it became the siderurgical center of the Peninsula, aided by British capital. The ancient marine tradition of the Basques, supported by siderurgy, facilitated the establishment of the only modern shipping industry in Spain. These two occurrences united to afford the Basques the opportunity to create the strongest banking industry in the country. The Basque bourgeoisie found itself amidst a feudal, backward hinterland—the rest of Spain. Basque banks have dominated most of the country's economy for a long time.

Catalonia's case is different. Since the twelfth century when it first began to acquire its own political personality, Catalonia has become a bourgeois country. The commercial and patrician bourgeoisie of Barcelona, in competition with that of Genoa and Venice, had the king as its executive arm and the nobility as its expansionist army. Its power was extended throughout the Balearic Islands, Valencia, Sardinia, Sicily, Greece, and Naples. But as the Catalonian and Castilian crowns were united at the end of the fifteenth century and the discovery of America shifted the center of gravity to the Atlantic Ocean, Catalonia declined. It rose again in the eighteenth century. The former patrician bourgeoisie had been succeeded by an industrial one, specializing in textiles. It was formed by the youngest sons of peasant families. These in turn were descendants of the serfs of the soil who were liberated by a fifteenth-century rebellion. Catalonia did not adapt to the Spanish oligarchic regime, but rather, in the nineteenth century, tried to change it. Barcelona was the seat of both the workers' movement and republicanism. The Catalonians tried to modernize Spain to echo their own modernization. They realized that their aspirations toward autonomy and their material prosperity could only be achieved in a capitalist Spain. These attempts were frustrated, since the bourgeoisie always feared going too far and thus being supplanted by the very active and energetic Catalonian middle class and proletariat. To protect themselves against this danger, the Catalonian bourgeoisie would always end up in an alliance with Spanish feudal forces. But, of course, there would emerge a conflict of interests which would split the alliance. Thus the Catalonian bourgeoisie would return to its desire to transform Spain. This process happened several times.

Thus the periphery has constantly progressed at a different pace from that of the center. The periphery has tended toward modernization, while the center has leaned toward immobility and traditionalism. The periphery is more or less bourgeois, the center, feudal. In the former, industry predominates, while in the latter, agriculture does. Add to all of these the class differences derived from the social structure, and one will understand that Spain is much more complex and less picturesque than the images the aroma of paella and the *olés*! of the spectators at the bullfight can evoke.

These diversities are also found, and logically so, in the Spaniards' way of life. They tend to reside increasingly in cities. Spanish cities are still relatively small, provincial. But with the mechanization of life, city dwellers have greater conveniences at their disposal than do inhabitants of smaller towns. Besides Madrid and Barcelona, which have exceeded two million inhabitants, there are ten cities with a population greater than 200,000. Valencia and Seville have exceeded the 600,000 mark, while Zaragoza and Bilbao are approaching 400,000. Several of these cities would double their population if the surrounding towns were permitted to consolidate to form one single municipality. But the puerile centralism of Madrid will not allow this, in order to maintain the capital's status as the largest city in the country. The housing problem is serious. Shantytowns abound, although hidden by high, large walls, where life offers no comfort other than television. Little by little the inhabitants of these hovels are being moved to enormous cheap-housing blocks. These are, at times, constructed by official "unions." But more often they are built by private companies that impose onerous conditions. The situation has become so serious that it is not rare to have to hold two jobs in order to pay the monthly installments to purchase the apartment. In a decapitalized country, this situation forces families to use up all their savings in the purchase of their living quarters, thus diminishing capital available for investment. Thus in the large cities only 30 percent of the families own their living quarters (almost always an apartment). In provincial cities, where ownership of a small house is more frequent, the figure approaches 60 percent.

Scarcely 16 percent of the families occupy dwellings with a surface larger than 110 square yards. There is running water in 96 percent of the dwellings in the Basque country, but only in 39 percent in Galicia. Some 20 percent of the dwellings (almost always in the country) do not have electricity; 72 percent do not have toilet facilities, while 79 percent do not have a bathroom. Despite the cold winters, only 26 percent of all living quarters have heat. The people who live this way belong to very different cultural levels. Ten percent of all heads of families are illiterate. Only 11 percent have enjoyed the benefits of a higher education. Probably one-half of all Spaniards, although they are technically classified as literate, almost never read or write. It is not surprising that as soon as economic opportunities arose, mass media became prevalent. Seventy-six percent of the families have a radio at their disposal while 38 percent have a television set. It is very common to find small towns with one or two television sets—one in the house of the administrator or the lord's estate and the other in a tavern. What remains after the rental or mortgage fee is paid goes toward payment of a washing machine, owned by 39 percent of the families, refrigerator, found in 35 percent of the dwellings, or car (one per every sixteen inhabitants).

One of the Spanish automobile factories, Seat (which operates under the patent of the Italian Fiat), reached the million mark in the production of vehicles in 1969. The development of automobile manufacturing (at lower prices than those of the world market for low horsepowered cars) came about prior to modernization of the highway network. This created greater traffic problems than in other European countries with more foresight. Such lack of planning is one of the characteristics of contemporary Spanish life. Everything has grown haphazardly, rapidly, without planning, but with enormous speculative transactions. This growth came to Spain some twenty years after it had come to other countries. Hence Spain had at its disposal the experiences of these countries, and could have adopted preventive measures so much more easily since its regime, being authoritarian, had no need to consult with anyone. But this was not done.

The great majority of Spaniards die within the same social class into which they were born (many even in the same house, and a great many in the same city). Only 6 percent of professionals are the sons of workers or country peasants. Only 4 percent of executives and company directors spring from such origins. Social mobility occurs only slightly more in Spain than in the most backward Latin American countries.

Every year Spain hosts millions of tourists. Most of them belong to the European middle and working classes. When the French socialist Leon Blum established, in 1936, the first paid vacations in the world, he also initiated an unforeseeable paradox. The trend began then that was to save, some thirty years later, the economy of a regime to which Blum was opposed.

But most Spaniards do not take vacations. Fifty-two percent of the inhabitants of Madrid do not leave the city during the hot summer of the plateau area. In eleven provinces some 85 percent of the inhabitants do not take advantage of a vacation to travel. Only 2 percent of all Spaniards are able to get away from both work and the city for more than forty days each year.

Spain has traditionally been a country inclined to violence: civil wars, riots, terrorism, police brutality, burning of churches, assassinations, executions, long political jail sentences. But this violence exists only in public life. In private life, despite the supposed passion of the Spaniards, violence is at a minimum. Spain occupies one of the lowest places on the list of crimes of bloodshed. Approximately

200,000 crimes are committed each year. Of these, 1,400 are directed against the security of the state (political crimes). Three thousand five hundred against decency (sexual crimes), 80,000 against property, 80,000 due to imprudence (mostly traffic offenses), and 20,000 against people (of which 800 are homicides).

## NOTE

1. Ignacio Fernández de Castro, *La demagogia de los hechos*, Paris, 1962, p. 197.

# 4

# *Before Spain*

In summarizing the history of Spain, the most difficult problem is protecting oneself from two tendencies: first, to utilize a deformed past to justify the present, and second, to judge the past with today's values. Nor is it simple to free oneself from the passions provoked by the polemics between different historical schools.[1] These have been strongest among prehistorians, perhaps because of the scarcity of material concerning Spain. There was a time when it was assumed that the first inhabitants of the Peninsula proceeded from Africa. There was another in which they were to have come from the Orient. What does seem to be proven is that the Neanderthalians occupied the entire Peninsula, which they reached by way of the Pyrenees. Then the Cro-Magnons lived there, followed by the Magdalenians, who left the rupestrian paintings in the caves of Altamira. After the great climactic transformations of the seventh millenium before Christ, other peoples appeared, who seem to have imported agriculture. It was probably Spanish copper that had attracted them, just as later it was tin that attracted the peoples that worked in bronze (nineteenth to fifteenth centuries B.C.), and later the Phoenicians. These established commerce with the Tharshis of the Bible in western Andalusia (tenth century B.C.). The Greeks established colonies in the northeast (seventh century B.C.), such as Emporion (present-day Ampurias).

Meanwhile, in the ninth century B.C., the Celts arrived via the Western portion of the isthmus Spain shares with France, the traditional route taken by invaders from the north. The Celts had diffused the use of iron throughout the entire northern portion of the Peninsula. Thus at the beginning of the historical era, one finds two great branches, the Celts in the north and the Iberians (the name given to the diverse inhabitants along the coasts) in the Andalusian and Mediterranean periphery. To facilitate matters, the inhabitants of the plateau region were called Celtiberians, although there is no proof that they were the product of a fusion between the two aforementioned branches.

It was in the heat of the Second Punic War (third century B.C.) that the Peninsula entered history. The Carthaginians had established themselves in various sites along the coast. They recruited many soldiers for Hannibal's troups. In order to counterattack them, the Romans entered the way of the Pyrenees and conquered the Carthaginians. Rapidly the Peninsula was occupied by Roman legions; it was divided into three provinces: Lusitania (west), Betica (south and center), and Tarraconensis (the Mediterranean and north). The presence of Rome lasted for seven centuries. The resistance of the inhabitants of the interior determined from the beginning the concentration of the population in cities. This in turn led to the development of municipal life. Roads, aqueducts, and temples were constructed, financed by the commerce of the provinces with Rome in metals, olive oil, cereals, and wines. The heads of the tribes became great landowners, while Roman capitalists acquired land. Thus latifundium worked by slave labor reigned throughout the entire Peninsula.

There were two basic social classes. The first was that of the *seniores*, the proprietors who resided in the cities or in their villas, and who participated in the mercantile capitalism of the period. The second was that of the *humiliores*, the masses that worked the land and struggled with serfdom, or a type of tenant-farming system. The *seniores* were considered Romans (Caracalla gave the "Spaniards" the rights of citizenship in 212 A.D.). In all, there were some six million inhabitants.

The gap between *seniores* and *humiliores* was bridged by the inhabitants of the cities, of local origin, but romanized. These were called the *hispani*, or Hispano-Romans. From this rank rose some of the illustrious men of Rome: the writers Seneca, Marcial, Lucan, and Quintilian, plus the emperors Trajan and Adrian. Soon the echo of Christianity resounded in the cities. Legend has it that it was brought to the Peninsula by the apostles Saint James, in the north (buried at Compostela, according to popular belief), and Saint Paul, in the Mediterranean region.

The fifth century brought with it a Germanic invasion. Rome was unable to forestall it and summoned the aid of the Visigoths, who had established themselves in the south of France. The Visigoths entered Spain as allies of Rome to combat the Germanics that had preceded them. They succeeded in forcing some to flee to Africa, namely, the Alans and Vandals. Meanwhile they managed to corner the Suevi in Galicia. The Visigoths finally established their capital at Toledo.

The Visigoths, or Goths, were a minority. They numbered approximately one hundred thousand, yet they governed the four million Hispano-Romans. The Goths divided among themselves two-thirds of the cultivated land. They lived apart (the cities were divided into an Hispanic section and a Gothic one). The Goths commanded and the *hispani*, especially the priests, governed. The church bridged the gap between the two sides. It is from this point in history that the long alliance between the church, the crown, and the latifundia is derived. The cities began to decline, while the monetary economy was almost paralyzed.

The system, which was never very strong, weakened within two centuries. The army, formed by discontented peasants, frustrated citizens, and commanded by lords who had become softened by their wealth, could not withstand the force of twelve thousand Arabs and Berbers who landed in the south in 711. These had come from Africa and were strongly inspired by Islamic expansionism, which was enjoying unprecedented success.

In less than five years, almost the entire Peninsula, except for the Pyrenean and Cantabrian fringes, found itself under Islamic dominance. This dominion was supported by the results of what can well be called a social revolution, during the heat of the invasion. The Hispano-Roman people rebelled against the estateholders and the rulers. The Hispanic masses retained their recovered lands. Only the lands of those who resisted or fled were expropriated by the Arabs.

The invaders originated from two distinct peoples: the Arabs and the Berbers. The former advanced a system of tolerance wherever they settled. The Hispano-Romans (who were called Mozarabs) preserved their religion, their language, and their municipal authorities. The Berbers, however, who were novices to Islam and hence more fanatical, were responsible for many more conversions (the converts were called *Muladíes*). Also, in the areas of Berber dominance, the life conditions of Hispano-Romans were more difficult. The existence of the two branches of invaders accounted for a division of authority and resulted in a mute civil war. This continued until an Omeyan prince, Abderraman I (765-788), a fugitive from the Orient where his family had just lost the caliphate, arrived in Spain and raised himself to power. He then proclaimed this portion of the empire as independent of the east. Abderraman III (912-961) established its own caliphate, with its capital at Cordova. This Caliphate lasted for two and a half centuries, and at certain times was the most wealthy, powerful, and advanced state of Europe.

The Goths who had taken refuge in the north organized bands that fought against the Arabs. The Gothic refugees in Asturias vindicated the continuation of the Visigothic monarch. While one fight was launched from Asturias, another was advanced from the Catalonian Pyrenees, with the aid of the Franks, who had checked the Arabs at Poitiers in 732. Charlemagne entered the Peninsula and established the Marca Hispanica in Catalonia. In the same way, in the middle of the ninth century, the kingdoms of Navarre and Aragon were formed.

The Arabs called in some Persian technicians, who extended an irrigation system throughout all the south and east. Nevertheless, they were unsuccessful in repulsing the slow advances of the northern Christians who had reached the banks of the Buero River and installed themselves at León (914). The Leonese kingdom, thus established, later absorbed those of Galicia and Asturias, which had been formed at the beginning of the Reconquest.

In order to contain the Arabs, soldiers were needed along the frontiers. The kingdom of León was poor. Therefore the new lands were populated with country peasants who were to be soldiers at the same time. To attract them, liberties and rights were offered. Hence a society very different from the feudalism prevalent in Europe was formed. Each small town was allowed to govern itself. Castile, which was a county that had declared itself independent of León in 961, affirmed the popular, democratic character of the society by this very declaration.

Meanwhile, Europeans were carrying on pilgrimages to Compostela, which is said to be the site of the tomb of the apostle Saint James. With the pilgrims came European cultural influences. By the middle of the thirteenth century, only the kingdom of Granada, in the South, remained of what had been the great Moslem State.

With the combined efforts of Castilians, Catalonians, Aragonese, and Navarrese in the struggle against the Arabs, came the first mention of Reconquest. This also marked a change of conditions in the recovered lands. No longer were they populated with free men, with peasant-soldiers, but rather, now that the Arabs were less dangerous, with lords who established a system of serfdom. Furthermore, Military Orders had been established in order to better manage the war.

These occupied extensive territory, which they devoted to pasturing. There then emerged a rivalry between the democratic, agrarian, Castilian communities and the aristocratic, cattle-raising economy of the Orders. Finally, the latter triumphed.

Thus the appearance of feudalism in Spain was accompanied by the emergence of latifundism. To this must be added the problem of assimilation of the masses of Islamized Hispanics and Jews that the successive conquests of Toledo and Seville left in Christian territory. In general, this assimilation was achieved with relative ease in the cities, but in the countryside it was never fully realized and provoked tensions that were especially manifested in anti-Semitism.

Meanwhile, along the eastern fringe of the Peninsula, events advanced in an opposite direction. The count of Barcelona had converted the Marca Hispanica into an independent kingdom in 898. The patrician mercantile bourgeoisie of Barcelona was the dominant factor in this kingdom. The Aragonese, fearful of their absorption by Castile, married the heiress to the throne to the count of Barcelona in 1137. Thus, the Catalonian-Aragonese Confederation was formed, with its monarch called the count-king. First, Catalonia was extended up to Provence, but the Crusade against the Cathars gave these lands to France (1213). Next, the country extended southward with the conquest from the Arabs of the Balearic Islands (1229) and Valencia, which were then populated with Catalonian knights and merchants. When Catalonia had run out of lands to conquer in the Peninsula, it turned toward the Mediterranean, and created a small commercial empire which was the rival of Genoa. Sardinia, Corsica, several Greek duchies, Sicily (1282), and Naples formed part of Catalonia.

The strong urban bourgeoisie mitigated the struggles between the nobles and the monarch, and eventually was able to count on the service of both. In the countryside feudalism along European lines predominated. In existence in Catalonia were the *Corts* (Parliament) of the three states (bourgeois, ecclesiastic, and noble). The king was, to a certain extent, a constitutional monarch, since he was not able to repeal any law legislated by the Corts, which met automatically, without need for the king to convene them.

In 1410 the Catalonian king died without an heir. Representatives of the Corts of Valencia, Aragon, and Catalonia elected his successor, a prince of the reigning dynasty in Castile. Not long afterward, Catalonia began to decline, not because of the presence of a monarch of a foreign lineage, but rather due to the excesses of the patrician bourgeoisie and nobility. Rebellions by the peasants and artisans erupted, resulting in the redemption of peasants from feudal bondage and the representation of artisans in the urban councils.

Until then, there had been occasional collaboration among the different kingdoms of the Peninsula against the Arabs, but also intrigues and even wars among these same kingdoms. A certain degree of unity was to be achieved with the marriage of a Catalonian infante, Ferdinand (1452-1516), to Isabella, the Castilian infanta (1469). The former rose to the throne legitimately, while the latter did so owing to a civil war which set aside the legitimate heiress. Thus, the union, for the moment merely a dynastic one, between Catalonia and Castile, was effected by the marriage of a Catalonian king, who had granted freedom to the peasants and constitutional rights to the artisans, to a queen, Isabella I (1451-1504), who owed her crown to the feudal nobility who had risen in rebellion.

The reign of Ferdinand and Isabella would not have had a great impact on history if it had not been for the coincidental occurrence of two crucial incidents. The first was the conquest of Granada (1492) after eleven years of battle, which marked the end of the presence of the Arabs in Spain. The second was the discovery of America by an expedition of three caravels headed by Christopher Columbus and financed by Aragonese and Castilian bankers (1492).

At the beginning of the sixteenth century, Spain had reached a moment in its history in which everything seemed to lead to the formation of a single nationality within a single state. It might be said that Spain was at the point of being born after having spent a long period of gestation under the Visigothic monarchy and throughout its division between Moslems and Christians.

Prior to other European countries, Spain had enjoyed an absolute monarchy during the reign of Ferdinand and Isabella. The country also had the advantage of the tradition of the Arabic and Judaic cultures (which had produced Renaissance ahead of Italy, since these cultures had transmitted the survival of the Greek and Hellenic cultures). Added to this was the advantage of two strong Christian cultures, already rooted in languages—Castilian and Catalonian. These had produced very characteristic literatures: poetry, theater, novels, and juridical and philosophical works influential in all of Europe of the period.

Furthermore, Spain, in reference to the period, had several advantages at its disposal. First, it possessed sufficient sources of wealth and varied mines that would suffice to meet the needs of the time. It also owned abundant land that allowed for population growth despite the constant wars and local rebellions. The Arabs had left as a legacy abundant irrigation projects and a flourishing artisanry, including the prosperous manufacturing of textiles, leather goods, and arms. The Jews had contributed an important banking experience plus a large number of professionals and scientists who were more advanced than those of the rest of Europe. There were chances, then, for Spain to become a united, absolute monarchy, with capitalist trends able to prevail over surviving feudal elements of an aristocracy exhausted in Castile by the civil wars and in Catalonia by the loss of its serfs.

Nevertheless, some four hundred years later, at the beginning of the twentieth century, Spain still cannot be considered a strong and stable unit nor a capitalist country, but rather one in which feudalism has survived. What happened to impede the birth of Spain, which in 1500 under Ferdinand and Isabella seemed an imminent fact? Three events, occurring within a few years, frustrated this possibility: the conquest of America, the expulsion of Jews and Moors, and the intervention of Spain in European politics.

The discovery of America logically effected a lasting influence on Spain. The Spaniards that conquered Mexico and Peru and established themselves in many other regions were second sons of *hidalgo* families—not noble but freemen—and people of the towns. These carried to the New World the municipal institutions to which they were accustomed. But this municipal democracy applied only to Spaniards, never to Indians. The crown divided the lands and those who received them were responsible for the care of the Indians that worked them. Yet this paternalistic intention was frustrated since the conquerors were eager to become wealthy. The crown, however, reserved for itself the control of the mines. Later on, the crown also controlled all commercial dealings between America and the rest of the world. All merchandise was forced to pass through the ports of Seville and Cádiz from five specified American ports.

A great deal has been written, much of it fantasy, regarding the conquest of America. There emerged in Anglo-Saxon countries what the Spaniards call the "Black Legend," which accused Spain of every type of crime. In reality, the Conquest was brutal and severe, but no more so than other wars of the period. Nor was it carried out with procedures not in vogue at the time. Nevertheless, voices resounded in Spain itself that raised doubts regarding the right of Spaniards to occupy the lands of other monarchs (as that of Francisco de Vitoria [1480?-1548], founder of international law). Other voices demanded respect and effective protection for the Indians (that of Bishop Bartolomé de las Casas [1474-1566]). Thus Spain was the first modern colonial empire and the first country in which anticolonialist doctrines emerged.

Faced with the problem, which was new to the world, of organizing distant lands, Ferdinand, his successors, and their advisors gave evidence of much political imagination. They established the Council of Indies in Seville, which legislated for the new colonies and acted as a Court of Appeals. They also established a House of Commerce (Case de Contratación), which regulated trade with the Indies and exploitation of their riches. Shortly after the discovery, America had thus become accustomed to a controlled economy, which is still strongly felt there, and to a paternalism that has still not disappeared from Spanish-American countries. Furthermore, America acquired the language, religion, and culture of Castile.

Conquest and colonization deprived Spain of its most dynamic people, those with the greatest initiative, since second sons were forced to make their own way through life, while the eldest son received the entire inheritance. Spain was compensated for this loss with the overwhelming abundance of precious metals from the New World. If the colonizers had remained in the Peninsula, they would have made these metals yield a profit in a capitalist sense, but of course there would not have been such metals for Spain. In the long run, the riches of America occasioned the ruin of the Spanish economy. This did not come about solely because of the loss of the country's dynamic element, but also because America's gold allowed Spain to get involved in European politics and spill more blood because of it. This in turn forced Spain to invest in military activities a capital which, had it been used in Spain, would have converted the country into one of the first in Europe with a capitalist society. Instead, a disdain for manual labor became general.

Two proverbs well describe the situation, indicating the way in which the Spanish themselves finally viewed what happened: "The father, a cattle raiser, the son, a knight, and the grandson, a beggar," says one, referring to the social aspect of life. And the other, which deals with economic life, affirms that the gold originated in the Indies, passed through Spain, and ended up in Genoa. That is, it went into the vaults of European bankers who had lent money to the crown for its European wars. Only Catalonia was spared this demographic bloodletting, since its citizens were not allowed to participate in the colonization, which was considered Castile's mission. This allowed Catalonia to recuperate from its crisis of the sixteenth century and return, in the seventeenth century, to its past prosperity.

On the other hand, Catalonia, whose monarch was likewise king of Naples, involved Spain in European matters for the first time. Ferdinand was forced to send armies to Italy, and from that point on, the soldiers of the Spanish *tercios* (infantry units) waged war for three centuries. The battle sites included North Africa and half of Europe. First, they fought against Italy and France, then against the Protestant German princes, later against the Turks and England, and once again against France and Germany. In spite of Spanish Catholicism, Spanish troops occupied and looted Rome. A French king, Francis I, was taken prisoner by the Spaniards, and a new country, Holland, emerged from the struggle with the Spanish army. The Spanish navy conquered its Turkish counterpart at Lepanto and was later destroyed by a storm in an attempt to invade England.

All this consumed the gold from America and placed the country in debt. It also deprived Spain of the capital needed to recover from the effects of the expulsion of Jews, ordered by the Catholic Kings (1492), and that of the Moors who had stayed in Spain (Moriscos), decreed a century later (1609). Spain was left without scientists and without what today would be called economists. Furthermore, the Spanish economy lost with the Moors its finest agriculturalists and craftsmen. But above all, Spain lost the sense of cultural and ethnic plurality, without achieving a sense of unity as compensation. Instead, it acquired a sterile religious unity, with the help of the Inquisition.

Paradoxically, feudalism became firmly implanted under absolute monarchy, a unique occurrence in the history of Europe. The successors of Ferdinand and Isabella, Philip the Fair (1478-1506) and Jane the Mad (1479-1555), ruled for a short time, 1504-06. But the son of the romantic couple governed for a long time and accomplished a great deal.

This son, Charles I (1500-58), grandson of Emperor Maximilian, had been educated in Flanders. He was elected emperor in 1519 (as Charles V), which emphasized the participation of Spain in European politics. His Flemish advisers, with a bourgeois mentality, at first encouraged an antifeudal policy, which incited rebellions of the nobility. The municipalities, fearing the loss of their *fueros* (or special local privileges), also rose in insurrection. Many democratic historians have tried to view this civil war, or war of the *comunidades* (municipalities) (1520-21), and the artisan uprisings of the *germanías* (guilds) of Valencia (1521) and Mallorca (1522), as democratic protests. In reality these were but an attempt by medieval institutions to survive. The king squelched these rebellions and destroyed the popular institutions, which were incompatible with absolute monarchy.

But the monarch did placate the nobles (those he needed for his wars) by granting them certain economic privileges. For example, he consolidated the institution of the *Mesta* (an association of cattle raisers) by means of which cattlemen, almost all of whom were aristocrats, could utilize enormous extensions of land to move their herds from winter pasturelands to summer ones.

The pressures of external wars prevented the monarchy from pursuing its antifeudal policy. On the other hand, it successively eliminated all elements of change that existed in the country: the converted Jews, the Moriscos, the heterodox. These elements were forced to indirect methods of expression, giving rise to the satirical character, at times sarcastic, of the splendid Spanish literature and art of the sixteenth and seventeenth centuries.

Nevertheless, the country did possess enormous vitality, since it otherwise could not have conquered America in less than twenty years, created there an efficient bureaucracy and new institutions, and brought very diverse peoples up to the standard of the "motherland." Furthermore, it could not have waged war throughout all Europe and continued to lose wars for three centuries. Nor could the country have inspired and sustained the Counterreformation (applying to the church the Spanish military experience with the Society of Jesus), or counteracted the softness of Rome with the relative purity and severity of the Spanish church. Spain, with all its weaknesses, was the great power of its era. For 150 years the world was forced to acknowledge the existence of Spain. Little did the world know to what small extent Spain actually existed in Spanish territory.

The history of Spain from the end of the fifteenth century until the middle of the eighteenth may be written in very different literary style: the epic for the conquest and colonization of America; the picaresque for Spanish society; the adventure story for the European wars; the sentimental saga for economic life; sarcasm for political life; and the psychoanalytical approach for the court.

Spain was not born as a unit when objective conditions favored its historic birth. Instead, these conditions led to a period of 250 years during which the appearance of Spain as such was simply postponed. Nothing that took place in the wars, in politics, or in the economy indicated even the least desire that this birth take place, nor the least awareness that it might have been possible or suitable. The country, behind the mask of great power, went adrift, mended its wounds, made challenging gestures, and lived, in fact, without going anywhere.

The Spain of this epoch was not officially called Spain. Nor did it possess one flag but rather many, one for each component. Nor did the country claim a capital. The court moved from Valladolid to Seville, from there to Barcelona, and then to Burgos or Valencia. Under the successors of Philip II, the country did not experience the sensation of possessing even a monarch, since the kings allowed themselves to be maneuvered by their favorites at court or by their wives' lovers, who in turn were mere instruments of the nobles. Never had a country been ruled by the nobles in such a complete and unrestrained manner as was Spain between the reigns of Philip III and Charles II. Nor had a country remained so immobile; it was administrated, but not governed.

To all the countries "united" under the crown, the king had to send viceroys; the Castilian public officials were viewed as foreigners. Furthermore, the king had to swear allegiance to the constitution of each of these countries. Each had its own customs, laws, monetary and tax systems, its own parliament and institutions. Spain was not a federation—which would be unity—but a simple dynastic union.

This superficial unity, a mere facade, would not have subsisted if the Catholic Monarchs and Charles I had not created an efficient state, with its rural policy (the Holy Brotherhood), its control of the military orders, and its scorn for the Parliament which was rarely convened.

The best instrument was the bureaucracy, which, in its time, was the most efficient in the world. It gave Spain its legalistic, rhetorical, and pompous spirit which it still preserves. Various councils (of Castile, Aragon, the Indies, and Finances) were formed in the court, in the same way as were chanceries and *audiencias* (high courts) for the administration of justice. After a fashion, the state and the king were separated, in the eyes of the subjects. Many times their anger was directed against public officials, while they respected the sovereign. The Indians of America, each time they rebelled, would shout: "Death to the bad government; long live the king!" In order to better control the nobility, the title of Spanish grandee was created. Thus the aristocracy was fossilized.

Philip II installed the councils in Madrid and, near the city, constructed an enormous palace, the Escorial, where he held his court. The bureaucracy continued to function in moments of crisis and decadence. It was a machine that whirled incessantly, but that, after Philip II, no longer produced anything.

By means of a series of chance events, Charles I found himself at the head of an empire, the likes of which had not been known since Rome: Castile with America, Catalonia-Aragon with Naples and interests in northern Africa, Burgundy with Flanders, and the German Holy Roman Empire. To sustain this empire, which Protestant rebellions soon began to undermine, many thousands of Spanish *hidalgos* and the lean budgets of Castile and Catalonia were needed. These were bargained for by the parliaments which were fearful of getting involved in conflicts in unknown countries. American gold financed military endeavors for a time. But already by 1550, this gold was mortgaged for more than ten years in advance. The German House of Welcher received the rights to exploit Venezuela; another, as collateral, received the mines of Almadén.

It was only in his old age that Charles I began to understand that the empire was unwieldy. He abdicated and left the empire to his brother, and to his son, Philip II, Spain and Flanders. Philip II, although he always spoke of religion, lived obsessed by the end of the month, by the necessity of paying the salaries of his soldiers and public officials. But still he did not renounce the European ventures; the war with France, the Turks, and the rebellious Low Countries. England grew into a rival, and the king was not able to cut down this flowering threat, since his Invincible Armada had failed (1588). Holland, upon separation (1597), replaced Seville and Lisbon with Amsterdam as the new center of world commerce. The war with Flanders was especially damaging. There Spain first attempted appeasement, later terror, and finally lost the Protestant provinces—but did preserve the Catholic provinces until 1713, when they went to Austria. This could be compared, to a certain extent, with the Vietnam War.

The astonishing fact is that, with all this going on, Spain still had reserve energy to devote to America. Half a century after the discovery, Spain had ended the conquest. Twenty years later, the administration was in regular working order everywhere; there were universities established in different places in the colonies. Ferdinand Magellan (1450?-1521) and Sebastián Elcano (1476?-1526) made their voyage around the world. The first African Negroes were imported to Cuba, where the Indian population had been destroyed by the Whites and by epidemics. Almost every Latin American city which is important today was founded at that time. The Philippines were conquered. Spanish missionaries were sent to Japan. Later on, with the French and English rivalry, it became necessary for Spain to battle pirates and organize armadas to defend the navigation which, twice each year, united the Philippines to Mexico, and America to Spain. Tobacco, corn, turkey, and tomatoes appeared for the first time in European cities, as did rubber, and later, potatoes.

Spain organized America and civilized it, but could not give the new land what Spain itself did not have. America possessed several ideal conditions which could have converted it into a mercantile society. Instead, Castile changed it to its own image, that is, a feudal society, from the lords down, and an authoritarian one from the lords up.

America transformed the world. And upset Spain. Seville, which had been the westernmost point in Europe, suddenly became the center of the world. For a time Spain prospered. Yet, already by the end of the reign of Charles I, inflation had set in. Under Philip II the inflationary trend became more intense, as did the gold hemorrhage. Under Philip III, the plague of 1600 aggravated the situation, while the coining of bronze replaced that of gold.

Philip II was a great figure. His successors were puppets. There is nothing worth mentioning about Philip III (1578-1621), except the loss of the Low Countries and the expulsion of the Moriscos. Philip IV (1605-65), the monarch that Velázquez unmercifully immortalized in his painting, had as his favorite the Count-Duke of Olivares (1584-1645). It was he who wanted to create forcefully the organic unity which previous kings had not achieved with their greatness. The result was a lost war with Portugal, which had been united with Castile for eighty years through inheritance. Now Portugal once again was independent. Another outcome was a twelve-year war with Catalonia (1640-52), which did not achieve the destruction of the autonomy of the ancient kingdom. Spain, in new wars, lost what was left of Flanders, Artoiq, Franche-Comté, and Roussillon. The country, which numbered eight million inhabitants in Ferdinand's times, scarcely reached five million at this point. When the heirless Charles II (1661-1700) became mortally ill, the European countries decided to put an end to the remains of Spanish power. France and Austria disputed the inheritance at the monarch's bedside. Charles II leaned toward the French and named as heir Philip of Anjou, the grandson of Louis XIV of France. Philip V (1683-1746) was accepted with apathy. The country was exhausted. But Austria and England were not so resigned. The war of succession which they provoked lasted fourteen years. They had especially taken advantage of Catalonia's lack of confidence in a monarch of such a centralist dynasty as the Bourbons. The Catalonians proclaimed the archduke Charles king. But as they were losing the war, they soon found themselves abandoned by the English. And even Charles, when he was elected emperor, abandoned them too. In 1714, Philip won the war[2] and Catalonia lost its institutions and even the official use of its language. Spain was transformed into a centralist monarchy. Of its enormous empire, Spain was left with America and the Philippines. But Spain remained with nothing of the European lands for which it had depopulated Castile and ruined the Spaniards. The empire had lasted for two and a half centuries. What would happen next with the country?

## NOTES

1. It would be useful to read the fundamental books of some modern historians, which, by the way, are excellent literary works: Américo Castro, *La realidad histórica de España*, Mexico, 1950; Claudio Sánchez Albornoz, *España, un enigma histórico*, Buenos Aires, 1956; J. Vicens Vives, *Approximaciòn a la historia de España*, Barcelona, 1952. The reader who would like to concentrate on details seen from a modern and objective point of view is advised to read Antonio Ubieto, Juan Reglá, and José María Jover, *Introducción a la historia de España*, Barcelona, 1963.

2. Gibraltar, however, off the southern point of the country and across from Africa, remained in the hands of England, which still possesses it today. The same happened to the Island of Menorca, although only for a few years.

# 5

# Emergence of Spain

Many Spanish historians tend to underemphasize the role of the Bourbon dynasty in Spain. It is true that attempts to modernize the country and society under several of the monarchs of this dynasty were due to the tenacity and vision of a few ministers and the influence of the period itself. But, after all, these ministers were selected by the sovereigns.

The eighteenth century witnessed the birth of Spain. Four monarchs—Philip V (1683-1746), Ferdinand VI (1713-59), Charles III (1716-88), and Charles IV (1748-1819, king until 1808)—covered this period and oriented a policy for unification of the country. The first of the line forcefully imposed this policy, especially in Catalonia, where he destroyed the ancient institutions. The other kings attempted to create a nation through social and economic measures, as a reflection of a mute struggle between feudal forces on the wane and growing bourgeois forces.

This eighteenth century was dressed in French culture, taste, and ideological influences. But, in contrast with what had happened on prior occasions, these external influences were utilized to study the local reality and confront its problems. They were not seen as models to be imitated, but rather as methods to understand.

The people reacted against French influence by intensifying their differing characteristics. This was true especially in Castile and Andalusia. This reaction reached the point of what is called *casticismo* (love of "purity" of customs). This *casticismo* was manifested in the popularity of the bullfight, flamenco, and the *majismo*[1] which Goya portrayed on his canvasses. Thus, what attracts today's tourist to Spain dates scarcely from the eighteenth century. Many other characteristics of present-day Spain, in politics, culture, economy, and even in language, are derived from this same century.

The important thing is that for the first time all the inhabitants of the country, without abandoning their national or local personality, felt themselves part of the same community. And this feeling is the basis of a nation. Spain was born under the Bourbons. Spain confirmed the fact that nationality is the product of the bourgeoisie, since the Bourbons, perhaps without clearly seeing it, fostered the change toward a bourgeois society.

This birth of Spain was even expressed in symbolic details: the present-day flag of Spain (one horizontal yellow stripe between two red ones) was created by Charles III; Madrid became a true capital and not simply the seat of the court; the national anthem was created, while the name of Spain was used on official documents. The population increased. Commerce, especially that of Catalonia, was resumed and prospered. The country acquired a new vitality. Reduced to its own borders and to America, it could now become more introspective and confront its own problems.

Catalonia, Valencia, Málaga, Santander, and Bilbao revived. The periphery progressed more rapidly than the center. In 1778, Charles III suppressed the monopoly that Cádiz had held over America. Hence, all the coastal Spanish cities turned their attention to the Atlantic. In a few years exports had doubled, the state escaped bankruptcy and was able to maintain an external policy independent of France, while there was money to spare for investment in new industries.

French culture became fashionable. The instrument of diffusion for the rationalist ideas was the Economic Societies of Friends of the Country. Portions of the church and of nobility, and the students, wanted modernization, agrarian reforms, and reforms in the colonial system.

The most urgent problem was the agrarian one. The population had grown by three million, and it was necessary to give lands to the majority of these people. Canals were opened, highways were built, and plans for internal colonization (one of them with German peasants) were undertaken. The privileges of the Mesta, the great organization of aristocratic cattle breeders which had asphyxiated Spanish agriculture for three centuries, were put to an end. But still there remained seventeen cities and close to ten thousand towns under feudal dominion, while three cities and seventeen hundred towns were under ecclesiastic control. There were some 150,000 beggars in the country. It was proposed that the wealth of the clergy be freed from mortmain, but what was actually done was little and slow. It was also proposed to the noble families that they renounce the *mayorazgo* (the right of the eldest son to inherit all the land and wealth of the family) in exchange for indemnities, but they refused. The nobility made sure that the only measure that would have been effective, mass expropriation of their lands, was not proposed. Yet the nobility was not able to impede prohibition of the guilds' practice to require proof of purity of blood from their members. Nor was it able to prevent the enclosure of common land to avoid its use by the nobles, the sale of royal lands, the simplification of courtly etiquette, the struggle against nepotism, the fostering of the merchant marine, nor, lastly, the increase by a quarter of a million of the number of manufacturers and merchants.

The ministers of Charles III, faced with several popular rebellions, blamed them not on the aristocrats, but on the Jesuits. The Jesuits were expelled from Spain and its colonies (1767), and the Company of Jesus was temporarily suppressed by the Holy See, which responded to pressures from Spain and France.

Spain's enlightened classes, as they were then called, advanced to the point of supporting the United States against England. Had it not been for the French Revolution, reforms might have been widely established. But the revolution instilled fear in the hearts of the reformers themselves. The minister of Charles IV, Manuel Godoy (1767-1851), suppressed most of the reform and preserved little more than the administrative dictatorship. The "enlightened despotism" had accomplished a great deal, but it had not allowed participation of the people in what it did accomplish. Its reforms were of the elite.

But the French ideas had already been deeply implanted. If there were few rationalist priests to be found, there were rationalist doctors, lawyers, and even industrialists. Godoy signed an alliance with France after Napoleon had placated the revolutionaries. The Franco-Spanish navy fought with Nelson's ships in the battle of Trafalgar (1805).

Napoleon, with the pretext of fighting against Portugal, which was an ally of England, requested and received permission for his troops to pass through Spain. When Charles IV and Godoy wanted to move the court to Andalusia because the French, at Murat's command, had virtually occupied Madrid, the people discovered the fugitive court in Aranjuez, and rioted. Charles IV abdicated in favor of his son, who rose to the throne with the name of Ferdinand VII (1784-1833). Ferdinand returned to Madrid, but Charles, having recovered from his fear, announced that he had only abdicated out of fright and annulled the abdication. Would the country now have two monarchs? Napoleon capitalized on the confusion in order to invite the two to Bayonne to discuss the matter. Once in the French city, they were made prisoners. Ferdinand signed his resignation, returning the throne to his father, while Charles renounced his claim in favor of Napoleon. The French leader handed the throne over to his brother Joseph, who although a temperate man, was nicknamed Pepe Botella (Joe Bottle) by the people.

These maneuvers left everyone in bad straits—everyone, that is, except the people. On May 2, 1808, the rumor circulated throughout Madrid that Napoleon had ordered the only two princes of the royal family who remained in Spain to be called to Bayonne. The people rose in rebellion and spontaneously began to murder Frenchmen. From the capital, the riot extended throughout the country.

Guerrillas, bands, and gangs of insurgents emerged everywhere. As was to happen more than a century later in the Civil War of 1936, the people viewed the defense of independence and social reforms as one and the same. It was impossible to have one without the other. The common people had reappeared in the country's history, from which they had been absent since the thirteenth century, when a retarded feudalism was established in Castile. The feudal forces needed a century and a quarter to again get rid of the people.

The people fought, but without thinking. A minority—aristocrats, intellectuals, and bourgeois—thought, but without fighting. This minority formed the local juntas and the Supreme Junta. In these groups were some who would have been on Napoleon's side had he not been a foreigner, and also uncompromising traditionalists. The war, almost always a guerrilla one, and with the help of England, lasted five years. If Napoleon had not had the Russian campaign, which indirectly determined the end of the war in Spain, it is probable that the invasion would not have ended. But it is likewise probable that the French would not have triumphed. Spain would have been a Vietnam for the empire.

The Supreme Junta decided to convene a parliament. From 1810 to 1812, the scene of the discussions was Cádiz, the last square mile free from invaders. A constitution was written. The Inquisition was finally abolished, as were the *mayorazgos*, the judicial jurisdiction of the lords, territorial privileges, and the medieval guilds. Thus, during the war, Spain was transformed into a constitutional monarchy.

This Constitution of Cádiz was very interesting. Alongside such naivetés as prescribing that Spaniards were to be "good and loyal," one finds glimpses of the future. Some of the latter included the recognition of autonomy for the American colonies, abolition of the servile condition of Indians there, and the establishment of guarantees for liberties in the constitutional mechanism.

It had some influence outside Spain. When, in 1820, a series of liberal governments was established in the various Italian states, the Constitution of Cádiz was adopted there, with scarcely any changes. Portugal did the same in 1822. Antonio Gramsci, a century later, was to comment upon this fact, saying that it was not proof of mental sloth or lack of preparation, but rather because "the Spanish situation was a model for absolutist Europe . . . and the Spanish liberals knew how to find the most appropriate and generalized juridic-constitutional solution to problems which were not only Spanish, but also Italian." Once again, Spain was outside the historical times; its liberal constitution anticipated the others of Europe. The first time in three centuries that the country had forged ahead of Europe was when the people spoke. The same thing would happen in 1936.

When Ferdinand VII finally returned after the withdrawal of the French, he was enthusiastically received. His first act in 1813 was to abolish the constitution. As the king gave over the government to prewar elements, and thus reestablished the absolutism that the people had repudiated at the same time as they did the French, he alienated the liberals and the guerrilla leaders who were left without any command. Both groups were found in the Masonic and Carbonari lodges. In these societies conspiracies to reestablish the constitution were plotted. In 1820 numerous troops destined to combat the insurrection of the American colonies found themselves concentrated in Andulasia.[2] A group of officials incited them to riot against absolutism. The king fought and was conquered. He then accepted the constitution.

Thus Spanish militarism was born. As can be seen, it was liberal in its origins. It was the product of the War of Independence and the decision of the country's feudal forces to close every door in the face of the new forces of society, which, of course, compelled them to resort to violence.

Ferdinand VII died in 1833. He left the throne to his daughter Isabella II (1830-1904), who was three years old at the time, under the regency of his widow María Cristina (1806-78). The most traditionalist elements refused to accept a woman on the throne. They rebelled in the Basque Country, and in parts of Catalonia, Aragon, and Navarre, proclaiming Charles (1788-1855), the brother of the dead monarch, king. A civil war began.

In order to oppose the Carlists (or Traditionalists, as Charles's partisans were called), the government was forced to become more liberal. In the cities, the people began to set fire to churches, while in the country, the peasants did the same with the monasteries, since both viewed the church as a supporter of the Carlists. With the introduction of the steam engine in 1833, an industrial proletariat came into existence. Its members most willingly listened to the extreme liberals. From this moment on, the people became anticlerical, although this does not mean that they were anti-Catholic.

One liberal minister, Juan Alvarez Mendizábal (1790-1853), a banker, seeing that conditions were opportune, proposed the application of something which the bureaucracy of Charles III had already suggested and which the Parliament of Cádiz could not put into effect: the freeing from mortmain of church properties. In 1837 the church's possessions were expropriated and sold. The government needed money for the war against the Carlists. The church's estates were purchased by the big landowners and the urban bourgeoisie, which reinforced latifundism. The liberals had not dared utilize the freeing from mortmain to give lands to the peasants. But many conservatives who had acquired property became supporters of Isabella II, whose government sold it to them. Thus the regime was bolstered.

In the liberal ranks a split took place. The Progressives appeared, along with minority groups of industrial workers, a few intellectuals, and low-ranking officers. A coup of sergeants pushed the regime toward the Left. The Constitution of 1837, which reflected this movement, was one of the most liberal that the country has had. Nevertheless, suffrage continued to be limited. Hence, the popular masses remained outside the political process, except for moments of violence. If they wanted to be heard, they had to initiate such action.

The civil war approached its termination through an agreement achieved by the Progressives. The Carlist leaders entered the army of Isabella, and the guerrillas returned home. General Baldomero Espartero (1793-1879), leader of the Progressives, felt the moment had arrived to seize power. He forced the regent to resign and had himself proclaimed regent (1841-43). The people triumphed without vote. But the doors of power had been opened to the generals.

The workers of Barcelona had been the force behind Espartero's impact. The rapidly industrialized Barcelona had become the political vanguard of the country. Espartero did not fulfill his promises, so the workers abandoned him. And they remonstrated. In reply, the general bombed Barcelona (1842). As a revenge, the following year, the Catalonian city supported the moderates, who, via a military coup, ousted Espartero.

Thus began a period of twenty-four years (1844-68) of domination by the moderates. This period was marked by a new constitution (1845). General Ramón María Narváez (1799-1868) was the central figure of this period. On his deathbed, he was asked by his confessor if he had pardoned his enemies, to which the general, raising his head, shouted: "I have no enemies. I have executed them all."

Under the moderates, the bourgeoisie prospered. The Crimean War opened new markets to Catalonian textiles. But this prosperity also gave strength to the proletariat, which had begun to organize. In 1855 in Barcelona, the workers declared Spain's first general strike, to support their demand for the right to unionize. There were peasant riots in Andalusia, where the new latifundists (buyers of clerical properties) proved to be even harsher than the old aristocrats. All of this led to a progressive biennium (1855-57), once again with Espartero, which was a short interregnum.

Following this period came the moderate Liberal Union, governed by General Leopoldo O'Donnell (1809-67). The queen allowed herself to be carried away by the advice of a few religious fanatics, and alternately by that of a few of her favorites. Thus she involved herself in politics. The people felt disgusted and disillusioned by the sterility of the protests and turned their back on politics. This permitted the moderates to reach an agreement with the Holy See. Through this pact, the latter accepted expropriation of the church's property, while the government agreed to use public monies to support both the costs of worship and the priests, to whom a salary would be given.

The way in which the railroad system was laid out after 1848 is an excellent example of the mentality of these moderate liberals. Madrid was the capital at the center. All railroad lines connected Madrid with the periphery. In order to travel from one end of the country to the other, one had to circle through Madrid. The centralism of the Bourbons seems child's play compared to the centralism of the moderate liberals of the nineteenth century. The latter was not so much a response to extreme patriotism as to the influence of the Napoleonic administrative concept. Exaggerated patriotism was merely used to justify this centralism. Spain was divided into provinces (fifty in all), each of which was arbitrarily marked on the map, without considering customs, language, or economy. The only relevant factor used in placing the boundaries was that it be possible to go from the capital of the province to its furthest point in twelve hours by carriage. There-fore, the flat provinces were extensive, while the mountainous ones, with their sinuous roads, were small. Not even the Second Republic dared tamper with this absurd division.

On the other hand, the economic policy of the moderate liberals aided the development of light industry in Catalonia and siderurgy in the Basque Country. Many new enterprises were established. Also, foreign investments began to arrive, especially for mining and siderurgy.

The moderate governments reorganized the administration and founded the Civil Guard, which was originally a rural police force, but which became a special force against agrarian riots and workers' protests. But the moderates had no program for the future. The mo-ment had arrived when the country demanded a greater impetus than needed to merely mark time. Administrative corruption (the bureaucrats were changed with each change in government), the queen's frivolity, foreign adventures (a war in Morocco, expeditions against Mexico and the American countries of the Pacific), all created an ambiance of contempt toward the regime. In 1868 General Juan Prim (1814-70), a Catalonian who had gained fame in Africa and who was a Progressive, rose in rebellion with the battlecry of "Spain with honor." He did not expect to head a real revolution. But the people rushed into the streets and Prim had the political sense to follow them. Isabella II left.

A month after taking power, the provisional government of Gen-eral Prim launched a warning aimed at those who wanted to pattern the regime along the lines of that of the United States, "only possible in the young countries, but not in those with long, indestructible tradition." This was also his reply to agrarian riots in Andalusia, where the peasants had occupied lands, to workers' strikes and de-monstrations in many cities, and to the formation of people's militias that controlled the municipalities. The government called for elec-tions with universal suffrage. The elections gave a majority to the Liberal and Progressive Monarchists, although with strong minorities to the Democrats and Republicans. Whom to place on the throne: a German, a Frenchman, an Italian? In any case, it would not be a Bourbon.

As negotiations regarding the future king continued, the Constitu-tional Assembly legislated; it established civil marriage and trial by jury. But it did not touch the essential problems: the agrarian situa-tion and the structure of the state (that is, unitarism or federalism).

Meanwhile, the masses organized. For fifty years up to this point, they had acted spontaneously or placed their confidence in the Progressives, who had never really served them. The year 1868 marked the beginning of the organization of workers. An Italian, Giuseppe Fanelli, a disciple and friend of Bakunin, visited Barcelona and established a section of the International Association of Workers, founded four years earlier in London, with Marx as secretary-general, and also branches of Bakunin's international Democratic Alliance. Marx's son-in-law, Paul Lafargue, visited Madrid, fleeing the repression that followed the Paris Commune, and helped organize socialist groups. A manifesto appeared requesting 500 subscribers to a workers' newspaper. This number was only achieved after two years. The paper, *La Solidaridad* (solidarity), was managed by one of the founders of Spanish anarchism, Anselmo Lorenzo (1842-1914). At the same time in Barcelona (1870) *La Federación* (the federation) was published by recently established workers' unions. In this same year the first Workers' Congress of the country was convened. One hundred delegates from all over Spain congregated in Barcelona. The antipolitical ideas of the Bakuninists predominated. The government prohibited the International. In Cuba a movement for independence broke out, which forced Spain to maintain a war of almost ten years in order to preserve one of the last colonies that still belonged to the country (the others were Puerto Rico, the Philippines, and several places in Morocco). The government, finding itself in bad economic straits, sold the copper mines of Riotinto to an English company for 92 million pesetas, a sum which would be redeemed with the profits of any two years of exploitation.

In the meantime, the Parliament elected a king: 191 votes for Amadeo of the House of Savoy (1845-90), the liberal and unpretentious son of the king of Italy; 60 votes for the Republic, and two votes for Alfonso of Bourbon, son of Isabella II. This election and the diplomatic maneuvers that preceded it were not distant from the immediate causes of the Franco-Prussian War. Prim was to receive the new monarch. But an assassination attempt on his life, seemingly by radical elements within his own party, was successful. Amadeo arrived in Madrid and found himself without the support of the only important figure that existed among his partisans.

The government of Amadeo was not able to control the situation. Aware of this, the Carlists began another civil war which was to last for two years. Almost no one was in favor of Amadeo, the son of a king who had imprisoned the Pope, according to the Catholics, and a partisan of reestablishing diplomatic relations with the Holy See, according to anticlericals. There was an attempt on his life, which failed. The nobility did not accept him. The workers rejected him. In 1872, another congress of workers, with delegates from 101 local federations, was held in Cordova. The anarchist Spanish Workers' Federation was founded.

The government proposed the abolition of slavery in the colonies, and a Colonial League was formed to oppose this move. New elections: the 60 republican candidates expanded their ranks to 100, but still constituted a minority. The Carlist war ended. Finally, in February 1873, Amadeo I, disheartened, abdicated. The people did not hate him nor did they love him, but rather felt a certain respect for this exceptional monarch who, several weeks before giving up the throne, refused to sign a decree suspending constitutional guarantees.

Both houses of Parliament met in convention to vote for the regime that would succeed Amadeo: a king—and in which case, who—or the Republic? On February 11, 1873, the Republic was proclaimed by a vote of 258 to 32. Estanislau Figueras (1819-82), an unpretentious Catalonian, was elected its first president. Amidst public festivities for the new regime, Amadeo left Madrid. The Republic did not owe its birth to the Republicans, but rather to the disappointed Liberal Monarchists. Many had voted in favor of the Republic to allow it to discredit itself, since they considered it premature. But the people would wait no longer.

For the first time, a change in the regime was to come legally, without bloodshed or violence. The new regime was to last eleven months, with four different presidents. Each of these leaders was a distinguished intellectual but a mediocre politician. All four were from the periphery of Spain.

The first, Figueras, realized that the Republic had invoked the mistrust of everyone: that of the Right, for fear of reforms, and that of the Left, for fear that reforms would not be carried out. The Republican ranks were divided into Moderates and Progressives. The former believed that the revolution had ended with the proclamation of the Republic; Figueras financed a coup attempt, but failed. The Carlists resumed the civil war in the north and in the northeast. The only country that recognized the new regime was the United States. The government organized volunteer militia, suppressing the system of compulsory military service. Spectacular and useless measures were adopted: secularization of cemeteries and abolition of titles (the nobility had emigrated en masse), but nothing was done with respect to the agrarian problem. The only energetic measure undertaken was the abolition of slavery. But no agreement was reached with the Cuban independence fighters.

Radical elements in Barcelona had proclaimed for several hours the Catalonian State, to compel the dissolution of Parliament and the election of a new Constituent Assembly. Pi i Margall, minister of the interior, was able to dissuade his Catalonian friends, which he was later to regret.

Parliament was dissolved. In June a Constituent Assembly was held, its delegates elected by universal suffrage; the Republicans held the majority. Figueras, weary of quarrels among his friends, sent a letter of resignation to the president of the new Parliament, and left for France. He had been in power for four months. None of his successors would last even that long.

The first to succeed him was Francesc Pi i Margall (1824-1901). The masses had confidence in him. In the cities and towns, the Republican committees spontaneously replaced the monarchic municipal councils. But the government reestablished the latter, since it considered legality of primary importance. The Andalusian peasants divided large estates among themselves, and the government sent the army against them. In some places local Republican-Leftist powers were formed, proclaiming themselves autonomous regions or *cantones*. The government also sent troops against these groups. The Moderates accused Pi i Margall of being too soft; a month and a half after accepting the presidency, he resigned.

Nicolás Salmerón (1838-1908), a professor of philosophy, succeeded him. Parliament approved a complicated law for the redemption of lands, which left the peasants exactly where they had been before. When he found himself faced with signing an order for execution, Salmerón, who had always been against the death penalty, resigned. His position of power had lasted less than two months. His successor was the leader of the Moderate Republicans, Emilio Castelar (1832-99), a professor of history and a pompous orator.

Figueras and Pi had tried, without much effort, to eliminate the remains of feudalism; Salmerón had wanted to subjugate them. Castelar tried to integrate them into the regime. He again sent the army against the peasants in the south, against the *cantones* in the east, and against the Carlists in the north. He authorized the formation of monarchic societies.

At the end of three months, General Manuel Pavía (1828-95), seeing that Castelar's support in Parliament was a minority, and that left-wing Republicans were reorganizing, prepared for a military coup. (It is not known whether this was done with Castelar's approval.) Castelar appeared before Parliament. He contended that with political liberty, democracy, separation of church and state, and the abolition of slavery, the Republicans should consider themselves to have accomplished as much as was possible for the moment. He further stated that as for federalism and agrarian reform, these could be discussed later on. By a vote of 120 against, 100 for, Parliament refused him its confidence. Pavía ordered his troops to occupy the Parliament building. The deputies sounded off with a few cries of "Long live the Republic," and dispersed. The date was January 3, 1874. The First Republic had lasted exactly 327 days.

Pavía gathered a group of personalities and asked them to form the government. He did not want the power. General Francisco Serrano, Duke of la Torre (1816-85), who had been Prim's ally, was saddled with presiding over the state, while another general headed the government. Legally, the country was still a Republic. Its master was the army.

For a year, there was a strong government. The autonomous *cantones* were eradicated, but no end could be put to Carlism. Fourteen hundred cantonalists were deported to the Philippines. The workers' press was suspended. The Alfonsonians (partisans of the restoration of the Bourbons in the person of the son of Isabella II) were led by an able politician, Antonio Cánovas del Castillo (1828-97), who believed in a paternalistic democracy and who sought a way to "reconcile Spaniards." On December 29, 1874, General Arsenio Martínez Campos (1831-1900) staged a military coup proclaiming Alfonso king, with the title of Alfonso XII (1857-85). Several days later, this monarch, from the English Military School at Sandhurst, signed a manifesto which promised a liberal constitutional monarchy, steeped in tradition. Cánovas formed the government. The Republic had failed because those who should have supported it, the middle class and the bourgeoisie, were weak and timid, and because it had not dared defend those who did uphold it, the workers and peasants.

## NOTES

1. The customs, dress, dances, and games of the *majos* and *majas*, the low people of Madrid.

2. The American colonies had benefitted from the politics of enlightened despotism. The condition of the Indian masses slightly improved, the administration was modernized. Under Charles III, a plan to give the colonies to different sons of the monarch and to organize a community of kingdoms was considered. The nationalist ideas impregnated the Creoles. When the French sent Ferdinand VII to Bayonne, the royal authorities vacillated in America, but the Creoles organized juntas and proclaimed independence, not so much from Spain, but from the court of Joseph Bonaparte. They sent delegates to

the Parliament of Cádiz. But meanwhile, the conviction arose that it was better to maintain independence even after the return of Ferdinand VII to Madrid. There was a long war between the royal troops and the improvised independence forces. Finally the latter triumphed.

# 6

# *Bloody Years*

For almost a century, except for brief intervals, Spain would be under tutelage. The Spanish people would be governed by elites. Only by bearing this in mind can the history of the country in the last one hundred years be understood. And it is only thus that its explosions, experiments, and failures can be explained without recourse to such easy clichés as "the Spanish temperament," "the Hispanic fury," and other such banalities.

From 1875 until 1918, Spanish political life was very peaceful, so much so that this period has received the well-deserved title of "the foolish years." Cánovas had a democratic constitution formally approved, but he established a practice which eliminated the people from government. Two parties, the conservative one of Cánovas and the liberal of Praxedes Mateo Sagasta (1825-1903) took turns at the reins of power. Elections were controlled by local caciques (political bosses),[1] and caciquism was accepted and recognized by all. Only in certain working-class and middle-class districts of several large cities would candidates opposed to the regime succeed. The opposition of the extreme Right was that of Carlist traditionalism (since the third Carlist war which began under the Republic was terminated shortly after the Restoration), while that of the Left consisted of the Republicans and later a few Socialists. Outside the system were the anarchists. The number of votes registered in the elections was small even after universal suffrage had been reestablished in 1890.

In 1878 the Socialist party was founded. It was led by a printer, Pablo Iglesias (1850-1925), who later became the first representative of his party in Parliament. The Socialists predominated, their ranks growing slowly, in regions where anarchism had not penetrated: the north, the Basque Country, the center, especially Madrid. They established their own unions in these regions, which in 1888 united to form the General Union of Workers (UGT).

The growth of the anarchist movement was faster. It had been banned by the Restoration but still enjoyed a great deal of influence in Catalonia, Valencia, and among Andalusian peasants. In 1881 in Barcelona, the Federation of Workers of the Spanish Region was founded, to unite the unions led by anarchists. From that point on, the movement incorporated two tendencies: syndicalist and pure anarchist.

The law forbade strikes, but it could not prevent them. Rather it forced the workers' movement into illegality and violent action. Their most frequent demands were the eight-hour day, the regulation of women and child labor, and the right to unionize. But the anarchists, and with them large masses of Catalonian workers and Andalusian peasants, had a broader objective: the establishment of an egalitarian society without authority. To accomplish this goal, they resorted to terrorist methods. In 1892, a bomb was thrown at General Martínez Campos, who escaped uninjured. Later, an anarchist threw a bomb into the Opera House in Barcelona; detentions, tortures, executions. Retaliation: bombs thrown at religious processions and military parades. Cánovas was assassinated by an Italian anarchist. Meanwhile in Andalusia there were riots. The police arrested and executed numerous members of a secret anarchist organization, the Black Hand. Fermín Salvochea (1842-1907) agitated and educated the peasants in the south, who worshipped him.

In 1885, Alfonso XII died, leaving an expectant wife. When her son was born, Queen María Cristina remained in charge of the regency until 1902. Naturally, nothing changed. Nor did anything change after 1898, when Spain lost its last colonies. Partisans of independence in Cuba had again risen in rebellion, in spite of a promise of autonomy which had already been granted to Puerto Rico. The United States, for expansionist motives, involved itself in a war with Spain just as the Cubans had almost achieved victory. Spain sued for peace. By the Treaty of Paris, Cuba was proclaimed independent (although due to the Platt amendment to its constitution, the island remained virtually submitted to U.S. influence). The United States acquired Puerto Rico and the Philippine Islands as colonies. In order to pay the debts incurred by the war, Spain sold to Germany the islands it possessed in the Marian Archipelago, except Guam which was conceded to the United States.

The loss of the last colonies had deep repercussions in Spain. The Catalonian bourgeoisie, which enjoyed large profits from commercial dealings with Cuba, lost this market, which added to its discontent with the politics of Madrid. The intellectuals began to analyze the causes for the decline of the country and suggest remedies for them. The military for their part, found in Morocco, where Spain still possessed limited territories, compensation for the humiliation the country had suffered with the loss of the war with Cuba. All that remained of the empire were a few areas in western Africa (Guinea, Fernando Poo, the Sahara, and two cities in Morocco).

Thus Spain was to enter the twentieth century burdened with problems which had survived from previous centuries, but which became more acute in the modern Western world where capitalism and industrialism predominated.

Most important was the agrarian problem. From 11 million inhabitants in 1808, the population reached the 18 million mark by 1900. Agricultural productivity in Spain was very low. Extensive (as opposed to intensive) cultivation did not permit its increase, and the government's irrigation policy was weak. In the south and center, the regions of least productivity, latifundia prevailed. In 1900, ten thousand families (many of them aristocratic) owned 50 percent of the cultivated land; 1 percent of landowners had 42 percent of the arable land. These lands were badly cultivated, many of them devoted to pasture for bulls or to hunting areas. When they were worked, it was done by agricultural workers who were forced to survive for an entire year with little more than some 150 days' wages. Each morning they would gather at the town plaza, where the landowner's foreman would come to select those who were to work that day. Naturally, those who belonged to socialist or anarchist groups were never chosen. If there were protests or strikes, the foreman, with the support of the Civil Guard, would have day workers come from another town.

In other regions the land was so subdivided that no single family was able to subsist on it. Galicia, which is a typical small-farm region, supplied almost half of the Spanish emigrants to Latin America. In Catalonia, a large portion of the peasant masses was composed of *rabassaires* tenant farmers of vineyards, from which they could not be dismissed as long as the vine lived. Phylloxera, which on two occasions destroyed the vineyards, left these peasants without any legal protection and provoked strong social conflicts.

All of this meant that Spain was a poor market for industrial products. It was in fact limited to the cities. This situation led to a second
problem: that of the industrial zones. In the Basque Country thrived a
steel industry supported by British capital. At the turn of the century,
nationalist tendencies appeared. These were based upon the differences between the Basque language and that of the rest of Spain, and
also upon the desire of the Basque capitalists and middle class for
greater influence in national politics. In Catalonia, where light industry, especially textiles, abounded, and where there existed an historic
tradition of political independence, there had been a cultural renaissance beginning in 1832. The Catalan language, which since the days
of Philip V had been banished to the countryside, once again became
the language of culture, spoken in the cities. Catalonian industrialists
searched for a way to have their influence felt in Madrid.
They especially hoped to attain a protectionist policy. Castilian and
Andalusian grape and cereal growers, who exported their products, opposed this move. Little by little, this led to the renaissance of
Catalonian national consciousness and to the organization of Catalonian movements in search of autonomy. The outcome of these
movements came at the turn of the century when the Regionalist
League was formed, composed primarily of the middle class.

This same problem of modernization also worried the intellectuals
belonging to the Generation of '98, thus named for the year of the loss
of the last colonies. Spanish intellectuals at the end of the nineteenth
century found themselves in a culturally arid Spain.

> *Impoverished Castile, yesteryear's might*
> *swathed in rags,*
> *scorns all that she does not know,*

wrote Antonio Machado (1875-1939), one of the poets of '98. As did
he, many others tried to understand their country. Miguel de Unamuno (1864-1936), a Hellenist and essayist, was an *avant-la-lettre*
existentialist who learned Danish in order to read Kierkegaard and
who, with his paradoxes, lashed out at Spanish inertia. The
philosopher José Ortega y Gasset (1883-1955) imported German ideas
and tried to teach Spaniards to place reason above their primary
sentiments. Joan (John) Maragall (1860-1911) in Catalonia asked that
Spain stop talking about glory and death. The sociologist Joaquín
Costa (1866-1911) defended the Spanish collectivist tradition and demanded that Spain adopt a "policy of school and kitchen." A
pedagogue, Francisco Giner de los Ríos (1840-1915), founded the Free
Institution of Learning in 1876. Here the children of the liberal middle
class of Madrid were educated into a progressive elite. The children of

well-heeled parents went to Germany and England to study, returning convinced that Spain needed to become Europeanized. They
hoped to attain this objective primarily through cultural action. The
corrupted politics of the "foolish years" (los años bobos) did not in the
least appeal to them and they had no contact with the workers'
movement. If the church appeared to them as responsible, to a large
extent, for the cultural backwardness of the country and the persistence of feudal customs, due to its near-monopoly on private education, the anarchists seemed to them simple and irresponsible dreamers, for whom they felt the scorn of any university graduate toward
the self-taught man.

What they failed to understand was that Spanish anarchism was an
inevitable, transitory phenomenon which could render some benefits
to the country. Anarchism is found in backward countries (at times
for technical reasons, as in France, at others for social reasons, as in
Italy or Argentina) with relatively weak capitalist enclaves. Anarchis-
tic messianism was forged into the peasant's mentality and brought
to it an awareness of his frustrations and means of action which the
peasant could understand: riots, terrorism, "taking from the rich to
give the poor," the secret sect. Furthermore, anarchism gave the
peasants who had been transplanted into the cities a hope that would
justify their uprooting. The anarchists, all things considered, including their fanaticism, were not dogmatic. They greatly respected the
culture and could have been incorporated into broader movements
for the modernization of Spain, had this modernization assumed a
social character and had they been taken seriously by the intellectuals. But they were left in isolation and thus were not able to overcome
the simplistic character of their ideas.

But the military did take the anarchists seriously. The anarchists
were of use to them as a pretext for intervention in the politics of the
present century. As we have seen, Spanish militarism sprang from
liberal roots. But with the Restoration, the army became conformist.
The Cuban war discredited and demoralized it so much so that, instead of reforming, it preferred to devote itself to minor operations in
Morocco and seek the protection of the court. The court responded
favorably, and in exchange, obtained the total adhesion of the military to the established system. The army became little more than a
bodyguard to those who had arrogated themselves the role of Spain's
guardians.

With Alfonso XIII (1886-1941), who had come of age in 1902, the
guardianship was to pass from the hands of the parties to the
monarch. As he opened the first meeting of his ministers, Alfonso

XIII announced: "From this moment on, I reserve the right to make all military commissions." He was sixteen years old. As he listened to the monarch, Sagasta, the leader of the government, must have thought back to the moment when the queen's chambermaid had placed the newborn infant in his arms, as he was the prime minister, and he himself had proclaimed to the court: "Gentlemen, we now have a king." Later on, he added to Cánovas, commenting on the helplessness of the infant: "We have the smallest quantity possible of a king."

Sagasta was mistaken. Alfonso XIII was the greatest possible quantity of a king that twentieth-century Spain could bear. In all probability, Alfonso XIII's problem was that he did not know how to gauge the point up to which he could go. To all appearances, he seemed a happy, crowd-pleasing, foul-mouthed, stately, playboy figure. But in reality he was a tragic figure. By temperament, he was an activist. Had he not been king, he more than likely would have entered politics. The ceremonial role of a constitutional monarch seemed to him a narrow one. Although many Spaniards considered him to be indifferent to the fate of the country, he began his reign with the evident desire to contribute to what was then called the regeneration of Spain. It is possible that he might have attained this objective had he not found himself imbedded in the quicksand of the cacique brand of politics, and had he not breathed the scorn for the common people that the aristocracy of the era spewed into the air. During his reign, several reforms were attempted that would have given social content to formal democracy had they been effected with the people instead of out of fear of the people. In a tutelar society he wished to be the only guardian. Finally, Spain became fed up with living under guardianship. This cost him the throne.

He reigned for twenty-nine years curdled with crises. The first was Barcelona's Tragic Week in 1909. In Catalonia the anarquist movement had grown rapidly. The powerful Catalonian Federation of Unions was formed, which, in 1910, joined unions from other parts of Spain and became the National Confederation of Workers (Confederación Nacional del Trabajo, CNT). Alongside the Catalonism of the bourgeois Regionalist League there was the Catalonist movement of the middle class, which was both Republican and moderate leftist. The government feared that this Catalonism and anarchism would merge. In order to separate the two movements, a young newspaperman, Alejandro Lerroux (1864-1949), a clever demagogue, was sent to Barcelona. There he formed a radical party whose youthful members were given the name of "barbarian youth." Lerroux insisted on the crudest anticlericalism ("lift up the novices' skirts and raise them to the level of motherhood," he said in one of his speeches). He knew how to draw in the little-educated masses, and he won over a large number of people from the anarchist ranks.

But Lerroux lost control of the masses when a few incidents in Morocco grew into a war which the people detested. One by one, shiploads of troops headed for Africa. In order to impede the embarkings, in July 1909 a large group gathered at the port of Barcelona. There were confrontations with the police. The people, exasperated, lashed out at their traditional enemy, the church. They burned dozens of convents. During a week, the city was at the hands of the workers and the army, who harassed people in the streets. Lerroux was traveling abroad. The press called these events The Tragic Week.

Hundreds were arrested, among them an anarchist teacher, Francisco Ferrer Guardia (1849-1909), founder of the Modern School. During this time the anarchists had created a series of schools supported by their unions, just as they had choirs, popular cultural clubs (Ateneos), publishing houses which produced works by Kropotkin and Bakunin as well as books dealing with sexual questions, vegetarianism, nudism, "the secret powers of the Jesuits," etc. In spite of an intense campaign in Ferrer's favor throughout the entire world, he was sentenced and executed (October 13, 1909). At that time, the Conservative Antonio Maura (1853-1925) headed the government. He tried to effect a program of modernization of the country. But the people identified him with the execution of Ferrer, which had really been imposed by the Catalonist bourgeoisie. From that point on Maura remained displaced from the political scene. Maura had made both unions and strikes legal and had promulgated the so-called law of the chair, which forced employers to furnish their women workers with chairs.

The Tragic Week had occasioned a rapprochement of the Catalonist bourgeoisie and the Madrid government. The year 1912 witnessed the outcome of this rapprochement with the establishment of the Mancomunitat de Catalunya, that is, a form of Catalonian administration based on a legal association of the four Catalonian provinces and their agencies, for the purpose of coordinate action. The Mancomunitat was not given the faculty of imposing taxes nor the power to legislate, and was therefore able to do little. Nevertheless, under the presidency of the leader of the Regionalist League, Enric Prat de la Riba (1870-1917), it modernized communications which linked Barcelona with the four Catalonian provinces and developed middle and higher education. The Mancomunitat was not autonomy, but it was perceived as the first step toward it.

In order to attain autonomy, the Catalonian bourgeoisie would have to struggle so that Spanish society would be converted from a feudal to a capitalist society. This would require applying pressure on the government for reforms. But the government had the police, and the police was indispensable for facing the anarchists. The Catalonian bourgeoisie was not willing to have a dialogue with the anarchists or to give the workers living conditions which would draw them away from anarchism. Therefore, Madrid was still needed. Furthermore, Madrid fixed the customs tariffs, and Catalonian industry, which was already anachronistic due to its family enterprises, needed this protection. The Catalonian bourgeoisie then was allied, though not with much stability, to the feudal forces of the court. Thus the possibility of the modernization of Spain, accelerated by the bourgeoisie's pressure, was lost.

It seemed that World War I would modify the situation. The country maintained its neutrality, with the court sympathizing with the Central Powers and the urban people with the Allies. But business was carried on with both sides. A class of nouveaux riches was quickly formed. The Germans organized a terrorist band to frighten those who sold to the Allies. The workers pressed to obtain part of the wealth which poured into the country; they did obtain some of it, enough so that in the anarchist movement there would predominate the revolutionary syndicalist tendency headed by Salvador Seguí (1886-1923), who wanted a society in which the labor unions would take the place of the stage.

The year 1917 presented a double opportunity to unify Socialists and syndicalists and overthrow the monarchy. The army was discontent, since the king favored his friends when granting promotions. Military Juntas of Defense were formed in Barcelona to protest against favoritism. By mid-year, the Catalonists, many Liberals, and Republicans suggested that Parliament draw up a new constitution, that is, they raised the possibility of changing the regime legally. When the government refused, the members of Parliament who favored this line of action met in Barcelona. The police broke up this meeting. Nothing happened because the Military Juntas of Defense did not support this Assembly of Parliamentarians. But strong feelings had been stirred in the country and in the court. Next, the two labor federations, UGT and CNT, formed an alliance and declared a general strike throughout the country, supporting a strike of railroad workers. Revolutionary syndicalism tacitly abandoned its antipolitical position. But the Socialists did not dare go any further and the alliance was dissolved. Francesc Cambó (1876-1947), leader of the Catalonian League, accepted a government post. The monarchy had been saved. The general strike had made the country tremble. There had been deaths, wounded, and thousands of arrests. The workers' movement had demonstrated that it was now a true force. Spain was entering a period in which everything would revolve about the workers' movement, on the one hand, and the national vindication of Catalonia, on the other.

If the two forces had merged, the country would have been able to change. But the Catalonian bourgeoisie was too frightened. The church organized Catholic unions, which the police later used to form what were called "free unions," but which were really groups of gun-toting gangsters to break up strikes, which were becoming increasingly frequent and violent. The CNT used its own groups of defense to combat the "free unions." Assassination attempts constantly occurred: one day an employer would be found riddled with bullet holes; the next day, it would be a union leader; the next, a gangster hired by the employers' association. The Archbishop of Zaragoza and the chief of the government, Eduardo Dato (1856-1921) were assassinated, just as Cánovas and José Canalejas (1854-1912) had been previously.

Among Catalonists there were groups which did not want Catalonism to be the monopoly of the bourgeoisie and the national vindications of Catalonia to be identified with those of the bourgeois league. One of them, Francesc Layret (1880-1920), a deputy and lawyer of the CNT, was felled by the bullets of a gunman. Later, Salvador Seguí was assassinated. In Parliament, a Conservative minister asked for more "workers' blood." The CNT reached a membership figure of 700,000, while the Socialist UGT claimed 110,000 members. The Socialist party split, and a minority group formed the Communist party in 1920; the CNT adhered for a few months to the Third International, but later on withdrew, in light of the increasingly dictatorial character of the Soviet government.

Meanwhile, the situation in Morocco was growing worse. In 1912, Spain and France had established a joint protectorate over this country, with Spain controlling the northern part, across Gibraltar. The army had begun "pacification" operations against the guerrillas of Abd-el-Krim. The king, via his generals, directed the progress of this exhausting war. In the course of an operation prepared by the monarch, there was a disaster on Mount Annual, which cost the lives of 12,000 soldiers (1921). Fifteen hundred survivors were taken prisoner. Abd-el-Krim asked for five million pesetas for their ransom. When the king found this out, he commented: "Chicken meat is really expensive." The indignation that followed was tremendous. The people had no faith left in the army, which claimed 11,000 officials for 80,000 soldiers. Parliament had no alternative but to launch an investigation. Everyone was certain that this would point out the king's responsibility.

Mussolini rose to power in Italy. The king began to make speeches in which he spoke of Parliamentary corruption and inefficiency of the political parties. The press pointed out that in Barcelona, the five-hundredth victim of terrorism had fallen. The king consecrated Spain to the Sacred Heart of Jesus.

Parliament indicted General Dámaso Berenguer (1873-1953), the high commissioner in Morocco, and one of the king's advisers. The palace felt the threat coming closer. The king reacted, and, through the efforts of a few military friends, he began to prepare a coup d'état. It was carried out on September 13, 1923, by General Miguel Primo de Rivera (1876-1930), captain-general of Catalonia. He promised the League to put an end to terrorism and the League supported him. The government did not resist. Twenty-four hours later, the general was in Madrid, where he formed a Military Directorate of ten generals and an admiral.

In his first public statement, the general announced that "this is a movement of men." This set the tone. Primo de Rivera was a bon vivant who sincerely believed he could regenerate Spain. He would not use terror but he would use censorship, especially to force the newspapers to publish his "unofficial notes," which he himself wrote in an effort to explain to the Spaniards the good intentions of the dictatorship. But the Spaniards were skeptical.

The workers' movement and the Republicans were caught off guard. They did not react. The CNT declared a general strike, but it failed. The directorate declared the CNT illegal. For the next seven years its activities were underground. Often these were undertaken with the cooperation of the more active Republican groups, in which such prominent figures as Lluis Companys (1883-1940) and Francesc Macià (1859-1933) were included. Companys was the lawyer for the CNT in Barcelona, while Macià was an exiled ex-colonel who had left the army to head a group of radical Catalonists. The Socialists, although they did not support the dictatorship, later on decided that one of their leaders should accept a post in the State Council, which the dictator had offered. The Socialists' desire to displace the CNT had become an obsession; they hoped that the dictatorship would do away with the anarcho-syndicalist organization. To a large measure, this explained their passivity.

Parliament was dissolved, army officials replaced the mayors, teaching in Catalan was forbidden, the Mancomunitat was dissolved, and trial by jury annulled. Military leaders occupied all administrative posts of the state. And the dossier regarding the responsibility for Morocco disappeared from Parliament's vaults.

The Military Directorate lasted two years, until the end of 1925. The opposition during this time was especially that of intellectuals. Miguel de Unamuno was dismissed from his university chair. The prisons were filled with anarchists. The government organized a sole political party, the Patriotic Union, which was never really popular nor did it dare adopt the external form of fascism. Primo de Rivera tried to negotiate in Morocco but failed. But when military necessity forced Abd-el-Krim to face the French, he was defeated with the cooperation of Spanish soldiers and taken prisoner. The war in Morocco came to an end after having involved Spain for nearly a century.

Shady deals were initiated from the palace (the dictator never took part in these as he was an honorable man). As a popular poet commented in one of the newspapers:

> The Spanish people are fools
> to whom it doesn't seem to matter
> that dirtier is the broom
> than the filth that it scatters.

But the people began to take note of what was going on. The still small ranks of the opposition began to grow. Toward the end of 1925, the Military Directorate abandoned its position to a Civil Directorate, in which the most prominent figure was the bright minister of finance José Calvo Sotelo (1893-1936). The Civil Directorate would, in its own way, try to modernize the country. It established, for example, a petroleum monopoly, with oil from the Soviet Union; it changed teaching methods to one single textbook per subject—compulsory, inexpensive, and biased; it reorganized the tax system; it built a broad network of highways; it established arbitration committees, to settle work conflicts and to "put an end to class struggles"; and it organized two simultaneous world fairs in Seville and Barcelona (1929). But at the same time, it announced a new penal code with hard penalties for political crimes. It also authorized the minister of justice to dismiss or transfer judges and magistrates. Furthermore, it granted to a U.S. company, ITT, the concession to modernize telephone services. The shady deals continued. The peseta, overburdened by debts contracted by the dictatorship to carry out public works, began to fall; it became necessary to contract a public loan of 350 million gold pesetas to support it, and later 151 million gold pesetas had to be sold for the same purpose.

Opposition grew. A handful of anarchists, apparently stirred up by a secret police agent, tried to penetrate the country but were machine-gunned down in Vera del Bidasoa: two survivors were executed by garrote, another committed suicide; a group of young left-wing Catalonists planned an assassination attempt against the royal train: the bomb did not explode; there were seven arrests, tortures, and long prison sentences. Francesc Macià organized an "invasion" of Catalonia, but an informer betrayed him and he and his group were arrested by the French police in Prats de Molló. Miguel de Unamuno was exiled; he escaped exile and established himself in France. The then-famous novelist Vicente Blasco Ibáñez (1867-1928), using the money from the sale of his novels to Hollywood, financed the printing of pamphlets and books against the dictatorship and tried to distribute them over Spain from an airplane. Artillery officers protested against promotions they considered illegal; the government dissolved the artillery branch of the army. Students held strikes and demonstrations, and their leaders were exiled. There was an attempted military insurrection in Ciudad Real. Later, the Conservative ex-minister José Sánchez Guerra (1858-1935) tried to get the garrison in Valencia to rebel and was arrested. A Catalonian Communist party was formed, independent from Moscow. In 1931 this party would become united with the Catalonian Federation of the Communist party, separated from it by its opposition to the line imposed by Moscow, and the two would form the Workers' and Peasants' Bloc (Bloque Obrero y Campesino—BOC), headed by Joaquín Maurin (1896-1973). The Iberian Anarchist Federation (FAI) was secretly constituted in 1927.

Corruption continued, and the people became more aware of it despite censorship. There were dirty deals concerning oil, telephones, railroads, and even gambling. This alienated the bourgeoisie. And when the effects of the worldwide economic crisis of 1929 were felt in Spain, the bourgeoisie entered the ranks of the opposition.

At this point, Primo de Rivera tried to "liberalize" the dictatorship. He convoked a National Assembly. He named by decree many professors and former politicians to fill its benches. Most of them did not accept. Even the Socialist party refused, despite the fact that it was the only party which the dictatorship allowed to operate, and the labor unions of the UGT were the only ones that functioned, although they were unable to do anything to defend the workers. There was a general strike in Barcelona in January 1928 organized by the anarchists. New conspiracies were discovered, and there were also new attempts at military coups. To confront the general discontent, the dictator requested the support of the army and ordered the captain-generals to sound out the general opinion of their officers. All the replies were unfavorable toward continuation of the dictatorship. The king was restless. Through a minister, Alfonso XIII ordered the dictator to resign, without even personally speaking to him, and he did so on January 22, 1930. A month and a half later, he died, saddened and disgusted, in a second-class Paris hotel.

To establish a dictatorship is easy. To get rid of it is most difficult, as Alfonso XIII now discovered. The king called to the government his friend General Dámasco Berenguer, chief of his personal guard, who reestablished the Constitution of 1876. He invited those who had been exiled to return and granted amnesty to political prisoners. Political lectures and meetings were authorized. The former parties reappeared, and with them, the old leaders. But they found themselves ignored. The people wanted change. The unions were reorganized. Various monarchist politicians declared themselves Republicans. Foremost among these was ex-minister Niceto Alcalá Zamora (1877-1949). José Sánchez Guerra, who still held a great deal of prestige, affirmed his allegiance to the monarchic system in a lecture, but, in citing the following verse, gave evidence of his new political views: "To no longer serve lords/who will become worms." He hoped to provoke the king's abdication and the coronation of one of his sons.

The students demonstrated and the government closed the universities. New political parties attracted the people: The Catalonian Action party, founded in 1923, but scarcely able to function at that time; Unió Socialista de Catalunya (USC), also founded in 1923, and which interested mostly intellectuals and white-collar workers; and BOC, which attracted many youths. Within the CNT there was a power struggle between the syndicalists and the FAI. The Socialist party almost doubled the number of its members. Cambó, of the League, and Santiago Alba (1872-1942), the politician against whom the dictator had directed most of his attacks, unsuccessfully tried to form a party of the Center. The peseta continued to fall.

On August 17, 1930, a group of Republican personalities met in San Sebastián to sign a pact which would commit the Republic to grant

Catalonia a statute of autonomy. The signatories formed a revolutionary committee that included leftist Republicans, Socialists, and Catalonists. Its greatest problem was to secure the aid of the CNT, without which nothing could be done. But a military insurrection was also considered, and sympathetic military men organized the Republican Military Union.

In October, an attempted coup by the air force of Madrid, headed by General Gonzalo Queipo del Llano (1875-1951) and the pilot Ramón Franco (1896-1938), failed. The latter was a popular figure for having been the first to fly across the South Atlantic in the plane *Plus Ultra*. The capital was "bombed" with manifestos. More strikes. Arrests. Student protests. Confrontations with the police. José Ortega y Gasset announced his Republican allegiance. Macià entered Catalonia and the police escorted him to the border.

On December 12 two captains, Fermín Galán (1899-1930) and Angel García Hernández (1900-30), rebelled in Jaca, in the Pyrenees. Both were arrested and executed. The coup had been part of a movement planned by the Revolutionary Committee, which later suspended it. But in Jaca this was not known. Great emotion throughout the country. Arrest of the members of the Revolutionary Committee. A general strike throughout Spain, which failed in Madrid, because a Socialist faction opposed the alliance with the Republicans. Many intellectuals formed an Association for Service to the Republic (Agrupación al Servicio de la República), headed by Ortega y Gasset.

After so much tension, it seemed that peace had returned. Berenguer wanted to take advantage of this pause to call for elections. The opposition rejected the idea of elections for fear of losing them; they had still not captured the mood of the country. In the cities the air was filled with hope. The people sensed that something new was coming. The only ones who did not realize this were the court and the Republican politicians themselves.

Berenguer, as a result of his failure, resigned in February 1931. Sánchez Guerra accepted to try to form a new government, but wished first to confer with the Revolutionary Committee. For this purpose he went to the prison, where he talked to the prisoners. They refused to be part of any monarchic government. An admiral, Juan Bautista Aznar (1860-1933), finally formed the government, which included politicians from the League and several monarchists. Thus the Catalonian bourgeoisie closed the door to the future in its own face. The first thing Aznar did was to announce municipal elections for Sunday, April 12. He was confident that they would have no political significance, since they would be mere administrative elections. On the other hand, he felt that they would alleviate the tension.

On March 20, the Revolutionary Committee was tried. After a political speech by each of the accused, they were condemned to a prison sentence of six months and one day. It was suspended, and they were freed. The public prosecutor had requested a fifteen-year sentence. New student demonstrations. Macià returned to Barcelona and formed a new party, Esquerra Republicana de Catalunya (Republican Left of Catalonia). The other politicians did not give it any hope of success.

The elections were drawing near; the united Republicans and Socialists presented candidates to oppose the Union of the Right, to which was added Cambó's improvised party of the Center. The Revolutionary Committee did not believe elections could change anything. April 12, 1931 saw 22,150 monarchic aldermen and 5,775 Republicans elected. But the number of votes received by Republicans in all the country's cities and the capitals of the provinces was almost as great as that which the monarchists gleaned from the towns and villages run by caciques. Since the Restoration, the average number of votes won by the triumphant candidate had been 23 percent of the registered voters. But in 1931 in Barcelona the Esquerra had gathered 47 percent, which came as a surprise to everyone, including the party organizers. The anarchists had abandoned their apoliticism to vote en masse for the Republicans. The people had been more perceptive than their leaders. They would continue to be so for the next five years.

## NOTE

1. The cacique was the chief of an Indian tribe in Spanish America. By extension, this name was given to the strongman, not necessarily a legal authority, who controlled a group of electors. The cacique would obtain favors for his people and also knew how to make life difficult for those who opposed him. Each party had its caciques. The custom spread so widely that even the Republicans had their caciques, although these based their forces more on personal prestige than violence or corruption. At its height, corruption was not so much based on bribery as on favors and privileges for one's friends. Many politicians died poor men, while many became poor through politics.

# 7

# *The Republic Revisited*

The Palace District in Madrid gave the voting majority to the Republicans: the servants had voted against their masters. Traditionally monarchic cities voted Republican. It was the same in the rich residential districts of Barcelona. The surprise was not confined to the palace. Manuel Azaña (1880-1940), an intellectual and member of the Revolutionary Committee had declared a few days prior to the vote: "It would be naive to expect anything to come from the elections." The naiveté of the people had placed the Republic in the hands of the very leaders who had demonstrated this lack of confidence in the people.

The most astute of the monarchic politicians, the Count of Romanones (1863-1950), went to visit his dentist, who was also the king's dentist, and of course had voted Republican. The count asked the dentist to see the monarch and tell him that the only solution was his departure from Spain. The king tried to save at least the dynasty. He ordered his minister of war to consult with the captain-generals to find out if the army was ready to defend the throne. The answer was negative. Admiral Aznar resigned and commented to the press: "The Spaniards went to sleep as monarchists and awoke as Republicans." The king announced consultations to form a new government.

The Revolutionary Committee made a declaration which asked for the change of the regime. As night fell, crowds filled the streets with shouts of: "Death to the king; let him depart." The first Republican flags appeared (horizontal stripes of red, yellow, and purple). The police were impassible.

On April 14, 1931, Romanones and Alcalá Zamora held an interview in the home of Dr. Gregorio Marañón (1887-1960), a famous physician whom from that day on the people referred to as "the midwife of the Republic." The count requested a truce of one week. Alcalá Zamora declared that the king should depart immediately for his own safety. They agreed on his departing from Cartagena in a battleship. Romanones went to inform the monarch. Meanwhile, in the Plaza de San Jaume in Barcelona (where the City Hall and the palace of the former independent Catalonian government of the Middle Ages are), people who were casually passing by stopped as they heard shouts proceeding from the balcony of the City Hall. There they saw a man raise a Republican flag. Then they heard a few sentences in Catalan: "Citizens, long live the Republic!" Lluis Companys, of the Esquerra, had just proclaimed the Republic without waiting for negotiations or indications from Madrid.

From the balcony of the palace across the square, Francesc Macià proclaimed the Catalonian Republic. In the Basque city of Eibar, the workers did the same. The people did not wait for orders from the Revolutionary Committee. The news circulated throughout Spain in a few minutes. In the Royal Palace they knew that with the Republic in Barcelona there was no possibility of manuevering or resisting.

By mid-afternoon, the streets of the cities and towns throughout Spain were filled with excited crowds with makeshift Republican flags. Street cars, taxis, and private cars were filled with chanting and flag-waving people. The monarchic flag and the crown at the top of the coat of arms disappeared from official centers and government buildings. Even military men went out into the street with a Republican flag. Large photographs, printed in haste, of the captains shot to death at Jaca four months earlier, appeared. The crowds sang the Marseillaise, since the Republic still had no anthem.

Whoever has lived through these moments of collective jubiliation preserves within himself a very stirring memory. The faith of the people, who believed that everything had been resolved with the king's departure, was extremely moving. Everybody had the certainty that the king would leave and that the will of the people was irresistible. There was no fear or tension to be found, only happiness. Civilians, policemen, and soldiers embraced each other in the streets in idyllic euphoria. The taverns served free drinks. Stores and factories were closed. Sirens reverberated nonstop. A few loyalists who shouted "Long live the king!" were given a few good-natured swats and they kept silent. The children played at being Republicans.

On the fences encircling the Oriente Palace in Madrid, signs were posted which read: "People, respect this palace, it is yours." General José Sanjurjo (1872-1936), a fervent monarchist and chief of the Civil Guard, was the monarch's last hope. But the general said to the king, "I guarantee order, but nothing more. We will not interfere in the matter of the regime. The mission of the Civil Guard is not a political one."

Nobles filled the palace. Alcalá Zamora telephoned a warning that if the transfer of power were not soon carried out, the Revolutionary Committee could not guarantee the king's safety. Shouts from the multitude which had begun to gather across from the palace reached the inner chambers: "¡Que se vaya! ¡Que se vaya!" (Let him leave!).

In the evening the king exited via the back door of the palace by car. At daybreak, he boarded ship in Cartegena. Once on board, he signed a document addressed to the country: "The elections held on Sunday have clearly indicated to me that I do not possess the love of my people. My conscience tells me that this aversion is temporary. . . . I do not renounce any of my rights, since they are not just mine; they are the trust accumulated throughout history. . . . I hope to know the authentic and adequate expression of the collective conscience and, as the nation speaks, I deliberately suspend the exercise of royal power, and I shall remove myself from Spain, recognizing it as the only mistress of its fate." The king had yielded, but did not abdicate (he would do so ten years later, in exile, in favor of his third-born son, Juan [b. 1913], the present Count of Barcelona, since his first-born was a hemophiliac and his second a deaf-mute).

The members of the Revolutionary Committee arrived by motorcade at the Ministry of Interior (which controlled the police) in the center of Madrid. When the news that the king had already departed Madrid was received, they went out onto the balcony and proclaimed the Republic. Until daybreak, the crowds paraded through the streets, singing and shouting. Not one shot was fired nor one drop of blood shed. At dawn, the royal family left by train. Political exiles began to return, as did thousands of Spaniards who had left their country to avoid taking part in the war in Africa.

For the second time, Spain had proclaimed the Republic without a glimpse of violence. Alcalá Zamora affirmed in a radio broadcast: "The entire world admires Spain." But the people sang: "He [the king] didn't leave; we threw him out!"

Marx, in a series of articles dealing with Spain, published in 1854 in the *New York Tribune*, wrote: "Spain has never been able to assimilate the very recent French procedure, much in vogue in 1848, of beginning and ending a revolution in the space of three days. Spain's attempts in this field are much more vast in extension and intensity. Her minimum revolutionary cycle is one of three years, and, often, it is prolonged for as many as nine years." The members of the Revolutionary Committee had not read Marx and were not aware that they were presiding over the initiation of one of these cycles. It would last exactly eight years, almost on a day-to-day basis.

The provisional government named Niceto Alcalá Zamora as provisional chief of state and government. Three Socialists were included in the cabinet (one in Finances, another in Justice, and the third in Labor), as were one Catalonian, one Galician, two radicals (moderate, from Lerroux's party), two right-wing Republicans, and two left-wing Republicans. For the first time in modern times, the minister of war was a civilian instead of a military man; there was no one in uniform in the cabinet. The military leaders rushed to place themselves at the orders of Alcalá Zamora. France recognized the new regime: the other countries followed suit. *L'Illustration* of Paris commented: "The dynasty has been overthrown, but the new regime is not a revolutionary one."

The Spanish aristocrats and bourgeoisie did not share this thought. The flight of capital was enormous. On May 10, rumors of a monarchist conspiracy were circulated; the people were stirred up, and they did what they have always done: they set fire to several churches in Madrid. The government was forced to send the Civil Guard out against the people. In other areas of the country, when news of what had happened in Madrid reached them, temples were set aflame also.

Meanwhile, press commentaries began to warn that it was necessary to give some substance to the Republic, although something had already been done along these lines, especially in Catalonia. Three government ministers went to Barcelona. After a lengthy discussion with Macià, the latter consented to replace his Catalonian Republic with an autonomous government, which would adopt the name of the former Catalonian institution, Generalitat. A statute legalizing this decision would be drawn up, voted upon, and presented to the future Spanish constituent parliament. The radical Catalonists stated that this was claudication; the Centralists felt that it marked the beginnings of the dismemberment of the fatherland. On his part, the minister of labor issued an order forbidding the contracting of workers from another town as long as there were local workers without employment; this was a severe blow against caciquism, since one of the caciques' most effective measures for getting the workers to vote the way they wanted was to threaten to displace them with workers from another town. But the problems were of such magnitude as to require broader and rapid measures.

Who would be able to undertake these measures? The men who began to lead the Republic and who, only a week earlier, never thought it would arrive, had been formed in the mentality of 1898. The novelist Benito Pérez Galdós (1843-1920) had written that "the Spaniard left his home in 1808 and has still not returned to it." The Republican leaders wished to make Spain as European a house as possible to return to. Europe was their model: the constitution which they formulated would be inspired by Weimar's, precisely when Hitler had begun to place it in jeopardy. Their solution for church problems would not differ from that which France had tried half a century earlier. The agrarian reform which they were to attempt was to find its inspiration in those of Eastern Europe of the prior decade. These leaders were intellectuals, without any previous political experience. They had a theoretical idea of the social problem, but they did not know the common people, nor had they lived side-by-side with them. To a certain point, they considered themselves guardians of the people.

Ortega y Gasset justified this elitist position: "It is one of the greatest crimes of the monarchy that it has left Spain useless for the monarchy itself and temporarily so for the Republic. It will be necessary to reconstruct the social tapestry thread by thread and knot by knot." He also underlined the basic problem of the new regime, to rescue the submerged masses: "The great cities were never monarchic since 1873—meanwhile the provinces remained inert. It was not that they were monarchic, but rather that they did not exist politically. And the monarchy's tactic was one of crushing, by making simoniac use of suffrage and elections, the restlessness of some cities with the provincial inertia. Everyone knew and even said that in the provinces there was no voting. . . . The monarchy has lived by speculating with national vices."

Manuel Azaña, "author of works which no one has read," as he described himself, Marcelino Domingo (1884-1938), a teacher, and Alvaro de Albornoz (1879-1954), a lawyer, formed the Republican left wing with its new Republican Alliance party, later called Republican Leftist party. For them, education was most important, and therefore the greatest enemy was the church.

The Center was composed of the former Radical party of Alejandro Lerroux. While under the monarchy, this party had provoked the mistrust of the other Republicans. This was due to its enmity toward the Socialist party, and its obscure origins (it was suspected that Lerroux had been sent to Barcelona at the turn of the century by the government to distract the masses from anarchism and Catalonism). In addition, several of its leaders had become popular for their propensity for shady deals. It was the tragedy of the Republic that its Center, which could have attracted the bourgeoisie, should have fallen into the hands of people of such low stature and shallow prestige. The most prominent figure among the radicals was Diego Martínez Barrio (1883-1962), a lawyer from Seville.

The right wing of the regime was headed by the new president, Niceto Alcalá Zamora, and by the son of the former conservative politician Antonio Maura, Miguel Maura (1887-1971), who was the new minister of interior; his family name stirred the suspicions of the working masses. This right-wing faction of the regime was sincerely Republican, Catholic (although it understood the necessity of the separation of church and state), and moderate in regard to the social question. It was not reactionary. It formed a small Progressive party.

The Socialists constituted a separate force. They had no thoughts of changing the social system, but only of making it more democratic. Above all, they aspired to be the decisive force. The anarchist CNT seemed to them the primary obstacle to their plans. They had experienced union leaders, as Francisco Largo Caballero (1869-1946), who managed the UGT, coupled with the political ability of Indalecio Prieto (1883-1962), who had no real Socialist leanings. Also included in their ranks were several worthwhile intellectuals: Julián Besteiro (1870-1939), a professor of logic, and the only Marxist in the party, and Fernando de los Ríos (1879-1949), a jurist. What the Socialist party was to do would be decisive for the Republic.

A second force which would be decisive was the CNT. At the heart of this organization two distinct branches disputed its course: the syndicalists, led by personalities of the heroic era, all of whom were workers who enjoyed a great deal of popular prestige, such as Joan (John) Peiró (1887-1942) and Angel Pestaña (1881-1937); and the anarchists, organized in the FAI and led by young men of action. These young leaders would not hesitate to stage a holdup to finance a strike with the booty. They included Buenaventura Durruti (1896-1936) and Diego Abad de Santillán (b. 1894).

The Basques had organized their Nationalist Basque party, which was Catholic and, at the moment, indifferent toward the matter of the regime. The Galician autonomists had their own party, which was called Orga. The Catalonians were divided into three parties: the League, on the Right; the Catalonian Action, a party of progressive intellectuals and bourgeoisie, in the Center; and the Esquerra, a party of the middle class, on the Left, whose leader Macià was the most attractive popular figure of the day, not only in Catalonia, but throughout Spain.

The Communist party was a group of little importance which had lost prestige since on April 14 it had launched the absurd slogan "All Power to the Soviets" in a country where few knew what a Soviet was, and where, naturally, not even one Soviet existed. On the other hand, the Workers' and Peasants' Bloc (BOC), although localized in Catalonia and still relatively small, enjoyed a certain prestige owing to its politically keen leader, Maurín, and its enthusiastic young militants.

The extreme Right was formed by several monarchic politicians (among them the count of Romanones, whom the monarchists reproached for having induced the king to leave), and the Traditionalists or Carlists. At the moment, they lacked strength, but they showed themselves to be active and soon formed several rather aggressive youth groups.

The dangerous right wing did not take direct political action. It included the top hierarchy of the church (only one archbishop, Emili Vidal i Barraquer (1868-1943) of Tarragona, seemed ready to accept the new regime) and the Catholic and monarchic press (especially *ABC* and *El Debate* of Madrid, and numerous provincial newspapers). As for the army, although most of its officers had declared themselves Republicans for the sake of convenience, it was a known fact that only a handful of generals and other officers were sincere in this declaration, and that the majority favored the return of the king. The question which constantly plagued both politicians and the people was, each time an important decision was made, what would the army do?

But for the time being, neither the army, the church, the big landowners (who exported their capital and left the workers jobless telling them "let the Republic feed you"), nor the monarchic nobles were able to do anything against the Republic. The people, en masse, including the inert provincial masses, were with the Republic.

The moment seemed propitious to solve the traditional problems of the country. These problems demanded what could be called a bourgeois solution, that is, a democratic revolution: the land problem, the problem of liberty, the problem of the army, the problem of education, the problem of the church, the problem of national minorities, and the problem of economic modernization. The Republic would attempt to solve them in different ways, according to the forces which were successively predominant.

8

# Laws and Realities

Once the Republic had been proclaimed, it was imperative that it be given legal structure and that the instruments for change be created. This task fell jointly upon the provisional government and the Constituent Assembly or *Cortes*, for whom an election was held in June.

The government adopted measures which seemed consubstantial with the proclamation of the new regime. For example, it abolished titles of nobility, lowered the voting age from twenty-five to twenty-three, and established provincial electoral districts, with 80 percent of the posts going to the candidature that received the majority, 20 percent to go to that which followed, and a runoff if no candidature obtained an absolute majority. As the government continued to prepare the bills it would present to the Cortes, it issued several decrees which would have decisive importance.

On May 7 a decree established Mixed Juries of employers and workers, presided over by a delegate of the ministry of labor, to resolve labor conflicts. This decree was the idea of the minister of labor, the Socialist Largo Caballero, and it reflected the UGT's way of dealing with social struggles. But it was evident that it was aimed at placing outside the regime the labor federation which was the rival of the UGT and which also outnumbered its membership, the anarcho-syndicalist CNT. The latter, from its inception, was a partisan of direct action and, by principle, opposed government intervention in labor conflicts. Rather than search for a flexible system which could attract and mollify the CNT and at the same time integrate it into the Republic, the Socialists, guided by their antianarchist obsession, established a system that the CNT could not accept. The Socialists knew that this would place the CNT in an inferior position, without realizing that it would also push the organization toward adventurism, which in the long run would place the Republic in jeopardy. The CNT accused the Socialists of taking advantage of their presence within the government to try to monopolize the labor movement. From this moment on, the radical faction, FAI, displaced the more moderate syndicalists, who if it had been possible, would have wished to integrate their movement into the Republic.

Meanwhile a commission of Catalonian jurists had drawn up an autonomy statute which was later debated by an assembly elected by the municipalities. On August 2, the Catalonian people ratified this statute with a vote of 595,205 in favor and 3,286 against, to be presented to the Cortes.

An urgent reform was that of education. An illiterate rate of 65 percent, the need for at least 50,000 new schools, the social and cultural lack of prestige of teachers, the backward and bureaucratized secondary and higher educational systems, constituted so many obstacles for a regime based on the political culture of the masses. The minister of public instruction, Marcelino Domingo, established a five-year plan for the construction of 27,000 schools, with 7,000 of them to be opened by the beginning of the following school term. Simultaneously, hundreds of scholarships were created and the university faculty was rejuvenated.

With this reform, the government had to face the religious problem, since the church was not ready to abandon its spiritual monopoly over the country. The minister of justice, the moderate Socialist Fernando de los Ríos, issued a decree which established absolute freedom of worship. The bishops published pastoral letters against the decree. The primate Archbishop of Toledo, Cardinal Pedro Segura (1880-1957), an intimate friend of the king, was the most outspoken in this position. The episcopate protested the secularization of cemeteries, the prohibition for military men to attend religious ceremonies with official representation, the exclusion of priests from the Council of Public Education, and the suppression of compulsory religious training in schools, unless the father of a student requested such instruction. Cardinal Segura even reached the point of expressing the clergy's loyalty to the monarchy in a pastoral letter. The government suggested to the cardinal that his absence from Spain would be to his advantage. The cardinal left, only to return later. Finally the minister of interior, Miguel Maura, himself a Catholic, had two civil guards accompany him to the border. The prelates collectively protested against the government and the Vatican suppressed the Seat of Toledo.

At that time, the church held 11,921 rural properties, 97,828 urban properties, and 4,192 annuities. There were 2,919 convents, 763 monasteries, 36,569 nuns, 8,396 friars, in addition to 35,000 secular priests. In total, there were some 80,000 clergy supported by the state. The above figures do not include the wealth of the Jesuits, who were adept at keeping their riches secret. Nevertheless, urban property owned by the Jesuits in Madrid was identified and found to be worth 36 million pesetas in addition to 112 million pesetas worth of rural property. One of their principal business agents held a position on the board of directors of forty-three corporations.

The government also faced the agrarian problem. By decree, it forbade the dispossession of tenants from rural farms for reasons other than lack of payment, since many rural proprietors had evicted their lessees who had voted Republican. Another decree authorized demands for reexamination of leases and contracts.

Another urgent problem, to which the basic instinct for self-preservation demanded immediate resolution, was that of the army. Even the monarchist general Emilio Mola (1887-1937) acknowledged in one of his books that "the army possessed deficient organization." The army was composed of 632 generals, 21,996 officers and chiefs, and 105,000 soldiers. In other terms, there was one officer for every four soldiers, more officers than the German army had as it entered the war in 1939, and more generals than the U.S. Army at the close of the war in 1945. Manuel Azaña, minister of war, took on this problem. First, he issued a decree which modified the oath taken by the military to the following: "I promise, on my honor, to serve the Republic well and faithfully, to obey its laws and defend it with arms." Those who would not sign this oath would be dismissed from the army "not as a sanction," as the decree read, "but as a termination of their contract with the government." All generals and officers did take the oath.

It then became necessary to reduce the size of the army. Azaña reduced it from sixteen divisions to eight. For this he established a voluntary retirement system for those who wished to take advantage of it. He granted them a retirement salary equal to that of the next highest rank attained. To finance the retiree's salaries, the government set aside 115 million pesetas per annum. Eager to intervene in politics, many Republican military men or Republican sympathizers retired, while the monarchists remained, since Azaña let each decide for himself. Naturally, no longer could civilians be tried by the military, except in cases where a State of War had been declared.

Social restlessness increased. The minister of finance, Indalecio Prieto, criticized the contract between the dictatorship and ITT, and the telephone workers went on strike. In Andalusia, Pedro Vallina (1879-1970), a physician, carried out an intense anarchist campaign among the peasants. At the Military Airport of Tablada, a conspiracy of corporals and sergeants to establish libertarian communism (anarchism) was discovered. The CNT was definitely in opposition to the Republic and intermittently went out into the streets.

On June 28, after an impassioned electoral campaign, the country elected the Constituent Assembly, composed of the following deputies:

| | |
|---|---:|
| Socialists | 116 |
| Radicals (Lerroux) | 90 |
| Radical Socialists (Domingo) | 56 |
| Esquerra de Catalunya (Macià) | 42 |
| Republican Action (Azaña) | 26 |
| Progressives (Alcalá Zamora) | 22 |
| At the Service of the Republic (Ortega y Gasset) | 16 |
| ORGA (Casares Quiroga) | 15 |
| Total: Republican Bloc | 383 |
| Agrarians and Basques-Navarrese | 21 |
| Catalonian League (Cambò) | 3 |
| Monarchists (Romanones) | 1 |
| Total: Opposition of Right | 1 |
| Federalists and Independents of the Left | 14 |

"We have to abbreviate the steps of history, taking a leap of four centuries, in order to catch up to those who have left us behind, to those with whom we must live," wrote Joaquín Costa, decades before. The Constituent Assembly should have made this leap legal. Instead of doing this, that is, letting the leap take place and later dressing it in legality, they tried to legislate it.

They began with the constitution. The Constitution of the Republic was chemically pure. It found its inspiration in that of Weimar, which, at the time, was on its last legs. Debate about the future constitution soon began and was stormy. Questions of federalism, separation of church and state, the social function of property, provoked great discussion. On December 6, 1931, the Constitution was promulgated.

According to its first article, Spain was "a democratic Republic of workers of all classes" ("of all classes" was an addition proposed by Alcalá Zamora to mollify the rhetoric offered by the Socialists). All powers emanated from the people. The Republic constituted an "integral state compatible with the autonomy of the municipalities and regions." (On this point, the Centralists' vices gained prominence over the traditional federalism of the Republicans, who were afraid of being accused of "selling out the fatherland" if they recognized the rights of the nationalities and established a federal system.)

Article 26 regulated relations between church and state; the latter had no official religion and existed separately from all denominations. Religious orders were submitted to a special law. Divorce was established. The public school system was to be the only one allowed, and it would be lay, free, and compulsory. Article 44 stated: "The wealth of the country, no matter who is its owner, will be subordinate to the interests of the national economy . . . and can be nationalized if social necessity requires it."

The organs of power were: only one House, the Cortes, elected by universal, equal, direct, and secret suffrage by those eligible twenty-three years of age and older, of both sexes. When not in session, Parliament would be represented by a Permanent Deputation, elected by the entire Parliament and of proportional composition.

The president was elected for six years by an electoral college composed of all the deputies plus an equal number of delegates chosen by the municipalities. The president could not be reelected, but could be elected anew six years after his term had expired and no active military men, clergy, or members of reigning families were eligible. The president would designate the chief of the government and could ask for his resignation; revocation was obligatory if Parliament did not give its vote of confidence to the government. The president could dissolve Parliament only twice during his term of office, and if he should exceed this limit, he would be dismissed from office. The president had the right to veto, but if a vetoed law were approved by Parliament in a second debate, it would be automatically promulgated.

The letter and the spirit of the Constitution were to be defended by a Court of Constitutional Guarantees, whose members were to be

elected in part by Parliament and in part by the professional associations, universities, etc. The president of this tribunal would be
named by Parliament.

Spain, by its Constitution, "renounced war as an instrument of
national politics" and incorporated within its legislation the
Kellogg-Briand pact. Spain could not abandon the League of Nations
without previous agreement of Parliament, adopted by absolute
majority. The Constitution recognized and guaranteed Spaniards the
enjoyment of all customary human rights.

Once this constitution had been approved, Parliament undertook
the discussion of two texts considered fundamental: the agrarian reform and the Statute of Catalonia. The latter was debated more vehemently than the former. Opposition from the Right and Center
prolonged debate from May until September 1932, when both texts
were approved by a vote of 414 for, and 19 against.

Many big landowners had gone abroad, abandoning their lands in
a state of uncultivation. No system of credit for farming existed while
the distribution of land remained as unbalanced as it was at the turn
of the century. Agrarian reform was intended to resolve a situation
which had placed the national economy in danger and kept the peasant masses in poverty. The law ordered the expropriation of lands,
with compensation, with an aim to establish 50,000 peasants in these
areas each year. This figure meant that the reform would have to last
at least forty years. An Institute of Agrarian Reform was given the
task of enforcing the law. The state granted credit to the thus-
established peasants, who could organize in collectives or cooperatives. Fifty million pesetas, minimum, per annum, would have to be
devoted to these rural placements. The reform would apply to farms
larger than 1,000 acres of dry land or larger than 75 acres of irrigated
land. The compensation was fixed by compounding the interest on
the taxable income. The reform was only applied to twelve provinces.

Many Spanish economists had defended the need for agrarian
reform. As early as the eighteenth century, Alvaro Flórez Estrada
(1766-1854), had proposed the general nationalization of land, just as
the Catalonian humanist Lluis Vives (1492-1540) and the Jesuit Juan
de Mariana (1536-1624) had done three centuries earlier. The legislators of 1932 did not go as far. The budgeted sums for placements
were never entirely spent. The Institute of Agrarian Reform received,
in its first twenty-eight months of existence (later, as shall be seen, its
activities were practically suspended), the sum of 108.3 million
pesetas; 74.1 million were not put to use. Meanwhile, the unem-

ployed peasants rioted and many fields remained uncultivated.

During the discussion of the Statute of Catalonia, the country experienced days of effervescence produced especially by the campaigns of the right-wing press, which presented the Republic as the destroyer of national unity. The deputies of right-wing factions led a systematic obstruction (a kind of filibuster). By the statute, Catalonia was constituted into an autonomous region. It possessed a parliament elected by universal suffrage, which in turn elected the president of the Generalitat, the name given to the system of Catalonian autonomous government. The Catalonian Parliament could legislate in matters of civil and penal law, local finances, public education, administrative and municipal government systems, and public order. The state reserved for itself control over international relations, the armed forces, control of the mint, customs, the general taxation system, and legislation of labor (this last was imposed by the Socialists who feared that Catalonian social legislation would strengthen the CNT, whose main thrust was precisely in Catalonia). The University of Barcelona was converted into an autonomous institution, governed by a council, half of whose membership was named by the state, the other half by the Generalitat. Catalan was the official language together with Spanish in the organisms of the Generalitat, in the administration of justice, and in education.

Neither the Law of Agrarian Reform nor the statute seemed appropriate to attract conservative elements to the regime. The rich sent their fortunes abroad, the aristocrats left, claiming to be persecuted. The Republican leaders tried to appease this lack of confidence, but their attempts only served to water down their measures. They did not understand that a new regime, in its beginnings, had to be swift in modifying the basic situation, and only later, when its actions were proven by the prosperity of the country, would it be possible to attract former adversaries. At the same time that the Socialists' policy exasperated the CNT and forced the latter into the hands of the messianic anarchists, there were frequent riots and public order became the principal preoccupation of the government. This alienated the favor of the most active part of the workers and peasants without attracting the Right.

This was clearly seen beginning with the approval of Article 26 of the Constitution, which established a special way of dealing with religious associations. These were forbidden any type of commercial activity and were submitted to general tax laws. In addition, orders which imposed the vow of obedience (to the Pope) besides the three canonic vows, were forbidden. The Company of Jesus was dissolved in accordance with this article, and its possessions were confiscated by the state.

Many Catholic Republicans felt offended by this article whose urgency was not absolutely evident, but which satisfied the anticlericalism of traditionalist Republicans. When it was approved, Azaña exclaimed: "Spain has ceased to be Catholic." The facts would show that he was quite mistaken. The Basque and the agrarian minorities withdrew in protest until the discussion of the Constitution ended. Alcalá Zamora and Maura resigned from the government. The president of Parliament, Julián Besteiro, in his capacity as acting chief of state, assigned the task of forming another cabinet to Manual Azaña. It was the same as the previous one, except for the two Catholic leaders.

Finally Parliament put an end to its debating of the Constitution and other basic laws. After deciding that they would not dissolve but rather continue as a regular Parliament, the members elected the first president of the second Spanish Republic on December 10, 1931, by 362 votes out of 410 cast. He was Niceto Alcalá Zamora.

# 9

# Two Years To The Left

The Republic, with its first president, left its provisional status. But the Republicans were still not aware of what they wanted it to be. For the next two years, a coalition of left-wing Republicans and Socialists would govern. The basic question was which of these groups would decide the foundation of the Republic. The Republicans of the Center (Lerroux and the Radicals, whose only radical element was the name itself), spoke of "broadening the Republic's base." To them this meant the incorporation of the forces of the Right which did not openly declare themselves monarchists. From a strictly Republican point of view, the new regime had to exist for everyone, and had to try to open its doors to conservative elements so that these might express themselves through the regime. Left-wing Republicans opposed this open door to the Right, but at the same time, they did not wish to open up the Republic to the anarcho-syndicalists. On the contrary, they wanted to undertake a systematic campaign against them—which would take the form of an endless spiral: persecution of the CNT, reaction from the CNT via riots and insurrections, new persecutions, new reactions, and so on, without any end in sight. This led to the predominance of the FAI within the CNT and the retreat of the moderate syndicalists. (This latter group was known as "the thirty," because of the number of signatures found at the bottom of the manifesto which announced their break with the anarchist-controlled CNT.) Nevertheless, this did not diminish the CNT's strength, which continued to be the most powerful union organization, despite the indirect support the UGT received from the government.

Alcalá Zamora, now president, gave the responsibility of forming the government to Azaña. Lerroux advised the Socialists not to continue in the cabinet, since their presence there was an impediment to the incorporation of the conservative elements within the Republic. Azaña dispensed with the Radicals and formed a coalition Republican-Socialist government, with a Catalonian, Jaume Carner (1867-1934), as minister of finance.

"Let's begin to govern," declared Azaña, as he presented his cabinet to Parliament. The first thing he did along these lines was to obtain the approval of a Law of Defense of the Republic, which permitted the government extensive powers to persecute those who challenged public order, in reality, the anarchists. Agrarian agitation and strikes increased. In Barcelona and Seville, the police (a new police force created by the government, the Guardias de Asalto, roughly translated as "storm troopers") applied frequently the *ley de fugas*, a nonwritten "law" which permitted the killing of prisoners with the pretext that they had tried to escape.

To counteract the effect of these measures on public opinion, Parliament named a commission which declared Alfonso de Bourbon guilty of high treason. But the forces of the Right did not wish to be incorporated into the new regime. They hoped to destroy it. The social agitation seemed to open the road to their plans. In Parliament, one deputy remembered that in Andalusia the day workers were singing an old refrain:

> *When will the God of Heaven see fit*
> *that the poor shall eat bread,*
> *while the rich shall eat shit?*

Factories closed down. Many lands remained uncultivated. The Republic was criticized from the pulpit. Peasants from Castillblanco, a town in Extremadura, massacred civil guards. In January 1932, the Catalonian anarchists staged an uprising in the mining basin of Fígols; the army squelched their efforts, while their leaders were deported to Bata, in West Africa, where Spain still held a few small colonies.

In Arnedo, the Civil Guard massacred strikers. There were so many protests as a result, that General José Sanjurjo was replaced as chief of the Civil Guard by General Virgilio Cabanellas (1862-1938), a Free Mason and a Republican. Strikes broke out among the miners of Asturias. Violence occurred between workers and traditionalists in Bilbao.

Yet in spite of everything, the peseta recovered. Military spending in Morocco was reduced, while more funds were poured into public education. Servicing of the public debt inherited from the monarchy absorbed 24 percent of the budget. In 1932, 7,000 schools and 200 institutes of secondary education (high schools and junior colleges) were opened. The number of army officers was reduced from 21,996 to 7,662. A divorce law was voted in, the legality of civil marriage was recognized, and mention in documents of illegitimacy was prohibited.

Juan March (1884-1962), a financier who had become rich by smuggling, plotted to regain control of the tobacco from Morocco, which the Republic had taken from him. He was arrested. The minister of finance affirmed: "Either March submits to the Republic, or the Republic submits to March." A few months later, the millionaire escaped from prison.

Lerroux again demanded the departure of the Socialists. Prieto answered him: "Socialism will not disappear from the scene until the Republic is consolidated." Before this happened, the extreme Right took the initiative. On the night of August 10, 1932, General José Sanjurjo staged a coup in Seville. The insurrection had been carefully prepared and should have been more extensive, since two military quarters in the north and two in the interior were to rebel simultaneously with Seville. But at the last minute the conspirators became frightened, leaving Sanjurjo alone in the attempt. In Madrid, groups of armed rightist citizens tried to take over the Ministry of War. After ninety minutes of exchanging fire, they surrendered, leaving hundreds of wounded and nine dead. In Seville, although Sanjurjo declared a state of war, the governor refused to obey the declaration: the unions (mostly CNT and some Communists) declared a general strike which paralyzed the city. When the soldiers sent from Madrid arrived, the coup had failed, due to the unions' efforts. Sanjurjo fled, but on his way to Portugal, he was stopped by several civil guards. The people of Seville set fire to the Círculo de Labradores (club of the big estate owners), a newspaper which had supported the insurrection, a church, and the club of the Employers' Association. The Civil Guard fired against the Republican demonstrators. Sanjurjo appeared before the judge and said that his movement was directed against the government but not against the regime. He was found guilty and sentenced to death. The president of the Republic, at the request of the Socialists, pardoned him, commuting the sentence to life imprisonment (thirty years). The monarchists arrested in Madrid, arms in hand, were deported to Villa Cisneros (the Spanish Sahara Coast), from which they escaped shortly thereafter. Azaña thought that by giving them the same treatment which he had given the workers of Fígols eight months earlier, the government would maintain its neutrality.

Official reaction to the unsuccessful coup was more rhetorical than efficacious. Parliament approved a law which permitted expropriation of the lands of the Spanish Grandees (high-ranking nobles) as a collective punishment for the uprising. The measure was juridically debatable and politically sterile. Nor was it enough to accelerate land reform.

Since several Spanish diplomats had expressed their sympathy for the ineffectual rebellion, Parliament retired a certain number of them. They were not missed, for in fact the Republic did not have a foreign policy. It did not capitalize on the sympathy which the new regime had awakened in Latin America. It had not modified its policy in Morocco, because if it had tried to offer the colonies autonomy, it would have encountered the opposition of France. A contract was signed with the U.S.S.R. for the purchase of petroleum, and diplomatic relations between the two countries were reestablished, yet no ambassadors were appointed. France enjoyed great prestige in Madrid, but the government refused to sign a treaty of alliance which Edouard Herriot offered during his visit to Madrid in November 1932. This action was taken despite the fact that it seemed a logical decision from the point of view of strengthening the regime.

When the feudal forces saw they could not destroy the Republic from without, they tried to destroy it from within. They felt that the vacillating attitude of the Republicans in power was alienating the masses. In the eighteen-month span since the proclamation of the new regime, there had been 400 persons killed in public disturbances (of these, 20 were members of the police force), 3,000 wounded, 9,000 arrested, and 160 deported. Furthermore, 30 general strikes had been registered and 3,600 economic strikes, while 161 newspapers had been suspended for short periods (only 4 of which were right-wing publications). "The harvesting of explosives is more important than the harvesting of wheat," ironically commented the CNT newspaper.

Nevertheless, the country was being governed, although it may have been under the trusteeship of the intellectual elite. The substitution of lay teaching for religious instruction was organized, which gave rise to new Catholic resentment. The Papal Nuncio, Monsignor Tedeschini, tried to smooth out the ruffled feelings of the prelates, which was no easy task, since the Spanish bishops considered Pius XI nothing short of a revolutionary.

In Catalonia, the statute was put into effect. The services of police passed to the control of the Generalitat, which handed them over to the most conservative and nationalistic group of the Esquerra, the so-called *escamots* (among whom fascist trends existed), who were dedicated to a systematic campaign against the anarchists. Elections to the Catalonian Parliament were held, with fifty-seven posts going to the Esquerra and seventeen to the League.

The minister of finance created a tax new in Spain: a softened income tax. Fiscal year 1932 ended with a deficit of 200 million pesetas. Forty percent of the budget had been absorbed by debts, bureaucrats pensions, the army, and the forces of repression.

Although they were expensive, the forces of repression did not turn out to be very efficient. In January 1933, there was a new anarchist movement in Andalusia and the Rioja region. In the town of Casas Viejas, storm troopers set fire to a stronghold of a group of anarchists, none of whom escaped the flames. The right wing took advantage of the incident to accuse Azaña of having given orders to take no prisoners. The Right and the Radicals kept up an extensive campaign centering around the excesses of Casas Viejas. The Radicals announced that as long as the government did not resign, they would obstruct (filibuster) all attempts to legislate. The parliamentary proceedings would take forever and it was necessary to have frequent recourse to the "guillotine" (the decision of the majority to end debate) to succeed in getting any new laws approved.

The organizations of the Right combined to form the new CEDA Spanish Confederation of Autonomous Right-Wing Groups. To head the organization they chose a former Jesuit student and a lawyer, José María Gil Robles (b. 1898). The minority of the right-wing parliamentary representatives from the cereal-growing provinces formed the Agrarian party, which declared Republican affiliation. CEDA stated its indifference to the matter of regime, which the Republicans interpreted as a refusal to work within the Republic. In fact, Gil Robles was trying in this way to attract the monarchists. But the latter organized their own party, Spanish Renovation. José Antonio Primo de Rivera (1903-36), son of the ex-dictator, founded in Madrid a party which acknowledged itself as fascist, the Falange Española.[1]

Lerroux achieved relative popularity among the frightened elements which did not belong to the Right—the middle class and the industrial bourgeoisie. No one remembered the demagogues' beginnings. The president tried unsuccessfully to come to a truce with the obstruction. He only achieved the truce temporarily for the approval of a law of public order to replace that of the Defense of the

Republic, which was even more biting then the latter. Pius XI published an encyclical condemning the law governing religious orders, while the bishops advised the faithful not to send their children to public schools.

On September 4, 1933, election of the members of the Court of Constitutional Guarantees took place. The candidates who were friends of the government secured five posts, while thirteen went to friends of the opposition. Among the latter was José Calvo Sotelo, who had been finance minister of the dictatorship. Lerroux, in Parliament, asked whether or not the government thought it could still count on the support of the majority of the country. Azaña felt that they could, but the President of the Republic did not think so. The government resigned. The task of forming the cabinet fell to Lerroux. The new cabinet consisted of ministers who represented all the Republican parties of the Center and Left, but no Socialists.

Lerroux annulled the law of municipal boundaries. Thus he hoped to pacify the big landowners and make further peasant strikes impossible. Prieto announced that the Socialists considered themselves free from all commitments to the Republicans and that they would never again, under any circumstances, collaborate with the government. Lerroux did not win the vote of confidence of Parliament. Another radical, Diego Martínez Barrio, replaced him. It was to Martínez Barrio that the president handed over the decree of the dissolution of Parliament. Elections were called for.

The right-wing groups appeared in bloc candidatures, often together with the Radicals. The Socialists presented themselves separately, and the left-wing Republicans were divided (there had been schisms within the Radical Socialist party and in the Esquerra). The anarchists launched an intense "no vote" propaganda.

The right-wing groups had large means at their disposal. In order to maintain some balance, the government forbade the use of aerial propaganda. The Union of the Right had, as its political slogans, amnesty for those condemned in the unsuccessful coup of August 10, anti-Marxism, and antilaicism. The Left and the Socialists stated that they wanted to save the Republic from radical corruption and clerical domination. The radicals offered to "broaden the base of the Republic." No one spoke of the real problems of the country. The elections were held on November 19. The results turned out favorably for the Right:

CEDA ..................................................... 87
Agrarians ............................................... 37
Right-Wing Independents ............................. 15

Traditionalists .......................................... 14
Spanish Renovation ..................................... 14
Basque Nationalists .................................... 12

TOTAL: Right-Wing Bloc  179

Radicals ................................................. 79
Catalonian League ...................................... 25
Conservatives .......................................... 14
Liberal Democrats ....................................... 9
Independents of the Center ............................. 6
Progressives ............................................ 1

TOTAL: Center  134

Socialists ............................................... 27
Esquerra ................................................ 22
Republican Action ...................................... 5
Independent Radical Socialists ......................... 2
Orthodox Radical Socialists ............................ 1

TOTAL: Left-Wing Bloc  57

Even in Catalonia the Right had won, although by a much smaller margin than in the rest of Spain. For the first time, a Communist was elected. If there had been proportional representation, the Socialists would have gleaned 133 posts and Parliament would have been Left of Center. Thanks to the electoral law of Azaña, inspired by his lack of confidence in the people, Parliament was not Right of Center. Beginning with this failure, one might say of the Spanish Republican Left what Giolitti said of a certain Italian politician: "He has a brilliant future behind him."

**NOTE**

1. This was not the first fascist group in the country. In 1931 a postal employee, Ramiro Ledesma Ramos (1905-36), had formed a Movement for the Renaissance of Spain, which combined with another group created in Valladolid by Onésimo Redondo (1905-36), of authoritarian unionist leanings. Together they formed the Juntas de Ofensiva Nacional Sindicalista (JONS). In February 1934, all these groups were united in the FE of the JONS, but Ledesma and Redondo went their separate ways in 1935, leaving Primo de Rivera as its head.

# 10

# *Two Years To The Right*

In its first two years, the Republic had not learned how to put an end to the remnants of feudalism within Spanish society. Now, during the next two years, it would try to absorb these remnants. In the eyes of the people the result would be that the Republic had become feudalized.

Having lost the elections, the left-wing parties accused the anarchists of having been responsible for their defeat by abstaining from voting. They had forgotten that, for two and a half years, they had done everything possible to exclude the CNT from the Republic. On December 8, 1933, scarcely three weeks after the elections, an anarchist movement broke out in various regions: fourteen police officers and seventy-five civilians were killed; there were hundreds of arrests and dozens of unions were closed.

Was it possible that the anarchists did not see that this was no way of establishing libertarian communism, as they called the system which they sought to introduce? Perhaps some of their leaders thought in terms of coming to the point of forcing the Republic to accept the CNT. Yet the anarchist masses really believed that via these tactics they would come to realize their dream, the destruction of the present society and the establishment of a more just one. This was evidently the product of lack of political education and peasant messianism. The Republic had not tried to remedy any of these causes, but instead had fomented and aggravated them with a policy of repression.

While on the streets workers and police battled frequently, the new deputies and political commentators discussed another problem: CEDA was the most numerous minority in the first regular Parliament of the Republic. But CEDA had almost exclusive contact with the monarchists, its elements originated from the monarchist camp, and, as a party, it had made no official declaration of allegiance to the Republic. Politicians of the Left asserted that opening a way for them into government would mean surrendering the Republic to its enemies.

Parliament assembled. Santiago Alba, now of the Radical party, was elected president of Parliament. Gil Robles, leader of CEDA, immediately reproached the Socialists for not having rushed into the streets after their defeat in the elections. This prompted Prieto to confess that they were experiencing tremendous pressure from the masses, who were anxious to reconquer the disfigured Republic. He also accused the Radicals of having procured the entrance of monarchist elements into the regime by virtue of their electoral alliances.

Lerroux formed the government on December 18, 1933. It was composed entirely of Radicals, plus two Progressives (presidential observers, since their party only accounted for one vote in Parliament), and two Independents of the Center. Lerroux announced that he would respect the legislative work of the constituents. CEDA supported the government and was attacked by the monarchists, who reminded Gil Robles of his declaration prior to elections: "If Parliament does not submit to our aspirations, we will dispense with Parliament." Fortunately Gil Robles was not of the same character as Il Duce, in spite of his grips to Italy and the fact that the youth of his party wore uniforms and greeted each other by raising their arms.

"The dictatorial threat is present in all sectors of the Right," claimed Prieto in Parliament. "The declarations of Gil Robles and of Lerroux have opened a revolutionary period. . . . We are telling the entire country that the Socialist party is publicly contracting the pledge [in case right-wing groups are called to power] to unleash the revolution."

Francesc Macià died on Christmas Day, 1933. The Catalonian Parliament elected Lluis Companys as his successor to the presidency of the Generalitat. In Catalonia there had been a homogeneous government during this entire period. The Esquerra had committed errors—persecuting the CNT and allowing the semifascist escamots to develop within its own ranks. Yet the party had taken root with the people. The Catalonian peasant felt himself represented by the Esquerra, which gave this party a degree of stability favorable to its goals. Cultural institutions, schools, and libraries multiplied; workers' cultural clubs were supported by the Generalitat, although they were part of a trend opposed to that of the Esquerra.

The Spanish Parliament set to work at once. Rights to retirement benefits were granted to priests, as if they were civil servants. Fourteen million pesetas were used for this purpose, while the budget for school lunches was reduced by 13 million. An ambassador close to the Vatican was named to see if an agreement which the Right demanded could be negotiated. At this time there were 600,000 unemployed workers. CEDA had asked in its election campaign for 100 million pesetas to fight unemployment. The Radicals offered one billion pesetas. The only thing achieved was to repeal the laws which required public works to be granted by contract bids.

In the streets the Falange had begun to act: assaults on the press of the left-wing newspaper *Heraldo de Madrid*, on the Socialist clubs or Casas del Pueblo, on student locales; the universities became shooting ranges; the Socialist party radicalized. Besteiro, leader of the moderate wing, was replaced as leader of the UGT by Francisco Largo Caballero, supported by the Socialist Youth. He began to make statements of a Marxist tone, defending the need of the working class to take power. In Catalonia, BOC launched a campaign for the establishment of a Workers' Alliance to unite all the proletarian organizations.

Diego Martínez Barrio, a moderate Radical, but one of steadfast Republicanism, at the time gave evidence of his lack of conformity with the policy followed by Lerroux, on resigning from the Ministry of Interior, and later announcing his separation from the Radical party. In the meantime, ORGA (Republican Party of Galicia), Republican Action, and the Independent Radical-Socialist party were fused into a single unit, the Republican Left, with Azaña as its principal leader. Later on, the Orthodox Radical-Socialist party and Martínez Barrio's group united to form the Republican Union. The minister of justice, an ex-monarchist, had to resign since he emitted slanderous remarks against the captains who had rebelled in Jaca in 1930; these remarks had occurred during the debate on the law to grant amnesty to those condemned for the rebellion of August 10. Parliament approved it.

The occupation of Ifni, a stretch of desert along the western African coast, which had been attributed to Spain but never claimed, was of little interest to the people. What was indeed of interest was the conflict which arose between the president and Parliament. In effect, Alcalá Zamora signed his amnesty decree, but sent Parliament a written allegation to have them realize that it would be dangerous to the morale of the army to place the rebellious and now pardoned leaders back in their positions of authority. The government did not wish to see this allegation published in the *Gaceta* (official bulletin of the Republic) but the president insisted. Lerroux then resigned.

Ricardo Samper (1881-1938), an obscure lawyer from Valencia, was chosen to succeed the radical leader. On April 28, 1934, he formed a government which resembled the former one, save for the absence of Lerroux. The attitude of Gil Robles and his party was still bewildering. Placed midway between the government, which demanded a previous declaration of Republicanism, and the monarchic opposition, Gil Robles reminded one of Hamlet, that is, if one did not remember Austria's Chancellor Dollfuss. One of the leaders of CEDA held an interview with the ex-king in Paris, while another did the same with the President in Madrid.

Catalonia was witnessing a widespread restlessness among the *rabassaires* (sharecropping peasants who worked vineyards). As one explained: "When my back begins to ache at noon, I have still not begun to work for my own family." The Catalonian Parliament voted a law of farming contracts which reduced the rights of the landlords by half. The Agricultural Institute of San Isidro (a landholders' organization), the League, and CEDA protested this law. Samper's government yielded to these protests and presented an appeal against the law to the Court of Constitutional Guarantees.

Right-wing forces had begun to speak of an agrarian counter-reform, at a time when there was a 50 percent reduction in the wages of Andalusian peasants, suspension of subsidies to workers' cultural societies, dispossession of 28,000 peasants in Estremadura from lands which had previously been given them, and the revealing pat answer given by landowners to peasants seeking work: "Eat the Republic." The UGT's National Federation of Landworkers organized a referendum: 70,000 members voted for a general peasant strike, with 350 opposing. The strike, in mid-summer, failed, despite the overwhelming enthusiasm that had accompanied it. The government had declared the harvest to be in the national interest and took military measures to squelch the strike. The police closed many Socialist clubs. The army began spectacular maneuvers.

While the conflict with Catalonia was gestating, another sprung up in the Basque Country. The minister of finance had decided to modify the economic agreement which had been in force in these provinces for decades. According to this agreement, the provincial administrations collected the taxes and turned over a determined sum to the state. The Basque Nationalists, supported by the Socialists, decided that the municipal councils should elect a commission which would replace the provincial administrations (since the latter were designated by the central government instead of being elected). Their purpose in so doing was to oppose the changes proposed by Madrid. The meeting of the municipal councils to elect these delegates was prohibited, but the elections took place in secret. The police arrested the candidates and a month later violently dissolved a meeting of Basque deputies and mayors.

In the meantime, the Court of Constitutional Guarantees, composed of a right-wing majority, had declared the Catalonian farming contract law unconstitutional. Two days later, on June 12, 1934, the Catalonian Parliament approved a new law which was merely a carbon copy of the previous one. The Madrid government secured negotiations with the Generalitat; the Catalonian and Basque deputies withdrew from Parliament. The Basques, who had started out as pro-rightists, had gone through an evolutionary process. They now accepted the Republic and saw the leftists as representing their only possibility for gaining autonomy for their people. The Catalonian landowners organized a collective visit to Madrid to protest the new Catalonian law of farming contracts. The workers of Madrid welcomed them with a general strike. For the first time there was a show of solidarity of the Spanish workers with Catalonian autonomy. Largo Caballero, without clearly acknowledging it, had adopted as his own a proposition which the BOC had defended since 1931, namely: neither the middle class nor the bourgeoisie were capable of carrying out the democratic bourgeois revolution that Spain needed since they were too weak and too easily terrorized; therefore, the working class must do so, by pulling in the majority of the middle class and the peasantry. Basically this was a Leninist theory. Largo Caballero soon became known as the Spanish Lenin.

One day Alcalá Zamora advised Azaña, Prieto, and Largo Caballero in private of the need of protecting themselves in case of a military coup. For their part, the leftist parties warned the president of the potential danger of seating CEDA in the government. But Alcalá Zamora, obsessed by his desire to have the Constitution revised and thus eliminate Article 26 (which dealt with separation of church and state), allowed himself to be convinced by CEDA's promises, in a revisionist sense. On October 2, Samper resigned. Lerroux was given the task of forming the government.

Months earlier, on March 31, 1934, monarchist leader Antonio Goicoechea (1876-1953), plus a general and a traditionalist leader, had spoken with Benito Mussolini and Marshall Italo Balbo in Rome. Later, the three signed a statement which gave witness to the fact that

> Mr. Mussolini, after having shown great interest as he was informed of the present situation in Spain and the aspirations of the army, navy, and monarchist parties, declared the following: First, that he is prepared to help in any way possible the parties struggling against Spain's present regime, with the purpose of allowing them to overthrow it and replace it with a regency which will restore the monarchy; Mr. Mussolini has solemnly repeated this statement three times, and we have answered him, as might be imagined, with a demonstration of our esteem and gratitude. Second, that he is prepared to give evidence of the sincerity of his intentions with an offer of tangible proof: he has proposed, with this end in mind, to immediately provide us with 20,000 rifles, 20,000 grenades, 200 submachine guns, and the sum of 1,500,000 pesetas in bullion. Third, that this contribution is but the beginning of the execution of his promises and that it will be augmented at the proper time, in more important proportions.

The message was clear: CEDA had to obtain power legally or, under the penalty of seeing itself overwhelmed by its Right, it had to adopt an attitude of rebellion against the Republic. The character of CEDA and the temperament of Gil Robles moved in favor of the first attitude. On October 4, 1934, Lerroux announced the formation of his government, composed of Radicals, Agrarians, Liberal Democrats, and three ministers from CEDA.

Immediately the Republican parties published various messages of protest, declaring that "the monstrous fact of handing over the government of the Republic to its enemies is an act of treason." In consequence, "they broke all ties of solidarity with the present institutions of the regime and affirmed their decision to have recourse to all means for the defense of the Republic." Even the party of Miguel Maura, an associate of Alcalá Zamora, sent a similar document to the president. Alvaro de Albornoz (1879-1954) resigned the office of president of the Court of Constitutional Guarantees.

What was the labor movement doing? A Workers' Alliance was formed in Catalonia at the initiative of BOC. It was composed of several small Catalonian workers' parties; the Communist party, which had criticized it and which had no real power, joined the alliance on October 4. The CNT had not joined, but the idea of the alliance corresponded so much to the aspirations of the people that when it declared a general strike on October 5, everyone followed suit. The alliance demanded arms, which the *escamots* of the Esquerra refused to provide, thinking that they and the police were sufficient. At that very moment, the *escamots* were arresting workers. The peasants had begun to assemble in the towns. The smell of civil war was in the air. On the evening of the 6th, after a silent demonstration by the Workers' Alliance, Companys, president of the Generalitat, called the people together to speak to them: "In this solemn hour, in the name of the people and the Catalonian Parliament, the government over which I preside assumes all faculties of power in Catalonia, and proclaims the Catalonian State within the Spanish Federal Republic; and invites the leaders of the general protest against fascism to establish in Catalonia the provisional government of the Republic." Companys, who was more of a politician and more daring than the Spanish Republicans, realized that if one broke with existing institutions, one must create others; to do otherwise was to play the fool. But no one in Spain followed his lead.

The de facto split between Barcelona and Madrid was transformed into a de jure break. Companys tried to communicate with the president, but to no avail. He did get to speak with Captain General Domingo Batet (1872-1936), a Catalonian, who refused to align himself with Companys, saying that he only obeyed the legal authorities.[1]

Batet, after consultations with Madrid, proclaimed a state of war. The workers were unarmed. Josep Dencàs (1900-52), leader of the Esquerra *escamots* and minister of interior (that is, of the Catalonia police), still refused to give them arms. Nevertheless, the only ones to return the soldiers' fire were groups of workers who had stormed several arms depots. The artillery fired on the building of the Generalitat, where the Catalonian government had secluded itself. At daybreak Dencàs fled the country. The army arrested the entire Catalonian government, the municipal government of Barcelona (except the Lliga and Radical councilmen), and began to round up the labor leaders. A colonel took over Companys's position.

The Catalonian middle class, proficient in democratic government, had failed to defend it. It is possible that the attitude of its leaders had not been opportune. Or perhaps it would have been more adroit to have accepted CEDA into the government and tried to incorporate it into the Republic. But passions had been running high. The Republicans were gripped by their failure to effect a democratic revolution. The workers tried to compensate for their disillusionment with the

Republican in which they had placed their confidence. The Socialists felt the bitter sting of having been abandoned by the Republicans when the latter had accepted their departure from government.

From that moment on, the initiative fell into the hands of the working class, which although divided, was animated by its intense desire to change the status quo. This was clearly demonstrated in Asturias, the mining region of the north, where the entire mining valley had risen in rebellion. A long tradition of struggle had prepared the miners for action. The Workers' Alliance, to which the CNT, the UGT, and the workers' parties belonged, provided them an instrument. The valley fell into their hands after a day and night of battles to capture the military quarters of the Civil Guard. The movement underwent a transformation from defense to attack. Their battlecry was that of the initials UHP (Union of Proletarian Brothers), which took root by virtue of its very naiveté. Mieres was their capital. An army of miners was formed which advanced on Oviedo, with dynamite as its main weapon. Several urgent measures were adopted: health, supplies, arrests of reactionary elements (none of whom were harmed). The arms factories of Trubia and La Vega fell into the miners' power.

What was Spain doing? Striking. A general strike in Madrid, with an exchange of gunshots and nothing else. Several strikes in towns and cities—but not in all of them. But no overall Spanish Workers' Alliance existed and, lacking unity in their objectives, the workers' movement did not follow the example Asturias had set. In Asturias, fighting continued. The Revolutionary Committee published a proclamation forbidding acts of pillage, which did not take place, and organizing the workers' army, which confiscated all food and clothing supplies. Two sergeants directed the technical aspect of operations. The government placed General Eduardo López Ochoa (1877-1936), a Freemason and a Republican, at the head of a column formed by the soldiers of the Spanish Foreign Legion and Moslems from Morocco. The battle lasted a week. The rest of the country witnessed the rebirth of calm, while the court martials began to function. The government appeared before Parliament and, of course, obtained a vote of confidence and 46 million pesetas for police expenses. Diego Hidalgo, the minister of war (who in 1931 had written a book in glowing praise of the U.S.S.R.), declared to the press: "The only argument against using African troops is the fact that in war they are merciless and do not submit to humanitarian laws."

In Asturias the resistance lasted for another week. The men put down their arms at the order of the Revolutionary Committee, which came after a meeting of their leaders, Socialist deputy Belarmino Tomás with General López Ochoa, who had pledged to execute no reprisals. The insurrection had come to an end. Repression had now begun. As he took over his task as special head of public order in Asturias, the colonel of the Civil Guard Luis Doval, declared: "I am resolved to spare the life of none of the revolutionaries and to exterminate the seeds of revolution, even in the wombs that bear them."

The right-wing press published trumped-up photographs of priests with their eyes yanked from their sockets, while not a single one had actually been harmed by the miners. The church hierarchy refrained from advertising the falsity of this campaign. Upon terminating the occupation, General López Ochoa stated: "The stories of the atrocities committed by the revolutionaries of Asturias are a product of a low and exaggerated campaign. I condemn what has happened in Asturias from the bottom of my heart, but I must also condemn the campaign to which the miners have been subjected. The revolutionaries did kill any and all who resisted them, but as a general rule, they did respect the lives of their prisoners."

Luis de Sirval, a journalist who was collecting data to inform the public of the repression, was assassinated in Oviedo by a lieutenant of the Tercio (Foreign Legion) who, of course, was never to be punished for this crime. The jails were filled within two days. The mining companies fired their workers en masse and only readmitted them after a police purge. Several convents were placed at the disposal of the authorities to be converted into prison and police centers. For a period of seven weeks, the entire mining valley lived under terror. The struggle had resulted in one thousand deaths and three thousand wounded. The repression was responsible for almost as many more. The Spanish jails were crammed full. More than thirty thousand men were arrested in all parts of the country by government orders within several months. Parliament reestablished the death penalty, which had been abolished in 1931. Enrique Pérez Farrás (1890-1949), commander-in-chief of the guard of the Generalitat, had been condemned to death, but Alcalá Zamora commuted the sentence to life imprisonment. Azaña was arrested in Barcelona and tried. Asturian Socialist deputies Ramón González Peña and Teodomiro Menéndez were condemned to death, and a severe struggle began between the president, who advocated pardon, and the ministers of CEDA, who were opposed to it. Sergeants Vázquez and Argüelles, who had been with the miners, faced a firing squad. The Generalitat was suspended. In its place the government named a rightist as governor. The *rabassaires* were forced to return to their landlords the fruit which, according to the law of farming contracts, belonged to them.

In Parliament, where neither Republicans nor Socialists were in attendance, the majority demanded greater rigidity from the government. As monarchist leader Antonio Goicoechea asserted: "It is necessary to retrace our steps taken since April 14, 1931." The government opened a subscription to which banks, corporations, and aristocrats contributed to recompense the police and troops. Dissent between CEDA and the president regarding the matter of pardon forced the government to resign.

On the occasion of the presidential consultations, the Socialists and the leftist Republicans resumed their relations with the institutions which had really never been broken except on paper. Lerroux formed (April 3, 1935) the government which Gil Robles had hoped would be given to him to preside over. It was composed of Radicals and a few technical experts. This government signed the pardons. Then Lerroux was able to negotiate with CEDA and managed to obtain its entry into the cabinet, with Gil Robles as minister of war. Five ministers from CEDA assured a complete program of counterreforms.

The country was "pacified": there were hardly any strikes, unions were closed down, salaries were lowered, and the opposition appeared to have been crushed. Gil Robles, of compromising temperament and parliamentarian spirit, despite his strong desire to be "chief," preferred to govern legally rather than initiate a coup d'état.

But conflicts of interest and party rivalries within the governing coalition prevented any long-range policy. Even in CEDA itself there were elements that understood that it would be impossible to retrace the steps the Republic had taken and that not everything which had been done should be condemned by the Right. In addition, the opposition was quickly reorganizing, the heat of sympathy from the prisoners acting as stimulus. Prieto advocated a new union of Socialists and Republicans, while Largo Caballero and the Socialist Youth defended a policy of revolutionary socialism. In the CNT, faced with the consequences that an electoral abstention would bring, a path was being opened for a current favorable to the revision of the anarchists tactics. Azaña regained popularity after a seven-hour speech in Parliament in which he declared that he had not taken part in the October movement in Catalonia (as usual, preoccupation with appearing more "patriotic" than the Right was evident). He spoke to 100,000 people in Valencia and to 200,000 in Madrid. In Zaragoza, the CNT, to show solidarity with the construction workers on strike, maintained the longest general strike in history: thirty-five days. No one paid any attention to parliamentary debates. The life of the country seemed to take place outside the confines of Parliament.

When the Supreme Court proclaimed Azaña not guilty, Gil Robles demanded that Lerroux replaced the magistrates. But the president refused to accede, out of respect for judicial independence. After Parliament had voted in a law which expelled all Freemasons from the army, a conflict arose between CEDA and the president. The latter refused to sign a law revoking another of Azaña's, which annulled pensions obtained on the basis of war merits gained during the monarchy (in fact, these were simply proof of the king's favoritism). The constitutional reform project of Article 26 did not make any progress. There was no time to discuss the budget, so quarterly extensions were voted.

But all this mattered little to the life of the country. What did matter was the renewal of social agitation: the streetcar workers' strike in Barcelona, whose consequence was a long series of burnings of trolley cars as reprisals for the firing of workers by the company; the trial before the Court of Guarantees of the Generalitat government, whose members were condemned to life imprisonment; student agitation in Catalonia; the radicalization of the Socialist Youth; the number of workers on strike, which rose to 689,000 for the year 1935; the participation of the League in the imposed and unelected Generalitat government.

In all this time, CEDA had only achieved two things: a reform of the mixed labor juries and an agrarian counterreform, which imposed on the state the obligation of paying for the expropriated lands according to a price fixed by the owners of the lands and not in accordance with its tax value. But the victory was Pyrrhic since the leftist Republicans, reintegrated into Parliament, announced that when the country returned power to them, this law would be annulled and the paid sums reclaimed. Thus it was not strange that no one in the government block seemed satisfied. Finally, Lerroux resigned.

The ex-minister of the monarchy and the minister of finance in Lerroux's government, Joaquín Chapaprieta (1871-1951), was given (September 25, 1935) the task of presiding over the new combination, which looked much like the former one. Its task was to reduce expenditures, reorganize the administration, and prepare a new budget. Several days later, the president received a letter from a Mr. M. Strauss, a Dutch businessman. The letter accused certain members of the government and of the Radical party of having accepted gifts (gold watches) in exchange for a promise to grant permission for a game involving a new model electric roulette wheel, christened

"Straperlo."[2] He further alleged that a trial model had been installed in the very office of the minister of interior, the Radical Rafael Salazar Alonso (1895-1936). Alcalá Zamora sent Strauss's letter to Chapaprieta. The latter asked the advice of his ministers, among whom was Lerroux himself, before handing the accusation over to Parliament.

A parliamentary commission of investigation proved the accusation to be true and advised that these facts be brought to justice. The Radical party, of which all the accused individuals were members, ordered its ministers to resign. Chapaprieta formed a second government on October 28; its composition was the same as the previous one, except that the radical members were second-rank figures.

The matter of Straperlo brought forth the indignation of the entire country. Many considered the parties which had collaborated with the Radicals as their accomplices. Left-wing parties accentuated their campaign, demanding amnesty, and stated that those who were keeping the prisoners in jail were the very ones that had been accused of corruption. In December a new scandal: the Nombela affair, as it was called, taken from the name of the public official who exposed it. This time it concerned irregular compensation awarded to a company of colonial public works. CEDA retired from government because Chapaprieta, in his eagerness to decrease the budget deficit (one billion pesetas), tried to increase certain taxes on inheritance and the sale of luxury items.

Gil Robles requested power, refusing to support any coalition that he did not head. The president in turn refused to hand over power to a man who had not yet made a profession of Republicanism. Manuel Portela Valladares (1868-1946), an Independent of the Center, formed the government on December 14, 1935. It was composed of Independents, Agrarians, Democratic Liberals, the League, and dissident radicals. It was to last for two weeks, until Parliament, returning from Christmas recession, refused its vote of confidence. It resigned on January 31. The same day, Portela formed a second government, having received this time from the president a dissolution decree of Parliament. The cabinet was composed of Independents and technical experts. Elections were called for February 16.

The two-year reign of the Right had come to an end. The people referred to the period as the "black biennium," but it should also be christened with the adjective *sterile*, especially when compared with the preceding two-year period. In the course of the latter, fundamental laws of the regime were approved, public works were realized, budgets were voted in, thousands of schools were created, and although with vacillations and contradictions, all this had begun to change the face of the country. Under the banner of Lerroux-Robles, Parliament had spent more time discussing scandals and questions of morality than legislating. Once the lack of honorability of the Radicals, which was known by all, had been brought out into the open to the point where it was impossible to continue collaborating with them, the parliamentary game fell apart. It was necessary to elect a new Parliament.

The electoral campaign was sparked by tremendous verbal violence. The only one who maintained a moderate tone was Azaña, who in his speeches defended the necessity of a strictly Republican government, that is, that the tactic of alliance with the Socialists be abandoned.

Tremendous neon signs in the cities asked for "All power to the Chief" (Gil Robles). CEDA hoped to obtain 300 deputies in the elections, that is, an absolute majority. In many provinces CEDA was allied to the monarchists, the Agrarians and the Radicals, although no right-wing block was presented. The only place where such a bloc existed was in Catalonia, with the alliance of the League, the Traditionalists, and the Radicals.

The Left formed a united bloc in the Popular Front. The pact had been signed toward the end of 1935 by the representatives of the Republican Left, the Republican Union, the Catalonian Esquerra, the Socialists, the Communists, POUM (the Workers' Party of Marxist Unification formed by the fusion in 1935 of BOC, Joaquín Maurín, and the Communist Left of Andreu Nin), together with several minor Catalonian groups. The Communists had not taken the initiative in the Popular Front, which had been suggested by Prieto and several Republicans.

The anarchists and the CNT remained outside the pact, but in their propaganda they indicated to the masses the desirability of getting the prisoners out of jail, in other words, to vote for the candidates of the Popular Front. The pact of the Popular Front established compromises of a legislative character that its signatories acquired and referred to as "indispensable prerequisites for public peace." These were: amnesty, revision of sentences dictated by the law of vagrants (which had served to condemn many workers' leaders and which had been proposed by Azaña), reinstatement of employees and civil servants who had been fired because of their political activities, readmission of workers who had been fired for political reasons, reparation to victims of the repression, revision of the Law of Public Order (another of the laws proposed by Azaña), reform of the Bank of Spain, a plan for the acceleration of agrarian reform, a plan for development of public education, and respect for autonomic legislation.

The Socialist party wanted inclusion into the program of the nationalization of the banking system and land, control of certain industries, and unemployment subsidies. The Republicans refused to accept these measures. Nonetheless the pact was signed, since above all it was necessary to put an end to the constant threat of a coup d'état. "The Republicans do not conceive of a Republic led by social and economic motives, but rather a regime of democratic liberty impelled by reasons of public interest and social progress," read the pact. Largo Caballero stated that "before the Republic, the duty of the Socialists was to introduce it; but once the Republic has been established, their duty is to bring in socialism."

Elections took place without incident on February 16, 1936. The first returns proclaimed the victory of the Popular Front. With the second return, the third Parliament of the Republic was composed of the following 443 deputies:

| | |
|---|---:|
| Republican Left | 80 |
| Republican Union | 37 |
| Socialists | 90 |
| Communists | 13 |
| Esquerra | 38 |
| POUM | 1 |
| Proletarian Catalonians | 1 |
| Syndicalists | 2 |
| **Popular Front Total** | **262** |
| Progressives | 6 |
| Centrists | 14 |
| Conservative Republicans | 3 |
| Radicals | 6 |
| Democratic Liberals | 1 |
| Catalonian League | 13 |
| Basque Nationalists | 9 |
| **Center Total** | **52** |
| CEDA | 86 |
| Agrarians | 13 |
| Spanish Renovation | 11 |
| Traditionalists | 8 |
| Independent Monarchists | 3 |

Right-Wing Independents  ..............................  8

                                          _____

                                          Right-Wing Total    129

The vote count gave the Popular Front 4,540,000 votes and 4,300,000 to the Center and Right.

The people began to demand the immediate release of the prisoners. Portela resigned on February 19. The Socialists advised a government of the Popular Front; Azaña, one strictly Republican. Alcalá Zamora placed Azaña in charge of the cabinet. In the cabinet there were only Republicans and one general (the first military man to occupy a ministerial position during the Republic). Azaña stated to *Paris-Soir*: "Before the elections we drafted a program of minimal reforms. We intend to carry it out. I wish to govern in accordance with the law. Nothing of dangerous innovations. We desire peace and order; we are moderates." Thus the Republic entered a new stage in its history. Since the feudal forces had failed to occupy it from within, they would now try to do so from without.

## NOTES

1. Two years later, when he gave the same answer to rebellious officers in Burgos, where he was captain general, his subordinates arrested and executed him.

2. Even now black market is called *straperlo* in Spain.

# 11

# The Plot

The attempt to incorporate the feudal forces into the Republic had failed. There was no other recourse but to eliminate them. The feudal forces realized this better than the Republicans themselves. Thus those same plans which had been outlined in consultation with Mussolini in 1934, which were not put into practice as long as the hope of feudalizing the Republic still existed, were now placed in the forefront.

The people surmised the content of these plans. Two days after elections the rumor was circulated that General Francisco Franco and General Manuel Goded (1882-1936) had been arrested for conspiracy. Portela published the following notice: "There is no grain of truth in such a rumor. Both generals are executing their duties and have given their complete allegiance, which I believe, since they are two soldiers whose word is worthy of such trust."

Azaña's government decreed political amnesty; to maintain legal formality, he submitted the decree for approval to the Permanent Commission of the dissolved Parliament. The majority of this commission was composed of the right-wing elements which had put these prisoners in jail. And these same elements voted in favor of amnesty. Companys and the member of the Generalitat government triumphantly crossed the entire country from the penitentiaries to Barcelona, to again take possession of the reestablished Generalitat.

The people, inspired by the old proverb *"A Dios rogando y con el mazo dando"* (literally, "Pray to God and give it to them with the sledgehammer"), began to take into their own hands the measures that for years they had longed for. These were really measures that the European nations and governments had adopted centuries or decades earliers.

Why did the separation of church and state, which was the norm in France, the United States, and the majority of civilized countries, continue to be grounds for constant aggression in Spain? Why did the federation of the different peoples within the Peninsula, which existed as such in Switzerland, the United States, and Czechoslovakia, have to be considered a crime against patriotism in Spain? Why did an agrarian reform which was much more moderate than those after World War I decreed by Czechoslovakia, Rumania, Finland, have to provoke rebellions and inspire protests? The people did not ask themselves these questions. They knew that they needed four things: land, freedom of conscience, national freedom, and an apolitical army. And they directed their attack against those who opposed these four things and were within their local reach.

From there, strikes in every city, churches set ablaze when they housed deposits of arms or were the site of political sermons; from there, on to the surveillance that the workers' organizations set up around the military quarters, then the battle between the working youth and the groups of the Falange, which grew with the addition of students and monarchists converted to fascism. On Sundays, shots rang out in the cities as people returned from their country outings. It was unfortunate that even the Socialist Youth wore uniforms (a blue shirt and red tie) in the face of the blue shifts of the Falangists. In April 1936, the former fused with the Communist Youth to form the Unified Socialist Youth (JSU). Leadership was soon taken over by the Communists in spite of their numerical inferiority.

Parliament elected Diego Martínez Barrio to preside over it. The Falange was dissolved by the government. The right-wing deputies, with José Calvo Sotelo out in front, declared that the government lacked authority, and that the only support of order was the army.

According to the Constitution, the president of the Republic could dissolve Parliament twice, and in this case, the new Parliament would investigate to see if the second dissolution had sufficient grounds. If this were not the case, the President was automatically removed from office. The dissolution of the Parliament which had been elected in 1933 was advised by all the heads of the parties which formed the present government. Furthermore, this dissolution had permitted the victory of the Popular Front. Yet this did not prevent that, on April 7, by a vote of 238 to 5, Parliament decided that the second dissolution had not been necessary. Alcalá Zamora was removed from office to satisfy several personal grudges and Prieto's desire to preside over the government, an impossible occurrence as long as Azaña was available. Alongside the popular pressure, then, the wheeling-dealing politicking.

Martínez Barrio, as president of Parliament, occupied the position of chief of state until April 26, 1936, the date on which the newly-elected electors and the deputies chose a new president. Gleaning 754 out of 874 votes, Manuel Azaña was elected president of the Republic. He took over on May 10. Santiago Casares Quiroga (1884-1950), a Galician who had the reputation of being an energetic man, came to occupy the presidency of the council, whose members had scarcely changed. Earlier Prieto—Azaña's great "campaign manager"—had made gestures toward forming a Republican-Socialist coalition government, but had failed due to the unanimous veto put forth by the Socialist party.

Meanwhile, rumors of preparation for a coup d'état grew rampant. The number of strikes and the land occupations increased. Prieto did try hard to placate the masses with his propaganda and to once again establish an atmosphere of confidence. In his declaration before Parliament, Casares announced that "against fascism, the government is belligerent." At this time, the Civil Guard fired on a demonstration in the Murcian town of Yeste; 23 were killed and 100 wounded. This occurrence, combined with landowners, sabotage, and the closing of factories, exasperated the masses. Assassination attempts were frequent occurrences. A judge named Manuel Pedregal, who had sentenced a falangist, was murdered. This was followed by a failed attempt on the life of the vice-president of Parliament, the Socialist Luis Jiménez de Asúa (1889-1970). The next victims were two editors of provincial newspapers; finally several Republican officers and tens of workers. A bomb was discovered which had been planted in Largo Caballero's house. Primo de Rivera was arrested for illegal bearing of arms.

General Manuel Goded—the same who, at a banquet in 1931, proposed a toast: "Long live Spain and nothing else!" indicating that he was not toasting the Republic—was sent as captain general to the Balearic Islands; General Francisco Franco was sent to the Canary Islands; General Emilio Mola (1887-1937) went as captain general to Navarre, the strongest Traditionalist center in the country. The cadets at the Alcázar Military School in Toledo protested against the government and burnt leftist newspapers. The people spoke of a conspiracy. The government published a notice which read: "The government has become informed, with great sadness and indignation, of the unjust attacks upon officers who are loyal servants of the constitutional power, far removed from all political struggles and obedient to the will of the people. Only a devious and criminal desire to undermine the army can explain the insults and attacks, both verbal and written, which have been directed against it. The government has applied and will continue to apply all legal force against those who persist in such unpatriotic behavior." It was to be discovered later that at this very time the generals had already formulated a plan for a coup in meetings at which the inspector general of the army, General Rodríguez del Barrio, had presided.

As the Right united in preparation for the military insurrection, the government was sending out its police to repress strikes and land occupations. For three months the streets of Spain resembled those of Germany and Italy in the weeks that preceded Hitler and Mussolini's rise to power. Amidst the parade in Madrid on April 14 for the fifth anniversary of the Republic, bombs exploded at the foot of the presidential grandstand.

One day in July, well-known Republican Captain Carlos Faraudo, was assassinated as he was out strolling with his wife. Not too long afterwards—while this crime had gone unpunished—Lieutenant José Castillo, leader of a group of police storm troopers and apparently a Communist, was assassinated in the street; the assassins were never discovered. That very evening, a group of police storm troopers who had been under Lieutenant Castillo's command, appeared at the home of Calvo Sotelo (whose speeches in Parliament had made him the visible leader of the Right and the one whom the Communists had surmised to be responsible for Castillo's death) and took him away. The next morning, his corpse showed up at the depository of Madrid's cemetery. All the members of the Permanent Commission of Parliament condemned the assassination of the monarchist leader.

In Barcelona the Generalitat police force discovered a rightist organization of arms purchasers. Casares Quiroga, upon receiving notice of this discovery, dismissed it as being "of no importance." In the midst of this agitation, a projected Statute of Autonomy was voted by plebiscite in Galicia, but Parliament, instead of quickly adding its approval, let it stagnate in a committee. What it did was discuss the problems of public order: from February 16 to June 15 there had been 160 churches burned, 269 persons murdered, 1,287 wounded, 215 assassination attempts, 113 general strikes, 228 partial strikes, and 146 bombs exploded. The government suspended several right-wing newspapers and other left-wing ones. It also shut down dozens of monarchist and workers' centers. Thus they thought they would maintain a balance.

In Parliament, Miguel Maura revealed some interesting data: "The Director of Police has made a very interesting survey, whose results include the following statistics: Socialists, 1,447,000 paid members; the anarcho-syndicalists, 1,577,000 members; Communists, 133,000; right-wing forces, 549,000." No one doubted that the time for a roll call was quickly approaching. The Republic was about to disappear as it was, as a regime which had tried to arbitrate and compromise. Either the right-wing forces would triumph or the workers would. No one believed that an intermediate situation could last very long. It was even recognized by its adversaries that the balance-sheet of the Republic was positive. The very workers who wanted to go one step further realized that they would not have been able to do so without the groundwork previously laid by the Republic.

On the political plane, there was no doubt as to the positive balance: a regime of representative democracy had been established, women had been given the vote, the destruction of caciquism had begun, the middle class and a portion of the working class and peasantry had been incorporated into the regime, and the church had been separated from the state. The debit side of the ledger included a weak constitution, the slow pace of redistributing the land and, above all, the exclusion of anarcho-syndicalists, which probably constituted the regime's worst error.

On the social plane, the balance was also a positive one, but with more shadows: the right to unionize and to strike existed, the peasants were protected by the township law, the standard of living of workers and peasants had improved, and several agreements with the International Labor Organization had begun to be applied. But, on the other hand, anarcho-syndicalism had been systematically persecuted, while the system of social security had seen no innovation.

On the cultural plane, the balance was definitely a positive one. This was a reflection of the conviction of the intellectuals who led the regime that education was the basis for the country's modernization. More than 25,000 schools had been created, thousands of teachers had been trained, religious instruction had been made voluntary, university life had been renovated, the cultural life had been made accessible to a small portion of the working masses. Perhaps the only black mark on this page of the ledger was the unnecessary and sectarian expulsion of the Jesuits.

On the state organizational plane, the balance showed one distinguished mark, the Statute of Catalonia, shadowed by several gray entries: delay to approve similar statutes for Galicia and the Basque Country, timidity of army reform, lack of administrational reform, increase in bureaucracy, lack of reform in justice administration, lack of vitality of the municipalities and provinces.

On the international plane, the balance was indifferent: Spain had participated more actively in the League of Nations and had occupied Ifni. But, on the other hand, the sanction against Italy for the occupation of Ethiopia had been enforced rather unenthusiastically, there had been no search for ways to democratize the Moroccan and colonial policies, and the Diplomatic Corps had not been Republicanized.

Finally, on the economic plane, the balance was not a bad one, considered from a capitalist point of view, which was that of the Republic: the standard of living of the masses had been raised, and consequently the domestic market increased, the peseta had remained stable, the Bank of Spain had been slightly reformed, while industry had been stimulated. On the other side of the ledger, however, all of these measures had been timid ones, agrarian reform had scarcely been started, the banking system still exerted an excessive and uncontrolled influence on the economy, while foreign commerce had not been coordinated.

But no one was happy: right-wing factions, because too much had been done; the leftists, because not enough had been done; the Center, because everyone was dissatisfied. Nevertheless, everyone had a better life (the very rich, at least, did not have a worse one). Perhaps the basic error of the regime was that it had offended too many sensitivities (especially in the religious field) while not wounding enough interests. If the regime had wanted to completely eliminate the influence of the church, it should not have become involved with the feudal large-estate owners at the same time; if it had wanted to destroy the influence of the latter, it should have left the church alone.

The Republic had come to power without violence. The only blood spilled was that of the workers, and the Republic's life was mortgaged by this blood. Its life was also mortgaged by its desire to incorporate the feudal classes; because of this desire it did not dare take away their economic power and completely put into effect the minimal social reforms. The Republicans had lost sight of the fact that with a feudal social system, only two things can be done: either destroy it or surrender to it. Spain was in need of a democratic capitalist system; this need demanded the destruction of the feudal system. This could have been done on April 15, 1931. By April 30, it was probably already too late. Spain was a living example of the fact that when a feudal system is not destroyed with one swift blow, it will never be destroyed and will come to prevail in the end.

The Spanish bourgeoisie had grown as a graft onto feudalism. After the bourgeoisie had failed to predominate in the nineteenth century, when it should have historically done so, it became a parasite of feudalism. The Republic could have given it independence, but it did not find a way to do this. Furthermore, the Republic lacked the support of the bourgeoisie itself, which was imperative to effect this independence.

In 1936, the Spanish bourgeoisie found itself in a state of complete impotence, owing to its alliance with agrarian feudalism. If World War I was able to give the Spanish bourgeoisie a dynamism which forced it to the foreground of the political scene, it was only a momentary thing. Lacking a tradition of leadership and a constructive history as a social class, the bourgeoisie became an accomplice of the stagnation of the country. Mining production had decreased, while industrial production did not increase in harmony with the world's pace; the transportation system developed slowly. Spain, which counted on thousands of coastal miles and an important market in Latin America, figured very low on the list of merchant marines.

The banking system was a reflection of the bourgeoisie. The official discount of the period was 2 percent in Germany and 2.5 percent in France, while it had gone up to 6 percent in Spain. Spanish money was the most expensive in Europe. "The Bank of Spain asphyxiated all economic initiative," stated Luis Araquistáin (1886-1959). Sixteen thousand people held all the stock of the Bank of Spain (an official institution), which repaid their capital with the benefits of any quinquennium in its history. The observation had already been made in 1920 that the bank obtained greater benefits precisely in every national crisis. In 1921, the year of the catastrophe of Annual, its dividend was 54 percent, and this was never less than 16 percent. In 1934, the year of the October movement, the bank's dividend was 130 percent. The stock reports also proved revealing: as the issues of the public debt increased, industrial issues proportionately decreased, that is, the capital took refuge in the government finances. Foreign trade presented a growing deficit.

The budget offered no consolation. Until the first decade of the twentieth century it had presented a surplus, but from then on the deficit had swelled until it came to 1 billion pesetas in the 1935 budget. The bureaucracy, from 1900 until 1936, had multiplied the number of its pencil-pushing office clerks by eight. Since 1900, the national revenue had been augmented by 55 percent, the budget by 513 percent. Almost one-third of the nation's revenue which totaled 17 billion pesetas, was absorbed by the state, which in 1936 had on its payrolls 54,000 police agents.

All this could be reduced to a fundamental cause: Spanish capitalism was a monopolizer in a country of reduced economic life. De facto monopoly of iron, in the hands of English companies; transport monopoly by the railroads, to whom the state constantly offered financial aid; a monopoly of gas and electricity, also in the hands of foreign companies; a monopoly of maritime transports. The Catalonian bourgeoisie, for its part, monopolized the textile industry as a clan. Paper production was mostly found in the power of a single trust. Coal production received state aid almost every year, since it was mined in such anachronistic ways as to render it unprofitable. War industries, in spite of Azaña's law controlling them, were in the hands of foreign stockholders (Vickers and Krupp), often partners in the same company.

And all this was jointly subjugated to the banking system. The Urquijo family of bankers headed 134 boards of directors. Ruíz Senén, a former notary public who had become a business agent of the Jesuits, held a seat on 43 boards, among them the most important press agencies, broadcasting, and publicity. Ignacio Herrera was the head of 22 corporations; Echeverría, 33; the count of Gamazo, 28; the Basque shipping magnate Sota, 18; the marquis of Ibarra, 24; the Catalonian Ventosa Calvell, 20.

In view of this lack of initiative of the bourgeoisie, one can understand that foreign capital, which was relatively small, could not have been absorbed by the national economy and that it was motivated by this very fact to yield to the tendency to function as if it were a colonial country. In this way it exerted an influence which was much greater than it should have been by virtue of its size. The Telephone Company constituted the United States' first foothold in Spain; England and Canada had been well-seated in the country since the middle of the nineteenth century and were in possession of huge interests in electric, streetcar, and dockyard companies, in military industries, and in Basque and Andalusian mining companies. Germany intervened in the chemical industries and in the dockyards, in addition to several electric companies: Italy, in the Pirelli rubber company; Belgium and Switzerland in urban transportation, utilities, several Asturian mines, and potash; France in gas, public transport, and Asturian and Andalusian mines. None of this would have been very serious if it had been balanced by an active indigenous capital.

The Republic had had two huge ballasts: the lack of Republicans and several strong personalities at its head. The Republican parties could not count on organization, but rather were simple crystallizations of opinion centered in several popular names. In order to support itself, the Republic was forced to lean on the workers' parties and the unions, but the programs of these groups and those of the Republican personalities did not coincide. In fact, the Republic wound up by not representing the interests of any class, and this made it vulnerable on all sides. On the other hand, the Republic had been constantly signaled by the presence of Manuel Azaña, a man of distinguished intelligence but of a bitter personalist temperament, and Indalecio Prieto, a man skilled in political maneuvering but excessively egotistical. "The tragedy of the Republic," declared Azaña to a friend, "is that I have no one with whom I can carry on a conversation." In its first phase of governing, the fight between Azaña and Alcalá Zamora constantly created artificial conflicts, which would be resolved by the absurd and unjust removal from office of the latter when Azaña once again took over. During the period of the opposition, Azaña promised the country the same policy as Lerroux, but with more decorum and intelligence. Azaña was the author of the very severe Law of Public Order, and also of the very soft military reform. This contrast resulted in perhaps the best political portrait of him by a workers' leader: "Azaña is a Jacobin mixed with a Kerenski."

Built on this unstable base, the regime found itself constantly at the mercy of enemies it had decided not to eliminate economically. It had not eliminated them politically because then the Republican leftists would have been left without a strong counterpart to face the working parties; it had not done so economically since the regime did not know if it would be able to stop the transformation of the social structures where it wanted.

This incapacity for initiative on the part of the Spanish middle class was so evident that it had given rise to the workers' desire to be the ones to take charge of orienting the economic life. Each worker felt himself to be at least as well prepared to manage the company where he worked as was the owner. This sentiment was not limited to a few nuclei of dogmatic militants, but permeated the whole workers' movement. And the latter did not simply consist of minority organizations, composed of a group of dues-paying members and a few leaders. The past events had pushed the masses into politics; the masses exerted greater control over their organizations than the leaders. In fact, the latter gave the impression of being towed along by the masses. In a country of 25 million inhabitants, more than half of whom lived in rural areas, 3 million people were organized in unions and workers' parties: almost one-third of the economically active population. The workers had taken stock of the Republic and of the social forces; they believed that they were the most powerful and the best prepared.

# 12

# Fear and Hope

In 1820, when the Liberals forced Ferdinand VII to accept a constitution, the people sang out through the streets of Madrid:

> *Swallow it, swallow it,*
> *swallow it, you who doesn't want it,*
> *the Constitution.*

To a certain extent, this same spirit animated a large part of the Spanish Right in the early summer of 1936. Clearly, what mattered to them was to recover lost privileges, prevent the loss of others, and reconquer the reins of power. But what happened above all was "to put the people in their place," to force the peasant to manifest his servility, the worker, to be submissive, the petite bourgeoisie, to be obsequious. The Spanish rightists had suffered so much fear that they could consider themselves liberated from it only when they could see the masses frightened and humiliated.

This state of mind of the right-wing factions must have seemed an obstacle to their leaders, since they knew that, one way or another, these were irreversible matters, such as the substitution of the monarchy by the Republic, the new dignity acquired by the man in the street, and the separation of the church and the popular masses. Discrepancies existed among right-wing leaders themselves. Some, especially the monarchists and aristocrats, partook of the "swallow it" spirit, so characteristically Spanish, while others, such as Falangists and some military, held more modern concepts. Nevertheless, they all collaborated in the preparation for attack on the existing powers.

The people had guessed that there was a conspiracy, if such overt activity could be called that. Its first phase was the frustrated coup of General Sanjurjo in 1932. Then, the discussion with Mussolini in Rome. In 1935 the plan had matured. The UME (Spanish Military Union), to which the majority of leaders and officers belonged, encountered as its only opposition the weak UMR (Republican Military Union). The foundation of those pledged to the conspiracy was formed by the aristocracy and the politicians of the extreme Right; its force of impact consisted of the Requetés (Traditionalists) and the Falangists. No one bothered the military conspirators. In 1935, General Franco was chief of the general staff, General Goded, chief of military inspection, and General Joaquín Fanjul (1880-1936) was undersecretary of war. They were not conspirators, but they permitted the conspiracy. On February 17, as the Popular Front victory became known, Calvo Sotelo visited Portela, the head of the government, and took him to a meeting of the conspirators at the Palace Hotel. There they asked him to turn over the power to the army. Portela, vacillating for a moment, refused. The conspirators did not insist, since at that time they did not dare step out into the streets without the aid of the cabinet.

The Popular Front government transferred several generals but did not keep them under surveillance. Franco went as captain general to the Canary Islands (which lay across from Morocco), Goded to the Balearic Islands (which faced Barcelona), Mola to Navarre (the most Traditionalist region in the country). Mola was the soul of the preparations, the center of a junta of eight generals, which would be transformed into a government when the coup had succeeded. They assumed it would be something similar to General Primo de Rivera's coup in 1923, without a struggle: no one spoke of fascism or of the threat of communism. The Falange, with small action groups, hoped to be able to lead the coup along the tracks of fascism. Primo de Rivera was in prison in Alicante, absent from the events being prepared.

In April 1936, the French ambassador in Berlin informed his government of a trip by General Sanjurjo to the German capital, "where he was received quite cordially." Two generals who had been Republicans until then, Cabanellas and Queipo del Llano, joined the junta in May. Admiral Francisco Salas (1871-1936) joined it in the name of the navy, which the Republicans had not even tried to dearistocratize. Calvo Sotelo, in Parliament, made efforts to dissipate suspicions: "When I hear of the danger of the monarchist generals, I smile to myself, because I do not believe that at this time, within the

Spanish army, which respects the Constitution, whatever the personal ideas of its components may be, there exists a single soldier ready to rise in rebellion against the Republic. And if one should happen to exist, I tell you with complete frankness, he would be either crazy or a complete fool."

The assassination of Calvo Sotelo forced the generals' secret junta to realize that if it did not hurry, it could arrive too late, because the man in the street, in a primitive and brutal way, would take the action which the government had neglected to take. The order to revolt came three days after the assassination of Calvo Sotelo. The uprising was to consist of drawing the troops out into the street proclaiming the state of war in "defense of the Republic," thus replacing civil authority with military personnel.

In Morocco on July 17, several trucks loaded with legionnaires distributed forces throughout the cities of the zone and occupied positions of command: military quarters, telegraph offices, and airports. General Franco, captain general of the Canary Islands, flew from Tenerife to Morocco. Immediately a proclamation was issued announcing that the army "had decided to reestablish order and appealed to the Republican sentiment of all Spaniards to be ready to participate in the task of restoring Spain." To accomplish this, a state of war was declared and the right to strike was suspended. Numerous workers' leaders were executed in the following two days.

The government of Madrid asked the general to set arms aside. No reply was received. On the afternoon of the 18th a government plane flew over Tetuán and dropped six bombs on the military quarters and the airport. Franco sent the following telegram to the prime minister: "Now that I have assumed my new responsibilities, I wish to protest vehemently against the most reprehensible act of the government to order its pilots to attack the civilian population, thus putting the safety of innocent women and children in danger. It will not be long before the salvation movement of Spain shall triumph and then I will demand an account for this act. The reprisals which we will take will be in proportion to the resistance that is offered us. We explicitly request the cessation of this useless blood-spilling on your part."

The minister of the governorate, as this telegram was being transmitted via official lines, announced to the press: "The government declares that the movement is limited to certain zones of the Protectorate [of Morocco], and that no one, absolutely no one, in the Peninsula has joined such an absurd undertaking." Several hours later, when "such an absurd undertaking" was in full swing throughout the entire country, an official note still tried to calm the people's alarm: "Thanks to the measures adopted by the government, the sweeping movement of aggression upon the Republic can be considered aborted. The government's action will be sufficient to reestablish normality." The government was more worried by the possibility of spontaneous mass action than by the rebellion itself. At seven o'clock in the evening, the government recognized the fact that there had been "acts of agression" in Seville, where General Queipo del Llano had already spent one day in power, with gunfire and executions throughout the entire city.

The Socialist party also published a notice: "The moment is difficult, but not one of despair. The government is certain that it possesses sufficient means to squelch this criminal attempt. In the eventuality that these resources should not be sufficient, the Republic has the solemn promise of the Popular Front, which is serenely and resolutely decided to intervene in the battle as soon as its intervention is requested. The government orders and the Popular Front obeys." Nevertheless, the CNT and UGT issued an order which declared a general strike indefinitely where the military had proclaimed the state of war.

From the 16th of the month, the unions and the workers' parties had their militants on the alert. Workers' groups, armed with old pistols, took turns patrolling around the military quarters. They wanted to prevent the troops from going out into the street. At dawn on Sunday, July 19, many cities witnessed bloody battles. A naval cruiser, crossing the Strait of Gibraltar, bombed the fort at Algeciras, which surrendered. Moorish troops and the Foreign Legion disembarked.

A military agent secured planes in London which would be used to transport troops from Morocco. An Italian military aircraft mistakenly landed in French Morocco; the pilot thought he was going to Spanish Morocco. Navarre rose en masse in rebellion at the orders of General Mola. The army occupied Burgos and executed General Batet who refused to join the rebels. In Valladolid, the Falangist stronghold there was fighting with the railroad workers. There General Antonio Saliquet took the city after the execution of General José Molero (1870-1936), loyal to the Republic. The Casa del Pueblo resisted and was destroyed; the governor had not given arms to the workers. In Avila, the governor was executed. In the rest of the small cities of the wheat-growing region, it was an easy matter: governors arrested, executions at dawn, the formation of groups which headed in trucks toward Madrid, which, by this time, General Fanjul should have already occupied. But in Madrid, General Fanjul found himself besieged within the military barracks of La Montaña. The minister of war had sent General Miguel Núñez de Prado to Zaragoza; he was discovered and executed. In Zaragoza the battle continued for four days; Cabanellas assured the union delegates that he would remain loyal to the Republic. Then he executed them.

In Seville, entire areas of the city were occupied by General Queipo's forces. Thousands were killed. As had happened in all the provinces where the governor had refused to arm the workers, the victory fell to the military. The miners of Riotinto, armed with dynamite, rushed to Seville's aid, only to be decimated. In Cordova and Granada, the governors had not given arms, and the military triumphed. In Cádiz, the battle continued all night long around the burning arms factory; the arrival of a cruiser in the hands of the rebels ended the struggle. In Málaga, after several hours of indecisive battle, the people were victorious. In Asturias, Colonel Antonio Aranda was in possession of Oviedo; the miners controlled the port of Gijon and the coal-mining zone. Bilbao remained on the side of the Republic. In San Sebastián, a battle was to be carried on for several days until the city fell into the hands of the military. In Galicia the military triumphed. Alicante was loyal, and from there a column went forth to recover Albacete, which had rebelled. In Valencia an uprising attempt was thwarted by a worker's attack on the military quarters. The military was successful in Huesca. In Guadalajara the military was in power for two days when it was vanquished by a worker's column which had been launched from Madrid. In Lérida, the garrison rebelled, a general strike broke out, and the rebels surrendered.

But it was to be Barcelona where everything would be decided. There, the struggle lasted a night and a day. Four military columns, to which civilians had been added, went out from the military quarters of the periphery. The workers and the Catalanists, armed with whatever they could find, met the troops. Companys placed himself personally at the head of the attacking guards; when they lost heart, he boosted their morale. The Civil Guard, which had remained neutral at the beginning, swung to the Republic when it saw that the military had been conquered.

The workers improvised tanks which they launched at top speed against the cannons. General Manuel Goded arrived from Mallorca by plane, took over the Captain Generalship, was trapped there and taken prisoner by the people. He was led to the Palace of the Generalitat and there, over the radio, he announced: "I inform the Spanish people that my luck has taken a turn for the worse. I am a prisoner. I say this to all those who do not wish to continue the fight:

consider yourselves free from your pledges to me." In the streets, cars bearing the red and black flag of the CNT made their way through the litter of human corpses and dead horses. Some churches had served the rightist civilians as shooting posts; soon almost all the churches and convents in the city were ablaze.

Meanwhile the military quarters of La Montaña in Madrid had fallen. Hundreds were dead. Churches were burning. The advance of the first military forces on the capital through the Sierra was announced. The workers, armed with booty taken from the barracks, rushed to defend the Sierra as if they were on vacation. They fought almost completely unprotected, scarcely knowing how to use the rifles and grenades, against well-armed professionals. They fought, and they conquered. They were routed only in those places where Republican authorities had not given arms to the people. There was no doubt at all: if many Republicans had not been so afraid of the people, the uprising would have been squelched everywhere within two days.

The military uprising had become a civil war, one which everyone thought would be short. The country found itself divided into two zones which corresponded to a social reality: the agrarian provinces (Galicia, rural Asturias, León, Old Castile, Navarre, Aragon, and Andalusia, with the exception of Jaén, Almería, and Málaga) in the hands of the military; the industrial provinces (Valencia, Catalonia, the Basque Country, mining Asturias, Madrid and the provinces skirting it to the south and east) were in the hands of the people— they could hardly be said to be in the hands of the government. The two zones were split: the military zone along the Portuguese border in Extremadura; the Republican zone along the French border in Aragon and Navarre.

The intensity and severity of the struggle had surprised everyone. The military had thought they would not encounter any resistance. But the resistance had been spontaneous. There had been no need for orders from the government. Without the masses in the streets, the government would probably have surrendered. Those few days of sporadic, extremely violent battles, brought out both the best and the worst of the Spanish character: solidarity, combativeness, tenacity, the desire to humiliate the conquered, cruelty, self-sacrifice for a cause, idealism, and fanaticism.

The rightists were especially moved to act by the fear of the future, the desire to compensate for past fears, and also by very deep religious sentiment. The people were certainly moved by a spirit of vengeance for the still-recent repression, but above all, by hope. It had been proved that things could be better—under the Republic they had been somewhat improved—which provided the people with impetus and impatience. For years the people had acted with tactics which were very often violent, since violence was the only mode of expression allowed them. They had acted more for ideals than for immediate objectives. Most likely a third of the strikes which had taken place in Spain during the twentieth century had occurred for reasons of solidarity rather than for concrete demands. The people were trained to think, feel, and act in idealistic terms.

Seventy-two hours after the uprising had begun, there had been not only military changes, but also political ones, within the two zones. The heroism and enthusiasm of the beginning hours had been followed by a general radicalization: in the republican zone, a shift to the Left; in the rebel zone, a shift to the Right. Forces which two days earlier had been underrated had now become decisive. Spain, in the heat of the Civil War, again became malleable. How would events and men transform it?

# 13

# *Everything is Possible*

A century earlier, the partisans of Ferdinand VII used to greet him with the cry (which was not at all sarcastic): "Long live the chains!" The military uprising had destroyed against its will all the chains, both within the ranks of the rebels and those of the people. Suddenly Spain was free of shackles, free of inhibitions, and free of limitations. Everything could be done. Attempts to do everything soon began.

The revolution had highs and lows, an ascending road. It had now arrived at its apex: the transfer of power from one class to another. On July 20, when a group of anarchist leaders visited the president of the Generalitat, Lluis Companys, the latter told them:

> You have conquered. You have always been persecuted, and I, with deep regret, I, who in past years have been your defender, was myself forced by political circumstances to also persecute you. Today you are the lords of the city and of Catalonia, because you alone have vanquished the fascist soldiers. I hope you do not find it distasteful that I remind you that you have not been without the assistance of many or of few men of my party and the aid of the police storm troopers. . . . You have conquered and everything is in your power. If you do not need me or do not want me as president, tell me now and I will be but another soldier in the antifascist struggle. If, on the contrary, you believe me when I tell you I shall abandon this position to the fascists only over my dead body, perhaps with my comrades, my name, and my prestige, I may be able to serve you.

The anarchist leaders, who represented almost the entire Catalonian proletariat, had spent half a century speaking out against the state and politics. Now that the state had fallen into their hands, they did not know what to do with it. So Companys continued as President of the Generalitat.

In Madrid, a brief government presided by Diego Martínez Barrio met on the night of July 20. They established communication with General Mola, with the intent of offering him a place in the cabinet in exchange for putting an end to the rebellion. Mola listened to the proposal without saying a word and hung up the receiver. Then the task of forming the government was entrusted to José Giral (1880-1962), a chemistry professor member of the Republican Left and a friend of Azaña.

In Catalonia, a Committee of Militias was created, composed of five members of the CNT, three of the UGT, four of the Esquerra and other Republican groups, one from POUM, one from the Unió de Rabassaires, and one from the PSUC (Unified Socialist Party of Catalonia), which had been organized three days after the coup with the union of the Communist Party of Catalonia and other small Catalonian socialist groups, and adhered to the Third International). The Committee of Militias was in effect a second power. It organized and directed columns of voluntary workers who were headed toward Aragon and established lines in front of Huesca and Zaragoza. Generalitat, in actuality, did not exist. In Valencia a Popular Council had been created, much along the same lines as the Committee of Militias of Catalonia.

The workers realized that they had saved Barcelona and that Barcelona had saved the Republic. This gave them enormous self-confidence. They would need it, since the situation soon became difficult. Many business owners had fled to France, or were in hiding, fearful of workers' reprisals. The workers themselves took charge of making the factories hum once again. Committees to manage the factories were spontaneously organized. Furthermore, since the Basque Country and its siderurgy remained far away and cut off from the rest of the Republican zone, it became necessary to improvise a war industry to furnish munitions and arms to the military. Although it was commonly thought that the war would be brief, everyone realized that it was a war. In order to start the wheels of the economy in motion, the workers discovered that their utopias were useful to them. If their unions had not spent decades dreaming about one day organizing an ideal society, they would have now found themselves ignorant of what to do. But from the store of dreams, projects, and fantasies came forth initiatives, ideas, and forms of organization. In addition, the workers felt the desire to be the masters. The military coup had created a situation in which they had to be the masters, not only for their own benefit, but also for that of the entire society. But this self-confidence of the workers frightened the Republican middle class.

There existed an atomization of power, with each committee of enterprise thinking itself master, each committee of a region, city, or town, considering itself the government. The old anarchist antiauthoritarian tradition and the governmental inexperience of the working class were reflected in this state of affairs.

An economic council was established in Barcelona. The council decreed the collectivization of all industries employing more than one hundred salaried employees. A committee of control elected by the workers managed each company. The assets and liabilities of the former business were inherited by the new one. All committees of control were coordinated by the economic council, which was responsible for the organization of the country's economy in all its orders. Foreign stock holdings in the collectivized companies were respected. Many of the owners who had not left occupied positions as technical advisors in their own companies.

With regard to the land, it fell to the men that worked it. Agricultural cooperatives, traditional in Catalonia, were developed until they controlled all the country's agrarian economy.

Bank accounts remained under government control. Silver money disappeared from circulation, and many city governments were forced to issue fractional paper money, which shortly thereafter was suppressed. Palaces and villas were systematically requisitioned for use as hospitals, homes for the displaced, and schools. In towns where the CNT was strong, reactionary elements took shelter in the UGT. The PSUC rapidly augmented its ranks, becoming a refuge for the middle class.

On the front, command was also atomized. Still, the enthusiasm compensated for the lack of experience, and chaos became organization. It was exactly what a paradoxical order by the anarchists expressed: "Let's organize the indiscipline." Unquestionably, things would have gone more smoothly and rapidly if the people had submitted to the government and limited their activity to carrying on the war, rather than undertaking political action. But the people wanted to do things for themselves. Furthermore, they lacked confidence in the government whose ineptness had carried them into civil war.

In the rest of Republican Spain, Catalonia's example pressured the government. In towns within latifundist regions, the peasants took over the land, often killing or imprisoning the administrators, and they organized it into collectives or cooperatives. In other places, the unions administered the land directly. Agrarian reform was realized in less than a week.[1]

The church remained radically separated from the state. Those bishop and clergy whose political activity was known were spontaneously persecuted in the first days, in spite of government attempts to save them (successful in a large number of cases). Churches and convents were burned; in many cases people removed their artistic treasures out into the street and then sent them to museums. Convents were converted into hospitals, palaces into schools and shelters.[2]

Automatically, the army had also been transformed. The government, with an eye to pulling out the rug from under the rebellious generals, had discharged the soldiers. Those who were in the rebel zone remained in their ranks. Those of the Republican zone went home and were replaced by militiamen (volunteers who had to present a signed guarantee of their organization in order to be given a weapon, and who also joined the column which pleased them most). Very few officers remained loyal and new leaders arose from the ranks of militiamen. These new leaders were given rather sketchy advice by the old professionals. Martínez Barrio was given the task of organizing a nucleus of the regular army in Valencia.

The problem of nationalities was resolved in the first session of Parliament. José Antonio Aguirre (1904-60), leader of the Basque Nationalist party, was transported from Bilbao to Madrid by plane, carrying a proposal for the Basque Statute, which was approved by Parliament. In Bilbao, a government which included Nationalists, Republicans, Socialists, and Communists was constituted, with Aguirre elected as president of Euzkadi (the Basque Country).

Finally, state reform was likewise the work of a few days. A large portion of high bureaucrats had escaped and had either joined the rebels or left the country. Most of the diplomatic corps went over to the side of the military. The government was forced to improvise a bureaucracy and a diplomatic corps with politically safe elements, even if their inexperience made them ineffectual.

Parliament met to approve the Basque Statute and give its vote of confidence to the new government. Many centrist and rightest deputies sided with the military; others had been murdered, like General López Ochoa, the conqueror of Asturias in 1934, and other personalities that the people considered dangerous. For men of the Right, jail became a refuge. For a month, the people exerted an implacable repression, often cruel and brutal, intemperate and unjust. Then Popular Tribunals were organized, whose juries were composed of representatives of the different parties and unions. The more traditional court martials sentenced to death and executed generals Goded, Fanjul, and other military who had rebelled and been imprisoned.

Within a few days, the atmosphere had completely changed. The bourgeois disguised themselves as workers. "Decent" people soon discovered "friends" whom weeks earlier they had despised as extremists, and from whom they requested the indispensable *avales* (guarantees of "good" political behavior) needed to obtain visas, passports, etc. Those who had been arrested remembered their Republican friends. Friendship and a certain degree of compassion overruled ideological differences. But they could not restrain those to whom the people referred as "uncontrollables," groups who took matters into their own hands. These groups were dedicated to vengeance, and at times even to blackmail, directed against known rightists or those who had been very harsh with workers or peasants. For example the landowners who had taken advantage of October 1934 to evict their tenant farmers, were the targets of visits from these "uncontrollables." Although there were hundreds of these cases, so much was said about them that people were under the impression that their number was well up into the thousands.

In two weeks, circumstances and the workers had joined to undertake, almost without realizing it, the reforms that Spain had been trying to accomplish for a century and a half, and had never realized. They were chaotic, incomplete, and at times contradictory reforms which needed to be coordinated. But the first essential step had been taken. Once the war ended, people believed, it would be possible to build a different society, one without exploitive latifundists and confining centralism. The defensive combat resulting from the uprising had been converted into a popular, offensive, revolutionary war. The conspirators' calculations had been in error. The lack of political culture in which they had held the country in submission for centuries, had now turned against them, manifested in a series of acts, some of them cruel, which they themselves had provoked.

Soon a divergence in the interpretation of the situation became evident. On one side the CNT, POUM, and the left wing of the Socialist party affirmed that the war and the revolution were inseparable. They further maintained the need to oppose the hosts of rebels an army capable of conquering, and this army had to necessarily receive its support from an economy opposed to that which supported the generals. Also, they felt that the support by the proletariat on the international level could counteract the generals' diplomatic maneuverings. On the other side, the Republican parties—Esquerra, the Basque Nationalists, the Socialists' right wing, and the Communist party—maintained that first and foremost the war had to be won, and then the country could decide if it wanted to stage a revolution. They felt it necessary to limit themselves to the defense of constitutional legality, so that the diplomatic corps could obtain the help of England and France. On August 16, one month after the outbreak, *Mundo Obrero*, the organ of the Communist party, wrote: "It is absolutely false that the present movement has as its objective the establishment of dictatorship of the proletariat, once the war is ended. It cannot be said that we have a social motive for our intervention in the war. Our only desire is to defend the democratic Republic."

It was necessary to resolve the duality of power. Either the proletariat would definitely take possession of the state, or the state would return to the hands of the middle class. But for the latter to happen, the situation had not matured sufficiently. On September 4, the Giral government gave way to a cabinet presided by the Socialist Largo Caballero, which was formed by three Socialists of leftist tendencies, three of rightist tendencies, two Communists, and five Republicans. Largo Caballero declared: "This government has been constituted by all the groups of the Popular Front, and all of those who form it have previously renounced the defense of their private principles and tendencies, with the objective of remaining united in one sole aspiration: to defend Spain in its fight against fascism." On the other side of the front a parallel process was evolving, but in an inverse direction.

José Ortega y Gasset had written in 1920: "The generals and colonels of the nineteenth century thought that the cry given in their barracks would resound in coinciding echos throughout the breadth of Spain. Those who cried out did not think that it would ever be necessary to fight zealously to win victory. They were, then, not going to fight, but rather take possession of the public power." The belief that stimulated the rebels in 1936 was much the same. Upon finding a resistance as unexpected as it was tenacious, their entire movement was dislocated on the political plane. In order to give the rebellion some degree of permanence, they were forced to search for some ideological basis for it.

On the military side were the two monarchist parties (Alfonsians and Carlists), still separated by dynastic questions. To base the movement on the principle of restoration would have been to divide it. There was one other group: the Falange. The Italians and Germans had already begun to send materials (on credit) and advisors. The best way to thank them for it was to give the movement a fascist character, which the politicians of the old regime accepted with the hope that it would take care of the dirty work (executions, street fighting, etc.).

But the fascist movement needed a leader. José Antonio Primo de Rivera was a prisoner in Alicante, in the Republican zone. Calvo Sotelo had been assassinated (furthermore, he had not been a Fascist proper). General Sanjurjo had died in a plane crash on the way from Lisbon to Burgos on July 20. In Burgos there was a junta provisional of generals presided by Cabanellas (who was to die soon). Mola could have been the leader, but his monarchist convictions had placed him in a bad light with the Falangists. Franco, the best military mind among all of them wound up being proclaimed chief of state in Burgos on October 1, 1936. He immediately formed the first government, which would be called Technical Junta. In it figures Agrarians, industrialists, Catalonians from the Lliga, and several generals. From this moment on, the political life of the rebel zone remained paralyzed. Months later (April 19, 1937), there came the unification of Traditionalists and Falangists, decreed by General Franco. Thus the single party of the Traditionalist Spanish Falange appeared, with Franco as its leader, just as he was chief of state. A movement of protest from the Falange purists, headed by Manuel Hedilla (1902-70), was suppressed and its leaders were exiled or jailed. The National Council of the new Falange was composed of twenty Falangists, five generals, eight Traditionalists, and the remaining members, which totaled fifty, were Conservatives and Alfonsian monarchists. After that there were only struggles of influence between Agrarians and industrialists, Germans and Italians, military and Falangists. The difference with the other zone was immediately evident: the rebel zone witnessed unity of command and political submission; the Republican zone, political discussion and dispersion of command.

In the first week of the war, the predominant characteristic of the rebel zone was terror. It was not an occasional terror, a sporadic outburst at the hands of spontaneous groups, but a legalized, organized, public terror. No one condemned it, which differed from what was happening in the other zone. There was not more brutality nor more cruelty, but there was more of a system. Furthermore, those who executed the terror were not uneducated, poor people, who had been persecuted and humiliated all their lives, but rich, educated, privileged people. Deputies, governors, workers' leaders, and leftists were executed. Those military who had not become party to the rebellion were also executed. The world press gave figures, which may have been exaggerated, but nevertheless revealed the impression received by the news correspondents: Seville, 20,000 dead; Zaragoza, 17,000; Valladolid, 8,000; El Ferrol, 3,000. Faced with the advancing rebel troops, the people fled en masse, creating a problem of shelter and food supplies in the Republican cities. Later on in the struggle, after the fury of revenge had passed, other characteristics were added: the organization of a new state, the preponderance of the church, the rise of the figure of Franco as the sole leader.

One simple fact, as told by Georges Bernanos, the French Catholic writer, revealed the tone of the moment. In Mallorca, the inhabitants received a printed form for communion: "Mr. ——— Mrs. ——— Miss ——— residing at ——— Number ——— Street, has fulfilled the communion Easter duty at the church of —. Do not forget to deposit your form in the box at the rear of the church, so that you are included in the census."[3]

The atmosphere was such that anyone could settle a private account, killing, for example, the poet Federico García Lorca (1899-1936) in Granada. Or, as happened in Salamanca, the elderly Miguel de Unamuno, after listening to the cry, "Death to culture!" hurled at a banquet by a general, became indignant and declared in public: "You will conquer, but you will not convince," and had to be protected against the anger of the guest invited by General Franco's own wife. Several days later Unamuno died in the confinement of his home.

In Granada, Cordova, and San Fernando, where there were Protestant communities, pastors were beaten and murdered. The bishops in the rebel zone, and those who had fled the Republican zone, published a pastoral letter in which they announced their allegiance to what they called the crusade to save Spain (July 10, 1937), inspired by the primate cardinal Isidro Gomá (1869-1940). Only the archbishop of Tarragona and the bishop of Vitoria, both exiled in Switzerland, did not add their signatures to this document. On March 22, 1938, the Burgos Junta returned the control and registry of births, marriages, and deaths back to the church.

From this moment on, to the anti-Marxist label given the war, and the nickname "Reds" given to the Republicans, were added the mottoes "Christian Crusade" and "fight for the salvation of Europe." Franco stated to a correspondent from the *Daily Telegraph* that he "planned to organize Spain along the lines of the German and Italian models, but still respecting national characteristics." Another time, he spoke of the "community of German, Italian, and Spanish arms aimed at Freemasonry, communism, and rotted liberalism."

Ex-king Alfonso supported General Franco as did his son, the infante Don Juan; the latter offered Franco his services in a letter dated December 7, 1936. Don Juan showed up in the rebel zone, but he was accompanied to the border; his presence could have politically divided the partisans of the Burgos Junta. The picture is complete if one adds to it that the peasants whom the Republicans had established on expropriated lands were expelled from these same lands, that salaries returned to the level of 1935, that the right to strike and the unions disappeared, and that censorship was established from the onset.

In Portugal, agents of the rebels worked zealously. At this time Gil Robles was their adviser until, months later, he would be left out by the newly-promoted leaders of Falangism. A brother of General Franco, Nicolás (b. 1891), was ambassador to Lisbon. In London, the duke of Alba, who was related to the English nobility, represented the interests of the rebels. Shortly thereafter, in November, Germany, Italy, Hungary, Portugal, and Japan broke diplomatic relations with the Republican government and recognized that of Burgos.

Despite all this, it was difficult to consider the rebels as fascists. It is true that they had adopted the external forms of fascism and its vocabulary, but their objectives were typically reactionary and their method of repression characteristically Spanish. In this light, Spain continued to act outside of history. In the zone which had already begun to be called "nationalist," life was lived in the seventeenth century with twentieth-century techniques. In the Republican zone, it was lived in the twenty-first century, with techniques and rhetoric of the nineteenth.

## NOTES

1. By May 1938, 2,432,202 hectares of land had been expropriated due to lack of cultivation, 2,008,000 for reasons of social utility, and 1,252,000 by virtue of provisional occupation. In regions of small property holdings, agricultural production was maintained, and the peasants got rich on the black market. In regions of large property holdings, where the peasants had never been property owners, production declined, except in Aragon, where the CNT had organized agricultural collectives which functioned well despite propaganda against them which Communists and moderate Republicans had unfurled.

2. According to figures of the church itself, provided after the Civil War, 13 bishops, 4,171 priests, 2,365 friars, and 282 nuns were murdered. On the Nationalist side, although actual figures were not available, numerous

Basque priests, who for reasons of nationalism had remained loyal to the Republic, were executed.

3. Georges Bernanos, *Les Cimetières sous la lune*, Paris, Plon, 1938, pp. 141-43.

# 14

# Ten Months of
# Creativity

Spain, since its appearance as such in history, had constantly been under a guardianship. First, that of enlightened despotism. Then, that of the Liberals and Conservatives. This was followed by the intellectuals of the First Republic and the various parties of the "foolish years"; then came the military and civilians of the dictatorship. Lastly, it was the guardianship of the intellectuals of the Second Republic. There had always been an elite which had told the country what it should do, and especially what it should not do.

Suddenly the elite found itself without knowing what to order and with no one to listen to it. Spain, in those early days of the Civil War, had left its tutelage behind. The Spaniards acted on their own, without asking anyone's opinion. They had reached the legal age of adulthood.

It was to be a short-lived legal age, since the elite soon recovered from its surprise and began to create new instruments which would again submit the country to guardianship. On the Nationalist side, these instruments worked well, but on the Republican side, the people refused to let themselves be subjugated. Hence in the Nationalist zone war was spoken of more than politics, while in the Republican side, politics, more than war, was the topic of the day. But on both sides the war was waged with a dog-eat-dog spirit, with that cruelty which characterizes civil wars.

In the first months of war, one saw an army fighting against a people, a description which is by no means exaggerated. The rebels counted on the majority of the military regiments, the Civil Guard, the Foreign Legion, the Regulars (the Moorish troops), and foreign technical advisers. Facing them was a handful of Republican officers and the mass of voluntary militiamen. For the first phase of operations, the columns of militiamen from parties and organization were sufficient. Attention should be briefly directed toward the evolution of these operations, which were simultaneously those of a civil war, a social war, a religious war, and an international war.

In the Mediterranean Sea were Mallorca and Ibiza, which the nationalist spirit of Catalonia tried to pull out from under the domination of the generals with an expedition, commanded by Captain Alberto Bayo (who later was Fidel Castro's trainer in Mexico). The attempt failed. The Republic preserved only the island of Menorca. With this, Barcelona remained exposed to the bombers which left from Mallorca.

On the north were Irún and San Sebastián, in the hands of the militia, which was exterminated once they ran out of munitions, while in the French border station of Hendaya a train filled with arms awaited permission of the French government to open the border. In the Sierra, opposite Madrid, the Nationalist forces were contained, due to the fortification which had been constructed by order of General Franco and Gil Robles in 1935. Facing Cordova and Granada, the Republican forces were unsuccessful in their bid to storm the enemy line. A group of rebels set up a stronghold in the sanctuary of Santa María de la Cabeza, from where they would resist for more than a year and a half.

In Toledo, Colonel José Moscardó (1878-1936), along with hundreds of officers and civil guards, entrenched himself in the old Alcázar. The government negotiated. When finally the decision was reached to blow up the Alcázar with the help of a group of miners skilled in the use of dynamite, it was already too late. The rebel forces had advanced toward Toledo, on the road to Madrid.

It was in the south and southwest that the rebel offensive took on greatest proportions, with an eye to joining its Castilian and Andalusian zones. From Seville, where General Queipo reigned with terror, the Moors and legionnaires advanced on Extremadura, trampling on the improvised militias of the towns, and crossed the Tajo River. The two rebel zones were now united. This had been possible due to the so-called Battle of the Straits won by the rebels with the help of the millions from Juan March, who bought airplanes to transfer the Moors from Africa to the Peninsula just as he had financed an Italian escadrille, commanded by "count Rossi" (Arconovaldo Ponaccorsi) in Mallorca. The Republican fleet[1] ruled the strait, but the first Italian and German planes protected air routes. In addition, the chief of international control at Tangiers demanded that the Republican government have the fleet abandon the waters of the strait (August 4, 1936). Nine Italian airplanes cleaned up the sea. General Franco now had the option of organizing convoys across the strait.

The peasants who had fled to Portugal were handed over to the military by the police force of Oliveira Salazar. Badajoz fell on August 14. Two days later, in the bullfight ring in the city, hundreds of prisoners were machine-gunned to death. The news of the fall of Irún, on September 5, followed on the 13th by the seizure of San Sebastián which was abandoned without destruction and with the defection of several officers of the enemy, was accompanied by that of the arrival of the Moors in Talavera. On September 27, Toledo fell. The Moors murdered the wounded in the hospital there and the Alcázar was liberated.

Meanwhile in Seville, the voice of General Queipo del Llano was heard every day over the radio: "Our valiant legionaires and Moorish Troups," he said on July 23, "have shown the Reds what it is to be men. By the way, they have also shown this to the Reds' women, who have now finally known true men and not castrated militiamen. Their kicking and crying like dogs will not save them." On August 12: "The Marxists are ferocious beasts, but we are gentlemen. . . . Mr. Companys deserves to have his throat cut like a pig." On August 18: "Eighty percent of the families of Andalusia are in mourning. And we shall not hesitate to adopt even more rigorous measures in order to insure our victory." On September 3: "If the bombing of La Línea is repeated, I shall give the order to shoot three relatives of each of the sailors of the Coast Guard crew who is responsible for them." On September 8: "I have given the order to shoot three members of the families of each of the sailors of the Coast Guard who have again bombed La Línea. . . . I would like to tell my daughter, who is in Paris, that we are all in fine health and that it would make us very happy to receive news from her."

General Juan Yagüe (1891-1952), leader of operations against Toledo, stated the following to a correspondent from the German agency DNB: "The fact that the conquest of Spain by our army has been so slow has an advantage: it gives us time to cleanse our entire territory of Red elements."

A Nationalist officer, who was taken prisoner on July 28, was found to be in possession of a confidential circular order from his staff which read as follows: "One of the essential conditions of the victory consists of breaking down the morale of enemy troops. In order to occupy territory it is necessary to instill a certain amount of terror in the population. The means employed must be spectacularly impressive. It is essential that in occupied towns information be gathered via the priest regarding important members of the population. Having seen the large number of women who are fighting on the enemy's side, the sex of the adversaries shall, under no circumstances, be taken into account. After the occupation of Madrid, machine guns should be installed in the bell towers and on the rooftops."

After the occupation of Madrid all measures for the victory parade were being taken. The legionnaires had already occupied Carabanchel in the outlying districts of the capital. The government decided to abandon Madrid, loaded its archives onto trucks and moved to Valencia, leaving the city in charge of a Defense Junta presided by General José Miaja (1878-1958) and formed by representatives of all parties and organizations. On November 7, the Moors took the trolley into the Ciudad Universitaria (the campus of the University of Madrid). But they met up with a resistance they had not expected.

The life of Spain had totally changed. The same people who, five years earlier, in April 1931, had sung and laughed as the Republic had been proclaimed, now killed and were killed with the same enthusiasm and for the same motives they had previously cheered. The people had seen themselves pushed into a total change of mood. This was visible in the daily life of the country. People greeted each other in a different way: on one side, with an extended open hand, on the other, with a closed fist. The traditional *adiós* was replaced by ¡Salud! (health) in the loyal zone and with ¡Arriba España! (up with Spain) or ¡Viva Franco! (long live Franco) in the rebel zone. To the civilians' suits were added the blue shirt and the Falangist beret or the militiamen's coveralls with picturesque adornments of Negus-styled beards, multicolored handkerchiefs, or insignias on the lapels. The abundance of stores and markets gave way to lineups in front of bread and meat stores in the Republican zone and in front of clothing stores in the rebel zone. Books of ration tickets made their appearance three months after the start of the war. Catalonia and Levante attracted thousands of refugees from Madrid and the occupied Andalusian towns. San Sebastián attracted thousands of well-to-do people who had managed to slip away from the fronts or had fled from the Republican zone. On one hand the unions and on the other the Falange had become essential characteristics of the political landscape. The radio broadcasts reached every home. The peasants of the Republican zone, who previously had reserved the best room in the house for the cattle, now occupied what had been the stable, while the animals lived where the people had.

When the militia men in the trenches laid their arms to rest, they learned to read.

The first bombing of Barcelona brought the presence of the war into the rear guard. General Mola, at the portals of Madrid, had given universal language a neologism as he declared: "Four columns are advancing on the capital. Inside Madrid is the fifth column of our partisans." Actually, as the battle took place in the outlying districts, fascist elements were hurling bombs from the rooftops at the civilian population while other rightists, who were more timorous, waited in the shelter of foreign embassies for the arrival of the Nationalist soldiers.

But the soldiers did not arrive. In the Casa de Campo, on the campus of the university, and the Model Prison, a new force had sprung up: the International Brigades. Men who had come from all over the world—the United States, the Balkan countries, Scandinavia, France, and England, German and Italian exiles, veterans of World War I and the revolutionary years, with whom some mercenaries and adventurers had mixed, had been gradually arriving in Spain, motivated by the same enthusiasm: to vanquish in this extremity of Europe the regime which had already taken over half the continent.

By June 1937, the International Brigades totalled 25,000 Frenchmen, 5,000 Poles, 5,000 British and North Americans, 3,000 Belgians, approximately 1,000 South Americans, 2,000 Balkans, and some 5,000 anti-Fascist Germans and Italians. Their leaders were Communists such as Tito, Kleber, Longo, and Beimbler, or Socialists such as Deutsch, Nenni, and Gallo. The French Communist André Marty was their general commisar with headquarters in Albacete. His own men referred to him as "the hangman." Many of the Communists who occupied positions in the International Brigades would return to their countries after World War II and, after having been involved in the leadership of the "people's democracies," would wind up being executed as "traitors and spies" when Stalin feared that the lessons learned in Spain would undermine their submission. But in those months of 1936, the International Brigades reflected the tension, enthusiasm, and hopes of the moment that the Civil War had spread over the world.

For years the Left and the workers' movement all over Europe had been losing ground, while fascism grew without opposition. But suddenly Spain halted this chain of destruction and began to fight. Spain made the fascist threat more evident and presented a profile of the war to come. For many it was the hope that the current could be reversed. For others, it represented a cause with which to identify. To the thousands of political exiles, Spain offered the possibility of giving battle in Spain to the regimes which dominated their own countries. For many Catholics who disagreed with Vatican policy, Spain seemed a proof of the validity of their position. Families were divided. In the universities, students fought each other either in favor of or against the Republic. In the factories, collections were made, with housewives collecting clothing and food for children who had been displaced by bombings. Committees were formed to take care of war orphans. Artists, poets, and intellectuals took a stand, formed committees and organized meetings. Newspapers sent correspondents, as writers came to visit the country and the combat fronts: Hemingway, Malraux, Thomas, Attlee, Vandervelde. For many, especially in the middle class, Spain signified baptism of fire for active politics. The generation which lived through those years with anguish and enthusiasm would be marked by the Civil War.

The Communists, with their efficient propaganda techniques, capitalized on this enthusiasm. Spain's war served them as bait to attract intellectuals and divide parties. It also afforded them an excellent diversion to distract the attention of the people from what was happening in the U.S.S.R., where the trials against the old Bolsheviks had begun. The Communists had taken the initiative of organizing the International Brigades, since until they had done so, foreign sympathizers aided directly the parties and unions with which they had affinity. Thus in the columns of the CNT there were anarchists from all over the world, just as the ranks of POUM included revolutionary socialists, ex-communists, and sympathizers (among them, George Orwell). The International Brigades were led by Communists—with a few Socialists and leftists serving as a cover, but the bulk of their members were not Communists and those that were did not constitute the leadership, but rather proceeded from the base of their own parties. With time, the International Brigades would see their ranks decimated by Stalinist sectarianism, which was to determine the execution of many dissidents as "traitors."

Each political tendency redeemed its honor in Spain. The Socialists, who had been pacifists everywhere, were vindicated by the Spanish Socialists. The anarchists, who had been on the decline everywhere, felt themselves rejuvenated. The Marxists who were not Communists, even the Trotskyites, saw an occasion for justifying their points of view. The struggle between the two great currents, the Revolutionary and the Conservative within the Republican ranks, had echoes in foreign parties.

A few months after the start of the Civil War, presses began to generate books, pamphlets, manifestos, and newspapers. Even now, some forty years later, there is still no end to printing everything which the Civil War has made people think, say, and remember. With the exception of the Russian Revolution, it is possibly the single historical event which has produced the greatest amount of printed material.

The Spaniards realized this rather vaguely. Echoes reached them via the visits of personalities and by means of food packages, and also because of the existence of the International Brigades, although their leaders kept them very removed from the civilian population. There was great confidence, more on the people's part than on the government's. Newspapers were filled with allusions to "proletarian solidarity" and the readers sincerely believed in it. For the militant, the Civil War was not only Spanish, but a part of the worldwide struggle against fascism. For many months, despite all the news items, they would continue to believe that proletarian solidarity would help them conquer. But this solidarity, aside from the International Brigades, was mostly evident in cans of condensed milk, which certainly manifested the sacrifices of those who had sent them, but were not enough to win a war. In the United States, 4 million dollars were collected; 16 million francs in France; 4 million crowns in Sweden; 70,000 pounds sterling in England; 11,000 pounds in Australia; even from the Orient came 5,000 Chinese dollars.

The French government helped immediately as long as the Popular Front was in power and as much as their English ally would allow them. The minister of aviation, Pierre Cot, was able to send Barcelona one hundred planes, that is, he authorized their sale through French companies. André Malraux, on his part, was successful in buying about twenty old airplanes for his Air Foreign Legion. The men of the International Brigades helped save Madrid, side by side with Madrilenians, Valencians, and Catalonians, in the early hours of the morning of November 7.

At that point General Franco, who a few days earlier had declared to *Paris-Soir*: "We will never bomb Madrid, because innocent women and children live there," ordered a daily aerial offensive against the capital, which used German and Italian planes. The battle from the air, which began on October 23, was to last four weeks; it was a general trial run for the blitz that London would experience five years later. The total results of one single day: 1,491 dead, 3,500 wounded, 430 unaccounted for, eight churches, fourteen schools, nine shelters, four hospitals, two museums, and 110 houses, destroyed.

Madrid posed the problem of foreign intervention in the Civil War. The first to intervene had been the Portuguese. Via Lisbon, Mola and General Franco could telephone each other daily (through a central exchange installed in the Hotel Aviz) while the territories of the north and south were not united. The Banco Espíritu Santo granted credit to the Burgos Junta. The arms factory at Barcarena supplied the rebels with grenades and machine guns until the arrival of German and Italian shipments. The German ship *Kamerun* docked at Lisbon with 8000 tons of war materials, as did the Swedish *Wisborg* with tanks and airplanes.

The Italian planes which landed by error on August 20 in French Morocco have already been mentioned. Those that followed did not make the same mistake. Italian arms arrived via Lisbon and El Ferrol. In Palma de Mallorca, the Italian legionary aviation, as it was called, established its base, from where it constantly bombed Barcelona, Alicante, Castellón, and Valencia. Later on, Italian experts and "volunteers," whom Mussolini had personally addressed in Naples and who were paid by the Italian government, rushed to the side of the Nationalists.

Nor did Germany hesitate. On August 3, the *Deutschland* docked at Ceuta and its commander dined with General Franco. The same *Deutschland* had forced the Republican cruiser *Libertad* to free the *Kamerun*, which the former had seized across from Gibraltar. German Junkers established the Nationalists' claim to air supremacy. For several long weeks, the Republicans had only very antiquated Breuguets at their disposal to combat the ultramodern German and Italian airplanes.

Most of the embassies in Madrid became refuges for rightist elements. In Alicante, Valencia, and Barcelona, foreign ships took on board any and all who wanted to leave Spain; the legal government offered no opposition. But in Seville, Vigo, and Cádiz, not a single foreign ship appeared to save the leftists who were being persecuted. The doors of all consulates were closed in the livid faces of the deputies, union leaders, and ordinary workers who sought asylum in vain.

The government called attention to the arms shipments from the Germans and Italians to the rebel zone. Washington, Paris, and London received message after message of protest. There were only two countries on the side of the Republicans: Mexico, who remained faithful to its traditional policy of opposing all types of intervention, and the U.S.S.R., which sent several technical advisers, guns, fighter planes, and small bombers, which the people christened "Moscas" (flies), "Chatos" (snubbed-nosed), and "Katiuskas."[2] These had a

difficult time arriving by ship, having to cross the entire Mediterranean, which had been seeded with Italian submarines that sank one
ship out of three. At the border in the Pyrenees, casks of arms bought
by the government in Czechoslovakia, France, and Sweden, waited
for the French government to allow them to cross the border. It was
only when there occurred some serious Republican setback which
placed the equilibrium of the war in the Peninsula in jeopardy that a
few hundred casks were allowed to enter, and then, it was only the
amount needed to reestablish equilibrium.

The diplomatic position of the democracies was one of nonintervention in the Civil War, since the victory precipitated by one faction
could unleash a worldwide conflict or at least shake the European
status quo. This was the position of the British Foreign Office, which
imposed it on Paris with the threat that if France were to find itself
involved in a conflict because of its aid to the Republic, London
would not support it. It should not be forgotten that there was at this
time an ultraconservative British government, some of whose members had demonstrated evident empathy for Mussolini.

On September 9, 1936, at the British initiative, the Non-
Intervention Committee was founded in London. Its members included France, Great Britain, the U.S.S.R., Germany, Italy, and a
number of smaller countries. The president of the United States,
Franklin D. Roosevelt, in January 1937 decreed the embargo of arms
destined to Spain, but not that of oil and trucks, which were sold in
large quantities to the Nationalists. For nine months, under the
chairmanship of Lord Plymouth, the delegates from half the world
would discuss the necessity of nonintervention in Spain, while German and Italian planes bombed nonstop, and Italian forces of artillery, tanks, and infantry marched on Málaga and Madrid. In fact, the
Republicans remained cut off from the world, while the Nationalists,
by way of Portugal and the sea, received every type of aid imaginable.
Furthermore, Italian submarines, the cruisers *Canarias* and *Baleares*,
and the battleship *España* prevented dockings at the Mediterranean
ports of Bilbao, Gijon, and Santander, including shipments of food
supplies.

The war had created a difficult material situation for the Republican
zone. Lack of manpower, the readjustment of agriculture to the new
economic system, and the fact of including the most populated cities
and two million refugees, were a cause of general scarcity. The soldiers' daily fare was lentils, the civilian population was severely ra-
tioned, the black market flourished in the cities, and the traditional
selfishness of the peasants pushed the early enthusiasm for the

struggle into past play. Inflation rose, while the shipments of food supplies sent by dozens of committees from all over the world were not sufficient to feed the 13 million people in the Republican zone. Of the 600 million dollars in gold that constituted the Republic's reserve, one portion went to purchase food supplies—lentils, sugar, wheat, canned meat, equipment for the soldiers, poor sanitary equipment, while the main part went to pay for the Soviet shipments. Burgos decreed a blockade; it was not successful as a total blockade, but it did exert a double influence: it deprived the Republicans of food supplies and gave these same supplies to the rebels. Since many shipping companies were in accord with Burgos, they advised the rebels of the passing of their ships and let them be seized, thus gaining a bonus from the rebels in addition to the price of the shipment, which the legal government had paid in advance with gold.

Since the beginning of the air battle of Madrid between foreign planes and men in the street, the Nationalist zone headed toward total war, while in the Republican zone the tension was divided between the battles at the front and those in the political arena. An important step was the entry of four ministers of the CNT into Largo Caballero's government (November 3, 1936), after having entered that of the Generalitat in September. The anarcho-syndicalists now began for the first time to have a role in political life. This had tremendous consequences. There were not only immediate ones, since they stabilized the situation in the Republican zone, but also long-range ones, since they promised to liquidate the ballast of apoliticalism at the heart of the Spanish workers' movement.

What Malraux had qualified as the "apocalypse of fraternity" was gradually settling down. The life of the rear guard acquired a new rhythm, in which bombings and alarms, the black market, and obstacles placed before workers' committees were normal characteristics. The Largo Caballero government was not a counterrevolutionary formation, but circumstances forced it to take measures of this character. Its first decrees sanctioning the occupation of lands and organizing worker control in industry (already established in Catalonia) tended to legitimize the masses' spontaneous conquests. Then the counteroffensive sprung from Catalonia, just as the offensive had: a decree dissolving the people's committees and establishing regular municipal councils with all the antifascist parties represented; a decree for the seizure of arms (that is, for disarming the workers of the rear guard); the law of collectivizations (which actually converted what had been worker and union property into state-owned property). At the end of the year, POUM was excluded from the Generalitat's government; six months later the CNT was likewise eliminated. And if still public services, transportation, and large industries were collectivized, a bank to make the measure viable was not created. Foreigners' rights were respected, and it was established that compensation to the owners of collectivized companies would be fixed subsequently. Juan García Oliver (b. 1901), the anarchist minister of justice (who had extended to the entire zone the People's Courts which had already been created in Catalonia by Andreu Nin) would later say in a meeting in Paris: "The international bourgeoisie refused to supply us with arms. It was a tragic moment. We were forced to create the impression that the masters were not the workers' committees, but the legal government. Had it not been that way, we would not have received anything at all."

In January 1937, a series of decrees from the Generalitat put an end to all new collectivizations, while another decree established that "the resistance of the committees to being dissolved will be considered a Fascist act and its instigators will be handed over to the courts." In Aragón the anarchists had proceeded to agrarian collectivizations, at times by forcing the issue, and had created a Council of Aragón, in fact an autonomous government. Soon the Aragón front began to receive some arms which until then had been refused to them. The different services of "public safety" (Control Patrols, the popular guard, and rearguard militias) were gradually dissolved. In their place there sprung up the SIM (Military Information Service), in which all parties participated at the onset. It would later come to be a state within the state, even to the point of dominating the state when the Communists controlled SIM in 1938.

The army was slowly reorganizing, with several formal changes: saluting with a closed fist, stripes instead of stars on the uniforms, the establishment of commissaries (in reality, simple party agents). Between the anarchists and the Poumists on one side, and the Republicans and Communists on the other, polemics regarding whether the army should be a regular or a workers' army ended. It was to be regular, although it was called Popular Army, with officers coming from the common people and advised by loyal professional elements: Cipriano Mera (1897-1975) was a Freemason; Valentín Gonzáles "El Campesino" (b. 1903), a peasant; Buenaventura Durruti (1898-1936), who died on November 20, 1936 under mysterious circumstances during the defense of Madrid, was a textile worker. Many "geographically loyal" elements of the former army fled to enemy ranks, while many sons of rich families were "camouflaged" to avoid going to the front, or else they went over to the other side. The fifth column worked with limited risks, while the technical superiority of the Nationalists' armaments grew. José Antonio Primo de Rivera was sentenced to death and shot in Alicante, in spite of his defense speech in which he condemned the generals' rebellion.

Shortly thereafter, the fronts, which had appeared stabilized, began to crumble in Málaga under the strength of the Nationalist squadrons and mechanized Italian troops which entered the city on February 8, 1937. By the next morning, eight Freemasons were hung in the public square. A week later, 5,000 workers had been shot. Italian and German planes gunned down some 30,000 civilians who were fleeing the city.

Nevertheless, the strength of the government was not diminished, since the people preserved their enthusiasm. The ugliness of the war had still not reached the point of dampening their spirit. In Asturias, the bishop of Mondonedo had gone in help of Oviedo, leading a column of seminarians, before the arrival of General Yague to raise the blockade which the miners had set up around the city. In Bilbao, the political situation was calm, since the Basque Nationalists held the power, with the approval of London, which made gestures toward a separate peace between Basques and Nationalists. On the Madrid front, the Germans, in a general tryout of an en masse attack, were cut down by machine guns at the shore of the Jarama River (February 17, 1937).

But if the Republican morale did not subside, neither did the Nationalists' decision to take Madrid lessen in its intensity. The prestige of Burgos grew abroad, the Nationalist peseta was quoted on the rise in March 1937, while the Republican peseta had gone down ten times its value, in comparison with the previous year; the shares of the Riotinto Mining Company, which sold its copper to Burgos in pesetas, rose on the international market. All this could be traced to the fact that it was commonly known that a great offensive against Madrid was being prepared from La Alcarria, with the objective of cutting off the central plateau from the rest of the Republican zone. The offensive began on March 8. The Italians, sporting black shirts, were at the front line of the attack. Twenty-eight planes manufactured in the U.S.S.R. shot down the motorized columns that advanced in the pouring rain along the highway from Guadalajara. Loudspeakers shouted Republican propaganda at the Italians in Italian (ready to face them were, among others, the Garibaldi batallions of the International Brigades), telling them to give up, that their leaders had deceived them. The disbandment was a general one, and a large number of Italians were taken prisoner. On March 8, Queipo del

Llano recognized the Italian defeat over the radio, not without some pleasure. The Republican forces reinforced their positions and Madrid was saved once again. The city would still have to ward off continual artillery and air bombings, but no further land offensive was to be launched against it. General Franco considered it more important to conquer the Republican industrial zones, the North, and Catalonia. And he was the undisputable chief. He was called "caudillo."

Meanwhile, serious political occurrences were gestating in Catalonia. The struggle between the PSUC (communist), which had increased greatly in volume, and the CNT and POUM, had provoked skirmishes and deaths on both sides.[3] On May 3, 1937, the differences broke out violently as police forces, at the command of a member of the PSUC, were sent to occupy the premises of the Telephone Company, where CNT workers controlled the buildings. In a few hours, Barcelona was covered with barricades. Within the CNT two tendencies could be distinguished: on one side, those in favor of forging ahead with the revolution to ultimately take over power (the "Friends of Durruti"), while on the other side were those in favor of maintaining the status quo. For six days, while the struggle raged between anarchists and Poumists, and the police and PSUC, the ministers of CNT constantly recommended by radio that peace be reestablished. While the people fought in the streets, President Azaña dictated the disheartened pages of his *Velada de Benicarló (Night Vigil in Benicarló)*. The Republic managed to have an army, but it never found a Cromwell.

Finally an accord was reached: each side would maintain its position and the workers would return to work, abandoning the barricades. Five thousand police storm troopers sent from Valencia enforced these conditions. It was already too late to impose a revolutionary change in direction on the worn-out masses, to whom the war and "what the rest of the world would think" were most important. During the struggles, Camilo Bernieri (1897-1937), an Italian anarchist, Kurt Landau (1896-1937), an Austrian Socialist, and a few weeks later, Andreu Nin, POUM's political secretary, were kidnapped and murdered by the Communists, among hundreds of other victims of this final effort to return to the hope that had accompanied the beginning of the war. The anarchists were late in realizing that the question of power is the essence of politics.

The Republican government withdrew public order from the Generalitat. Days later, the Communist ministers resigned from Largo Caballero's cabinet when he refused to outlaw a worker's party (POUM). President Azaña, at his residence of Benicarló, assigned

Largo Caballero himself with the formation of another government. Largo Caballero had planned to and did offer to constitute a cabinet composed exclusively of the two labor federations, but the Republicans and right-wing Socialists refused to accept this solution and he finally declined. He was succeeded in his task by his minister of finances, Juan Negrín (1889-1956), an intelligent man of tremendous vitality, a moderate Socialist until that point, and from then on a faithful instrument of the Communists. His government was composed of right-wing Socialists, Communists, Republicans; a Basque Nationalist, Indalecio Prieto, was minister of national defense. The CNT and the Socialists who followed Largo Caballero's views were noticeably absent.

From this moment on, no one spoke anymore of revolution, but only of war, of national independence, of defense of the fatherland. The revolutionary forces had been squelched and were not to exert any influence again. POUM was outlawed. The only thing that would remain of those ten months of enthusiasm and revolutionary creativity would be the nostalgia for that hope of the days in July. The twenty-three months of battle to come would be months of fighting just for survival, not to create something new.

After the ten-month taste of being of legal age, Spain once again fell under the yoke of tutelage.

## NOTES

1. In the navy, the seamen, as soon as they had received news of the military uprising, had attacked the officers, killing some and imprisoning others. In some ships, among them two armored destroyers, the officers managed to keep sailors under control and thus the ships remained on the side of the rebels. The portion of the fleet which stayed with the Republic was almost immobilized for a few days due to a lack of technicians, but soon the committees of command which had been established on board found ways of compensating for the deficiency. Nevertheless, the Republican fleet never demonstrated much efficiency.

2. See chapter 16 for more detail on foreign intervention, especially the Soviet one.

3. POUM warned that the Communists were preparing a provocation and tried to place the CNT on the alert against it. But it also stated that if it could not be avoided, it would remain beside the CNT, even though it already seemed too late to reconquer the revolution. In any case, POUM was not strong enough to determine events.

# 15

# *Two Years of Despair*

The revolution now subdued, the Republican zone embarked on a series of long agonies. One, a military agony, which exhausted the country, another, a political agony, which increasingly concentrated power in the hands of Negrín and placed him in the hands of the Communists. Another agony was the intimate one of many leaders, who asked themselves if they had followed the right road. The anarcho-syndicalists began to repent for having tried to calm down its masses in May. The Republicans would soon repent having played into the hands of the "forces of order"—the Communists—when they realized that they proposed no relief for the country. The Catalonians and Basques would repent for not having placed themselves alongside the anarcho-syndicalists and Largo Caballero, when they received proof of the centrist character of Negrín's brand of politics. The Republican military would come to repent having listened to the advice of a handful of Soviet advisers, when they discovered that their aim was the liquidation of the Republican army. More than a few foreign friends of the Republic would become dubious when they saw that Negrín allowed a handful of Spaniards (the POUM's members) to be used to justify Moscow's trials. Western politicians would begin to vacillate when they saw that their policy of neutrality had different results from what they had hoped. But not one of these agencies would serve any purpose.

It is possible that had the revolutionary forces won in May, or if the confrontation between them and the counterrevolutionary forces had never come about, the war's destiny might not have been different.

But it would have come to the denouement either in better condition or sooner. The overwhelming amount of suffering and destruction would have been less, and the country would have saved itself the humiliation of having its politics dictated and being used as a pawn by Soviet diplomacy.

In May 1937 the Spanish Civil War ceased to be a great historic adventure and became an amazing but hopeless resistance. No one believed that the war could be won. At most, it was hoped that a negotiation or mediation could be reached, or at worst, that the war in Spain would be joined to the world war already coming. Negrín's entire set of politics, in the measure that his allies the Communists would allow him to have a policy, tended toward joining the war in Spain with the approaching world war. The Negrín government, which the Communists christened "the Victory Government," would rule, with several changes of ministers, for the rest of the war. Its primary preoccupation would be to "reestablish order" in the Republican zone. The civil war was entering its international phase.

Spain's problem had become an international one. Nations found themselves divided between partisans of General Franco and friends of the Republic. The latter organized meetings, demonstrations, and collections; their objective was to force their governments to give up the nonintervention policy and see to it that the legal government of Spain regain the possibility of exercising the right to acquire arms and receive them. (Up until this point the government had been permitted to buy arms, but these did not reach their ports of destination.) The two workers' internationals and the labor unions were also with the Republic, at least in their propaganda. Freemasonry adopted an ambiguous attitude: Ybon Delbos, for example, a high-ranking Mason and France's minister of foreign affairs, was in favor of nonintervention. On the other hand, several conservatives (the Duchess of Atholl in England, Jacques Maritain and François Mauriac in France) were on the Republic's side. There were many trips to Barcelona and Madrid made by celebrated personalities, and innumerable articles and speeches. But Spain's war forced the weakness of the international workers' movement into the open, just as it served to show the contradictions between the masses and their governments, the democracies' fear of Fascist aggression, and the security with which the two Fascist powers felt themselves masters of the situation.

The legal government's demand for arms fell on deaf ears, despite the fact that France had accepted important contracts long before July 18, 1936. Edouard Herriot visited Léon Blum several times and convinced the Socialist leader to refuse shipments of planes and arms. "I am heartbroken," declared Blum. In spite of nonintervention, the French government was able to send a few cannons and planes to the Republic, but this was under cover and in insufficient quantities.

London maintained a trenchant attitude, but it permitted its ships to accept cargo for the government, without guaranteeing them the protection of the British fleet. Mexico placed itself unconditionally on the side of the Republic and the U.S.S.R.; once its ambassador, Marcel Rosenberg, was in Spain, and also sent several ships loaded with arms. Mexico's aid to the Republic consisted especially of rifles bought in the United States while the Soviet Union's included oil, cannons, machine guns, (there were also some from Czechoslovakia), tanks, and airplanes (the Republic never had more than 300 bombers and combat planes at its disposal at any given time).

Sympathy for the rebels was not manifest in the masses, but rather in several parties, such as the English Conservative party, Action Française, and in totalitarian countries. Portugal created a Legion to fight alongside General Franco; Ireland sent out 1,000 volunteers who returned home after two months; Germany and Italy did not stop sending arms and materials. For instance, 1,930 cannons, 10,000 automatic weapons, 240,000 rifles, 8 million rounds of ammunition for howitzers, 324 million other rounds of ammunition, 7,000 automobiles, 4,300 trucks, 800 tractors, 700 tanks, 1,414 airplane engines, some 17,000 tons of bombs, 2 submarines, 4 destroyers, were the figures of war materials which Mussolini's government later admitted having sent the Burgos government. No one knows for certain the exact figures regarding Germany's shipments, but the debt with Germany in 1939 was approximately half that with Italy.

All these shipments were made behind the Nonintervention Committee's back. The U.S.S.R. declared to the committee that it would consider itself free from obligation if they were not observed more rigorously (October 1936). But the U.S.S.R. never broke relations with the committee. For months the diplomats debated and finally reached an agreement to establish maritime control over the Spanish coasts, with observers from all the committee's member countries. Beginning on April 20, 1937, Italian and German squadrons patrolled the Mediterranean, while the French and English kept watch over the Cantabrian and the Atlantic. The U.S.S.R. refused to participate in the control. This did not prevent the smuggling of arms on a large scale, nor did it prevent Mussolini's delegate to the committee, Dino Grandi, from declaring that his country would not withdraw a single "volunteer" from Spain. The control flag (white with two black spheres) waved in the empty breeze.

In Geneva, things were simple. Before the League of Nations, the "socialist" Julio Alvarez del Vayo (1891-1975), Spanish minister of foreign affairs, denounced the "juridical monstrosity of neutrality" in September 1936, in December 1936 (before the Special Assembly requested by the Spanish government), and in January 1937, while refusing two attempts of mediation undertaken in the London committee. In February 1937, the Spanish government sent a message to Paris and London, proposing an active part in the reconstruction of the national economy, once the war was ended, in addition to a modification of the borders of Spanish Morocco. That is, Spain offered these powers a participation in its national life in exchange for their aid. London and Paris preferred to let Hitler and Mussolini obtain this participation.

Resolutions were adopted in the League of Nations' meetings, all of them inconsequential, save for one which was to establish a procedure for the evacuation of refugees in the embassies of Madrid to other countries. At the Special Assembly in May 1937, the Republican government presented a "White Book" with proof of the German and Italian intervention on the Nationalist side. The assembly condemned the violation of the rules of war, but abstained from saying that it was German and Italian planes which had violated it. In 1938, when it became necessary to select the nonpermanent members of the council, Spain was not reelected. During this same period an agent of General Franco in London, the Marquis del Moral, wrote his friend, the English Conservative leader Lord Penrith: "Can you help us to reinforce British neutrality?" Meanwhile, the Burgos radio announced that the bombing of Barcelona, on the same date, was "dedicated to the visit of the British revolutionaries Attlee and Noel Baker to the Republican zone."

At this time the offensive against Bilbao had already begun with the German bombing of Guernica, which devastated the symbolic city of Basque liberties. Almeria had already been bombed by the German ship *Graff Spee*, in reprisal for the dropping of several bombs on the *Deutschland*, anchored in the port of Palma de Mallorca. Valencia had already received some bombings from Heinkels and Fiats, to "celebrate" the meeting of Parliament which had given its vote of confidence to Negrín's government.

Republican and leftist deputies, together with a few centrists, were present at this meeting. Those of the Right could be found on the other side of the trenches. Nevertheless the number present was constitutionally sufficient to insure that the decisions made were legal. But these were merely idle discussions for diplomatic consumption.

Months later, subjected to almost daily bombings, Barcelona would suffer through thirty-six continuous hours on the alert, with the following results: 1,200 dead, 3,000 wounded. Meanwhile, during this same period, Burgos was only visited twice by bombing raids from the Republic; Sevilla was visited once, and Zaragoza four times. By 1938 the situation seemed to have been stabilized, as much from a military as from a political point of view.

General Franco governed without opposition. Trade agreements with Germany and Italy normalized to a certain degree the economic life of the zone, which lacked only several manufactured items. The political and cultural life was dead. In the Republican zone, a general displacement of the anarchists from all positions of responsibility coincided with the rise of the Communists, the replacement by the government police of the Executive Council of the UGT—which was akin to Largo Caballero's policies with one which was more in line with Negrín's objective—the disappearance of the militias, which had given way to a regular army, and the scarcity of foodstuffs.

The growing Communist influence was due to several factors. Its principal cause was the nonintervention policy which forced the Republican army to depend on Soviet arms for survival. The Communists continued to take advantage of this dependency to impose conditions which became increasingly severe and which were always backed up by the Soviet Embassy. The naiveté of the right-wing Socialists and the egocentricity of Indalecio Prieto, who thought he could use the Communists to get rid of Largo Caballero without being dominated by them, gave the Communists the springboard to power. Finally, the Communists counted on the support of a considerable number of the middle class who were Republican in sentiment, partisans of order, and frightened by the revolutionary measures of the early months. These people saw the Communists as a new force of order. These groups, at the beginning, had shown themselves to be as brutal as the revolutionary militants; but as time had passed, they found it very comfortable to believe, as Communist propaganda continued to tell them, that brutality was the exclusive work of the anarchists, thus blaming the latter for the repression, the burning of churches, the executions.

The position adopted by the Spanish Communist party during the Civil War was only apparently paradoxical. The people who wanted change or revolution knew where to go for it—the CNT, the left wing of the Socialist party, or POUM—whereas those who considered themselves liberal or moderate had no such refuge, since the right wing of the Socialist party and the other Republican parties were weak. Hence the Communist party was the right place for them; it offered them a politics of "order." For simple political motives, then, the Spanish Communists had to adopt this brand of politics, which allowed them to grow from a small party with no influence into a powerful organization, supported by its positions in government and in the army and by the fact that only the U.S.S.R. supplied the Republic with arms. But even without this motivation, the Communist party would have adopted a position of "order" since it was the only position consistent with the line mapped out in Moscow to attract allies from the Right and Center, without doing anything which might frighten the Western powers. If the U.S.S.R. felt forced, in order to keep its image, to send weapons to Spain, this aid could not be presented as one of revolutionary action, but rather only as an act of defense of democracy. Hence the Spanish Communists, who never displayed any independence with respect to Moscow, made great efforts from the beginning to present the Civil War merely as a defense of democracy and national independence. In order to achieve this, they tried to asphyxiate revolutionary aspirations. Stalin was not only the one who buried revolution in the U.S.S.R., but was also responsible for its interment in Spain.

But the Communists could not work miracles. They had themselves used the routings suffered by the Republican forces when Largo Cabellero was the leader of the government to their advantage, ascribing these to Largo Caballero and revolutionary politics, and with this ascription, ejecting him from power. Now that power was theirs and they would shortly control the Political Commisariat, the command of the best-supplied forces, the SIM, and the police force, things still did not go better on the fronts. The Nationalists undertook an offensive against the north, at the beginning of which (June 3, 1937) its organizer, General Emilio Mola, died in an airplane crash. The Nationalists had air, artillery, tank, and sea superiority. The Republican navy, with the armored cruiser *Jaime I* destroyed by an act of sabotage, found itself practically bottled up in the port of Cartagena. The only factors on the side of the Republic were the mass of soldiers, the enthusiasm of what was left of the first columns of volunteers, and an upsurge of new military men who had sprung from the Popular Schools of War and had come from factories, fields, and universities. Five hundred Republican soldiers against 500,000 Nationalist soldiers; the latter group included legionnaires, Moors, and, in 1938, Blacks from Ifni and Guinea.

Bilbao had been subdued by a land and sea blockade. The iron belt of fortifications was broken because several of the technicians who had built it had defected to the Nationalist side, with the plans for the fortifications in their hands. Bilbao fell without anything happening to the industrial installations of the city. The Basque bourgeoisie salvaged its property. The government of Euzkadi decided to move to Bayonne, France. After the Nationalist cruiser *España* had been sunk, Santander also fell. Terror reigned in the north from July 19, 1937, the date on which the Italian Division Black Arrows entered Bilbao and began to distribute white bread to the people, until August 26, when three "republican" envoys (officers of the police, which had previously killed the officers of the army who had refused to surrender) appeared before the chief of the Italian forces outside Santander to hand the city over to him. Many Basque Nationalist priests were shot to death, just as the Catholic Catalonian Nationalist, Manuel Carrasco i Formiguera (1890-1937), who had been taken prisoner as he sailed to Bilbao, had been executed in Burgos.

The government knew that it could not avoid the fall of the north. The only thing possible was to try some type of diversion. In Brunete (near Madrid), the Republican forces fought for three days and managed to break the front, but could not penetrate it. In Aragón, they took Belchite, a key position for the defense of Zaragoza, but they were not able to advance from there. The Nationalist offensive against Asturias was accelerated. On October 21, the fifth column, which reached an accord with the police, took possession of Gijón, preventing the evacuation of the bulk of the northern Republican army. The Republicans could now count only fifteen out of fifty provinces and 11 million inhabitants out of 25 million.

Meanwhile in the Nonintervention Committee, discussion centered around the withdrawal of volunteers as an indispensable condition for the government of Paris and London to recognize the Burgos Junta as belligerent. The official Vatican daily, *L'Osservatore Romano*, condemned the position taken by Catholics such as François Mauriac, Jacques Maritain, and Georges Bidault, in favor of the Republic. It also stated that the Nationalists were in the right.

After the collapse of the northern front, the government moved from Valencia to Barcelona. The stated reason for this move was to reinforce Catalonia's war production and to be present in the region where the anarcho-syndicalists were stronger. Prieto, from his Ministry of Defense, organized a secret assault on Teruel. The attack began on December 15, 1937, just as Burgos was preparing a repetition of its unsuccessful offensive from Guadalajara. For two weeks the Nationalists resisted from the seminary in the city, but finally surrendered. But the Republicans did not have reinforcements with sufficient war materials to continue the offensive. After seventy days of uninterrupted battle, Teruel once again was in Nationalist hands.

The operations of Teruel, which had been realized with an enormous spirit of self-sacrifice, had been prepared by Prieto, who was familiar with the true situation. What was his objective, since Teruel was not an important strategic position? He wanted to demonstrate that the Republic still had the capacity for a considerable offensive and was in a position to prolong the war, thus inducing the powers to impose a mediation to end the war. Furthermore, Prieto felt that his personal political position was weakening, as much due to temperamental incompatibility with Negrín (the two were extreme egocentrics) as to the Communists' desire to get rid of him, since as long as he was in the Defense Ministry they would not be the exclusive masters of the army. Prieto was not a submissive person, as were Julio Alvarez del Vayo, minister of foreign affairs, or Julián Zugazagoitia, minister of the interior, for example, who had placed the police force at the disposal of the Communists in order to persecute POUM and the CNT. The Communists had to eliminate Prieto with the help of Negrín, just as they had previously eliminated Largo Caballero with Prieto's help.

The hope that the Republicans had in their grasp for a moment, was now vanishing. Prieto's mediating position was eliminated and Prieto himself left the government, in which Negrín, the Communists, the Negrínist Socialists, and the Republicans continued (April 5, 1938). Now that they could no longer put Prieto to good use, they covered him with a campaign of falsehoods and Negrín sent him as special ambassador to Chile where a president supported by the local popular front had been elected. From this moment on, until both were dead, Prieto and Negrín would be engulfed in extremely violent polemics, which would divide the Socialist party even more.

The harassed CNT, in constant struggle for survival, was still strong enough for the Communists to dare not try an open attack against them. Instead, they constantly undermined the CNT's positions, making the organization the target of permanent propaganda campaigning, blaming the CNT for every military failure. The representative character of the government was to be seen as still weaker when, in August 1938, the Basque and Catalonian ministers resigned in protest against Negrín's centrist policy. His modus operandi cut back more and more on the rights of the Generalitat, since the latter had refused to collaborate in the mute persecution of the CNT and because its president, Lluis Companys, protested against the brutality demonstrated by SIM, which was now totally in the hands of the Communists. The manifestation of this brutality was not only directed against the members of the fifth column, but also against the Republicans and workers who had not allowed themselves to become instruments of the Communists.

The fifth column showed itself to be more active with each passing day, animated by the military successes of the Nationalists. The Nationalists, despite the serious blow caused by the loss of the cruiser *Baleares*, which had been sunk by the joint efforts of the Republican air force and navy, were preparing a large-scale offensive, to the sea. For five months, the hand-to-hand combat continued. Castellón on the Mediterranean coast fell on June 16, 1938. A week later, the rebel forces found themselves almost at the gates of Valencia. But in Valencia the Republicans had organized a line of defense, and the Nationalist army was well held in front of Sagunto. On the other hand, near Aragón, the Republican front was broken. The Nationalists trespassed on Catalonian soil and took Lérida, but their advance was detained there. The Segre and Ebro rivers now formed the Catalonian front, which remained separated from the south-central front, whose command the government had delegated to General Miaja. Barcelona, the victim of daily bombings, led a miserable life, almost completely without electricity, since the thermal centers were located directly beneath the Nationalist cannons on the banks of the Segre.

Although Prieto had been eliminated by the accusation that he had severed a negotiation, Negrín followed his policies. In May 1938, the government addressed some feelers for a mediation. It published the points that the government felt were basic to the reestablishment of peace: a democratic Republic, respect for regional liberties, and amnesty. There was no reaction from the other side. Later, at the coronation of George VI, the Spanish delegation, headed by Julián Besteiro, spoke with Anthony Eden and informed him that the government was ready to accept any arbitration of the great powers. France proposed an international arbitration meeting, but Italy refused the invitation and the war continued.

The chief of the General Staff, General Vicente Rojo (1894-1967), organized a most daring maneuver imposed by the Soviet technicians, which was destined to fail. On July 25, 1938, the Republican troops crossed the Ebro River and caught the Nationalists by surprise.

They advanced up to Gandesa. The battle was fought desperately for four months. The young (eighteen to nineteen years old) inexperienced recruits accomplished miracles of courage and tenacity. Yet the inferiority of the materials and the lack of reserves led to the abandonment of the battle of Ebro. The last protective forces returned across the river on November 15, 1938. The battle had cost the Republicans 70,000 casualties. The Republican army was in a state of ruin.

The people were now convinced that there was no longer any hope. Everything was lost. The common man was tired, hungry, and disgusted with Communist sectarianism and the attitude of some control committees, which had gradually become actual black market committees as the revolutionary morale lost ground. The fifth column grew. The government wished to reestablish the cult of Catholicism, but it was not able to do so because the church refused to play their game. The Executive Committee of POUM was tried toward the end of 1938 before the Special High Treason Tribunal. Its members were condemned to fifteen years imprisonment, and the party was dissolved for having carried out its own policies; but the sentence did not support the accusations of espionage and collaboration with the enemy, which had been formulated by the Communists. The Communists had failed in their attempt to set up "proof" that the "anti-Soviet conspiracy" was a general one, and not limited to the U.S.S.R., and that the confessions of guilt by the revolutionaries were not a phenomenon of the Stalinist regime.[1]

The difficulties of daily life, the lack of food, the alarms and all-clear signals took their toll on the frazzled nerves of the people in the street; this was more accentuated in Catalonia than in the south-central zone, but this distraught feeling was quickly spreading. The peasants lost faith in the money issued by the Government (Burgos had announced over the radio that it did not recognize it), and supplies in the city markets dwindled. In spite of all this, in 1938, when the Republican 46th Division found itself isolated in the Pyrennes, after a steadfast resistance, it entered France, where it was disarmed, and 97 percent of its members asked to return to Barcelona instead of remaining in France or joining the ranks of those who clearly would be the victors.

The Control Committee studied a plan for the withdrawal of volunteers. Italy, attempting to force their hand, announced on October 8, 1938, that it would withdraw all who had accumulated more than eighteen months of combat—a total of 10,000 men, according to Dino Grandi. Ten thousand men would also be withdrawn from the International Brigades, since the Republican government felt itself forced to make the gesture, even though for each volunteer that stayed in the loyal zone, there were five in the Nationalist zone. The League of Nations calculated the number of volunteers in the Republican zone as 12,673.

The battle of the Ebro had absorbed a very large amount of materials. Now, in December 1938, when General Franco announced his offensive against Catalonia, the Republican government had neither reserves nor arms in sufficient quantity at its disposal. Hatred toward England and France was very intense at this moment, as the people considered them responsible for the Spanish catastrophe due to their nonintervention policy.

While disorganization took possession of demoralized Catalonia, General Franco promulgated laws with a view to the day after victory: a rationing law, a labor law, and he created the Social Aid (an imitation of the Nazis' Winter Aid) and the National Unionist Center (CNS), the sole "union" organism, controlled by the Falange and including employers, technicians, and workers. In January 1938, General Franco had already promulgated the Organic Law of the State, or Constitution. The National Council of the Falange, the Council of Ministers, and the CNS were the three branches of what was called the "New State." Ramón Serrano Suñer (b. 1901), General Franco's brother-in-law, was named minister of interior. The international position of Burgos was reinforced. Already in November 1937, London had sent a commercial agent to Burgos. Chamberlain declared in the Commons: "We will allow certain countries to run the risk of getting their fingers burned." And as Eden stated, also in the Commons: "In the course of the first nine months of 1938, Spain has purchased from England the value of 2,800,000 pounds, of which 2 million were from the rebel territories." Toward the end of 1938, the Daladier government sent a right-wing senator, Léon Berard, to Burgos as an observer.

Belgium withdrew from the Nonintervention Committee. Eden reassured the deputies that England and General Franco would get along perfectly well in the future. The countries of the Balkan entente recognized the Burgos Junta, which now maintained diplomatic relations with twenty-six countries.

On December 23, 1938, the rebels attacked on the banks of the Segre and Ebro rivers. Ten days later, General Moscardó's troops coming through the north, and General Yagüe's through the south, found themselves before the last orographic defenses of Barcelona. The Republicans tried to set up a front but their army, weakened by the battle of Ebro, with a scarcity of weapons and almost without air power, became more scattered as the days went by. Reus and Tarragona fell, despite diversionary operations in Brunete (in the center) and Extremadura. Barcelona fell without offering any resistance on January 26, 1939. Trucks loaded with white bread followed the tanks and the Arab and Italian troops. The first arrests were made on the 27th. The use of the Catalan language was forbidden, the Generalitat supressed.

Parliament, or what was left of it, met in Figueres. Negrín let forth one last appeal: "We have mountains of weapons which have just arrived." Presidents Azaña and Companys, on February 7 crossed the border on foot. At the border, Negrín made proposals of mediation to the English and French ambassadors. Four hundred thousand men gradually filtered through the Pyrennes. The highways were strewn with weapons and corpses. On the other side of the mountains, the gendarmes corralled the multitude toward concentration camps. Some of those in the concentration camps asked to be sent to Franco's Spain, while others enlisted to go out to fight in the south-central zone, since this zone still resisted and Negrín, along with several other members of his cabinet, had gone there.

On February 24, the French Senate, by a vote of 323 to 261, approved the recognition of General Franco's regime. England did the same, while the other countries, save Mexico and Russia, followed suit. Azaña resigned as president on February 27. As prescribed by the Constitution, Diego Martínez Barrio, President of Parliament, succeeded him. But London and Paris announced that the only Spanish government they recognized was Franco's. Marshall Pétain was named ambassador in Burgos. Menorca surrendered to a British battleship; on board was a messenger of General Franco.

In the south-central zone, everyone knew that the end of the war was imminent. There were no reserves of personnel or weapons. Negrín wanted to continue the war; according to him, a worldwide conflict was on the threshold and it was now just a question of resisting and thus awaiting the outbreak of this war. Then Spain would find itself automatically on the side of Germany and Italy's enemies. But the question was: How to resist?

Negrín knew that resistance was impossible. In fact, while still in France, he had ordered that no more food be sent to central Spain. What he wanted was to pass the buck of ending the war to somebody else. To that end, by a decree dated March 5, 1939, he named Communists to all high military posts. The other parties considered this move a coup d'état, and organized a National Council of Defense in Madrid, presided by Colonel Segismundo Casado (1893-1968) and the Socialist Julián Besteiro as principal. It also included Socialists, Republicans, and CNT and UGT representatives. The National Council of Defense published a manifesto which announced Negrín's dismissal. A Communist Army Corps went from the front to Madrid where an anarchist corps confronted it. In Valencia, the Communist forces' march on the city failed. In the navy base of Cartagena shots rang out in the streets from three different forces for several days: the Communists, the Defense Council and the fifth column. A convoy invasion, sent by General Franco in haste, was scattered at the last moment by the coastal batteries recovered by the Republicans only five minutes before the convoy had neared shore. Meanwhile, in Madrid, the struggle had ended in victory for the council forces, with two Communist leaders executed. From Rabasa airport in Alicante, Negrín and his ministers departed with Dolores Ibarruri (b. 1895), "La Pasionaria." What remained of Republican Spain lay in the hands of the council.

The council announced its desire of reaching an agreement with the Nationalists and thus end the war. On March 18 Besteiro gave a radio address to Burgos, requesting a "suitable and honorable" peace. Gradually the prisoners were released. The council asked General Franco to guarantee the integrity of the national territory, to respect the lives of all those who had fought against him, to promise no retaliation, to withdraw the Italian, German, and Moroccan troops, and to grant a twenty-five-day period during which those who wished to could leave the country. Lists of those who wanted to emigrate were being drawn up in the unions and parties. Several shiploads of émigrés embarked in Alicante and Valencia. From Cartegena, the navy fleet, in a moment of irresponsibility, had set out to sea in the direction of Bizerte. Burgos agreed to negotiate with the council on March 22. On the 23rd, two colonels from Madrid arrived by plane in Burgos and began negotiations. General Franco demanded that the entire Republican air force be turned over within three days. But since there was not enough gasoline and since many pilots had gone into hiding, this condition could not be met. On the 26th, General Franco ordered an offensive. Negotiations had broken down. The only promise from General Franco was: "The only ones who have anything to fear are those whose hands are stained with blood." The soldiers, who for a month had been savoring the promise of peace or the prospect of emigration, now received the order to "resist." The order was in vain. Some officers committed suicide, while others went into hiding or surrendered. To avoid any more futile deaths, the council ordered surrender without struggle.

Casado telegraphed Lebrun and Chamberlain requesting that ships be sent to evacuate all those who had opted for exile. On the 28th, the 300,000 men who had defended Madrid surrendered. The council (with the exception of Besteiro) moved to Valencia. The people, scattered throughout the country, made their way to the coast. In Gandía, Casado and several military men boarded an English warship. Miaja left by airplane. The port of Alicante constituted the point of the funnel from which people hoped to leave. Brigades en masse, politicians, peasants, committees, union leaders, workers, 20,000 men in all, congregated at the port. No ships to leave with. The rest of the city was in the hands of the fifth column.

On the dawn of March 30, nearly all of Spain, except for the port of Alicante, was in the hands of the Francoist troops. In Alicante, a young boy had climbed up to a lookout post, at the top of the breakwater, to watch for the ships that did not come. Along the docks, people threw luggage, jewels, books, papers into the water. Many flung themselves into it. By late afternoon, amidst a light rain, the Nationalist troops entered the city: the Italian division Littorio, commanded by General Gastone Gambara, took possession of the port. And when the young boy, from his lookout post, saw the Italian tanks and cannons and heard the cries of "Duce, Duce!," he hurled himself into the sea.

**NOTE**

1. For more details regarding POUM, see the following chapter and also George Orwell's *Homage to Catalonia*, London, 1938.

# 16

# Twenty-Five Million Pawns

It has been said that the Spanish Civil War was a general trial run for World War II. Some of the arms and tactics that would later be used in Europe were tried out in Spain. In the political field, the Communists applied several lessons they had learned in Spain to their gradual takeover of Eastern and Central European countries after 1945. In Yugoslavia, although the Yugoslavs never recognized the fact, several of the anarcho-syndicalist experiences of workers' control were also applied.

None of this would have been possible without the intervention of three countries in Spain's affairs: Italy and Germany on the side of the Nationalists, and the U.S.S.R. on the side of the Republic. It was a tragic paradox: the Italo-German intervention made possible the Nationalist victory, since without the aid of these countries in the early weeks of the war, the probabilities of victory rested with the Republicans. But this intervention was much more military than political. General Franco did have the ability to maintain his independence of decision, both during the Civil War and World War II, in spite of the fact that the aid received from his allies was by far superior to that which the Soviets gave the Republic. On the other hand, the Republican leaders, once they had discarded Largo Caballero from government, did not know how to maintain their independence regarding pressures from local Communists and Soviet advisers. This occurred despite the fact that the majority of the Republican political and even military forces opposed this intervention. In any case, the Soviet aid came too late to permit a Republican victory from the beginning, was never sufficient to allow them to win the war, and determined the end of the fighting when it suited Soviet diplomacy.

These interventions proved that in a country of certain importance in the modern world, a civil war will be inevitably converted into a playing field for international interests. They also proved that what is called disinterested aid, for reasons of ideological solidarity, does not exist when the aid is given by nations. These interventions demonstrated also the uselessness of such systems as the League of Nations and the Nonintervention Committee, which are not based on popular sovereignty but on the collaboration of nations. This proof, followed by similar proof in the Ethiopian war, disqualified the League of Nations long before World War II would bury it.

Some figures concerning the German and Italian participation in Franco's movement have already been cited. Eight hundred documents found in Berlin after World War II and published by the U.S. State Department, allow the addition of some accurate data: as of July 1938, there were some 20,000 to 25,000 German soldiers in Spain, in addition to another 7,000 engaged in the air force. One must not forget the seventeen Junkers sent to Tetuán on August 1, 1936, which allowed General Franco to transport numerous troops (15,000 men in ten days) in incessant trips to the Peninsula during decisive moments. In November 1936, the Condor Legion (of aviation) was organized, made up of three wings of JU 52s, three wings of Heinkel, twelve Heinkel 70 aircrafts, a naval wing of Heinkel 50s, five heavy anticraft batteries, and two light ones. This legion was commanded successively by generals Hugo von Sperrle (Guernica and Bilbao), Wolkmann (battle of Ebro), and Colonel Wolfam Von Richthofen (Catalonia). In two and a half years, German instructor's corps trained 55,000 officers of the Nationalist army.

Other figures will give an idea of the inequality of weapons between the two factions. By the middle of 1938, the proportion of war materials (was always favorable to the Nationalists), was as follows: light-weight artillery, four to one; airplanes, eight to one, heavy artillery, eight to one. In the battle of Ebro, General Franco pitted 1,400 cannons against the 120 of the Republicans. Burgos saw 600 to 650 Nationalist aircraft as opposed to 100 to 130 Republican planes. After the battle of Ebro, the proportion became: lightweight artillery, ten to one; heavy artillery, twelve to one; tanks, thirty to one; aircraft, fifty to one.

The Italian aid to General Franco was perhaps less useful militarily, but did have useful repercussions in the diplomatic field. On the other hand, it also awakened certain resentment among the Nationalists themselves. The CTV (Corpo di Truppe Volontarie) was frequently referred to as "When are you leaving?" There were some 40,000 Italian military men in Spain and Italy's participation in the Civil War cost some 6,000 deaths, a loss of aircraft and cannons. Italy was especially valuable to the Burgos Junta in the Mediterranean, since the "unidentified" submarines which captured or sunk many ships carrying supplies to the Republican zone were Italian. Fascist leader Roberto Farinacci was in Salamanca in 1937, apparently to negotiate for the designation of the Duke of Aosta as king of Spain, in spite of the king of Italy's opposition to such a move. He was not successful.

Another useful source of aid, although not readily admitted, was England. Official British agents were always on the scene in Burgos, attempting to arrange Burgos' acceptance of credit in British sterling to pay for the Italian and German supplies, in the hope that were this offer accepted, after the end of the Civil War General Franco would find himself free of all pledges save with the British. Meanwhile, British and American petroleum companies supplied the necessary oil for the offensives of Franco's troops. The mines of Riotinto (in the Nationalist zone) never ceased production, and its minerals—exported to Germany just as was the iron from the north in the second phase of the war—did not cease their production of dividends to the British stockholders.

It is necessary to sum up the Stalinist infiltration with greater detail than Fascist intervention, since the latter is recognized by everyone, while what is known about the Communist intervention is based mostly on Nationalist propaganda. During the first months of the war, Moscow sent only technicians and agents. Three of these formed the troika which effectively directed the policy of the Spanish Communist party: the Italian Palmiro Togliatti (Ercole, Alfredo), the Russian Stepanov, and the Argentine Vitorio Codovila (Medina), who had already been the agents of the Communist International in Spain. The Frenchman Jacques Duclos and the Hungarian Enro Gerö (Pedro) were added to this group on occasion. André Marty was general commisar of the International Brigades and the depiction of him by Hemingway in *For Whom the Bell Tolls* was not a distorted one. Emilio Kleber (Lazar Stern) commanded the International Brigades in which many foreign Communists met death on matters of internal discipline, often as an echo of the Moscow trials. It has also been said that the Soviet generals Koniev, Rokossovski, and Berzin (Goniev) were also present in Spain.

Jesús Hernández, Communist minister of public instruction, tells the story that once, in 1936, upon complaining that the U.S.S.R. had sent sparse quantities of war materials and pointing out that the military uprising, in those first months, could have been liquidated in short order if the Republicans had weapons at their disposal, Jacques Duclos told him that the U.S.S.R. feared that if it sent too many arms this would alarm the governments of Paris and London, with which Moscow maintained friendly relations. Duclos affirmed that this opinion had been expressed to him by the Soviet ambassador in Paris.

The shipments of Soviet arms to Spain were parsimonious; they did not begin until November 1936, when there no longer existed a way of striking down the rebellion with one blow, and they were never sufficient to cover the needs of the fronts, but rather only to continue support of the war with no possibility of winning it. The Soviets determined to whom the arms should be given. There is a case of a ship loaded with Soviet arms which was ordered to let itself be captured or sunk by the rebels before it reached refuge in Barcelona for fear that in Barcelona the CNT would get a hold of the arms. This same reason accounted for the virtual paralysis of the Aragonese front (defended primarily by anarchists and militiamen from POUM), notwithstanding that with enough armaments it would have been possible to break it open and bring about the union with the Basque forces in the north. Many of the Soviet arms were near-antiques. On occasion, the Soviets forced German airplanes, which had fallen in Republican territory, to be turned over to them, although the government wanted to trade them for arms with France and England. Even before the Munich Conference, Stalin wanted to enter into negotiations with Hitler. The former felt that his abandonment of Spain would be interpreted in Berlin as a guarantee of good faith and the lack of Soviet aspirations west of the Reich. For this reason, the Soviet military advisers imposed the battle of Ebro, which in two months liquidated the Republican army and all the government's materials and human reserves. In a similar way, and for reasons of prestige, Valentín González (The Peasant) a brutal Communist military leader, had to continue uselessly in Teruel, so that the Communists could say that Prieto had ordered the abandonment of a site which could still have been defended.

After the loss of Barcelona, Negrín went to Madrid. There the Communists imposed on him the coup d'état which provoked, as a reaction, the formation of the National Defense Council. But the extraordinary fact was that the Communists, who possessed the majority of the military force and positions of command in the south-central zone, did nothing to support Negrín's coup. For Moscow, it was a question of ending the war in Spain without incurring the responsibility of ending it. Manuilsky, leader of the Communist International, later justified this policy before the few Spanish Communist leaders admitted to the U.S.S.R., offering as proof the typical argument that, in the long run, what was suitable to the diplomatic interests of the U.S.S.R., was suitable to people everywhere. And when the Soviet government was asked to open the doors of the "fatherland of the proletariat," at least to the exiled Spanish Communists, the government refused.

During the war, the most distinguished Soviet agents were: Marcel Rosenberg, in the embassy; Vladimir Antonov-Ovseenko, an ex-Trotskyite, in the Barcelona Consulate (he led the political offensive against POUM, of which his ex-comrade Nin was political secretary); Artur Stashevsky, the commercial attaché (he actively intervened in the transfer of Spanish gold stock to the U.S.S.R.). All without exception were eliminated in 1938-39 (Antonov, deemed officially insane, was committed to an asylum). Ilya Ehrenburg, the only one who survived, was given the task of winning over the intellectuals.

The Nationalist elements in Morocco, represented by Abdelkader Torres, in 1936 and again in 1937 proposed to the government of the Republic to organize an uprising in Morocco in exchange for the necessary materials and money. Such a rebellion would have cut into the supply of Moorish soldiers to General Franco. The government was afraid of creating difficulties for itself with France and England and refused the offer, thus putting the finishing touches to a policy of indifference and mistakes in the protectorate. In addition, the Soviet military in Spain offered their opinion that, militarily, a rebellion in Morocco would not be useful to the Republic's cause. They also opposed the use of guerrilla tactics by the Republic, obviously because they would not be able to control the bands fighting behind Franco's lines.

The effective increase of Communist party membership was obtained through two distinct procedures: coercion (threats at times, and very often promises of posts in the army, since whoever held a Communist card would obtain protection and advantages, while those who did not would always run the risk of being sent on the most dangerous missions), and through a policy of flattering the petite bourgeoisie. Furthermore, in every political party, no matter how small, with the exception of the CNT and POUM, there were factions which played the game of the Communists. At the end of the war, these factions predominated in several parties, even in the Socialist party, in which Negrín and Alvarez del Vayo openly carried out the Communist policy.

The question of the Spanish gold given over to the Soviet Union can be summed up as follows: on October 25, 1936, 7,800 strongboxes filled with gold bars and coins, which formed the bulk of the Bank of Spain reserves, were shipped from Cartegena, unloaded in Odessa, and sent to Moscow. Negrín, then minister of finance, had obtained a decree from the government and the president which authorized him to place the Spanish gold in safekeeping, without specifying where this might be. He personally directed the loading of the gold, which was done in secret. The four bank employees who accompanied the shipment were retained in Moscow until the end of the war. Later, they were sent to four separate destinations in Latin America. The Soviet civil servants who received the Spanish gold all disappeared (Grinko, the minister of finance; Marguliz, Grosbank's manager; Kagan, submanager of the same, and Stashevsky, Communist Attaché). Immediately after the arrival of the Spanish gold, Soviet propaganda initiated a campaign informing of the increase in gold production in the U.S.S.R.[1] At this point it is unavoidable to compare the cost of military aid to both sides. At the end of the war, Franco owed Germany and Italy 600 million (of 1939) dollars for materials sold on credit while, for a much smaller amount of materials, the Republic paid in advance to the U.S.S.R. 500 million dollars. The conclusion is self-evident.

The French Communists benefitted directly and handsomely from the Spanish funds. The French Communist party administered 2,500 million francs in 1937 for the purchase of war materials, without ever rendering any accounts; the Parisian pro-Communist daily *Ce Soir*, was founded with money from the Spanish Republic. The twelve-ship fleet *France-Navigation* was acquired by agents of the French Communist party with Republican money. Yet at the termination of the war in Spain, its administrators, who were French Communists, refused to return them and did not allow their use either to fetch Spaniards waiting at the port of Alicante, or to take the exiles to Latin America. Only one of these ships, the *Winnipeg*, was leased to a group of exiles; thus the Spaniards had to pay for the services of a ship which had been purchased with their own money.

Orlov, of the NKVD, led groups of Communist Spanish police, which were beyond all government control. The NKVD organized the persecution of POUM after the events of May 1937, and was directly responsible for the assassination of Austrian left-wing Socialist Kurt

Landau (an ex-Communist), Socialist Mark Rhein (son of the Menshevik Rafael Abramovich), Trotsky's ex-secretary Erwin Wolf, Italian Anarchist Camillo Bernieri, and numerous POUM militants (aside from those who were "spontaneously" murdered in brigades commanded by Communists and later publicly branded as traitors).

The NKVD managed the kidnapping of Andreu Nin, the political secretary of POUM. For fourteen days, in a house in Alcalá de Henares, Nin was tortured by men from the NKVD. When they became convinced that he would not sign any form of confession, they killed him. It was impossible to hand him over to the government's police force, since his corpse presented evident traces of torture. In view of this, another agent of the NKVD, the Italian Vittorio Vidale (Carlos Contreras in Spain, and before that, Eneas Sormenti in Mexico) had the idea of having him "kidnapped" by Germans from the International Brigades (who later "disappeared" in combat) and to have the rumor circulated that Nin had been "saved" by Gestapo agents. For this reason, when militants from POUM, who were in hiding, wrote on the walls: "Government Negrín, where is Nin?", the Communists added the phrase "In Salamanca or in Berlin." Orlov, later on, when he was in the United States, denied that he had participated in Nin's assassination. In any event, whoever was the immediate executor of the crime is of no importance, the responsibility was a collective one of the Soviet and Spanish Communist leadership.

Lastly, it is necessary to accurately clarify the political personality of POUM, since a large part of the Communist propaganda in Spain revolved around this party. The POUM was created in 1935 by the union of the Bloque Obrero y Campesino (BOC), with some 7,000 members headed by Joaquín Maurín, and the Communist Left, with some 200 members, led by Andreu Nin. Trotsky severely criticized this fusion and the policy of the POUM during the Civil War. Small Trotskyite groups, both Spanish and international, tried to infiltrate POUM in order to "Trotskyize" its politics, but were unsuccessful. Although POUM was on the side of the CNT during the time of the events of May, which it did not provoke (due to a lack of strength and its belief that they were a Communist provocation), there was never any real alliance between the CNT and POUM. The anarchists felt that, at least until 1938, the persecution of POUM by the Communists was an internal matter—"arguments within the Marxist family." But POUM denounced the Moscow trials and Soviet intervention in Republican politics—for instance, the dismissal of Nin from the Catalonian government was imposed by Antonov-Ovseenko under menace of suspending Soviet aid. And this was unforgettable in Moscow.

In the trial for high treason and espionage to which Negrín's government subjected POUM due to pressure from the Communists, a great many labor and Republican leaders testified guaranteeing the behavior of POUM leaders being tried. An empty space covered with flowers among the accused leaders represented the place that Andreu Nin would have occupied, had he not been assassinated. Some international labor leaders (Louis de Brouckère, Fenner Brockway, James Maxton, Marceau Pivert, Norman Thomas) sent delegations to pressure the minister of interior in Negrín's government, to do everything possible to save Nin. The Negrin government did not dare oppose the will of the NKVD.

The trial, held in Barcelona in October 1938, ended with an acquittal of the charges of espionage and high treason (based on declarations from Victorio Sala, an agent provocateur, and on a map of Madrid behind which appeared an "N" written in ink, which the prosecuting attorney tried to represent as Nin's signature). However, the members of POUM's executive committee were sentenced to fifteen years in prison for their participation in the May 1937 events. The party was also declared illegal. Those sentenced were released at the last moment, just as Franco's troops were spotted outside Barcelona. This was not due to orders from the government, but to the initiative of the jailers themselves. The Communists tried to have them remain imprisoned in Barcelona so that it would be said that they had gone over to the enemy side.[2]

It is necessary to recount all this so that the character of the Stalinist intervention in Spain and the frame of mind produced by the Popular Front's politics can be accurately understood. The Popular Front succeeded in silencing, even some Socialists, all over the world, the case of POUM, just as they had before with the Moscow trials, so that the anti-Fascist front not be broken.

In passing, it is of interest to point out the enormous influence that the Communist propaganda machinery had. The Communists called the members of POUM "Trotskyites," since for them this was anathema. POUM was by no means a Trotskyite party, as the most casual examination of its program and activities would prove. But in all the literature written about the Spanish Civil War, POUM is referred to as Trotskyite or semi-Trotskyite, even by scholars who do not consider this adjective anathema and who supposedly should be able to distinguish between political nuances. The adjective, by virtue of being repeated by Communists, simply penetrated everyone's mind. This had as a further consequence to present as sectarianism what was one of the clearest examples of idealism and tenacity under the most adverse circumstances. To belong to POUM after 1937 was suicidal; yet there were very few defections among POUM members. At the end of the Civil War, POUM's ranks were emaciated due to the murders committed by the Communists; yet its convictions and the will to defend them remained intact.

The men of Negrín's government, by the end of the war, were much less intact. They had not dared oppose the persecution of POUM nor set limits to the Communist intervention, not even when this intervention resulted in failure of their attempts to end the war. In fact, there were several attempts to come to a mediation. Curiously, the first attempt was initiated by Mussolini's representative to General Franco, Randolfo Cantalupo, together with an agent of his, Count Francesco Cavalleti. By means of a Jesuit, Cavalleti entered into discussions with Aguirre, president of the autonomous Basque government, to ask for the surrender of the north in exchange for a guarantee to allow the Basque leaders to flee with no reprisals. The attempt failed.

In August 1937, there was also the so-called Pact of Laredo between the Basque Nationalist leaders and the leader of the Littorio Division, General Manzini. By it, the Basques promised to free the prisoners, to surrender their weapons, to maintain order, while the Italian general was to allow those who wished to leave to do so with no reprisals, while the Basques would not be forced to fight on Franco's side. The text of this agreement was posted on the street corners of Laredo by the Italians. The Spanish Nationalists were opposed to the fulfillment of the conditions stipulated by the Italians once the Basques had fulfilled their part of the bargain. Thus the very soldiers of the Littorio carted the arrested Basques off to prison.

Largo Caballero, when he presided over the government, offered concessions to Paris and London in the protectorate of Morocco, in exchange for the aid of the two powers to the Republic or, at least, for a mediation that would leave the Republican regime intact. On March 20, 1937, London answered by rejecting the proposition. Paris followed suit.

Prior reference has been made to Prieto's position, which was favorable to mediation after the taking of Teruel and also to Besteiro's attempts in London to come to a mediatory intervention from the democratic powers.

There was still one more curious attempt. When in 1938 Negrín attended the International Congress of Physiology—his professional area of specialization—in Zurich, he had a conference with messengers from Hitler, which was held in a small Swiss town. He proposed that Germany withdraw all support to General Franco, and in exchange Negrín agreed, once the war was over, to establish in Spain a regime favorable to the diplomatic position of Hitler or at least neutral, in case of a world war. Moscow opposed the negotiations. Stalin wished to be the one to sacrifice the Spanish Republic on the altar of his pact with Hitler.

## NOTES

1. The retention of this quantity of gold, which overpaid for the arms shipments made to Spain by the U.S.S.R., is one of the reasons for Moscow's never recognizing the Spanish government in exile after 1946, while many of the satellite countries did. In 1957, Moscow announced that the cost of the arms and the aid to the Republic were higher than the value of the gold remittance, and thus Spain was in debt to the U.S.S.R.

2. For more detail about POUM see Victor Alba's *Histoire du POUM*, Paris, 1975.

# 17

# *Franco's "New State"*

On April 14, 1931, the Second Spanish Republic had been proclaimed. On April 1, 1939, it came to an end: "Today, with the disarmament and imprisonment of the Red army, the national troops have reached their final objectives. The war has ended. Burgos, April 1, 1939. Year of Victory. Francisco Franco."

After 986 days of combat, the war had been terminated. The Republic had disappeared from the Spanish stage. The Republicans' weakness (which had brought the war), SIM's excesses under Communist control, the abandonment by Western democracies, the U.S.S.R.'s obvious betrayal, the daily, nerve-racking discomforts of the recent months, all contributed to creating an atmosphere in the country which can be described by the following sentence heard in many streets and houses: "It matter not who comes along, as long as the war is ended." The war did end, and along came General Franco.

At this time, Franco could have won the acceptance of the disillusioned masses, since their natural leaders were now in exile. Had he carried out a policy of goodwill, he could have at least counted on popular passivity for a few years. But General Franco was incapable of carrying out such a strategy. The forces which had supported him now demanded payment for their support. The nobles claimed their lands, the church desired complete spiritual power, the army aspired to domination of the state, the Falange laid claim to public positions. After having won the war, General Franco found himself condemned, by the very contradictions of his position, to lose the peace.

He found a country devastated by the war and cities with large areas destroyed by his own air force. But he also found an agriculture which had improved despite extreme poverty, and an industry which was better managed and ran more smoothly than it had prior to the war. Yet he also found a country (or rather, that part of the country which had constituted the Republican zone) deprived of technicians, specialized workers, and intellectuals. Most of these had gone into exile. Had they not, they would have found themselves in jail within days after the end of the war, since they had formed the framework of the Republican army and the economy.

But above all, he found a country weakened by the excessive loss of blood in both zones. There was not one family which had not been affected by the war. Statistics would more than likely show that one out of every fifty Spaniards had died, in one way or another, as a direct result of the Civil War. In the three years of war, 380,000 were killed. The atrocity of this figure can be seen if one remembers that the United States, which had sent half a million soldiers to Vietnam within a ten-year period, had lost less than 60,000 men. There are no truly valid statistics available. One evaluation which seems accurate is that of the American Gabriel Jackson.[1]

| | |
|---|---|
| Killed on the battlefields | 100,000 |
| Civilians killed by aerial bombings | 10,000 |
| Killed by disease and hunger (due to the war) | 50,000 |
| Killed by reprisals in the Republican zone | 20,000* |
| Killed by reprisals in the Nationalist zone | 200,000 |
| Killed by execution or disease in the prison camps after April 1, 1939 | 200,000 |
| Total | 580,000 |

*According to Nationalist propaganda, this figure should be exactly 85,940.

For the entire year of 1939, envelopes which did not bear "Long live Franco! Year of Victory" would not be processed by the post office. Hundreds of thousands of men (the exact figure can never be known) were kept in concentration camps, later to be taken to jail, court martialed, and sentenced. The sentences imposed by the military were generally classified into four degrees: six years and a day, for aid to the rebellion; twelve years and a day, for inciting the rebellion; twenty years and a day, for supporting the rebellion; and the death penalty, for rebellion. When a man sentenced to death was pardoned, which, if it occurred, came about after fifteen to twenty months of awaiting the firing squad, a thirty-year prison term still lay before him. The state's police force, that of the Falange, the Civil Guard, and the Military Police, were placed at the disposal of private citizens, making arrests at the drop of a simple denunciatory statement, with proof unnecessary. After a lengthy legal process, usually two to three years, the accused would appear before military judges, having to prove his innocence through the efforts of a military defense attorney. Thus the accusation was considered sufficient proof of his guilt, although the accused was never told who had made the accusation against him. The Freemasons were subjected to a different type of legal proceedings, before a special tribunal. A Tribunal of Political Responsibilities imposed sentences of confiscation of possessions and fines on those who had been leaders or simple members of the "Red-Separatist-Masonic-Liberal" parties and unions. Julián Besteiro, arrested in Madrid, was condemned to death. His sentence was commuted, but he died shortly thereafter in an Andalusian prison.

Apart from this cold, bureaucratic repression in which torture was part of the modus operandi, there was also the personal repression prevalent in small towns, manifested by corpses found in ditches, women whose heads were shaved, prisoners' children handed over to religious schools. By the end of 1939, official statistics showed 217,000 prisoners in Spain. The government broke off relations with Chile from July to December 1940, since the latter's embassy gave refuge to Republicans, just as it had the Nationalists during the war. This was the only embassy which did so, although only for a short time.

The state had placed itself unconditionally at the service of its supporters. The bureaucrat who wished to be promoted, denounced his superiors; the factory owner who sought to get even with the former union shop stewart had him arrested; the landowner who wanted to raise the rent, had his lessee arrested to be free to do this; the parish priest who held aspirations of riding his flock of obstinate sheep, the doctor or lawyer who coveted the clientele of a more prosperous competitor—determined by serving such self-interests, the state had cut itself off completely from the people. On every street of every small town one could find a man, woman, or child who denounced, accused, and cudgeled his fellow man. All of this was politically wise, since it made the people feel themselves to be accomplices of the new regime, which they needed for protection, once they realized that by their accusations they had created enemies. Mistrust was prevalent.

Meanwhile, on March 15, Franco congratulated Hitler on his occupation of Czechoslovakia. On the 27th of the same month, he signed the anti-Komintern pact and presided at the victory parade. After this, German and Italian "volunteers" left the country. Spain owed Germany 300 million gold marks, in spite of the shipments of minerals and cereals it had made during the hostilities. Spain owed Italy 5 million gold lire, which in May 1940 it promised to pay by means of 5,000 treasury bonds of 1 million each. Its debt with England totaled 5.5 million pounds sterling, which it would pay in 1941-42. The remaining debts were to be paid after World War II to the governments that would succeed Mussolini and Hitler.

The Burgos government now put into practice the legislation that it had been preparing in the last months of the war. The Basque and Catalonian statutes, the divorce law, the sentences handed out by the courts in the Republican zone, etc., had been declared void. This government encountered a Catalonia which, along with Madrid, had borne the brunt of the war, was tired, and its main leaders were now in exile. A simple gesture showing respect for Catalonian folklore, language, popular dances, would have sufficed to begin a policy which might have led to integration. But there had been too much separatist rhetoric to allow the possibility of such a policy. Catalan was forbidden and repression became collective. Thus the door was closed to a type of centralist solution, that is, integration. Instead, an attempt to absorb was made by force, which, as will be seen, ended in failure.

The press was completely in the hands of the Falange, which controlled and named all editors and managers. The workers' cultural clubs became quarters for the Falange, sports clubs had supervisors from the Falange, and public libraries were expurgated by censors. A double censorship, political and religious, was established to authorize the publication of books. After some months of bread being sold without rationing, coupons reappeared (January 25, 1941). Rationing was in three categories, depending on the material resources of the consumer.

José Luis Arrese (b. 1905), a Falangist leader, gave a revealing speech toward the end of 1939: "We must demonstrate to the world that we did not oppose the Socialist revolution because it was violent, but rather because it was stupid and treacherous. When they said they had come to burn down the hovels to put the people in palaces, as you have already seen, they burned down the palaces and left the hovels. Those of us who felt the heartbeat of rebellion in our breasts, will never accuse them of having been incendiaries; we, too, shall be incendiaries, setting fire with a torch to that which displeases us."

But it was not the hovels which were burned down, but the palaces and temples which were reconstructed.

The way in which what they called "social justice" can best be understood is through Franco's own words, spoken in January 1940. As he reviewed the economic situation of the country, he said, among other things: "And if fish imports decrease, we have corbine in the Gulf of Guinea, which, although not very palatable, will satisfy our humble classes' needs." This mentality inspired the life of the New State. As again spoken by General Franco: "The country is tired of rotted liberalism, Judeo-Masonic-Communist plutocracy, we will give it a New State, in harmony with the new forms prevailing in the world."

In July 1937, General Franco had explained to a United Press reporter what his state would be: "Spain will follow the structure of the totalitarian regimes, as in Italy and Germany. It will be dressed in corporative forms and will do away with the liberal institutions which have poisoned the people. As in every empire, special attention will be given to the hierarchical principle, love for the fatherland will be required, social justice, and the protection of the middle classes and the workers will be stimulated. It will be inspired, then, in the norms of Italy and Germany, but with clearly defined national characteristics. It will be a tailor-made suit for Spaniards." The inspiration of the Fascist regimes was manifested in the organization of the state, which was the following:

1. His Excellency the Chief of State, Generalissimo of the armed forces, the National Leader of the Falange, the Caudillo of Spain, by the grace of God, to whom correspond "the power to establish juridical norms of a general character." The chief of state enjoyed the complete range of legislative, executive, and judicial powers, named all those who would be given positions in government, commanded all military forces, and signed all decrees. The council of ministers, over which he presided, was designated by him. He directed the Falange, the only political party allowed, whose leaders he named and whose national council he presided over. As the Falange's program read, General Franco "is solely responsible before History and before God."

2. The Spanish Traditionalist Falange was composed of hierarchies. That is, in the terminology of the Falange, it was formed by leaders and affiliates. The latter wore blue shirts, greeted each other in the Roman manner, and were organized into armed militias. There were sections for everyone: Flechas y Pelayos for children; the Youth Front for adolescents; the Women's Section; the Spanish University Union

(SEU); Social Assistance for charity; Education and Rest for recreation; Brotherhoods of Peasants; and Vertical Unions for employers and employees. The combination of unions pertaining to this last group composed the National Unionist Center (CNS), directed by the Falangists. Its members paid dues which were deducted from their salaries. Membership was compulsory in order to be able to work. All positions of authority were filled by those at the top; there were no elections of any kind. Franco appointed the leadership of the CNS.

The reader must not think there were no elements, especially among the Falangists, who sought social transformations. They repudiated capitalism and spoke of correcting its vices and abuses to build a "national unionist" society. But they lacked a concrete program, wished to attract the anarcho-syndicalists, at which they failed. In addition, they suffered from deep contradictions: they considered the religious sentiment of life, and not work, as the basis of their ideology, they praised Phillip II's Spain and abhorred that of Charles III. Modernization was not their concern; they wished to bring the country back to medieval institutions, which seemed more Christian to them. In any case, these elements did not manage to give the regime the revolutionary character which they proclaimed.

Naturally, there were no authorized strikes, collective bargaining, nor any way of defending oneself against the state. The state of war proclaimed by the military in July 1936 continued in force in Spain until 1956, together with all its consequences; censorship, both of publications and correspondence, and courts-martial.

3. Later on July 18, 1942, a Parliament was created by decree. Some of its members were named by the Falange, the "unions," the episcopate, and the universities, while others were designated by the chief of state, General Franco. Their role was merely advisory, although officially it was designated to be a legislative one.[2]

4. The economy was managed simultaneously by four different agencies. First, there was the Ministry of Industry and Commerce; second, the national leadership of the various unions of the CNS; third, a network of military committees—military industries, naval, bridge, and highway construction, minerals of military interest, etc. Later, the National Institute of Industries (INI) was created, which established companies with government investments. This multiplicity, with its orders and counterorders, inspections, quotas, waybills, authorizations, etc., was prone to every type of injustice, underhanded dealings, and corruption. Thus, it was not strange to see large trusts formed and enormous fortunes amassed overnight.

On the cultural plane, lay institutions disappeared, numerous private schools were shut down, many teachers were fired for political motives, journals and dailies diminished both in number and press run, the university system found itself completely subjected to the Falange and the church, with its *colegios mayores* (dorms) directed by priests, and its programs of study dictated by the state. At all levels, political education (based on the Falange's program) was compulsory. Religious censorship was absolute; books such as *Luther* by Funck Brentano and the *History of Philosophy* by Van Aster were suppressed. The budget for public instruction was diminished, while the publication of books, which soon became luxury items, declined. Film censorship filled the screen with "friends" rather than lovers and "illnesses," instead of suicides.

Under this rule Spanish lifestyle acquired the signs of a collective nightmare. No one trusted his neighbor, since everyone lived in fear of being denounced. In order to be able to eat, one had to resort to the black market (*straperlo*) or steal raw materials or tools from work sites. Young people, who had not known the Republic, grew up in complete indifference and apathy. The worker, with his 1936 salary having been increased by scarcely 50 percent, faced a cost of living rise which had quadrupled. Thus, of necessity, he resorted to expedients which would have repelled him before the war, especially moonlighting or the twelve to fourteen-hour work day. The church undertook moralizing campaigns which consisted of imposing that women's bathing suits reach the knees, of sending the yellow card of prostitutes to the fathers of young girls discovered in movie theaters in male company, of publishing in the newspapers the names of people found in *casas de cita* (locales used for clandestine meetings between people of the opposite sex). The point to which the church ruled in Spain can be seen in the fact that the head of the prison chaplains, the Reverend Martín Torrent, could write a book, published with the permission of the bishop and imprinted in the prison printshops, in which he said: "When will I die? Oh, if I only knew, echo the intimate voices of millions and millions of consciences. But then, the only man who has the incomparable good fortune of being able to answer this question is the man who is sentenced to death: 'I will die at 5 o'clock this very morning!' Can greater grace be given to a soul that has marked his entire life along a road leading further and further away from God?"[3] Divorce was abolished as was civil marriage. Later, even divorces granted during the Republic were annulled, so that many people did not know exactly what their legal marital status was. The head of censorship said to a publisher who complained that his business was on the verge of bankruptcy because of the books banned from publication: "I prefer to see you ruined that for you to lose your soul for publishing reprehensible books."

A new phraseology appeared in the press and in speeches. Foreign nouns were forbidden, such as *restaurant, grillroom, cocktail,* etc., while a series of baroque phrases covered the walls of the city: "Through the empire to God"; "Not one home without fire, nor one Spaniard without bread"; "God, Fatherland, and Justice"; "Service and Sacrifice." José Antonio Primo de Rivera, whose corpse had been moved to the Escorial and buried alongside the kings, was glorified and his writings became evangelical. People spoke of the "imperial will of Spain" and of the "spirit of permanence of Falangism." The country had three national anthems, the "Marcha Real," the Falangist "Cara al Sol," and the Traditionalist "Oriamendi." In the street, the people had to greet each other with their arms outstretched, returning two salutes to the other's three, while they shouted: "Franco, Franco, Franco!" This also occurred in the movies, the theater, or in sports arenas whenever the national anthems were played or a photograph of Franco appeared on the screen, while official propagandists and scholarly texts referred to him as "sent by Divine Providence." Spain was a "chosen country of God." The national coat of arms was changed, while the motto, written between the claws of the imperial eagle, read: "One, great, and free." One point of the Falange's program proclaimed: "There is no need to speak of rights, but rather of duties." Every chief of police was a member of the military, every governor was a Falangist and at the same time the provincial head of the Falange. All schools, institutes, libraries, prisons, universities, "unions," youth centers, sports clubs, had an assigned delegate of the Falange and a chaplain. And when the chief of state, naturally in full uniform, received a delegation of "union" leaders which had been named by him and shook hands with them as they left, the press published a photograph of the scene with headlines that read: "This, indeed, is real democracy."

In order to travel about the country, one needed a safe-conduct from the police. To study, one needed permission from the SEU. To exhibit one's paintings, one needed the Falange's written guarantee of good conduct. To publish books, one needed the permission of the under-secretary of propaganda. All Spaniards were carefully classified into three pidgeonholes in the municipal archives: supporters, indifferents, opponents (to the regime).

It is difficult to believe that the New State could have survived the end of World War II, had it not been for General Franco. His adversaries were accustomed to considering him as merely a military man.

But the reality of the situation showed him to be a great politician, one who knew his people well. He was cold, patient, capable of compromise and adaptation, with a brand of old Catholicism as the substance of his political personality. Franco adopted the external forms of fascism, since they were in vogue and politically advantageous. But what he really sought was a Spain populated by obedient, hard-working, and suspicious Spaniards. The best proof of his political qualities can be seen in his resistance to pressures from the Axis powers to enter the world war, and afterwards to maintain the regime in the face of international pressures of the postwar era. He lacked a social conscience, as does every Spaniard whose Catholicism is of a pre–Civil War vintage. His military life (he was possibly the Spanish military man most interested in the technical problems of his profession) had not allowed him to develop a sense of liberty. He sincerely believed that he had been sent by Providence to guide his country.

The son of an administrator in the navy, General Franco was considered a brilliant strategist. He began his career in the Military Academy, was promoted in Morocco, where he was instrumental in the creation of the Tercio (Foreign Legion), and became the youngest general in Europe. He had been dubbed "Franco, the African." A fervent Catholic, he married into a Catholic family. He always lived in a military environment, with the characteristic ambition of any intelligent Spanish military man. Under the monarchy, Franco was destined to be nothing more than an instrument of the king. Thus, he accepted the Republic, if not with fervor, with proper demeanor. But when the High Military Academy in Zaragoza, of which he was founder and director, was suppressed, he manifested his disconformity with the direction taken by the regime. Gil Robles named him chief of the General Staff in 1935, and it was he who had the idea of sending the Foreign Legion and the Moorish soldiers to Asturias. In the General Staff, he began his apprenticeship in the ways of government, which he used to his advantage in August 1936, when, after Sanjurjo's death, he was proclaimed leader of the Nationalists. Free from all ideological ties with the Traditionalists and Falangists, he was clever enough to combine the efforts of both factions and adapt the newly-born Falangist doctrine to his personal taste. On the other hand, he also knew how to inspire the fear of communism in all his allies, although it was a nonexistent danger in Spain. Thus, he presented himself as the lesser of the two evils, as the "last safeguard against communism."

He governed personally. He directed both internal and external politics and was clever enough to balance the opposed interests of the

Allies with those of the Axis. Without hesitation, he applied the theory that the end justifies the means. For him, the end meant a return to the era of Phillip II, with "an empire, a cross, and a sword." He named those who filled all high positions in the country, and he knew personally all military men of rank. In everything else, he was almost an ascetic. From his palace in El Pardo, his cold personality, lacking in cordiality in his treatment of others, marked the recent years of Spain's history.

World War II afforded him the opportunity to manifest this personality in full force. It often seemed that the regime was consistently falling into Hitler's hands. But although there were many elements within the regime that exerted pressure for Spain to openly proclaim itself on the side of Nazi Germany, General Franco wished to keep Spain out of the war. He managed to do this via concessions to the Axis, but without any real participation in the war. It is difficult to decide whether he did this for reasons of opportunism, conviction, or because he felt it impossible to subject the country to a new bloodbath. Thus Spain did not enter the war, although in official propaganda it was completely on the side of the Axis, while popular opinion was on the side of the Allies.

Immediately after the Civil War, there was an intensive pro-Nazi propaganda, which on occasion led to parodoxical situations. For example, Serrano Suñer said in one speech: "We are only the enemies of Russia's friends." This sentence was pasted on posters on every wall in the country, only to be torn down hastily two days later, since the U.S.S.R. and the Reich had just signed the pact of August 1939. On the walls of the city, the Falange wrote: "An Anglophile, a Red," which was the same as saying that all those on the side of the Allies were on the side of the Republic since they were called "red" and were enemies of the New State.

On September 2, 1939, Franco made an appeal that the war remain localized, and he declared Spain a neutral country. He knew that Spain could not intervene, since he could not possibly assure the loyalty of his troops nor that of his rear guard, although he could count on steady military and political frameworks. His relationship with the Axis was close, and his condemnation of democracy, which, in his own words, "would carry England to defeat," left no doubt as to which side had won his sympathy. The fascist sentiment of the regime became more acute. But the economy told a different story.

Since Spain needed cotton for the textile industry and petroleum for transportation and the army, on March 18, Ramón Serrano Suñer, General Franco's brother-in-law who was minister of foreign affairs, cosigned a commercial agreement with Sir Samuel Hoare, the British ambassador. In 1940 and 1942, Spain repaid the debt of 5.5 million pounds that had been contracted with London during the Civil War. Since Spain's gold and currency were in Moscow, plus the fact that French and English courts rejected the claims from Franco's government, leaving the deposits in the name of the Republican leaders who officially retained them (except for 8 million pounds deposited in Mont-de-Marsan), the government was forced to pay for the importing of wheat, oil, cotton, etc., and export products needed by the country. Products of military interest such as wolfram, mercury, potash, and also certain foods, went to Germany and Italy. When the latter entered the war in June 1940, Spain's position of neutrality became simply nonbelligerent.

After having received, with all due pomp and ceremony, Count Galeazzo Ciano in 1939 and Heinrich Himmler in 1940, General Franco held a conference with Hitler in Hendaya (October 23, 1940) and with Mussolini in Bordighera (February 12, 1941). He also spoke with Marshal Pétain. General Franco managed to stay out of a compromise that would have let the Germans march through Spain and attack Gibraltar, which was what Hitler wanted. That same year, 1941, saw the first pardon of political prisoners, which reached some 40,000 who had been condemned to six-year prison terms.

[In a speech made on July 14, 1941, Franco said: "Democracy and liberalism are hackneyed expressions. The triumph of Nazism is evident to everyone. The absurd conflict, the result of the declaration of war made by France and England, has reached its logical end: the Allies have lost the war." When the United States entered the conflict, General Franco wrote President Roosevelt warning him of the mistake he was making, since the victory by the Axis was inevitable/

Franco also evolved a policy of alliance with Portugal, by a treaty of March 17, 1940, and the pact established an Iberian Bloc (February 1942). He signed an agreement with the Vatican in June 1941, which gave the concordat of 1851 renewed vigor. That is, the state was to provide its subjects with a Catholic education and refrain from making any legislation regarding matters about which the church had definite opinions, without first consulting the Vatican.

Since the beginning of hostilities Franco had taken advantage of the momentary weakness of the democracies in order to deal with two important issues in his international imperial politics: Tangiers and Gibraltar. The city of Tangiers and surrounding area were submitted to an international regime by the Convention of Algeciras of April 1906, with the guarantee of eleven European powers, the United

States, and the sultan of Morocco, who would continue as nominal sovereign of the zone. In November 1923, the plenipotentiaries of England, France, and Spain signed a protocol which established the internationalization of Tangiers. Five years later, in 1928, at Italy's request, the statute was revised, to allow greater intervention to the signatory powers. Then on June 13, 1940, Spain declared its nonbelligerent status, and twenty-four hours later, Spanish troops occupied the city and Tangiers was incorporated into Spanish Morocco by a decree of November 23, 1940. In February 1941, England and Spain signed a provisional agreement by which the latter promised not to fortify the zone, while the former affirmed that the annexation would not be disputed by the signatory powers by reason of circumstances. But the London government reserved the right to do so in the future. The customs of Tangiers was included into the system of Spanish customs shortly thereafter, while foreign civil servants were fired. Nothing more was said about Tangiers until after the war.

Gibraltar became a lever in the hands of General Franco. It had been occupied in 1704 by the British, who were fighting against Phillip V. It remained in their hands from that point on, to the evident displeasure of the Spaniards. A neutral zone separated Gibraltar from Spanish territory. General Franco had the political prisoners build several fortifications in front of this zone. During the war, Allied squadrons used Gibraltar as a supplies depot, making passage through the strait difficult for German and Italian submarines. In 1941, the streets of Spain were filled with groups of Falangists who claimed "Gibraltar for Spain."

With the entry of the U.S.S.R. into the war, Spain partially abandoned its nonbelligerent status. On the day following the German attack on the Soviet Union, Serrano Suñer declared in a speech that "it was the Soviet Union's fault," announcing creation of the Blue Division, commanded by General Agustín Muñoz Grandes (1896-1970), to fight against the U.S.S.R. on the side of the Germans. The volunteers of the division were to die in large numbers. They also were to receive both German and Spanish decorations, to be pensioned by the Spanish state and, for months, to constitute the strong point of propaganda. Meanwhile, on November 25, 1941, Spain had signed the renewal of the Anti-Komintern Pact, and in August of the same year, a trade agreement with Germany which served to send some 50,000 Spanish workers to the Reich via the CNS.

Several times in the course of the war, the Allies protested in Madrid. After an unsuccessful Falangist attack on the British Embassy in June 1941, Serrano Suñer was removed from office. This occurred shortly after Franco had given a speech in Seville in which he offered Hitler, in order to defend Germany "from the Asiatic hordes, one million bayonets, if he needed them." It was a criminal occurrence that precipitated Franco's decision to get rid of his brother-in-law. On August 15, 1942, the monarchist general José Enrique Varela (1891-1951), a staunch enemy of the Falange, was the target of an assassination attempt as he left the church in Begoña. The aggressor was executed the next day. It was rumored that several Falangist leaders had organized the attempt, instigated by what the people called "*cuñadismo*" ("big brother-in-lawism"). Thus the silent struggle between the army and the Falange provided General Franco with the desired opportunity which left both Varela and Serrano Suñer out of office. On September 3, the count of Jordana (1876-1944), a minister during the dictatorship and a member of the Burgos Junta, was named minister of foreign affairs.

[When the Allies disembarked in North Africa (November 8, 1942), the American ambassador visited General Franco. He handed him a letter from President Roosevelt which assured him that the Spanish nation had nothing to fear from the Allies and that they were undertaking this operation to prevent the Axis from doing so. At this time, the United States, in an attempt to impede the sale of Spanish goods to the Axis, bought what Spain had to offer at a better price.

Things began to go badly for the Axis. In May 1943, General Franco offered his services as a mediator to put an end to the war, but no one accepted the offer. In a further attempt, he wrote a letter to Churchill in which he stated that, as Germany was virtually vanquished, there were only two "virile powers in Europe: England and Spain," and proposed an alliance of the two against the Soviet Union. The British Cabinet of War took notice of the letter, sending a copy to the Soviet government and answering that such a proposition did not interest it.] When Mussolini fell, there was a moment of panic, and the press published articles against those who "were packing their suitcases." The press went on to state that "if there were no other sources of hope, there would always be faith in the Divine Providence, who, after having given us General Franco, can never abandon us."

[In August, the British ambassador visited General Franco and asked him to close down the German Consulate in Tangiers and withdraw the Blue Division. In January 1944, after having received no satisfactory answer to these requests, the U.S. Department of State suspended shipments of petroleum to Spain. Finally, in May 1944, General Franco yielded to this pressure, withdrew his volunteers, named Muñoz Grandes chief of His Excellency's Military House, closed down the German Consulate in Tangiers, and reduced the shipments of wolfram to the Reich. At the same time there took place in Barcelona an exchange of prisoners between the Allies and the Axis.

The landing on the beaches of Normandy sent a chill of panic up the spine of the officials. It was feared that the French Resistance Forces, which included numerous exiled Spaniards, would come running en masse into Spain, with the Allies imposing a change in regime. But nothing of the kind happened.

In April 1945, General Franco tried to jump on the bandwagon of the victors. With the pretext that the Japanese in Manila had murdered several Spaniards, Franco broke off relations with Tokyo and even sounded out the possibility of a declaration of war to see if it would be well received in Washington. The only thing he achieved was to remind the Capitol of his congratulations to the Mikado on the attack of Pearl Harbor and to the Philippine quisling Laurel when the Japanese proclaimed him president of the Archipelago.

Lord Templewood (Sir Samuel Hoare), who had been ambassador to Madrid during the war, wrote that Spain had not entered the conflict due "to the hostility, which grew from day to day, of the Spanish people, toward intervening in the conflict and, later, to the routs suffered by the Italian Army in Greece, and to the existing differences with respect to the booty of Africa, which, besides Gibraltar, included the concession of a part of French Morocco to Spain." He went on to explain that: "Since my first discussion with General Franco, when he asked me, as we sat beneath the portraits of Hitler and Mussolini, why England had not withdrawn from the hostilities, knowing, as she should have, that she could not win the war, until my last visit, when the pictures had been replaced by new ones of the Pope and Salazar, four years have passed. During this time, except for a few months, England lived in uncertainty, not knowing what would happen the next morning."

The people maintained their sympathy for the Allies, based exclusively on political motivations. Thus, they forgot the Allies' attitude during the Civil War and helped, in a disinterested way, to save the elements of the French Resistance and Allied Forces heading to Portugal or Gibraltar from France and who, when discovered by the Spanish police, spent several months of waiting and humiliations in the concentration camp of Miranda de Ebro.

A thousand other details clearly indicate toward which side the sympathies of the Falangists and the New State were leaning. For example, there is the case of the Italian ships brought to the Balearic islands as Italy fell. It was only fifteen months later that Spain handed them over to the Allies, in contrast with what France had done in 1939, that is, turn over to Franco immediately the vessels of the Republican fleet which had been sheltered in Bizerte.

In 1946, when Admiral Raeder was interrogated by the Allied judges during the Nuremberg Trials, he stated that in 1941 General Franco and Hitler were agreed to attack Gibraltar, but that in order to reinforce his internal position, Franco asked that Hitler provoke British intervention, which would allow Franco to help Germany. Hitler did not want to risk a war in the Peninsula against England, in which, as he perceived it, he would also have to contend with a large portion of the Spanish people.

Franco's position is also very clearly revealed by the correspondence that changed hands between the two fascist leaders. This was discovered by the Allies after the fall of Germany and was published in a U.S. Department of State *White Book*. On August 8, 1940, the German ambassador to Madrid, Von Stohrer, wrote to his minister that "Spain has offered to enter the war on the side of the Axis at the right moment." This is confirmed by a letter from Franco to Hitler dated September 22, 1940: "Only our isolation and the lack of the most indispensable resources for our national existence keeps us from getting into the action. . . . I share your opinion that the attack and the occupation of Gibraltar should be our first operation. In this regard, our military policy in the Strait since 1936 has been directed by our foresight of the British intention to protect and defend their bases. . . . The material that you have offered me will be tremendously useful. On our part, we have been preparing this operation for a very long time. . . . I would also like to thank you, dear Führer, for your offer of solidarity. I respond to it by my affirmation of indefectible and sincere affection for you personally, for the German people, and for the cause for which you fight. I hope, in defense of this cause, to be able to renew the former bonds of comradeship between our armies."

Almost one year later, on February 26, 1941, General Franco wrote to Hitler: "I will always be a faithful partisan of your cause. As you do, I consider History's destiny as having united us, that is, you, Il Duce, and myself, with an indissoluble bond. . . . We maintain today our perpetual position with resolve and the firmest conviction. You should not give birth to any doubt concerning my absolute fidelity to the political idea and the realization of the union of our national destiny to that of Germany and Italy. I want to dissipate all shadow of doubt and to declare myself ever-ready at your side, completely and steadfastly at your disposal, united in a common historical destiny. If I should ever renege on these promises, it would mean my suicide and that of the cause which I have directed and which I represent in Spain."]

When Franco wrote to Hitler of "the lack of the most indispensable resources," he was not inventing some pretext, nor was he exaggerating. The government found itself without gold or currency. Nor did it have any way of reconstructing the devastated country other than its own means.

The first measure of the victors, on the economic field, was to suppress the value of all money issued in the Republican zone. This reduced prices suddenly. Salaries returned to the level of 1936. At the end of two years, the cost of living index had tripled, while salaries continued at the 1936 level. In 1946, the cost of living was 450 percent higher than in 1936, while salaries had merely doubled.

At the same time that the Jesuits had returned to the country, divorce had been abolished, the lands had been returned to their owners, farm laborers had returned to occupy the place of animals in their homes, and in the factories and mines, the workers fainted from hunger. This last situation came to the point that in many industries dispensaries had been installed solely to give a glass of milk with cognac to the worker who was too weak to continue working without this stimulant.

The cultural situation is reflected in the following list of topics of books published in 1945: art, 44; military art, 49; philosophy, 57; liturgy, 69; Falangism, 81; sociology, 3; dogmatic theology, 102; the remaining publications, which totaled 3,432, were novels, 80 percent of which were translations.

There was nothing extemporaneous, then, in the fact that General Franco, in times in which panic reigned among his followers, for example when Mussolini fell or when the Allies landed in Normandy, would insist on repeating to them a sentence of his which dated back to 1939: "Our Crusade is the only struggle in which the wealthy who went to war returned even wealthier." The profits from the war were never controlled, while political prisoners, for the lowest salaries imaginable (which went mostly to the state), were placed at the disposal of the companies which had been contracted to reconstruct the devastated zones.

The Spaniard of this period had the feeling of living as one who had been kidnapped, no matter what his political ideas may have been, since rightists were as exposed as leftists to the threat of a denunciation or fine, although the consequences for rightists were less severe. The police force (that is, the three police forces: military, Falangist, and civilian) was omnipotent. One could not appeal any measure taken by the state. In 1946, the jails were still well stocked, and there were three concentration camps and 137 work camps for political prisoners.

A detailed look at the economic life of the regime is in order. After the fall of Barcelona, in 1939, a group of French, Belgian, and Swiss capitalists headed by Belgian ex–prime minister Paul Van Zeeland, proposed to General Franco their financing of the reconstruction of the country. The war had scarcely touched industrial productive capacity; what had suffered most from the bombings were houses and communication lines, whose repair could be relatively rapid, but which in fact took ten years to complete and was mainly the task of political prisoners. The offer was rejected.

The wheels of industry were immediately set into motion and enjoyed certain continuity, due to shipments of cotton and petroleum from the Allies. In contrast, agriculture suffered considerable decline due to lack of workers—who had either emigrated or been imprisoned. The production of wheat, in 1946, reached only 70 percent of what it had been in 1935, while that of potatoes reached only 52 percent.

Exports made the situation bearable. In 1940, for example, a trade agreement was signed with Argentina. Another factor was the British purchase of oranges, mercury, oil, and wines, which allowed the acquisition of cotton and machinery. The government did not exercise any measures against foreign capital at work in Spain. It nationalized the Telephone Company paying it with dollars, and then conceded to a branch of IT&T the monopoly of all materials needed for the Spanish telephone system.

The state's budget granted more than half of its expenditures to the armed forces (the army, police force, and Falange). The growing deficit imposed government floating of bonds whose interests burdened the budget by 2,110 million pesetas (in 1946, the year to which these figures refer). Money circulation, which in 1936 was 4.5 billion, rose in ten years to 18 billion. While the circulation of paper money had quadrupled, the production of goods had not reached its prewar level. The public debt, which in 1935 was 19 billion pesetas, rose in 1946 to 36 billion. The army continued to grow: in 1940, after the end of the Civil War, there were 38,177 officers; in 1945, there were 41,089 (of which 306 were generals, in contrast with the 311 generals of the U.S. Army in the same year).

This situation shared common features with that of the entire postwar world, but since it was much worse than in the rest of Europe, one must place the blame on the procedures the government adopted to alleviate it, which were nothing more than new means of opening the door to the black market. Thus it was that a journalist, Josep Pla, who had supported the New State from its beginnings wrote: "One would be mistaken to believe that the only cause of what is happening is due to the greed of the people. No. There is a second cause which is as important as the first, a cause which resides in the general situation, which is characterized by the few who inevitably get richer, while the rest steadily grow poorer."

## NOTES

1. Gabriel Jackson, *The Spanish Republic and the Civil War, 1931-1939*, Princeton, 1965.

2. After 1966, by virtue of a reform of the fundamental laws, 108 of the 564 members of Parliament were elected by the heads of families, the only Spaniards who were allowed to vote.

3. Martín Torrent, *¿Qué me dice usted de los presos?* Talleres Penitenciarios de Alcalá de Henares, 1942, p. 68.

# 18

# A Paralyzed Country

Throughout the previous chapter the reader must have felt submerged in a world of incoherence, further burdened by a confusing accumulation of data. This was exactly how the Spaniards felt about their own lives, whatever their ideology. They did not view their country's recent history which was in a sense their own biography, as an ordered whole, classified into categories of internal politics, international politics, economy, etc. Instead they saw it as a hodgepodge of very different and often contradictory facts. If these pages have not succeeded in reproducing this same impression for the reader, he/she will never come to understand the Spaniard of today, formed and deformed by the events described.

This sensation was most evident among those opposed to the New State. When the world war broke out, General Franco felt quite insecure with regard to his rear guard, should he enter the war, in spite of the fact that opposition to his regime had not yet become organized. Little by little, the Civil War was idealized in the memory of the masses, Spanish irony immediately recognized the ridiculous side of the regime, while the economic situation placed the people against the regime. In 1940, when the Gestapo turned Lluis Companys, Julián Zugazagoitia, Joan (John) Peiró, and other Republican leaders who had sought refuge in France, over to the Falangists, the people found out what was going on, despite the government's precautions to maintain absolute secrecy regarding their arrival in Spain. When these prisoners were shot to death, the first clandestine manifestos appeared, signed by Republican and workers' parties.

At first, the opposition was simply an amalgamation of groups which could be found in prison, in factories, and on the street. Gradually, these groups began to achieve some degree of harmony. In 1942, the first underground newspaper, *Front de la Llibertat* (freedom front), appeared in Barcelona. In 1943, the workers' parties had formed their committees, while the unions were beginning to function in secret. In 1944, the National Alliance of Democratic Forces was constituted by the union of these groups. Those who joined were: the Socialist party, the Socialist Youth, and POUM, forming the Marxist sector; the CNT, FAI, and the Libertarian Youth, forming the libertarian sector; the Republican Left, the Republican Union, the Federal party, and the Esquerra, forming the Republican sector. The Communist party supported, at this time, the thesis of the National Union, in which they wanted to include all anti-Franco, military, and even Falangist elements.

In 1944, this National Union sent to Spain, via the Aran Valley, groups of Spanish guerrillas who were past members of the French Resistance movement. They came poorly armed and with assurances made to them regarding the support of the people when they entered the Peninsula. The Civil Guard received them, killed several dozen of them, threw others into prison, while the rest managed to escape back to France. Meanwhile, the Communists had sent to Spain several of their leaders who supported a rather unorthodox position and all of them fell into the hands of Franco police denounced by agents of the party. The National Union discredited the opposition in Spain, while in France, it served to divide the Spanish parties in exile, in each of which there emerged a pro-Communist group. The Falangist state feared the end of the war. Its "adaptation" was insufficient, while the people faithfully awaited the Allied victory, to which they contributed as much as their exhausted strength would allow.

Toward the end of 1945, the workers in Manresa, Catalonia, staged the first strike in the New State. The workers of other manufacturing cities, namely Madrid and Valencia, followed suit. Throughout the country, the CNS and the governors were forced to make promises, while the state established extra rations for the workers (only to be removed as soon as order had been reestablished). A new wave of strikes. New arrests. In the mountains of Castile and northern Andalusia, groups of guerrilla attacked the Civil Guard for a period of several months. The Communist party dissolved the National Union, but it was not admitted into the National Alliance of Democratic Forces. In 1946 both Catalonia and Euzkadi saw the creation of the parallel National Councils of Democracy, which united all the Catalonian and Basque parties and organizations. As time passed, these organisms were either dissolved or died off due to lack of outside support. Arrest became more frequent, and in 1952, opponents to the regime still faced the firing squad.

The disappointment that came with the realization that the end of the world war was not to precipitate the fall of the regime, nor even an increase in the perspectives for success of the opposition, isolated the latter amidst a tired, hungry, disoriented people. A new generation emerged, a generation that had passed through the schools of the regime, and thus knew nothing of Spain's modern history nor even recognized the names of the most prominent Republicans.

In this way, the initiative passed to the monarchists. These, who had supported General Franco in the Civil War, began to move, encouraged by certain British support. The Duke of Alba (1878-1953) invited the principal aristocrats in Seville to his daughter's debut. Shortly thereafter, Don Juan, Count of Barcelona, son and heir of the former Alfonso XIII, made statements in Geneva regarding the throne and offering a constitutional monarchy. General Franco, in order to discredit this enemy, promised in several statements that he would reestablish "the traditional regime of Spain" at the right time. Don Juan moved to Lisbon, spoke with the leader of CEDA, Gil Robles, who had broken off with General Franco in 1937. A group of generals, the most renowned of whom, Alfredo Kindelan, was exiled and later pardoned, were in favor of the restoration, while the Duke of Alba left his position in the London Embassy. For a short time, in light of the support the monarchists seemed to enjoy among the Allies, there were negotiations between them and the Alliance, but with no concrete results. In August 1946, the Alliance would confirm in a manifesto that in order to fight against the regime it would not reject any coalition.

General Franco kept a strong grip on the power reins. The bourgeoisie, tired of fines and regulations, would have abandoned him without a second thought, if the recollection of their complicity in the rebellion had not bound them tightly. If the church faced within it the protest of one segment of the Catholics, the high ecclesiastic hierarchies published pastoral letters each time General Franco was attacked abroad, defending his regime and speaking of the Civil War as "our Crusade." An example of such tactics can be seen in the pastoral letters of the Spanish primate Enrique Pla y Deniel (1876-1967) at the end of World War II, and of the archbishop of Granada, stating that with General Franco's regime the social problem in Spain had been resolved. The church continued to dominate the country. A single example will suffice to show to what degree it exercised this domination: in 1946, the Superior Junta of Cinematographic Orientation was created, which censored movies and directed all national production of same. Three Falangists and three ecclesiastics made up the junta, while the latter were the only members who had the right to veto. Nevertheless, there was tension with the state. For example, in 1942 the state forbade the diffusion of the pastoral letter written by the bishop of Soria against the paganism of the Nazis. The *Osservatore Romano* was prohibited in Spain during the war, to keep the public from finding out about the setbacks suffered by the Axis.

The Allied victory led General Franco into giving the regime a face-lifting: conditional liberty to thousands of prisoners, who on leaving jail were exiled from their former places of residence and subjected to police surveillance; removal of censorship from foreign correspondents (but not for the domestic press); suppression of the Falange's militias; suppression of the arm-raised salute and obligatory singing of the Falangist anthems, to avoid "misinterpretations," as the decree read.

At the death of the count of Jordana, he was succeeded in the Ministry of Foreign Affairs by José Félix de Lequerica, an ex-Traditionalist and the ex-ambassador to Vichy, who was followed a short time later by Alberto Martín Artajo, leader of the Catholic Action, about which it was said: "Before, the ministers changed their cassocks; now the cassocks change their ministers." It was taken for granted that no one resigned, unless General Franco notified those who were "in the way" by a letter announcing their dismissal and "thanking them for their services." Serrano Suñer, for example, in 1942, found out through the press that he had resigned twenty-four hours after his replacement had been signed in by Franco.

Next came a series of declarations by General Franco to the foreign press: "Spain is an evangelical democracy; Spain is headed for an organic democracy; Spain will have a social monarchy; the problem of the monarchy will be settled when the nation's interest demands it." Likewise, orders were given to form the electoral census, announcements were made concerning municipal elections, and a plebiscite spoken of to determine whether the monarchy should return. General Franco entered into negotiations with Don Juan via his brother Nicolás, ambassador to Lisbon. No agreement was reached, since the pretender to the throne wanted to succeed General Franco, but without inheriting Falangism in the process. Rumors spread of conspiracies among the generals.

Tangiers was subjected to an international regime, after Spanish troops were evacuated due to pressure from the Allies, with Spain to remain excluded from Tangiers as long as there were no change in regime. The declarations of Potsdam and the United Nations (which will be examined later) did little more than assure Franco's continuance in power, since they showed that there existed no real desire to remove him. Trade exchanges with the Allied countries increased. Negotiations with the U.S.S.R. were discussed. When Cristino García, leader of the French Resistance and a Communist, was sent to Spain by his party to assassinate a dissident, Gabriel León Trilla, was arrested and executed because of his participation in the Civil War. The French government then closed off the border in the Pyrennees (February 1946) and the Falangist students increasingly demanded the release of Petiot, a new Landru who at that time was being tried in Paris. In light of the division among the Allies, General Franco presented himself as a defender of the West: "Recently Spain has come into a role in the world. The defense of our independence not only serves our supreme interest as a nation, but we also constitute the most steadfast bullwark against communism."

General Franco concentrated troops in the Pyrennees to make the people believe that they were under the threat of invasion. According to a memorandum from the U.S. government, in July 1946 there were 150,000 soldiers stationed along the Pyrennees border, among them Moors and legionnaires, with 350,000 additional men in the rest of the Peninsula. Fugitive quislings from all over Europe took refuge in Spain. And while the government turned over Pierre Laval, since France vigorously demanded it, it also stowed away Léon Degrelle, Abel Bonnard, Otto Skorgeny, and others. The state declared that it had to retain German property to compensate for the expenditures incurred by having sent the Blue Division. The Allies were forced to exert strong diplomatic pressure to finally achieve, in 1946, the recognition of the Allied Committee of Control as a representative of Germany and with it the return of the German possessions that could not be hidden. Meanwhile, the Allies demanded payment of the debt that General Franco still owed to Mussolini and Hitler. In the course of 1945-46, Spain signed trade agreements with Switzerland, Sweden, Holland, and Argentina, and partial trade agreements with France, England, the United States, and Belgium. But all this was not enough to have Spain admitted into agencies other than those in which its presence was indispensable for technical reasons, such as Civil Aviation and the International Court of The Hague.

Another indication of this evolution was the attempt to give Catalonism a folkloric outlet by authorizing sardanas (typical Catalonian dances) and popular songs, which had been forbidden until then. The government allowed Catalonian theater and even the publication of several art and poetry books in Catalan.

Toward the middle of 1946, there was some agitation taking place in Morocco. The Party of Moroccan Unity presented a plea to the United Nations to investigate the situation of "more than one million Moroccans who lived under conditions of serfdom and isolation, under the threat of bayonets." General José Enrique Varela, the high commissioner, promised improvements and reforms.

These events were denounced in several underground newspapers, and in manifestos distributed at the risk of death. Despite the tremendous disillusionment that came when the end of the world war had not signaled the end of the regime, there was still confidence that pressure from the Allies, or that even a coup by the monarchist military, would depose General Franco. The opposition and those in exile drew up elaborate plans for what would come after Franco, yet no one proposed a viable means of getting rid of him. This accounted for the weakness of the regime's enemies and the strength of the caudillo.

In 1947, the Socialist Indalecio Prieto, an exile living in Mexico, tried to establish an alliance with the monarchists. He went to France to test his position through the Congress of the Socialist Party in exile. He held discussions with Gil Robles afterwards. They agreed that Spain's regime, once General Franco had fallen from power, would be decided freely by the Spanish people. While this pact with the improvised Confederation of Monarchist Forces generated confusion and divided the Socialists from the Republicans who had emigrated from the country, General Franco held an interview with Don Juan aboard a yacht in the Cantabrian and agreed that Don Juan's son Juan Carlos was to study in Madrid. Meanwhile several other pretenders to the throne were encouraged by Franco to air their claims to the throne. Toward the end of 1950 Prieto returned to Mexico, and the monarchist-Socialist entente practically came to an end, although the monarchists continued to agitate within Spain.

In July 1945, General Franco had affirmed that Spain was heading toward a "traditional, organic, and Christian monarchy." In March 1947, he announced that he had prepared a law of succession. On July 6, 1947, by a referendum voted upon by the heads of families, this law was approved and a Council of Regency was established in February 1948. This council was composed of bishops, magistrates, and Falangist leaders. Shortly thereafter, General Franco attacked the Bourbons in a speech, since Don Juan did not accept such a law of succession (which gave Franco the right to grant titles of nobility, for which a very high tax rate was established). He reinforced these measures with municipal elections in which there was only one slate of candidates for whom only the heads of families could vote. The official "unions" were to insure that all electors voted.

There were strikes in Catalonia, and when the Falangists staged a demonstration of their strength one day in March 1951, due to a brief strike in several of Barcelona's industries, the strike became a general one, propelled by underground groups, and the movement escaped the control of the Falangists. For four days the city was paralyzed, the people demanded better food supplies, and only after the strike had ended (although it was soon followed by partial strikes in Vitoria, Valencia, Madrid, and Pamplona, and another general one in Bilbao) the authorities dared arrest the strike leaders. Then the Communists tried to claim responsibility for it.

This incredible fact—a general strike amidst a clearly totalitarian regime, comparable only to the strike of June 1953 in East Berlin—revived worker opposition. But this opposition would end up once again in disappointment, as it became evident that neither the Republican government in exile nor the international workers' movement would lift a finger to sustain it. Yet in December 1953, another strike broke out in Bilbao (aside from numerous strikes in enterprises which took place in many cities as the months went by). The workers in the Basque dockyards left off work for a week when the management refused to pay the Christmas bonus. The repression of the Catholic unionists (Basque Workers' Solidarity) coincided with the signing of the Concordat with the Vatican, which will be discussed later. The Falangist CNS, shortly after this, requested admittance into the International Confederation of Christian Unions, but was refused, in spite of a gesture in favor of the admission made by the pope's nuncio in Brussels.

As hopes that the regime would be replaced vanished, and people began to realize that Franco was not a man who would give up power, political opposition diminished, at least for a time. In inverse proportion, social opposition increased, despite the fact that the workers ran a greater risk than the middle class when they openly expressed their aspirations. Peasant discontent did not find any channel for expression, outside of a growing emigration to the large cities, where they formed shantytowns which were carefully hidden by municipal authorities with masonry fences. The CNS "unions," which included both employers and workers, continued to be the regulatory instrument of the working world. The workers found themselves virtually defenseless—and this in a country in which the worker had been accustomed by a century-old tradition to rely only on the union for protection.

Since the official "union" did not appeal to the worker, membership dues were deducted directly from the paycheck and handed over to the "union" by the employer, something unheard of in Spain before. The order of command within "unions" went from top to bottom: the national union leader was named by the head of the Falange, Franco, and in turn named the leaders of the twenty-four national unions. These then designated the provincial leaders, and these the local leaders, etc. Working conditions such as schedules, salaries, and benefits, were decided by the minister of labor. Within each union there was a tribunal which pronounced judgments when workers or employers presented complaints; a large number of these tribunals' decisions were favorable to the workers, but they did not really alter their living conditions, which were miserable. The static low salaries, in contrast with continually rising prices, forced many workers to look for two or more jobs in order to make ends meet. Only the system of social security, which in theory was sound, compensated somewhat for this situation. It was managed by a National Institute which had been created by the Republic. A point system, in the form of bonuses, which did somewhat augment the incomes of workers with large families, created rivalries and division among workers.

A salary raise was promulgated on January 1, 1954; it ranged from 10 to 15 percent. From 1948 to 1954, the cost of living had risen from 483 to 579 (index of 100 for the year 1936). Prior to this, salaries had been at an index of 183 with respect to those on the eve of the Civil War. Almost four-fifths of the total number of buildings in the country were built before 1900, as was revealed in a general census of buildings and living quarters in Spain. In 1956 there were 796,420 families who lived in only one room, with 1,320,820 living in only two rooms.

The situation in the countryside was not any better. In those places where small farm holdings prevailed, the peasants, thanks to the black market, had become richer. But in places where latifundism reigned, the misery of the peasants can be seen by citing a few simple figures. In 1900, the total population living in towns larger than 10,000 inhabitants came to almost 6 million people, or one-third of the total population. In 1950, the corresponding population was 14.5 million, or more than one-half the total population of Spain.

For those who understand the meaning of the term *caciquism*, the interpretation of this phenomenon will be easy. Spanish industry had not increased from 1936 to 1950. Taking as an index of 100 industrial production during 1922-26, production reached a level of 103.7 in 1935, 91.9 in 1940, 97.0 in 1945, and 124.7 in 1950. (This last index was increased by the increment in mining industries which were not located in urban zones. In the other industries, the index was always less than that of 1935.) Agrarian production had diminished to an index of 64.3 after reaching 52.1 in 1945 and 97.3 in 1935. There seems to be no further proof necessary of the two statements which already seem unquestionable: first, that Spanish industry did not have need of more manpower, and second, that the country people who migrated to the cities did not do so searching for jobs.

Why then did they leave their towns to go to the cities, and once there, how did they make a living? The answer to these two questions is what characterizes the situation in the Spanish countryside, not economically, but socially. Leaving aside the percentage of peasants who went to the city due to a spirit of adventure or desire for change—which was the case especially among the young, who, upon completing their military service did not wish to return to their small towns—the rest of the people who had emigrated from these towns were composed of: (1) Those persecuted for political reasons who looked to the city in an attempt to hide out. (2) Those who lost their possessions through legislation or through the simple decisions of local authorities (during the Civil War, agrarian reform was applied with great rapidity in the Republican zone, benefiting millions of peasants who, after the end of the war, found the lands they had received during the fighting taken from them; in addition, they were looked upon unfavorably or were persecuted for having accepted them). (3) Those whose possessions had been destroyed (due to the war, many people found themselves with neither a home nor their workshops; if they did not have the means to build them or to work their fields while living in another home, they too, were forced to migrate). These people lived in the cities without producing and without resources. They were employed for short periods, became street vendors, or dealt in the black market.

Only the church could make public denunciations of this situation, and it was only after 1949-50 that the church seemed to realize what was happening. Thus, the archbishop of Valencia in 1950 stated at a meeting of employers: "A survey we have made among the workers reveals that 76 percent are hostile to the church, 23 percent have acquired the habit of pilfering on the job, without considering it to be of any moral importance, and 42 percent exist under miserable conditions." He went on to add: "The masses, the large masses of workers, are not on the side of the church, which they hate. But they feel an even stronger hatred toward their employers. A great many workers stated that they gained nothing from burning down churches, while they did gain much more from robbing banks and businesses." One year later, the same archbishop declared that "the worker finds the employers and the rich a hindrance." Nevertheless, "the worker begrudges the confidence he gives to the [official] union since he feels the union to be a political entity; deep down inside, he thinks about a change, without knowing which one. He feels that the legal salary is a salary of hunger." The bishop of Cordova was even more explicit when he wrote a pastoral letter in April 1952: "The worker is worse off than twenty or thirty years ago."

In 1953, a survey undertaken by the National Ecclesiastical Advisory Board of the official "unions" revealed that "the great majority of Spanish workers have not evolved as was desired to a more Christian sentiment toward life." It went on to show that "the economic straits in which they live greatly troubled their spirit, while their bitter life leads them to preferably worry about material aspects, with scorn for all institutions, whether of the church or state, which do not resolve their most urgent problems." The results also showed that workers preferred to see the priests removed from politics, that they considered the church to be more receptive to capitalists, and that they were in favor of the separation of church and state.

Why this sudden interest by the church in social questions, in a country where social Christianity had never managed to take root? It came about due to many members of the church who had begun to worry about the possible consequences of its identification with the regime. Several examples will suffice to demonstrate the extreme this identification had reached. In March 1952, Pedro Cardinal Segura, the archbishop of Seville, published a pastoral letter asking that "the Protestant heresy be uprooted from Spain's soil." (Since 1945 the government had authorized the functioning on a private basis of a few Protestant churches, for the 30,000 Protestants in the country.) The cardinal attributed the government's tolerance to the desire to win U.S. favor. In April 1951, the same prelate had forbidden the dancing of fox-trot and samba in the Seville Fair. In June 1952, Francis Cardinal Spellman, the archbishop of New York, held a lengthy discussion with General Franco on the occasion of a Eucharistic Congress. While the congress was in progress, there were hundreds of preventive arrests. In May 1953, the general director of police ordered that, while sunbathing on a public beach, one had to wear the *albornoz* (a type of hooded cloak). In December 1953, the Cortes approved a modification of the law of elementary education, granting the church and religious institutions the faculty to confer professional degrees on school teachers.

All this explains why, despite the return of some intellectuals to Spain, the cultural situation was cloaked oppressively in gray. The newspapers were the only reading material that was relatively inexpensive and within the reach of the masses. In 1952, there were 104 dailies and close to 2,000 magazines and journals. The total output of the dailies was 2,000,000 copies. Madrid held first place in the number of daily newspapers with eight; Barcelona was second with seven. Four provinces did not have any dailies. The classification of the magazines and journals was as follows: 304 official journals and magazines dealing with the Falangist movement; 512 dealt with religious topics, 114 social and "union" magazines (these were official publications); 129 cultural; 43 dealing with law and legislation; 78 scientific and technical; 108 which dealt with agriculture, industry, and commerce; 55 medical, pharmaceutical, and veterinarian; 30 dealing with tourism and travel; 92 on movies, theater, sports, and radio; and 208 news and literary magazines.

An idea as to the quality of these publications is provided in the description with which Juan José Pradera, national press delegate of the Falange, characterized them in a speech in November 1953: "Monotonous and boring." Pradera added: "The fact that all Spanish newspapers publish the same news, edited with the same syntax, and coming from the same sources, is the cause of this monotony."

In this framework of intellectual stupefication of the masses, the church began negotiations to consolidate its influence. Traditionally, the king of Spain had the right to name the bishops and the primate. This right passed to the government of the Republic and then to General Franco, who came to an agreement with the Vatican on June 6, 1941, by which he would submit a list of six names for each vacant ecclesiastical position. Rome would then select three and from these names General Franco would select the one he pleased. The state paid a salary to priests and subsidized 1,391 religious schools. In addition, the teaching of Catholic religion was compulsory in all schools. All schools had compulsory religious censorship of books and magazines. There was a religious adviser on every newspaper staff, just as there was one in each prison, military headquarters, university, "union," and each group of the Youth Front.

On August 27, 1953, Spain and the Vatican signed an agreement in

Rome, "in the name of the Most Holy Trinity," in whose thirty-six articles it was stipulated that the Catholic religion "would continue to be the only one in the Spanish nation." It recognized the full capacity of the church to acquire and own wealth; religious holidays were compulsory; the creation of an ecclesiastical patrimony was to be studied, which would assure the financial support of worship and the clergy; while these expenditures would be the state's responsibility, all religious possessions would enjoy tax-exempt status; the clergy and members of religious orders would be exempt from military service; it was agreed that, in criminal charges against clergy and members of religious orders these would be tried by civil courts as long as the local bishop authorized it; the church could demand a tithe from the faithful; Catholic religious buildings were inviolable; religious decisions taken in regard to matrimonial questions would be honored by lay authorities; teaching would be adjusted to the Catholic dogma; bishops could demand that books and publications against the dogma be forbidden; the teaching of Catholic religion would be compulsory and the state would see to it that this measure be fulfilled; the state would stimulate the teaching of Catholicism via the mass media; the state would ensure assistance at religious ceremonies in military quarters, orphanages, asylums, hospitals, etc. In exchange for all these concessions, the Vatican granted that: priests would offer daily prayers for Spain and the chief of state; Spanish could be used for beatification ceremonies; privileges for Spain contained in *Hispaniarum fidelitas* (a papal bull of August 3, 1593) were confirmed; among these were the system for naming bishops by a list of three candidates submitted for selection, and that which allowed Mohammedans and Jews in the Spanish colonies to practice their respective religions; members of other religious sects in Spain would have to request permission to practice their cult, and such worship had to take place at a site twenty meters away from the street; the so-called crimes against the faith and its ministers were again in effect (these included blasphemy, punishable by eight months detention, and insults against the clergy, punishable by six years in prison), after having been repealed for more than a century. Teaching freedom continued to be abolished, since the church had to give its approval to all scholarly works.

   This agreement served to calm down opposition by the church, especially that of Cardinal Segura, to all agreements made with the United States, a Protestant country. The church had managed to recover its preeminence among the bourgeoisie, which it had lost in the nineteenth century, and had only partially recovered in the twentieth. The middle class was impregnated with a type of Catholicism more ritualistic than moralistic, while in the towns, everyone went to mass, although no one knew the depth of religious sentiment this reflected. Only in the working-class regions was religious alienation evident, since the bishops themselves recognized it. But in a certain way, the church felt itself to be isolated.

The New State was also isolated on the international plane. Madrid tried to be admitted to the Marshall Plan. But Madrid was not successful, as much because the other Western nations opposed it as because American technicians felt that the economic rehabilitation of Spain would cost too many millions of dollars. In addition Truman had expressed his "repugnance" for the regime on several occasions. The exiles also opposed Spain's entrance into the plan, instead of suggesting that aid to Spain be given through mechanisms which would reach the common people directly. Negrín, from his exile, was the only one in favor of Spain's inclusion in the plan.

Madrid sought another help. It signed an exchange agreement with the government of General Perón of Argentina, and received Eva Perón with an affectionate welcome in 1949. But since Buenos Aires had sent wheat and wool, while Spain had not delivered the machines it had promised, Argentina stopped its shipments after 1950. Many shipments had been detoured to Italy, without disembarking in Spain, to pay the Italian Republic for the debt contracted with Mussolini.

Another means which General Franco wanted to use to force the Western governments to negotiate with him was the establishment of an active friendship with the Arab countries. But this pro-Arab policy proved sterile, just as the emphasis on Hispanity was fruitless in Latin America.

At this point, Madrid turned toward the U.S.S.R. As early as 1946, the London *Financial Times* reported that the Spanish government had allowed Spanish merchants to enter into business on an individual basis with the Soviet Union and that, via Iraq and Transjordania, Soviet goods had been received; other purchases were negotiated in Buenos Aires with the Soviet Trade Mission. In Rome and in Cairo in 1950, via Czech diplomats, an Hispanic-Soviet trade agreement was negotiated, which was never signed, since just at that time the Senate in Washington granted the first loans to Spain. Alongside these contacts, an exchange took place, toward the end of 1949, between Spanish pyrite and Russian wheat. Later on, Spanish mercury was sold to various "popular democracies," as were textiles and oil.

In November 1950, the United Nations heard the British delegate,

MacNeil, make the accusation that while the English Labor government had forbidden the shipment of airplane engines and arms to Madrid, the Communist government of Poland, in November 1948, had sold General Franco 500 engines and propellers. In 1953, the Madrid press praised Soviet anti-Semitism and the Prague trials. In May 1954, Madrid obtained the release of 280 Spanish prisoners, volunteers from the Blue Division which had fought against the Soviet Union in World War II.

During this period, the Spanish regime found itself diplomatically and economically cut off from the rest of the world. The great powers felt that world public opinion, still heated by the memory of the war and the Resistance, did not look with sympathy on Madrid's regime. Without doing anything effective to urge its replacement, they made gestures which were simply symbolic and which, for the moment, allowed General Franco to reinforce his control of the country. The Republican exiles had called for and supported these gestures, giving the illusion that they could overthrow the regime. This was against all lessons learned through history, since the exiles did not take into account that it was the Spaniards who had to suffer deprivations much more than the regime. The exiles, for example, congratulated themselves on the fact that Spain was not included among the countries which would be benefited by the Marshall Plan, without thinking that this would bring about an economic recession in the country with repercussions even after the regime ended.

In Potsdam, the Three Great Powers (the United States, Great Britain, and the Soviet Union) had confirmed (on a proposal by Stalin) their desire to keep Spain isolated from all international contact as long as no democratic regime was established in the country. The Constitutive Assembly of the United Nations, meeting in San Francisco, adopted the same attitudes, excluding all countries considered satellites of the Axis, Spain among them. Later on, in London, the first General Assembly of the United Nations, which met in February 1945, approved a resolution proposed by Panama to exclude Spain, whose regime, according to the Potsdam declaration, had been installed by the Axis. In May 1946, in a meeting of the Security Council in New York, the Polish delegation presented a proposition asking for a break in relations with Spain. The Australian delegate proposed an investigation prior to such action, and a subcommittee was named. In June, the Security Council discussed the report from this subcommittee, and the United States proposed that the matter be carried to the floor of the assembly. Gromyko, the Soviet delegate, opposed this move "so as not to give birth to a dangerous precedent," and vetoed the agreement of the majority of the members of the council to allow the assembly to decide if and when relations should be broken with General Franco. The matter was thus tabled. In November, the Polish delegate convinced the Security Council to remove the Spanish question from the agenda and presented to the assembly a demand for a diplomatic break with General Franco. Before this happened, Trygve Lie, secretary-general of the United Nations, advised the assembly that it consider the Spanish problem, "a permanent cause of friction." In addition, the Belgian delegate Paul Henri Spaak presented an indictment against Franco for having given asylum to the Belgian quisling Léon Degrelle.

It was becoming increasingly clear that internal opposition and the Republican exiles were not suggesting any viable means of overthrowing the regime. As the influence of the European resistance decreased and the Spanish situation became more stable, interest in showing opposition to the Franco regime diminished. Thus, in 1946, the United Nations had recommended to its member countries the withdrawal of their ambassadors from Madrid. Not all members complied with the recommendation, which was repealed in 1950. The United States voted in favor of the repeal of the 1946 agreement, while Great Britain abstained.

The following is a listing of votes cast in successive years in the United Nations regarding the matter of Spain:

| Year | For isolation | Against isolation | Abstentions |
|------|------|------|------|
| 1945 | 51 | 0 | 0 |
| 1946 | 34 | 6 | 13 |
| 1947 | 29 | 6 | 20 |
| 1948 | 14 | 21 | 16 |
| 1949 | 15 | 26 | 16 |
| 1950 | 10 | 38 | 12 |

The Spanish minister of foreign relations, Martín Artajo, commenting on the 1950 decision to send the ambassadors back to Spain, stated that "Spain has the right to be compensated for the economic losses suffered due to the unjust and stupid isolation." At the same time, the UN Assembly agreed to allow Spain to belong to the specialized agencies of the United Nations. In November 1952, several ranking officials of UNESCO, whose publications had been forbidden in Spain, resigned in protest for the admission of Franco's regime.

In October 1952, Great Britain lifted the ban on the exports of military materials to Spain, selling it aviation engines worth half a million pounds sterling. It was only in NATO and the European Parliament that Spain's isolation was upheld. Spain was not admitted into these agencies, despite the fact that Portugal had proposed its entry several times.

Madrid had an able lobby in the U.S. Senate. In April 1950, by a vote of 42-35 the Senate rejected a motion to allow Spain to be admitted to the Marshall Plan. But by February 1951, the U.S. Congress authorized loans to Spain not to exceed 65 million dollars. These loans were requested through the Eximbank. In April 1952, official negotiations began for a treaty between Spain and the United States. After several economic and military missions, a Spanish-American economic-military agreement was signed on September 26, 1953.

The Pentagon found itself strongly influenced by strategic concerns, and thus set aside political considerations. It considered the Iberian Peninsula as a natural air carrier far from the U.S.S.R. Through the treaty with Spain, the United States now had at its disposal one naval base and several air bases, several carbureting and atomic bomb depots. American soldiers stationed in Spain would not wear uniforms and were to try to limit their contact with the civilian population. Spanish authorities promised to guarantee the external security of the bases and airports in which the Americans had their armed forces, while the internal operations were under American jurisdiction. The United States did not promise to defend Spain in case of attack. The placement of the bases was decided jointly, but the United States made use of them as it saw fit. American journalists would have the right to receive and transmit reports without having to submit them for censorship, a privilege which was denied journalists from all other countries. At the same time, the United States granted Spain a determined amount of credit (about 226 million dollars in 1954) which was subject to the approval of the U.S. Congress.[1]

Naturally, this agreement provoked many protests, especially in the United States. The Spanish parties in exile announced that, if they should return to power, they would not recognize the treaty. The aversion of the Spaniards, including the Falangists, toward the United States grew steadily. Today it is a general feeling.

Immediately after signing the agreement, the Falange Congress met for the first time since 1939. The reason for the meeting was that Franco wished to point out that his ideology had not changed because of the treaty. In order to combat "the decadence of the American contagion," the Falangist Congress launched this slogan: "Every Falangist must be half monk and half soldier!"

On the other hand, General Franco was made to promise in the pact "to encourage competition and to place obstacles in the path of cartels and monopolies." Since 1951, when by the Benton Amendment, the U.S. Senate had placed the condition on all loans to Spain that this country reestablish freedom of enterprise, a large portion of the Spanish bourgeoisie had begun to make waves. The bourgeoisie wanted to see to it that the U.S. aid not be monopolized by the state. The Falange answered with a campaign for the redistribution of income and an increase in the income tax. This silenced the bourgeoisie.

As much in an attempt to distract the attention of the masses from these political quarrels, as to reinforce its international position, the Falange promoted a spectacular reaction to the announced visit of England's Queen Elizabeth II to Gibraltar. In January 1954, Miguel Primo de Rivera (b. 1904), in his capacity as ambassador to England, visited Eden to tell him that there would be a "national protest" if the Queen went to Gibraltar. There were student demonstrations in Madrid, organized by the SEU.[2] The result of all of this for the Spaniards was their conviction that the regime had been reinforced. An atmosphere of uncertainty had prevailed in the country since 1942, when they had seen that the Axis was going to lose the war. The uncertainty had now ended. Franco was there to stay.

## NOTES

1. Additional data complete this report: from 1953 until 1964, the year in which U.S. aid to Spain had almost ceased, Spain had received from the United States, for different purposes, a total of 2 billion dollars, of which 600 million was in military aid. The cost of the bases constructed by the U.S. Army, Navy, and Air Force in Spain was some 500 million dollars.

2. Gibraltar was occupied by the English in 1702, during the Spanish War of Succession. The Utrecht Treaty ended the war and recognized this occupation. In 1727, Phillip V had tried to recover the rock by military means. Again in the same century, there were several other attempts, some military and others diplomatic, and London proposed the exchange of Gibraltar for some other Spanish possession, since at the time England was not aware of the strategic importance of Gibraltar. After adopting several pressure methods and trying to negotiate directly with Great Britain, Spain took the problem to the United Nations (1964), which decided that Gibraltar was a colony and that sovereignty should be returned to Spain. The United Nations also advised direct negotiations between the interested parties to put an end to the dispute. London held a plebiscite among Gibraltarians (1967), who by an overwhelming majority decided to continue the status quo, but with greater

autonomy. Madrid offered to respect the basic guarantees and human rights enjoyed in Great Britain, although these were withheld from Spaniards. But there was no agreement, so in 1969, the Spanish government adopted new pressure tactics, such as closing the frontier with Gibraltar and withdrawing all Spanish laborers who worked on the rock.

# 19

# *Obsession with the Future*

As soon as Spaniards became convinced that no different future lay ahead for them, they began to concentrate their efforts in the present in a much more intense way than was necessary to merely survive. They observed the new prosperity and the consumer society that had begun to prevail in Europe. They wanted something similar. The regime recognized this new state of mind and changed its course in an attempt to satisfy it. It realized that this new spirit, far from threatening it, might rather strengthen the regime.

On the political field, concern with replacing the regime was succeeded by the worry about what would come when Franco was no longer on the scene. This led, along narrow and zigzagging routes, to what was called the "liberalization" of the regime. On the economic plane, the worry over subsistence was followed by the desire to live a better life. This led, in different cautious stages, to control of the economy by technicians trained after the Civil War, and also to the reinforcement of the large banks' dominance in industry; this constituted what was referred to as "economic liberalization," which preceded political liberalization.

The forces of the regime did not accept these changes easily. They alleged that these changes constituted a concession to pressures exerted by the Republican exiles. In reality, the political exile was completely ineffective. Before speaking of what was happening in Spain, it is best to sum up the causes of the exiles' failure, which resembles the failure of other groups of exiles, such as the White Russians and the anti-Mussolini Italians in the past, and the anti-

Castro Cubans of today. Perhaps it is more appropriate to attribute these failures to the simple fact that they were attempted in exile rather than to political or ideological reasons.

Of the half million men and women who had crossed the border in February 1939 (280,000 members of the Republican army—including 10,000 wounded—50,000 male civilians and 170,000 women and children) almost one-fourth returned to Spain within a few weeks, thinking that they had nothing to fear since they had not been politically important, nor "had they stained their hands with blood." Those who remained in France were shut in concentration camps.

Only the political leaders were able to enjoy mobility throughout France. In the atmosphere of the emigration, where disillusionment, panic at the sight of the gendarmes, and obsession with one's papers reigned, ideological divisions were personalized and refugee camps were filled with pamphlets and manifestos. Prieto accused Negrín, Negrín accused Prieto, the anarchists accused the politicians, the Republicans accused the anarchists, the Catalonians and Basques accused the centralists. Manuel Azaña resigned from the presidency (he died one year later) and was replaced by Diego Martínez Barrio, the president of Parliament, who convened the Parliaments' Permanent Deputation. On June 26, 1939, the Permanent Deputation declared that Parliament was neither ended nor dissolved, that the Republic was the legal regime in Spain, and that the Permanent Deputation would inspect the administration of what remained of the national patrimony. What did remain was the following: personal accounts in the names of several Republican leaders, in Swiss, French, British, and American banks; the gold deposited in Moscow; and a deposit of gold and jewels in Mexico controlled by the Mexican government. Two organizations of assistance were formed: JARE, animated by Prieto, and SERE, established by Negrín. The latter created several industries in Mexico to employ exiles. The former was able to pay the passage of Spaniards to whom Mexico was willing to offer refuge. With the German occupation of France, this assistance came to a halt, and exiles found themselves having to rely on their own meager resources.

Nevertheless, the Mexican Embassy in Vichy tried to save and send off to Mexico as many Spaniards as it could. On the part of the Communists, there was an effort to select only Communists and their fellow-travelling companions. Several committees, mostly American, were dedicated to helping the refugees, who were obsessed with visas and the unreal adventures with the false papers acquired through traders from Marseilles.

Gradually, the immigration groups in Latin America became stabilized and participated in the economic and cultural life of the country, while many exiles became naturalized citizens. But a logical and tragic phenomenon occurred. The exiled man could not adapt himself to the low standard of living of the Latin American worker. And since the unions had placed certain obstacles to his working as a salaried employee, he wound up becoming a foreman, shopkeeper, or establishing his own business. It is easy to imagine the moral repercussions of this situation for those with social concerns, who found themselves of necessity, in order to subsist, forced to have recourse to the exploitation of the workers of the country that had given them refuge. These men, while continuing to be faithful to their ideals in their groups of exiles, had to behave like any other boss before the local workers. The intimate tragedy of abandoning the ideals for which they had risked their lives, with an end to preserving life itself, had been one of the basic causes of the political sterility of the Spanish emigres.

The exiles were not sterile in the countries in which they became established. In Latin America, they participated in the economic development of each country and, above all, to their intellectual life. In twenty-five years more than 2,000 books were published in Latin America by Spanish intellectuals. They have founded twenty publishing houses and seventeen journals; they have held eighty-seven university faculty positions, and they have translated more than 4,500 works.

Several hundred Spaniards were admitted to the United States, and several hundred more to England, and a small number to the U.S.S.R., while some 60,000 were scattered throughout the Latin American republics (30,000 of these in Mexico), 30,000 in French North Africa, and the rest in France where some 40,000 are still alive.

The French government demanded that Madrid be responsible for the support of the exiles. But Madrid kept its purse tightly closed. During the summer of 1939, Spaniards worked in the fields, badly exploited by farmers of the Midi. Then workers' companies were organized, and these accounted for works of fortification at the beginning of the World War II. On more than one occasion during the debacle, they dropped their shovels, picked up rifles, and fought against the Germans. After this, many thousands of Spaniards were taken to the Reich as forced laborers, or they were put into French prisons. Meanwhile, many others participated in the Resistance movement, 16,000 of whom died in deportation camps. And some realized fruitful gains in the black market.

Narvick witnessed the participation of Spaniards who had enlisted in the French Foreign Legion. The Allies had barely disembarked in North Africa, when a corps of Spaniards was formed in the Free French Forces. This corps participated in the battles at Bir Hakeim, and later in the Normandy invasion. In France, the Spaniards were part of the maquis, worked with the Resistance movement and organized escape routes through the Pyrennees in contact with groups within Spain. "For every five maquis, there were two Spanish Republicans," acknowledged Anthony Eden in the House of Commons. When the Leclerc Division entered Paris, the first tanks which arrived at City Hall bore the names of Spanish towns painted on the iron facade. The political life of the exiles flourished in their aid to the liberation of France. Everyone worked, enjoying, at last, legal status.

At this point, the inevitable result of every emigration, especially inevitable after the successive catastrophes of a civil war and a world war, occurred: the parties became divided. In the CNT the partisans of political collaboration fought with those who were still antipolitical. In the Socialist party, followers of Prieto, Largo Caballero (who died in Paris in 1946 on his return from a German camp), and Negrín were at odds. The UGT was also divided along these three lines. The Republican parties were divided between opponents to communism and sympathizers. A Socialist movement which had split from POUM sprang up in Catalonia.

The division appeared deepest among the Communists. On the one hand, the PSUC lost all its Catalonian content (although it had been merely rhetorical), and one of its leaders, Joan (John) Comorera (1895-1960), was expelled. He returned to Barcelona, was betrayed by his comrades, arrested, tried, and died in prison in 1960. In the Spanish Communist party the crisis began in Moscow, scarcely after the end of the Civil War, among the only ones who had been admitted into the U.S.S.R.: the leaders. Dolores Ibarruri (La Pasionaria) and David Anton received the command; José Díaz, secretary-general of the party, committed suicide. Enrique Castro Delgado and Jesús Hernández (minister of public instruction in 1936) separated from the party as soon as they were able to reach Mexico. Hernández embraced Titoism. All of these internal struggles had tragic repercussions as they offered a pretext for sending some bothersome militants or leaders to Spain, where the man sent was denounced to Franco's police by Communist agents.

Related to this was the matter of the Republicans imprisoned in the U.S.S.R. The student pilots, sailors, and teachers in charge of youth colonies in the U.S.S.R. at the end of the Spanish war, all wound up in forced labor camps (especially in the Karaganda camp). A few of these were released in 1948-50 as a result of a campaign undertaken in their behalf by the Spanish Federation of Deported Persons.

A Spanish Junta of Liberation was created in Mexico. It was inspired by Prieto and lasted only a few months. In August 1945, the Parliament of the Republic was convened in the municipal building of Mexico City (which was declared to be in a status of extraterritoriality by the Mexican government). This Parliament had a sufficient number of deputies to pass resolutions, although there was no representative from the Right. Parliament elected as president of the Republic Diego Martínez Barrio, who several days later gave José Giral the task of forming the government in exile which was greater in Paris. This government included representation of the Socialists, the Republican parties, the Esquerra, the Basques, and a political faction of the CNT. In 1946, its ranks were broadened by the entrance of a Communist minister, and as a representative of conservative Republicans came Rafael Sánchez Guerra (1905-64), a former private secretary of Alcalá Zamora, recently released from a Spanish prison.

Indalecio Prieto stated that the Socialists would not refuse to accept any solution which, although it might be outside the Republican legality, would force General Franco out and give the Spanish people the possibility of choosing their regime. This statement led to negotiations by the president of Cuba, Ramón Grau Sanmartín, who proposed to the Latin American republics that they send General Franco an offer to control a plebiscite in Spain. The suggestion received no reply. This was not the first attempt to put an end to the Franco regime. In 1944, the conservative Republican ex-minister Miguel Maura undertook negotiations in Paris to form a transitional government. The negotiations failed.

The Republican government in exile proclaimed its loyalty to the Constitution of 1931, its desire to pacify Spain, and its relationship, in fact a passive one, with the National Alliance of Democratic Forces, which was at work in the interior of the country. The government successively obtained several recognitions: Mexico, Guatemala, Venezuela, Panama, Poland, Yugoslavia, Rumania, Hungary, Bulgaria, Czechoslovakia, but not that of the U.S.S.R., since this would have meant the return of the Spanish gold. The French government, in 1946, agreed to name Giral an unofficial representative, while also sending a note to London and Washington proposing that they undertake joint action. The consequence of the note was a communiqué from the three powers condemning Franco's regime and inviting the Spaniards to free themselves from him.

But not one of these efforts was fruitful. The gestures of solidarity were many—the closing of the border between France and Spain for some time in 1946, because of the execution of Cristino García for instance—but none brought any practical results. A democratic regime could be pressured by such gestures, but more than this was needed to overthrow a dictatorial regime, especially one headed by a politician with as much ability and sense of power as General Franco.

While the verbal anti-Franco offensive continued in the diplomatic centers, the workers' movement witnessed an upswing in the anti-Franco campaign. The Council of the World Trade-Union Federation met in Moscow and proposed a boycott against Spain which was to begin on June 18, but due to the opposition of the British delegation, the boycott was reduced to a protest campaign. In October, the Congress of Trade Unions, by a vote of 4,500,000 to 1,300,000, rejected the policy of the labor minister of foreign affairs, Ernest Bevin, concerning the Spanish problem. Bevin's position, which was also supported by the U.S. State Department, was that they "detested General Franco's regime," but limited their efforts to an invitation to the Spanish people to free themselves from it. An International Socialist Conference held in Paris in August, condemned General Franco one more time. Several Latin American legislative bodies asked their governments to break off relations with Spain, but the smaller nations preferred to leave the initiative to the big powers.

Meanwhile in France, the Basque government in exile, which had never ceased to function since the loss of Bilbao, was reorganized, while the Generalitat was reconstituted, the former under the presidency of José Antonio Aguirre, the latter under that of Josep Irla, president of the Catalonian Parliament, since the president of the Generalitat, Lluis Companys, had been executed in Barcelona.

As this was going on, the Republican government-in-exile sent protests to the United Nations. This government was headed by Félix Górdon Ordás in 1954, after having been presided by the Socialist Rodolfo Llopis (1946-47) and the Republican Alvaro de Albornoz (1947-52). In 1960, General Emilio Herrera succeeded Gordón Ordás. When Diego Martínez Barrio, the Socialist vice-president of Parliament, died in France in 1962, Luis Jiménez de Asúa (1889-1970) assumed the presidency of the Republic, while the historian Claudio Sánchez Albornoz (b. 1893) was given the leadership of the government, which by then had become a purely symbolic position. In 1970, at the death of Jiménez de Asúa, José Maldonado succeeded him as president of the Republic in exile.

The exiles continued to live enclosed in their groups, with scarcely any contact with the life in Spain, except for workers' organizations that maintained relations with the militants of the same organizations that were active in the Peninsula, at the price of trials and very severe sentences. In 1950, the French government dissolved the Spanish Communist organizations in France (a purely perfunctory action) and placed one hundred Spanish Communists, who had been involved in the CGT Communist wildcat strikes, under forced residence. None of them accepted the offer of being expelled to a "popular democracy." In 1960, De Gaulle's government forbade the exiled press to function, in payment for vigilance by the Spanish police over certain members of the OAS who had taken refuge in the Peninsula, but it was published under the responsibility of French sympathizers.

The apparition of a spontaneous opposition in Spain around 1955, an opposition which owed nothing to the ideologies of the pre-1939 era, nor to the aid of the exiles, changed the situation completely. The émigrés realized that Spain was not the same as it had existed before 1936. They knew that should they return someday, they would no longer play a leading role in the politics of the country. They understood that those who had continued to live in the Peninsula for all those years, without ever losing contact with the people, would be those who could interpret their feelings. They also realized that the Civil War, with all the brutality and its sequel of repression and hunger, was a nightmare for almost all the inhabitants of the Peninsula. But most important, they had spent years outside the country, a country which they no longer really knew, a country where no one outside their family circle would remember them, a country where their friends had died or had changed. Their interest in Spain and their passion for the country did not wane. But the door had been opened to the conviction that it was essential that Spaniards be allowed to decide from within the country. This feeling of separation was felt less in the workers' organizations, since they were the only ones who had been legally organized within the country and the only ones that had maintained a solidarity and a more active contact with their members who lived in Spain.

In March 1957, opposition groups within Spain sent to the émigré organizations a document which outlined a possible alternative: that General Franco be replaced by the monarchy without previous electoral consultation, or that the monarchy be submitted, then, to a plebiscite. The émigré organizations (except for the Communist party) answered in May 1957 that they rejected both, but would accept a third possibility, to which they would pledge their support: that the form of government be selected by the Spanish people. The émigrés had decided not to make the automatic reestablishment of the Republic a condition to any collaboration with the political forces in Spain.

But a portion of these internal forces did make the automatic reestablishment of the monarchy a condition to any action against the regime. In fact, they would not move at all if the Socialists, anarcho-syndicalists, and Republicans did not accept this reestablishment and if the first of these groups, at least, did not agree to form what could be called the left wing of the monarchist regime.

Little by little, strange rumors began to filter into the country; one, that the son of Martín Artajo, the Catholic minister of foreign affairs, had converted to Protestantism; another, that sons of several Falange leaders had participated in secret anti-Franco meetings. In fact, in most families that supported the regime, the children diverged from their parents' beliefs, as they sought a solution to the problems they discovered, problems to which their parents had closed their eyes.

The same thing happens when one studies a language: after a long period during which it seems that one is not learning anything, suddenly one day, the learner begins to speak in the new tongue, badly, hesitatingly, and with errors; but he is understood. This day, the day of the invention of liberty by the generation that had not lived through the Civil War, the generation which had not been taught anything unbiased about the Republic, was the day of the burial of the philosopher José Ortega y Gasset.

When he died in Madrid in November 1955, an attempt was made to link his name to the regime. The students rushed to his burial and, before the grave, spoke of the university students without a university. Pedro Laín Entralgo (b. 1908), dean of the University of Madrid, sent to the noteworthy members of the regime a confidential document, which revealed the spirited state of the youth and recommended more freedom in education. In February 1956, the students addressed a letter to the minister of national education, requesting the removal of the Falangist SEU and the convocation of a National Student Congress. February 7 brought student demonstrations to the streets of Madrid: the Falangists were pitched against the non-Falangists (namely, the Socialists, monarchists, and many without any specific ideology). The Falangists attacked several private schools accused of being "liberal." The disturbances continued until the 11th. On this day, the government suspended two articles of the so-called Constitution, which granted certain guarantees, but which in practice had never been respected. The rector, Pedro Laín Entralgo, and the dean of the Law School were dismissed from their positions. The government accused the students of participating in a Communist conspiracy, but after a month had passed, General Franco replaced his minister of education (Julio Ruíz Jiménez, a Catholic). Some students left the country, while others were arrested. The Communists, using to their advantage the propaganda that the government was creating for them, tried to claim paternity for the student protest, but the manifesto which the students published expressly excluded the Communists.

When the Soviets occupied Hungary, the government, in spite of its verbal anti-Communist position, forbade demonstrations of solidarity with the Hungarian people, after a student demonstration of solidarity in Barcelona which ended with cries of "Long live liberty!" In February 1957, the students in Barcelona requested that the use of Catalan be authorized in the university and that SEU be dissolved. They had called for a congress to examine the university situation, and in spite of the official ban, they held the congress for several hours on university grounds. The Falangists then carted off several students. There were many arrests. Later, those arrested would be expelled from the university and fined. The sum total of these fines was collected by voluntary contributions from all over Western Europe.[1] The students who had left the country informed the exiles of the situation. For the first time, the two Spains had really gotten to know each other. As time passed, some contacts between intellectuals in exile and those within the country were gradually established.

As can be expected, there was disorientation and frequent changes of position within the youth groups. But the will to transform reality and seek solutions persisted. From the recognition of the university problems, an awareness of the country's general problems was reached. The Jesuit Enrique María Laburu characterized the students as follows: "They are antibourgeois, they deny the branding of the Civil War as a Crusade, and they vehemently reject the myth that to be Spanish is to be Catholic; they still do not know what they want, but they know very well what they do not want; what now exists in Spain." The impossibility of meeting openly produced a proliferation of clandestine small organizations, some thirty in total. In the program of all of them social problems were the main issue.

The discontent even had repercussions within the Falange itself. While some groups, those of the founders or "old shirts," proclaimed themselves to be antimonarchists and organized demonstrations with cries of "Death to the King!", other groups tried to establish contact with the nuclei of the opposition.

In reaction to what was happening, a decree reorganized the

Falange, while Minister José Luis Arrese tried to get a series of decrees approved which would modify the structure of the state and give the Falange total power. Within several weeks, there were many intrigues concerned with this project, until finally the non-Falangist group in the government was victorious. From this moment on, the Falange began to lose its political influence.

Another demonstration of discontent was the evolution of several famous Falangists, the most renowned of which was the poet Dionisio Ridruejo (1912-75), who had fought in the Civil War and in the Blue Division. By March 1956, while the government suspended the magazines *Insula* and *Indice*, Ridruejo sent a letter to Martín Artajo protesting against the lack of intellectual liberty and stating that he did not think that the defects of the regime, from which he had separated in 1943, could be corrected. In May 1957, he made several declarations to the Cuban magazine *Bohemia*, which gave evidence of his status as a democrat. Ridruejo spent five months in prison.

The church noted that at the same time that the youth were escaping from under the yoke of the regime, they were also escaping from the influence of Catholicism. With the students, the church tried to reinforce the politics of coercion. Its attitude was different toward the workers, whom the church had never attracted. The Workers' Brotherhoods of Catholic Action (HOAC), accused of being rivals of the Falangist official "unions," stated that in February 1958, 89.6 percent of the workers were anticlerical, while 41.3 percent were antireligious. The Catholic Working Youth, in an unofficial probe it made among 40,000 working families, stated that boys under 14 years of age worked very often, with a workday which often exceeded legal limits; that the lack of proportion between the day wage and the cost of living forced many families to go hungry, driving their members to hold down two or three jobs; and that there was wide unemployment, especially in agricultural areas.

From this background, a series of illegal strikes broke out in most cities, with new forms of combat, such as the strike of streetcar passengers when a fare increase was ordered in 1955 in Madrid and Barcelona, January 1958 in Barcelona, and in February in Madrid (those arrested for these protests were sentenced to twelve to eighteen years in prison). In none of these strikes and protest movements did the Communists exert the least amount of influence. But as the government systematically attributed the responsibility of these protests to the Communists, it also gave them a prestige that their own activity would never have won them. The regime, seeing its dominion over the workers, students, and intellectuals dissipating, wanted to see Communists interwoven into these groups, not only to be able to ascribe to the Communists whatever action these nonconformist forces undertook, but also so that the efforts of these groups be sterilized by including the Communists among their ranks. For this reason some distinguished Communist visitors such as the Cuban poet Nicolás Guillén, the Brazilian novelist Jorge Amado, the Chilean poet Pablo Neruda, found themselves well publicized in the Falangist press, and many Communists were given authorization to return to Spain. The Communists, on their part, were divided as of 1960 into pro-Soviet, pro-Chinese, and pro-Italian groups, while several of their leaders were expelled in 1965 for their sympathy toward the "policentralist" position.

Strikes were frequent occurrences in spite of the fact that "unjustified work stoppages" were illegal. There was a general strike in Pamplona on April 9, 1956, followed by strikes in the Basque Country and in Barcelona. The wage increases ordered by the government, namely one of 15 percent in April 1956, and another of 6 percent in September of the same year, were not sufficient to calm the workers' discontent. In 1967 there was a strike among Asturian miners. On September 3, there was a sit-down strike in many industrial plants in Bilbao. In March 1958, the Asturian miners again went on strike. In Barcelona, thousands of workers stopped work, as did those in Bilbao, while students in Barcelona, followed by those in Madrid, Valencia, and Zaragoza, declared themselves on strike.

The strike not only meant running the risk of imprisonment, but also the loss of one's job. Each time a strike broke out, the workers who participated in it were fired; if later on they were reemployed, they lost their seniority and other benefits. In Asturias, grocery stores were closed down, so that the strikers would be moved by the threat of hunger to return to work. In Barcelona, there were 450 strikers arrested.

The ICFTU (International Confederation of Free Trade Unions) denounced before the International Labor Organization the lack of union freedom in Spain, plus the fact that striking was illegal. In March 1958, the government took a short step backward and had a law approved which authorized negotiations and collective labor contracts; it was no longer the state that would fix salaries to its own taste.

The church found itself divided. One portion of it, namely, the lower clergy, several bishops, and the Jesuits, turned toward social Christianity. Its counterpart was composed of the lay organization Opus Dei, founded in 1928 by the Reverend José María Escrivá de

Balaguer, and was comprised of 50,000 members in seventy-three countries, with 20,000 members in Spain. Opus Dei energetically opposed the Jesuits, while several of its lay members (who took the vows of chastity, poverty, and obedience) entered Franco's Cabinet in 1956. For seventeen years they directed the economic policy of the country. As a group, the Spanish Catholics became less and less associated with the regime, starting in 1956. In a pastoral letter written in May 1956 the primate of Spain condemned totalitarianism.

The monarchist ranks were also divided. Some led by the newspaper *ABC*, were in favor of a monarchy of Franco's inspiration. Others were in favor of a monarchy which, if not liberal, would simply have a popular facade, while a few other members were partisans of a frankly liberal monarchy. The Falange saw itself divided between those who tended toward a monarchy and those who were definitely opposed to it.

Don Juan vacillated and changed tactics. In November 1954, he called together the most illustrious among the Spanish nobility to come to Estoril, with his daughter's debut as pretext. On the 21st of the same month, in the municipal "elections," the monarchists obtained 17 percent of the vote in Madrid and a few thrashings at the hands of the Falangists. In December 1955, Don Juan and General Franco met in Cáceres to discuss Juan Carlos' education. Don Juan stated to the *ABC* that "Spaniards should be united in the ideals of the [Franco's] movement." But in 1957, Don Juan seemed again decided to accept no transaction whatsoever. There were arrests of monarchists who had communicated with Republican exiles. In a visit that a group of Traditionalist leaders made to Don Juan on December 20, 1957, to offer him their support, Don Juan promised to uphold Traditionalist political principles.

Some military men wanted to serve as a bridge to the monarchy, but they dared not take any step, since they were afraid of being overrun by the Left. Only if the Republicans, Socialists, and anarcho-syndicalists declared their readiness to collaborate with the monarchy, could they perhaps launch an attempt to overthrow the regime. But they did not want to run the risk of having the question of the regime be determined by an electoral decision.

After having been in power for twenty years, the same thing happened to Spain's regime that has happened to all dictatorships: the regime had ceased to represent the interests of the class or coalition of classes that had brought it to power, and became a simple caste regime, which represented itself. The regime endured due to the fear of its ex-allies to play the role of sorcerer's apprentices.

In different ways, General Franco affirmed his determination to remain in power. In December 1954, he had Parliament approve the recommendation that his grandson (General Franco's daughter had married the marquis of Villaverde, a physician) bear the last name of his grandfather, rather than that of his father. Thus, instead of bearing the name Francisco Martínez Franco, he would be known as Francisco Franco Martínez.[2] Before this took place, coins had been issued bearing the words: "Franco, Spain's Leader through the Grace of God." On July 18, 1957, a site some forty kilometers from Madrid was officially opened, which had been christened Valley of the Fallen, an underground cathedral. For thirteen years, 700 political prisoners had labored in its construction, at a cost of 75 million dollars. It was to be the caudillo's mausoleum.

The regime had not foregone the use of terror, although it exercised its implementation with more caution. In 1955 Tomás Centeno, a Socialist leader, was beaten to death in the dungeons of the police. At the beginning of this same year, the government promulgated an amnesty which allowed exiles to return. On November 19, 1956, Lieutenant-Colonel Ricardo Beneyto faced the firing squad after he had returned to Spain in the belief that the amnesty was a true one. On the other hand, General Vicente Rojo returned in 1957 and no one bothered him. He had been a colleague of General Franco's at the Military Academy. In 1957 there were still 6,349 political prisoners.

General Franco did realize his political isolation. In February 1957, he tried to extend a few bridges. He changed the government. Exit the remaining Falangists from the ranks of the ministers. Enter members from Opus Dei and a few military men.

The international politics of the regime had also taken a new turn. When France began to have serious difficulties in North Africa, Franco did not hesitate to widen them. The leaders of the Moroccan Istiqlal counted on money from Madrid, arms from Ceuta, and made many trips to Spain. The Algerian Nationalists were also given aid prior to 1958.

By an agreement with Madrid in 1880, the Algeciras Act of 1906, and the French-Spanish Treaty of 1912, the Moroccan Empire remained under the protectorate of France, which delegated to Spain the protectorate of northern Morocco, where 220,000 Spanish civilians lived. From its inception, the Falange had maintained that Spain had been betrayed in Algeciras. During World War II, Fernando María Castiella (since 1957, General Franco's minister of foreign affairs) reclaimed Algiers and Morocco for Spain. When in August 1953 the sultan was dethroned and replaced, Madrid protested in Paris for not having been consulted. Relations with France, which already were rather cold, became frozen. Toward the end of 1955, France put the sultan back on the throne and negotiated Morocco's independence with him. Madrid announced that it would not recognize any agreements in which it had not played a part. After an exchange of letters between the sultan and General Franco, the former went to Madrid in April 1956. An agreement was signed through which Spain accepted the incorporation to Morocco of its protectorate zone, while Ceuta and Melilla preserved their Spanish sovereignty.

When the Suez crisis developed in October 1956, Spain unsuccessfully tried to mediate. Its objective was to reinforce its good relations with the Arab countries and to win France's friendship. The idea of a Mediterranean pact was advanced but failed.

On June 19, 1957, the Istiqlal alleged that the local leaders of their party had been arrested in Ifni, a Spanish possession. In April and May 1956, there had been a rebellion in Ifni, with many killed on both sides. Morocco aspired to declare Ifni part of its territory.

Given that France also found itself in conflict with Rabat over territories in the Sahara, there was a sudden thaw in French-Spanish relations. In November, the situation in Ifni grew more serious. Irregular Moroccan forces (from the so-called liberation army) entered Ifni. The conflict was extended into the Sahara. Madrid sent reinforcements. Militarily, the attack was withstood, but Rabat continued diplomatic pressure. Finally, after long negotiations, Ifni was surrendered to Morocco in 1969.

Morocco had been a difficult test for General Franco: on the one hand, it had alienated the sympathy of a portion of the army; yet it had given him the opportunity to demonstrate that he did possess the essential characteristic of a politician: the wisdom not to persist in the impossible. He displayed this same characteristic in his dealings with other countries.

In October 1954, Franco attended the maneuvers of the U.S. Sixth Fleet. At that same time, General Muñoz Grandes visited the United States. In April 1955, James A. Farley, president of the Coca-Cola Company, received the Order of Isabella the Catholic. Through a bilateral agreement, the United States promised to supply Spain with an atomic reactor. In May 1956, Martín Artajo went to Washington to request loans and to seek Spain's entrance into NATO; he was unsuccessful in both requests (the latter refusal was due especially to the opposition of the Norwegian, Belgian, and British governments). On December 23, 1957, John Foster Dulles, the U.S. secretary of state, visited General Franco after the close of a NATO meeting. Dulles stated that "he could appreciate the fact that there existed a true spirit of friendship and cordiality [between Spain and the United States]."

Relations with the U.S.S.R. were less publicized. It has already been shown that these relations had been begun years earlier. Trade with Poland had remained active since 1949. Beginning in June 1955, Soviet delegates could be found attending international conferences in Spain; before this date, these delegates had been refused an invitation. On September 23, 1955 in New York, Molotov declared to the correspondent from *Arriba* that "the pact of European security which the Soviet government is proposing, naturally includes Spain, if it wishes to participate."

In June 1956, Moscow, by means of the Finnish legation in Madrid, offered General Franco the establishment of diplomatic relations and the extension of ample credit. In October, 557 repatriates returned to Valencia from the U.S.S.R.; most of these had been given refuge in the Soviet Union as children during the Civil War.

In December 1956, the Madrid government announced that Negrín, before he died, had arranged for the documentation relative to the shipments of gold made to the U.S.S.R. in 1936 be turned over to the Spanish authorities. *Pravda* hurried to state that the gold sent by the Republican government had been spent entirely in the payment of Soviet aid to the Republic, which still owed the U.S.S.R. the amount of expenditures outlayed for the refugees (all of whom were Communist leaders and numbered very few) and the children given refuge in the U.S.S.R.

In 1957, Spain signed several commercial agreements with satellite countries: Poland, Czechoslovakia, Hungary, and East Germany. In September 1957, General Franco stated that he would view with pleasure the withdrawal of Western forces from Germany. But what was most significant was the speech made by General Franco when the U.S.S.R. launched its first artificial satellite. On October 8, 1957, General Franco stated: "This could not have been accomplished in a country divided against itself, nor in a country where order did not reign." He added that "the political unity and the continuity of authority and discipline have made this Soviet scientific success possible."

The place where General Franco scored an international victory was the United Nations. On January 13, 1955, Spain sought admission to the United Nations as an observer country. It was granted. (The Republican government in exile had enjoyed this status from 1945 to 1950.) Spain had already been admitted into several specialized agencies. In December 1955 the UN General Assembly, with the pro votes of the United States and the U.S.S.R., and with very few abstentions, admitted Spain to the United Nations, together with a series of other countries whose admittance had been blocked for years, at times by the Soviets, at others by the United States. Almost at the same time, the Interparliamentary Union, meeting in Helsinki, admitted both Spain and the Soviet Union.

The paradox of this admission of Spain into the United Nations is that the Spaniards, both within the country and in exile, and world public opinion, had so soon forgotten that the U.S.S.R. had voted the same way as had the United States, namely, in favor of Spain's admittance. All the resentment was directed against the United States. This general disillusionment was, to a certain extent, a homage to the prestige that, despite all, the United States enjoyed among Spaniards.

This opening of doors made it possible for those within the regime who were partisans of certain gradual transformations to increase their influence. Due to this possibility, a basic change not in the substance, but in the form, of the regime was initiated in 1957. The first results of American aid had begun to be felt. Foreign investments began (especially from Germany and later from America). In 1960, the standard of living of Spaniards was changing. This was not so much due to the action of several ministers who had prepared a development plan under the direction of Laureano López Rodó (of Opus Dei), as to the general tendency of all Western Europe, which had repercussions in Spain, to income from tourism, which was constantly on the rise, and to remittances from almost a million Spanish workers who had emigrated to Germany, Switzerland, Sweden, Holland, and France, also on the rise.

At this time, 42 percent of the active population still depended on agriculture, which accounted for 26 percent of the gross national product; 27 percent were involved in services, which accounted for 41 percent of the GNP, the rest were engaged in industry, which accounted for 33 percent of the GNP. The total GNP in 1962 was 13 billion dollars. Since the end of the war, owing to several laws of "colonization" (never of agrarian reform), 16,000 colonizers had received lands (some 30,000 acres). Irrigation works had been resumed, at a pace of some 75,000 acres irrigated per year, following the plans elaborated by the Republic. Reforestation had been undertaken. In industry, some progress had been made, but the production index was much lower than if it had grown at the same rate as those of the rest of Western Europe.

Some 7.9 percent of the country's population received 36 percent of

the national income (these were landowners and upper bourgeoisie);
9.3 percent received 18.4 percent of the income (the middle class); and
82.8 percent received 44.6 percent of the national income (peasants
and workers). At the same time, 92.1 percent of the less favored of the
nation accounted for 60 percent of taxes. Wage earners received
barely 10 percent more than the amount constituted by profits of
industrial companies. The average income of the Spaniard was less
than that of the average Italian, for example, while in 1936, it had
been greater.

On the other hand, 79.8 percent of the mountains and pasturelands
of Spain were in the hands of 2.9 percent of landowners; 60.7 percent
of the dry lands were owned by 18.1 percent of the landowners, while
70 percent of irrigated lands were owned by 25.4 percent of the landowners. In 1934, the Spaniard consumed 3.7 kilograms of cotton per
year in clothing; in 1960, the amount used was 2.3 kilograms. To buy
a kilogram of bread it is necessary to work for 59 minutes, as compared with 41 minutes in Italy and 12 in England. In 1935, 1.2 kilograms of paper were used per inhabitant per year; in 1960, the figure
was 0.9 kilograms. Sixty-three percent of the state's income came
from indirect taxes, which, as everyone knows, come especially from
the poor man's pocket.

Notwithstanding, the working class is gradually approaching a
standard of living more acceptable than it was prior to the Civil War,
and which had grown worse until around 1960. As one walks along
the street, it is now impossible to distinguish the worker from the
employer by his mode of dress. Workers' homes have begun to make
room for a television set and a refrigerator. Even in apartments
shared by several families (the housing problem is still very serious)
and in the hovels found along the cities' boundaries, this phenomenon still occurs. Of course, the Spaniard pays for these "luxuries"
with a workday of ten, twelve, or even fourteen hours. It is still
necessary, in order to live half-way decently, that all members of a
family work, or that the principal wage earner work a shift and a half,
or two, often in different companies. But the young workers do not
realize that their new-found comfort is overpriced; they are only
aware that they are enjoying it.

In 1974, the annual per capita income reached 2,000 dollars (it had
been 600 twenty years before). But the inequities of distribution of
income persisted, although somewhat disguised by the increase of
the general standard of living. In certain regions, there was a comparable change for the peasantry. In those places where there had been
irrigation works, the small landholdings had been consolidated and

peasants lived a better life. The problem of latifundism and the day laborer still persisted as a dramatic one which saw little relief, even with the en masse emigration of peasants from Andalusia, Extremadura, and Castile to the large cities.

This, naturally, has changed their mentality, despite a certain nostalgia and admiration for the memory of former struggles. Before 1960, the strikes' objective was to avoid a decline in the standard of living. From that year on it became that of attaining a greater share in the benefits of the moderate economic progress.

Strikes broke out in 1962 and subsequent years among the miners in Asturias and the metallurgists in Bilbao and Barcelona. They were important and spontaneous strikes; although the Communists and Catholics tried to manage them, they reflected a state of discontent among the workers who did not respond to ideologies but to concrete facts. The situation was serious enough to warrant that the government finally accede to present a law concerning strikes, which was approved after a long debate (it was the first time that a government project was debated in the Cortes and that the press reported the debate). By this law, strikes with an economic objective were legalized, while all other strikes were still forbidden. Naturally, the law allowed much latitude to the authorities in classifying strikes and likewise in repressing those that they pleased. The same thing occurred with a law abolishing press censorship (1966) and establishing severe punishments (fines, suspension, prison) for newspaper editors who published texts which were contrary to the official ideology or to the security of the state.

This entire picture reflects what has been called the policy of liberalization, initiated in 1965 with a change in government and the replacement of the minister of information, Gabriel Arias Salgado (who had occupied this position since 1937) with Manuel Fraga Iribarne. This policy had two basic objectives: to present an image of the regime that would make it acceptable to the European institutions into which the government had requested admittance, and to prepare for the future, for the moment in which Franco would disappear from the scene. To ensure continuity of command, General Franco named General Agustín Muñoz Grandes vice-president of the council. More books written in Catalan were allowed to be published, while certain intellectuals were permitted to make statements abroad without being punished. One group, which revolved around the leadership of Professor Enrique Tierno Galván, even felt that it would be possible to organize a tolerated opposition. The Christian Democrats were organized in 1965; their main voice was heard through the magazine

*Cuadernos para el Diálogo*, managed by Joaquin Ruíz Jiménez, an ex-minister of General Franco.

On June 1, 1962, during a European congress held in Munich, former leaders of the exiled groups and old and new leaders of the internal opposition came together, discussed the situation, and approved a common declaration. Gil Robles and others, when they returned to Spain, were forced to choose between exile (which would be a short-term one) and banishment to isolated towns. Munich had had the virtue of proving to the Spanish people that the hatred of the past had been eradicated among the forces of opposition. But for the moment, none of this would suffice to open the doors of the Common Market to Spain. In 1968, the agencies of the Common Market decided to initiate discussions with the Spanish government, and in 1970 a trade agreement between Spain and the Common Market was approved.

The international policies of the country continued to change. There was, to a certain degree, a "meeting of the minds" with General de Gaulle and his points of view concerning Europe; the Gibraltar campaign was emphasized when the British government granted autonomy to its colony; religious freedom was recognized by law, echoing decisions of the Vatican Council, although earlier censorship had forbidden the printing of portions of John XXIII's encyclicals; despite pressure from the United States, trade with Fidel Castro's Cuba continued, with Spain sending ships, cars, and other products to the island.

The pressure exerted by the exiles had been gradually lessening, while that from the internal opposition was on the rise. In January 1965, student demonstrations in Madrid and Barcelona demanding the suppression of the SEU, were echoed by professors and students from all over the country. The government yielded a little, modifying the structure of the SEU without suppressing it, and during the summer vacation period it dismissed five professors who had participated in the student demonstrations. Abbot Aureli Escarré (1908-65), from the Monastery of Montserrat, declared to *Le Monde*, the Paris newspaper, that he demanded democracy for his country. At the end of a year, the Vatican ordered him moved to Italy. This did not impede the tendency toward change and greater social conscience in the heart of the church; such preoccupations had already been demonstrated years earlier in several pastoral letters and, since 1961, in several documents written by Basque and Catalonian priests. The year 1967 witnessed new student demonstrations which had now acquired a violent expression; eight universities were closed, and the minister of education was replaced, while the existence of a Democratic Union of Students, although illegal, was tolerated; this organization would vanish when the generation of students responsible for its inception had left the university. The SEU was replaced by official associations which everyone ignored. In 1968, a university reform was initiated, while in 1970 an education law was approved which tried to reorganize the entire educational system; there was a rather lengthy discussion of the law in Parliament and in the press.

All this was a manifestation of a general atmosphere of discontent due to the fossilization of the social and political structures. People thought about the future. They knew that the regime would endure as long as the Generalissimo was alive. But there were some who wished to see the regime changed to make way for a liberal monarchy or a presidentialist republic, while others hoped that the military or a king would assume the responsibility of continuing the regime, without any change whatsoever. Since no one had been able to acquire any political experience, no one knew what the people thought or desired.

The suppression of censorship had greater effects than had been foreseen: the newspapers began to publish news of the strikes, student agitation, and even, in 1969, of a great financial scandal (the Matesa affair) which affected some high-ranking civil servants and bank officials. Books by Marx, Lenin, and Guevara, and even—something of a miracle in Spain—books on sex education began to roll off the presses. Even books on the Civil War, which were more or less objective studies, were published. The movie censorship bureau allowed most foreign films to be shown, while books sent from abroad were allowed to enter the country by mail.

This had surprising results, which were not always positive ones, for the opposition. For example, ways of thinking and fighting could be seen in the youth which did not correspond to the Spanish reality, but rather were an imitation of movements abroad. Among the students, tactics of confrontation began to dominate, which neutralized their pressure for the betterment of the university, while dividing the student movement into many rival factions which competed to demonstrate that each was more radical than the others. A left-wing nationalist separatist movement, the Free Basque Fatherland (ETA), sprung up in the Basque Country which tried to unite the Basques of France and Spain. The movement had the support of many priests, and it employed terrorist methods. Among the workers more spontaneity was shown, as Workers' Commissions were formed within enterprises; these commissions elected their own leaders and tried to fulfill the functions that the official "unicns" did not. Progressive Catholic elements predominated in many of these commissions, while in some of them, Communists captured the power and then the workers abandoned the organizations. There were new strikes in Asturias, Madrid, and Catalonia.

The church experienced a still deeper division among its ranks. The young clergy, which was concerned with social issues, helped the workers' commissions, and in Catalonia and in the Basque Country, participated in the nationalist demonstrations. Even the hierarchy began to oppose the regime and enforce the Vatican II decisions.

In 1967, General Franco took a step toward "normalization" of his regime. By a referendum, a law was approved which eradicated the Falange, replacing it with a National Movement of lax organization and vague principles. Political associations could be formed within the movement (but none existed yet in 1973). Although the people viewed this with skepticism, it was possible that from these associations the parties of the future could conceivably arise. This was not a sign of weakness, since in January 1969, as a consequence of a confrontation between a group of students and a general, a state of siege was declared for two months. The state showed the people that a mere flick of the wrist could bring back censorship, deportation of opponents to the regime, etc.

In July 1969, a new and very important step was taken: General Franco convened Parliament and announced on television that he had decided to designate the infante Juan Carlos (the son of Don Juan) as his successor. General Franco had taken great precautions to have it noted that this did not mean the restoration of the old monarchy, but the "instauration" of a new monarchy through the National Movement. The successor, when he was sworn into this position, promised to support the principles of the movement and took the title of Prince of Spain. The monarchists (the majority of whom were partisans of Don Juan) were disappointed, but almost none of them hesitated to climb on the Juan Carlos bandwagon. One noteworthy occurrence: several members of Parliament dared to vote against Franco's decision to name Juan Carlos as his successor.

In 1969, General Muñoz Grandes, vice-president of the government, became seriously ill and Franco decided to replace him. People suspected that the offensive against Opus Dei led by ministers José Solís, an old-time Falangist, and Manuel Fraga, a "liberalizer," would succeed. But Franco appointed his only intimate friend, Admiral Luis Carrero Blanco, not vice-president, but president of the government. Franco remained in a more distant position, supervising instead of directing. Fifteen of the eighteen ministers were changed. Solís and Fraga were out. The Opus Dei was in force. The Falange were eliminated. The only serious protest was the suicide of a Falangist leader, Francisco Herranz, who shot himself in front of a church in Madrid.

Laureano López Rodó, the economic planning commissary, and Gregorio López Bravo, minister of foreign affairs, both from the Opus Dei, appeared to be those who most inspired the new government, which made efforts to accelerate the modernization of the country. This government could be classified as an authoritarian technocratic one. The trade agreement with the Common Market served for the government to eliminate small and antieconomic companies. The inflation, which was more serious but did not seem to worry the government very much, served as a means of capitalizing the companies which arose from the fusion of previously existing enterprises. Although the balance of foreign trade continued to be on the debit side for Spain, this was compensated by invisible income (23 million tourists in 1970, and 1 million Spanish workers in Europe who sent their savings back to the country). Foreign investment grew and was more diversified (mostly from the United States and Germany, and to a lesser degree from France, Italy, and England). Trade with the Soviet bloc countries increased, and commercial treaties were signed with several of them, while the U.S.S.R. established trade offices in Spain.

At the same time that pressure from the Gibraltar affair was lessening and Madrid's pro-Arab position became less strident, the renewal of the treaty with Washington concerning the American military bases was negotiated; this treaty had been extended twice since 1963. In August 1970, a new agreement was signed by which the United States was bound to defend Spain in case of aggression, as Madrid had requested, but on the other hand the United States did recognize Spanish sovereignty over the bases and granted several loans.

Student agitation declined, owing to fragmentation into dozens of minuscule groups and to their isolation in the country. But worker agitation grew: miners' strikes in Asturias, construction workers on strike in Granada (with four of them killed by the police during a demonstration), strikes of metallurgical workers in Barcelona and Bilbao, and farm workers in Jerez. The Falangist leaders of the CNS, who were removed from the government in 1969, proclaimed themselves as part of the opposition.

The opposition could be classified into three groups: first, the opposition which was tolerated (the Christian Democrat *Cuadernos para el Diálogo*, the Socialist Tierno Galván, the monarchist J. M. Areilza), whose members wrote letters of protest (for example, one to the U.S. secretary of state, William Rogers, on his 1970 visit to Madrid, which the secretary refused to receive, and which resulted in heavy fines for those who had signed the letter). This opposition counted on the support of many businessmen, the bourgeois Catalonists, and a segment of the church.

Next there was the very active Communist opposition, whose militants went to jail, but whose leaders were never persecuted. There was a deep division in the Communist party that followed the Soviet line, from which a former leader, E. Claudín (a partisan of policentralism) separated in 1967. The party condemned the 1968 Soviet occupation of Czechoslovakia, but in 1969 fully submitted itself to Moscow's control. Meanwhile, Moscow had resuscitated an ultra-Soviet faction in the heart of the party, which was opposed to the secretary-general, Santiago Carrillo. The Communists held important positions in the press, the editorial boards, and in several official "unions." They were looked upon with favor by almost everyone, and the bourgeois and progressive Catholics flirted with them. But the Communists had relatively little penetration into the workers' and peasant groups, despite the fact that they had abundant means to propagandize their position. Many thousands of Spanish youth had, for a short time, passed through the ranks of the Communist party, only to leave them with feelings of disgust or disillusionment; many of them simply went home and closed the door on further political involvement. In addition, there were also pro-Chinese Communists groups, Trotskyites who were divided along the three lines of division of the Fourth International movement—Castroites, Guevarists, independent Maoists, etc., all of which merely existed among the students.

Lastly, there was what could be called the latent opposition, which was that of the people. Although the memory of the Civil War and, above all, that of the terror which accompanied it in the Nationalist zone and followed it in the Republican zone, together with the necessity of working long, hard hours, or holding two jobs in order to get the mere semblance of an acceptable standard of living, maintained the workers in their indifference (to which radio and television, controlled by the state and, without a doubt, of the lowest quality in the Western world contributed), there were constant signs of protest and restlessness. There were attempts to channel and intensify these expressions by the small anarcho-syndicalist nuclei, postcouncil Catholics, and Socialists who had been freed from control by the exiled. The results of their efforts in political education would be seen on the day in which the workers could be freely organized. This type of work was also accomplished among the peasants, but still on a minor scale, due to the special difficulties of the means to do so. One must not think that this task of political education was very extensive, nor that it was coming close to breaking down the compartmentalization of the social classes, the isolation of students, and the tolerated opposition with respect to the country's submerged masses. Yet it was the only thing that was upsetting to the police and was the most severely persecuted. The nationalist movements of Catalonia, Galicia, and the Basque Country became very active.

There were no prospects for radical or profound changes in the near future. From the pressures that surrounded General Franco, one triumphant one had emerged: the technocratic tendency, which many term a result of the Opus Dei, since many of those who followed this tendency were members of this religious institution. For the first time in the years that Franco had been in power, he did not play arbiter, but rather took sides. Together with his government, he indicated the tone and direction that he wanted for the future monarchy. All that remained was that which was basic to Franco's personality: his traditional authoritarian Catholicism. Although people continued to speak of the almost infinite number of illnesses from which Franco supposedly suffered, he was strong and mentally alert.

All of this added sparks to the *tertulias* (café discussions) and press comments; yet the people exhibited absolute indifference. Since there were no political parties, the voice of the people could not be heard. In addition, although living conditions had slowly been improving and the second development plan (1967) promised an increase of 25 percent in the national income, there were persisting situations that worried the people more than the petty politics in which they had no participation. These included the fact that, in the south, mass emigration to the cities continued, while the land remained in the hands of the aristocrats, which they devoted to hunting and the raising of fighting bulls, or which they sold to the nouveaux riches, who saw it as a status symbol. In the center of the country, the fields had been depopulated, whole towns abandoned, and production continued to decline. In the industrial regions, workers enjoyed a better standard of living, but at the price of not having a free moment as they continued to work long hours or hold down two jobs. The middle class resented the fact that workers were beginning to live like the petite bourgeoisie. The capitalists were unhappy since foreign capital continued to bear increasing weight on the national economy.[3] In the army, young officers who had not lived through the Civil War, were annoyed that the "old-timers" figured in all the boards of directors and monopolized all the important positions.

It is not surprising that the Spaniards, who have been subjected to more than thirty years of controlled information and education, do not know the recent history of their country. But what *is* surprising is that they seem indifferent to knowing it, even though many books have been published. This indifference is generalized. The "old-timers" remember the Civil War as a hazy period of hunger and fear; the young see it as a pretext for adults to boast. The Spaniards share this cutoff with history with the rest of Europeans; but the causes of World War II have disappeared in Europe, while the basic causes of the Civil War continue to persist in Spain.

This mimicry with respect to Europe is accentuated among university students. If, between 1956 and 1966, these seemed concerned about the country's situation and problems, the new generations, following the model of the European "new" Left, seem to have broken off with the country, or current society, attending to nothing else but their own generational problems. The total alienation among the youth of the different social classes is much greater in Spain than it is in any other country.

In a survey made in 1969,[4] the results showed that 48 percent of the Spanish youth are not at all interested in politics, only 4 percent are very interested, while the rest merely show partial and intermittent interest in national issues. Among students, 27 percent are somewhat interested in politics, while the figure among the peasant youth is 6 percent, and among the workers, 13 percent. Thirty-six percent of the youth of all classes consider the most important thing for the country is that there be justice, while 22 percent see development to be of primary importance. One explanation for this indifference toward politics can be found in the answer to another of the survey's questions: 69 percent of the youth feel that they have no influence at all on political decisions, while the rest feel that they exert a slight influence. Furthermore, all of them agreed that the only way to resolve personal problems is to mobilize friendships. Yet even in the light of that answer, 49 percent felt Spanish society to be a just one. Among those who considered it an unjust society, the figures included 46 percent of the students, 12 percent of the peasants, and 35 percent of the workers.

Regarding more concrete questions, the survey showed the following results: 27 percent felt that the private enterprise system was the best, while 17 percent wanted nationalization of the large companies and 16 percent wanted the entire economy to be socialized; the rest had no opinion whatsoever. Fifty-eight percent aspired to Spain's entrance into the European Common Market, while 40 percent felt that adults were not promoting development, and 45 percent thought that, in any case, the youth could do a better job of promoting it. These young people saw the objective of their existence to be in the life of the family (although only 36 percent of the men responded in this way, as compared to 56 percent of the women). Fourteen percent never read a newspaper, while among those who did, more than half merely consulted the sports and entertainment sections.

Many people thought that all this should be corrected. But no one knew how to correct it nor who should correct it, since no one could participate in decision making. This accounts for the fact that the present seemed blurred, and the future, provisional. Today resembled yesterday, while tomorrow appeared to be only a bridge to the day after tomorrow. And, deep down inside, everyone was somewhat afraid of the day after tomorrow.

## NOTES

1. Since then, student strikes—sometimes professors' also—have been quite frequent, as have been student demonstrations. The police used to send young plain-clothesmen into the classrooms to watch and inform on students.

2. According to Spanish tradition, a child has two last names: first, that of his father, and second, his mother's maiden name. Franco had only one daughter and no son.

3. Some 1968 figures indicate the importance acquired by foreign capital: of the nearly 8 billion pesetas that foreigners invested in Spain in that year, 26 percent was American capital; 22 percent, German; 20 percent, Swiss; 10 percent, Italian; 9.5 percent, British; 4 percent Dutch; and 3 percent, French. As far as the areas of investment are concerned, foreign capital played an important role in the chemical industry (25 percent) the rubber industry (10 percent), the food industry (9 percent), commerce (9 percent), and the construction industry (9 percent). According to law, the participation of foreign capital could not account for more than 50 percent of any given company, unless authorized by the government. But government did authorize it in many cases. In fact, the most important companies in the country were under the majority control of foreign capital. *Mundo*, Bercelona, August 23, 1969, pp. 27-39.

4. *La Vanguardia Española*, Barcelona, April 27, 1969.

# 20

# *A Long Deathwatch*

With the government Carrero Blanco began the long deathwatch of Francoism. The Falange had already passed away in its transformation into the National Movement. But the Falangists—the prewar "old shirts," now few in number, and the more numerous "new shirts" of the postwar period—were still alive. They occupied important positions in the administration, on the police force, in the army, and especially in the official "unions." Although no longer in the government, they continued in the above-mentioned positions, still affirming their loyalty to the old principles. One of these men, José Antonio Girón, Franco's minister of labor for almost twenty years, spoke of the "pending revolution." Yet he did not try to explain why it had not occurred during the quarter of a century during which they were in power. Actually, speaking about it only served to show that they had not exercised power when they had it. It was Franco who had controlled the reins and Franco was no revolutionary.

Falangism had not been the topic of discussion in Spain for a very long time. Francoism had taken over. It was more of an attitude than an ideology: a rejection of democracy, liberalism, and all types of pluralism—religious, national, and political. It was also characterized by a tight hold on traditional norms of conduct, on the "wonders" of yesteryear performed by Mussolini and Hitler (in whose memory annual masses were celebrated in several Spanish cities). This rhetoric was underlined by a tenacious grip on political offices, privileges, the habit of giving orders without accounting to anyone, a superiority complex viewed as "due" the victors, and a nostalgia for victory itself, for the times in which having won the war was almost synonymous with a title of nobility. There was also an underlying resentment as the fruits of victory, which had been enjoyed for a long time, were lost. Nothing remained of the spirit of the New State, although its institutions, which had been adopted, continued. As a last resort, these institutions were clung to, any change in them meeting with opposition; political parties, elections with universal suffrage, or freedom of the unions were dirty words.

Carrero Blanco was a Francoist. Yet he realized that Franco's death would also mean the demise of Francoism if precautions were not taken to maintain it. To this purpose he dedicated the years he spent in power. He was the first president of the government (up until that time Franco had been president, while Muñoz Grandes was only vice-president). Carrero was the first to be named in accordance with the norms established by the constitutional reforms, i.e., as one of the list of three candidates that the Council of the Realm submitted to the chief of state who, in turn, selected the head of government, who was to retain the post for five years.

Comprised of five hundred legislators, of which only one hundred were elected by the heads of families from among candidates who had to be active members of the National Movement, Parliament acquired relative importance. Debates began in Parliament with governmental approval, since the apparently modern parliamentary activity in some of the sessions was viewed as indicative of its possible continuance after Franco.

The government soon ran into a weighty problem: nine militants of the Basque ETA were condemned to death by a martial court convened in Burgos in December 1970. The police demanded the execution of the condemned men since they had been apprehended for having murdered police officers whom they had accused of torturing prisoners. Demonstrations in many cities asked for the pardoning of the condemned men. Many people who had never before intervened in politics spoke out now. The politicization of a considerable segment of the urban population occurred rapidly. The exiles, who organized the customary protest demonstrations abroad, were surprised to see their ranks swell with the presence of thousands of workers in Paris, Geneva, Frankfurt, London, Brussels, Amsterdam, and Stockholm. These workers had likewise been politicized. For years Spain had seen no political executions, and the Spaniards did not want to return to postwar habits. Thirteen governments (the United States not among them), the pope and the Spanish bishops asked for the pardoning of the condemned men. Finally, shortly before Christmas 1970, Franco commuted the nine death sentences to life imprisonment, while allowing the other nine sentences to long prison terms dictated by the council to stand. The foreign protests alone did not account for this rare act of clemency. The kidnapping of an honorary consul in Bilbao by the ETA was also an influential factor.

Many members of the politicized masses returned to passing the time watching soccer games and television, although a significant number continued their activities in clandestine politics. This was less dangerous than it had been in the past, although arrests and sentencing continued at the hands of a special tribunal, the Tribunal of Public Order. Penalties could range up to twenty years for illegal organization and up to twelve years for illegal propaganda (distributing manifestos).

The Opus Dei dominated everything. The Falangists were furious, and at times sounded like members of the opposition. The Opus Dei asserted that it did not interfere in politics, although it did not prevent its secular members from holding political office. The activities of the ministers of Opus Dei justified the name given to its secular members by England: the Octopus Dei. Belonging to the Opus Dei opened every door, made official favors accessible, and resolved problems. Many people, especially from professional ranks, hurried to enroll in the Opus Dei, whose technocratic spirit flattered their elitism. It looked like its reign would be a long one, since the Opus Dei was to oversee the transition. At that time Franco was increasingly showing his age, while the effects of Parkinson's disease were becoming more evident.

It might be said the government repeated Louis Philippe's mandate to his supporters: "Get rich." Highways were built, exporting was subsidized, the building of enormous housing units and hotel complexes was encouraged, and the entire Mediterranean landscape was completely ruined. Madrid, Bilbao, and Barcelona began to figure in the list of the twenty cities in the world with the worst air pollution. Barcelona became only second to Calcutta in population density. Fantastic business deals were made while foreign investments quintupled. The government had the use of a Planning Commission in addition to full powers, as is the case with any dictatorship. Thus it could have coordinated development and protected the environment. Yet it did neither of these. There were soccer teams that paid up to a million dollars for a foreign player. Strikes became more rampant as did illegal demonstrations and clandestine political parties (in 1972 there were no fewer than thirty-seven).

Nevertheless, something happened that made the dreams of permanent power of the Opus Dei vanish. This "something," which surprised and worried the entire country, was the attempt on the life of Admiral Carrero Blanco on December 23, 1973. A bomb had been placed under the street leading from the exit of the church where he went to pray every morning. It exploded when his car rode over it. The car flew through the air, winding up on the roof of the church. Carrero and his chauffer were blown to bits.

Several days of panic followed. Many people did not sleep in their own homes. The first vice-president of the government, Torcuato Fernández Miranda, an old Falangist, took charge in the interim. Several ministers asked for reprisals, mass arrests and even police missions were to be sent abroad to eliminate the perpetrators of the assassination (members of ETA who claimed responsibility for the act). But it was reported that the chief of staff, General Manuel Díaz Alegría, considered a liberal within the context of the regime, cautioned that the army would not tolerate a blood bath.

Just as the people thought that they were on the threshold of a period of regression and police repression, Franco surprised everyone. From the list of three candidates submitted to him by the Council of the Realm, he chose the least likely candidate, whose name appeared only to round out the list—Carlos Arias Navarro. Arias had been minister of the Department of Interior (police) in Carrero's government. For this reason, many thought he would be the sacrificial lamb for not having protected the admiral (who had always rejected such protection).

Arias had been mayor of Madrid and had shown considerable efficiency in curbing municipal corruption. Prior to this he had held positions in the repressive machinery of the regime, in the Department of Interior and, after the war, he had served as military prosecutor in Málaga. He had been a second-rank Francoist until he was named mayor of Madrid.

Suddenly the country found itself governed by a man unknown to the masses. On February 12, 1974, all of Spain knew who he was after he had spoken in Parliament and on television, disclosing his government's program. This program had Franco's prior approval, since it was inconceivable that the caudillo would not decide the policies of his president of government. This program consisted of a promised "opening" (*apertura*), that is, more freedom of expression and, in the future, free elections and political parties, all of which would allow Spain to enter the European Economic Community. The people named these promises the "spirit of February 12."

Unless Franco wrote some very candid memoirs (it is known that he dictated some reminiscences, but no one is familiar with them, in contrast to the script he edited for a film about him in 1968 which was produced but which few people went to see), what prompted him to change course will probably never be known. Yet there can be little doubt that he was responding to the wishes of at least the great majority of Spaniards under fifty years old, that is, those who had not lived through the Civil War.

Immediately the "establishment" of the regime was divided into two camps: the *aperturistas* (in general, those under fifty) and the *antiaperturistas* (the surviving Francoists from the Civil War and those who had been in power before 1969). The people believed that they were heading toward a rapid democratization. In the Ministry of Information, Pío Cabanillas allowed the press much more freedom and authorized the publication of many books that had long been awaiting official authorization. New satirical magazines appeared. Even movie theaters experienced a relaxation of censorship. It was no longer necessary to organize motor caravans to travel to Bayonne and Perpignan, French cities near the border, to spend the weekend viewing half a dozen movies which were prohibited in Spain.

Perhaps the government felt that a little freedom would make people happy. In any case, it was the pretext that the *antiaperturistas* used to win Franco over again. These elements, in favor of maintaining the static regime, were popularly referred to as the "bunker" (reminiscent of the place where Hitler offered his last desperate resistance and died).

The beginnings of the "opening" were not easy, despite the popular support that hailed it and the margin of credit granted it by the opposition. Scarcely a month after taking over the presidency, Arias had to face a serious problem. Josep Puig Antich, a youth from an anarchist group in Barcelona, was condemned to death by a martial court. He had been accused of murdering a policeman. Everything seemed to indicate that in the shoot-out between Puig Antich and the police who were going to arrest him, one officer was killed by a stray bullet from the gun of a fellow officer. The martial court refused to allow a post mortem to be performed on the dead officer to determine if the wound could have been inflicted by the accused. Since Puig Antich belonged to a small, non-Marxist group, the numerous groups claiming to be Marxists and Communists did not actively become involved in the case. They neither protested nor organized any campaigns until after Puig Antich's execution on March 3, 1974. But there was agitation, although the people understood that this execution was a consequence of Carrero Blanco's death and that it had been imposed by the police.

The world economic crisis owing to inflation and the oil problem had repercussions in Spain. Prices spiraled while the government, in an attempt to offset the uneasiness of the people, allowed wages to increase, at times faster than prices. Nevertheless, strikes became more frequent and more exposed to public opinion. The press could now print news of the strikes, conflicts between strikers and police, and the firing of strikers by companies.

The "opening" became even more complicated as a result of events in Portugal, where a military coup in April ended Marcello Caetano's dictatorship. It was of little consequence that the Portuguese military, who suddenly awoke to find themselves "revolutionaries," were acting out of guilt for their behavior in the African colonies. The people hailed the Portuguese "revolution" with indiscriminate fear and enthusiasm. The *aperturistas* used the revolution to their advantage by pointing out that if Caetano had liberalized more the regime inherited from Oliveira Salazar, there would not have been a revolution. Those of the "bunker" claimed that as soon as liberalization had begun the revolution became inevitable.

Meanwhile, in the Spanish Sahara, the situation became more complex. Morocco and Mauritania claimed the area, opposing the Spanish position that the Saharans be granted self-determination. Each of these two countries claimed a section of the desert territory rich in phosphates. An anti-Spanish party supported by Algeria, the Polisario front, asked for immediate independence and organized guerrillas. The people began to fear that Spain would become involved in a colonial war. They were well aware that such a war marked the beginning of the gestation period of the Portuguese "revolution."

Arias and his ministers continued to speak of the "opening." The press, radio, and books reflected this fact, although this was not the case with the treatment of strikers. Unions were still controlled by the old Falangists who now formed the "bunker." Nobody saw the possibility of an authorization of political parties.

It is possible that the "opening" would have continued had it not been for an apolitical accident: Franco's illness. The events that put an end to the "opening" were known by all, even though they were never published in Spain. In June 1974, Franco suffered an attack of phlebitis and had to be hospitalized. He was in such serious condition that Arias convinced him to hand over power to the prince. The latter presided over the meetings of the Council of Ministers and acted as chief of state for six weeks. It was thought that he would now retain that position until Franco's death. But Franco recovered and went off to vacation in Galicia.

An official meeting of the ministers discussed what would have to be done if Franco wanted to govern again. Cabanillas proposed that if this happened, the government would oppose it and, as a last recourse, would resign. All the ministers agreed, but one of them went to visit Franco and informed him of the agreement.

In November, Franco called Arias in and handed him a stack of magazines with pictures of nude women, telling him that Cabanillas would have to resign from the Ministry of Information. Members of the "bunker" had prepared this "dossier" for Franco, who used it to eliminate the minister who had taken the initiative to try to keep him out of power in the role of retired dictator. Of all the ministers, only Barrera de Irimo, the minister of finance, resigned in a show of solidarity with his colleague in the Ministry of Information. The members of Cabanillas' staff also resigned. This was the first time since 1939 that there had been resignations. The new minister of information (who had been undersecretary of interior, the ministry which oversees the police) promised that there would be no "closing." Yet there came a storm of fines and suspensions of magazines, while many books encountered obstacles to publication.

There was another victim of Franco's illness: the prince. When Franco made public his decree which returned leadership of the state to himself, the prince was left in a ludicrous position in many people's eyes. But he said nothing. In time, however, his silence literally became golden, since many Spaniards interpreted it as proof of his maturity and ability.

With the elimination of the most committed *aperturistas*, the people's disappointment grew. The opposition began to move further and faster. The old Socialist party (PSOE) had maintained small groups headed by those in exile. A new wave of youth joined it, sent delegates to a congress meeting in Toulouse in 1969, ousted the leadership in exile, and moved it to Spain. From that moment on, with Felipe González and Pablo Castellanos as leaders, the PSOE grew and became the other force of democratic opposition, aside from Christian democracy with its moderate wing led by Gil Robles and its left wing (which was also moderate) led by Ruiz Jiménez. In addition, Dionisio Ridruejo and Antonio García Ruíz had formed a Social Democratic party. These three forces formed a Democratic platform to coordinate their efforts.

The official Communists, with Santiago Carrillo at their head, began to branch off from Moscow, since they had condemned the 1968 Soviet invasion of Czechoslovakia. They sent delegations to China, Yugoslavia, and Rumania. They sided with their Italian colleagues in their criticism of Cunhal and Moscow. Heavy subsidies from the Italian, Yugoslav, and Rumanian parties placed a professional apparatus at their disposal in Spain. Promising democratic pluralism[1] and independence with respect to Moscow, the Communists organized a Democratic Junta in Paris, with Rafael Calvo Serer from Opus Dei and Enrique Tierno Galván from a small Popular Socialist party composed of professors and students. The European press began to pay a great deal of attention to Carrillo, while the Spanish press spoke mainly about Ridruejo and González. The Democratic platform showed its readiness to give Juan Carlos a certain amount of trust, in the future. The Democratic Junta bridged the gap with the past by supporting Don Juan, the prince's father, who delivered "democratic" speeches in Estoril, proclaiming himself a more liberal successor than his son. Yet many suspected that the two were in agreement and that when the time came, Don Juan would switch his support to his son. No one could conceive of any measures that could force Franco or the army to accept Don Juan.

Further to the Left, although their elitist character should classify them as extreme Right, there were a series of some thirty groups—in constant subdivision—of Maoists, Trotskyites, and pseudoanarchists. Composed almost exclusively of students, some groups resorted to pedantic propaganda which was completely unintelligible to the workers, while others employed tactics of terrorism. Among the latter, the most important were MIL (International Libertarian Movement), to which Puig Antich belonged, ETA, and FRAP (Patriotic Antifascist Revolutionary Front). Not one of these groups numbered more than fifty members except ETA, which was divided into a nationalist Marxist faction and a Trotskyite faction (the latter involved exclusively in propagandizing).

The opposition also appeared very active in professional organizations of architects, engineers, lawyers, and doctors (which in Spain have an official character) with elected leaders. Once one of these associations was won over, it became a loudspeaker for the opposition with relatively few risks for those who spearheaded the verbal attacks. After 1974 a number of neighborhood associations were formed, tolerated by the government probably because it was felt that letting out some steam through them would divert their members from political action. The reverse happened: many of these associations took political stands. Communists and militants of the smaller groups were active, hoping to penetrate among the workers not in the factories, but in their places of residence.

There was even opposition within the army. In 1975, the government arrested eleven military men, captains and commanders, all of whom were also lawyers, engineers, or other professionals. They had formed a Democratic Military Union. The opposition was happy about this, not wanting to see it as a possibly threatening sign, not only because it reinforced the "bunker" in its fears, but also because it foreshadowed a new politicization of the army in the future.

All these groups tried to be active among the workers and in the official "unions," but only the Communists, Christians and the PSOE and some isolated Trotskyst or Maoist militants succeeded. When in 1974 the small "liberalizing" wing of the CNS succeeded in having elections call in the "unions," some 40 percent of the shop stewards elected belonged to opposition groups. Among the workers, especially in Catalonia, there was a renewal of interest in the old CNT, but its militants were too old to take advantage of this sympathy.

The opposition, especially the smaller groups, counted on the help of priests and many religious associations (Catholic Action, Catholic Workers' Brotherhoods, Catholic Youth Workers). Many Basque priests cooperated with ETA. The ecclesiastic hierarchy, which met periodically in an Episcopal Conference under the presidency of the archbishop of Madrid, Enrique y Tarancón, published pastoral letters and studies which highly criticized the regime and Spanish society, calling for democracy, liberty, social justice, etc. In churches and convents opposition groups and strikers found a haven for clandestine meetings. Priests held demonstrations (in 1966, more than a hundred in Barcelona were beaten by the police for having gone to the chief of police to protest the tortures inflicted upon a student who had been arrested). The monastery of Montserrat, in Catalonia, became the site of sit-ins and hunger strikes. In 1974, the Episcopal Conference publicly recognized that the church had "sinned" by taking sides during the Civil War. It was certainly no easy confession to make.

Of course, it was not the entire church that adopted this position. Nor were all Catholics happy with this aggiornamento which, at different times, accounted for the arrest and imprisonment of more than one hundred priests. The serious conflict in 1974 between the Arias government and the bishop of Bilbao, Monsignor Añoveros can also be attributed to it. An attempt was made to deport the bishop because of a pastoral letter he had written. The bishop refused to be deported.

The police did not dare use physical force to make him comply.

In the long run, this attitude of the church has favored the opposition. It also has presented the future danger of intervention of the church in politics, which the Left has traditionally opposed. There is also a virtue in this attitude. It has shown that the regime's support of the church was not based on the tenets of religious faith. Instead, it can be attributed to the fact that the church had defended the privileges of the regime's partisans. As soon as the church began to criticize these privileges, many traditionalist Catholics began to accuse the bishops of being "reds," badger priests, and demand their incarceration. Since within the regime opposition from the extreme Right had arisen due to the "opening," the "bunker" was now composed of traditional Francoists who were sheltered particularly in the official "unions"; a Fascist group which was more concerned with propaganda than with action, centered around the notary Blas Piñar and his weekly *New Force*; the Spanish National Syndicalist party (PENS); several Groups for Syndicalist Action (GAS); and some members of the police force, especially from the political police, who facilitated the functioning of PENS and GAS. There was also a very active group with an unlikely name: Guerrillas of Christ the King. These organizations, whose membership included many youths, specialized in attacking opposition members, burning bookstores which sold leftist literature, stashing bombs in religious sites deemed liberal and, in general, trying to frighten the partisans of change. For example, they "paid a visit" to the homes of several artists and destroyed their furniture. These groups relied on impunity. Many people suspected that the very police force which was to bring the perpetrators of these acts to justice were collaborating with them.

Under Franco, violence had never been absent from Spain, but until 1969, it had been an official violence. From that date on, violence was also dealt from the hands of the opposition in the form of terrorism by small groups, especially ETA. Television, although controlled by the government, had contributed to this new outbreak of violence. In order to paint an image of Spanish violence as a mere plaything when compared to that of other countries, television had propagated the acceptance of violence and its use by both right- and left-wing groups. This dissemination of violence became so great that at times it seemed that the country was populated only by terrorists from either extreme.

The people who were not involved in terrorism had the uncanny ability to guess who the authors of the violence really were. Thus in

1974 when a bomb exploded in a café next to a police station in Madrid, the general reaction was that it had been a provocation to justify repression. The people knew that the police force harbored many elements from the "bunker" who used this influence to their advantage, demanding a strong policy of law enforcement as a reaction to agression against the police.

Meanwhile, the government presented Parliament with a law of local rule, designed to somewhat democratize municipal life and allow a relative amount of administrative decentralization. Parliament, particularly its members named by the official "unions," managed to squelch all reforms. The law that was approved showed no signs of liberalization. Perhaps in an attempt to candy-coat the pill, the government presented another project which was quickly approved in December 1974. It allowed the organization of "political associations" within the National Movement, which in order to function had to adopt the principles of the movement. This meant that there would be no political parties and that the opposition would continue to exist illegally. Only a few elements from the "bunker" accepted the formation of such associations. The opposition, and even the *aperturistas* removed from government in November 1974, rejected them. The latter group, centering around the figures of Cabanillas, Areilza, and Fraga, formed, as a challenge, a business corporation for research, FEDISA. The government did not dare oppose it. There was then one open opposition within the regime.

In March 1975, Arias changed five ministers of his government and, at Franco's suggestion, asked José Solís, an old Francoist with a "union" background, to join his staff. Solís was put in charge of the National Movement. He was the organizer of the "political association" that had the greatest number of Francoists. José Antonio Girón organized the former Francoist combatants in the Civil War.

In the north, ETA showed signs of renewed activity. Several policemen were killed. The government declared a state of emergency in the Basque Country. Thousands were arrested. Members of FRAP began to murder policemen indiscriminately, that is, without identifying the torturers or the more brutal ones. Many thought that they were acting on advice from agent provocateurs serving the "bunker," who had secretly infiltrated their ranks. These murders only served to antagonize not just the political police, but also the entire police force, which felt threatened. In response came true police insubordination, with policemen beginning to act on their own initiative. Some officers were sent to France to pursue terrorists there, place bombs in the homes of exiles and in Spanish bookstores in Paris, etc. This provoked several incidents with the French government.

To hide the fact that the government no longer controlled the police, an Antiterrorist Law went into effect in September 1975. This sanctioned the tactics employed by the police. A result of one such "tactic" was a series of arrests and the confessions of those arrested. In September 1975, this led to several court-martials. At these, it came out into the open that those arrested had been tortured and that in some cases it was impossible to prove that those accused had actually participated in the acts attributed to them. It was common knowledge that the army was not pleased with having to play the role of executioner. Eleven were sentenced to death. Franco commuted only six of these sentences. The five executions were carried out by the police, not the soldiers (September 28). Apparently, the army refused to take charge of the executions. The executions (two members of ETA and three from FRAP) caused a tremendous uproar in Western Europe, although scarcely an eyebrow was raised in the United States.

Europe witnessed a general movement of protest, not in favor of the terrorists, but rather against the way in which the trials had been held, leaving doubts with regard to the guilt of some of those who had been condemned to death. There were demonstrations in many European cities, with emigrant Spanish workers participating in them. Demonstrating mobs destroyed the Spanish Embassy in Lisbon. Other places saw Spanish banks and businesses destroyed. The only concession that the Spanish government made came on September 27—the executions were now to be carried out by shooting rather than by garrote. Twelve European governments removed their ambassadors from Spain for several days. Mexico ended postal communications with Spain and unsuccessfully called for a meeting of the United Nations Security Council (although this attitude of the Mexican government was primarily due to internal politics). Only the United States did not protest.[2]

The European Economic Community decided to suspend negotiations for a trade treaty with Spain. There had not been such a strong reaction against Francoism since 1948, when the regime was isolated in the United Nations. Franco answered exactly as he had thirty years earlier—he organized a mass demonstration of his own in front of the Oriente (royal) Palace. There a rejuvenated and smiling Franco blamed the protests on a "Masonic conspiracy." The prince, in the shadows, wore his poker face. There were "patriotic" demonstrations. One woman who commented that these demonstrations were also illegal was arrested and tried in Madrid. Hours after the patriotic demonstration, FRAP terrorists killed four more policemen.

It is quite possible that the manipulation of nationalist sentiments aroused by the European protests temporarily reinforced the "bunker." But at the same time, the weakening of the Communists in Portugal opened prospects for the opposition, since it showed that the exit of a dictatorship did not necessarily have to lead to Communist rule, as the adversaries of the "opening" tried to make people believe. In spite of the executions and the sudden activity of the "bunker," the desire for an "opening" persisted.

Why did the desire for change become so general after 1960 and not before, despite the fact that before material conditions in the country had been worse? The answer is a multiple one. One can begin precisely with the fact that prior to 1960 material conditions were quite poor. History shows that it is not desperation or misery that generates the desire for change, but rather frustration. Until 1960, Spaniards were too concerned with simple survival to think about politics. When the situation began to improve, frustration set in.

Many factors contributed to this frustration. First and foremost, one factor must be noted, since it is the one most easily forgotten— the potential desire for liberty that is inherent in man and which seizes the smallest favorable opportunity to show its face. Added to this desire is the fact that the population of Spain has risen from 25 million in 1936 to 35 million today. More than 65 percent of the people were born after the Civil War. Cities have grown while the countryside has been depopulated. Spain has gone from an agricultural nation to an industrial one, although most of its exports still come from the countryside. American economic techniques have been imitated indiscriminately.

The lack of first-hand experience in the Civil War facilitated the formation of illegal groups. These in turn led to the desire for change prevailing even among the youthful members of the regime's establishment. Nonpolitical changes (which Franco unsuccessfully tried to avoid) in the church, in religious freedom, in sexual practices, in relations between parents and children, even in dress and language (often in imitation of Western Europe and the United States or inspired by what was going on in these countries), made political and social change seem possible and the desire for them became more evident.

When the government's promotion of Opus Dei and capitalism, together with the improved standard of living, showed that changes, no matter how slight, were possible and conceivable, the desire to increase them and accelerate them became prevalent. Finally the moment arrived when it came to light that the greatest obstacle to change, the greatest protector of immobility—Franco—would disappear. For many, it was preferable to stick with those who sought inevitable change than with those who opposed it in vain. The fear of what would happen after Franco caused many to want it to happen while Franco was still around as insurance against dangers and adventures. Franco and his supporters did not want to play this role of safeguards of the future, so they entrusted it to the institutions that they had created. They sought to enjoy absolute power until the last possible moment. The inherent risks of post-Francoism as seen from the perspective of the Francoists and many non-Francoist moderates would have been avoided or lessened if Franco had retired, or if he had allowed a more genuine and profound "opening," or, in the last extreme, if Franco had died earlier, for example in 1970.

The last five years have reinforced the resistance to change and the pressures for change, that is, the country has polarized. Franco's last month of life, with the long deathwatch and the shift toward the "bunker" that preceded it, made a gradual though rapid change much more difficult. Therefore it increased the risks of disappointment and the risks of an unrealistic reaction from those who had been disappointed.

According to a press release, Franco had suffered from a cold in mid-October. This mild affliction became something much more serious. After several days of confinement in the Pardo Palace, he was moved to a hospital when he suffered a stroke. He then underwent three operations. The government found itself facing three serious problems: terrorism and pressure from the *aperturistas* and the "bunker" at the same time; the Sahara; the illness of the caudillo. Arias spent his days going from the hospital to the Palace of Government and from the negotiation table with the Moroccans to the bedside of the stricken leader.

When they operated on Franco, three or four extra editions of the dailies hit the street. The country's life revolved around the hospital. The fear of what might happen after Franco's death was tempered with a certain amount of indignation of the tenacity with which the doctors insisted upon keeping Franco artificially alive—even to the point of freezing him—and also with the fear that a war with Morocco would break out in the Sahara.

In 1974, Spain had placed the problem in the hands of the United Nations, which sent an investigating committee whose evaluation was inconclusive. The International Court of The Hague also handed down an inconclusive opinion. Morocco and Mauritania did not want the United Nations to resolve the problem. They did not wish to see self-determination by the Saharans, which Madrid advocated, since it would mean that Spain had more possibilities of preserving its material interests in the Sahara, especially with regard to the potassium deposits.

King Hassan II had announced a peaceful "green march" (the color of the Moroccan flag) by Moroccans to occupy the Sahara. Solís, a friend of Hassan, went to Rabat to negotiate (displacing the minister of foreign relations, which caused the speculation that the "bunker" was ready to yield the Sahara at any price to avoid a colonial war which could turn out like that of Portugal). Moroccan ministers went to Madrid to continue negotiations. Many members of the military were distressed by rumors about dirty deals with regard to the Sahara, secret investments in Morocco, and also by the possibility that the government would allow the colony to be occupied without defending it.

By the second week of November, Franco's condition had grown worse. The government decided that the powers should pass to the prince. It seems that the latter had refused to accept them earlier for fear of a repeat performance of 1974, that is, should Franco recover, he would reclaim power, again leaving the prince looking like a fool. But the Sahara matter convinced him to accept. The first thing he did, after meeting with the Council of Ministers, was to go to the Sahara to speak to the Spanish troops stationed there, ordering them to be prepared to stop the "green march" by force if necessary. With this gesture, the prince won the support of the army.

A few days later, on November 15, a government decree declared that the regional languages (Catalan, Basque, and Galician) were national languages that should be protected "as a part of the national heritage." The voluntary teaching of these languages was authorized. It was not very much—a mere gesture which engendered no enthusiasm, although it did allow many places where these languages had been taught secretly to begin to do so openly. In any event, in the regions in which these languages are spoken, they were not given official status, which was reserved for Castilian. But the decree did authorize the use of these languages in the meetings of municipal councils (in actuality, this had always been done, since many members of these councils spoke Castilian poorly; now it could be done legally).

At the same time that agression from the "bunker" increased, so did arrests of members of the opposition. Within the opposition, negotiations began to effect more coordination between the Democratic Conference and the Democratic Junta, although no concrete results were attained. On the other hand, the steps that some members of the opposition took with regard to the small activist groups were fruitful, since their activities decreased for some weeks. The main fear of the opposition was to give the "bunker" pretexts for taking over the government immediately after Franco's death, an event which could only come to pass if the army became alarmed by an outbreak of violence from the radical opposition.

On Thursday, November 20, five weeks after being stricken, Franco died, three days before his eighty-third birthday. The radio and television, which had dedicated many hours to his illness, suppressing all sports and entertainment programs for those five weeks, now spoke only of Franco for an entire week. For seven days the country functioned in slow motion.

During these seven days ceremonial acts took place to mark the end of one era and the beginning of another. Everyone knew that the era that was drawing to a close had been paradise for some, hell for others, and limbo for the majority. No one could possibly know what the era that was about to begin would bring. Some thought it would be a mere continuation of the previous period, others that it would be completely different; the majority thought it would gradually separate itself from the preceding era.

Franco's slow march toward death seemed to have been a month-long recapitulation of the long deathwatch of Francoism of the last few years. In both cases, life was prolonged artificially. It is said that Franco's daughter, the marchioness of Villaverde, had an argument with the thirty-two doctors (among them, her husband) because she wanted to unplug the machines that sustained her father's life and suffering. "Will the king be able to unplug the machines—the institutions—that sustain the life of Francoism and the suffering of the nation?" the people asked themselves. Spaniards tried to guess at the future from the gestures of protocol that characterized the events of those seven days. These events can be summarized in a few lines.

On the morning of November 20, the head of government, his face distorted, appeared on television. He announced the death of the caudillo at 4:40 A.M.[3] He then read a letter (no one knew in whose possession it had been until then) written or dictated by Franco shortly before he fell ill or in the beginning stages of his illness. The letter reported that he who was still chief of state, head of the movement, and generalissimo of the armed forces, asked Spaniards to continue united, in peace, in support of the king. It further requested that they not forget that "the enemies of Spain and civilization are watching." He also asked the forgiveness of everyone in the same way as, in his words, he had forgiven those who had declared themselves his enemies, although he believed, he added, that the only enemies he had were the enemies of Spain.

The body was moved from the hospital to the Pardo Palace, and from there the following day to the Oriente Palace. Hundreds of thousands of people filed by, some old-timers dressed in Falange uniforms, their arm held high, while others wore their military uniforms. Others paraded in silence. Some wept.

## NOTES

1. For instance "Luis," an underground leader of the Spanish Communist party, said in the *New York Times* (October 29, 1975): "We do not renounce a single one of the bourgeois liberties. If the bourgeoisie can dominate in freedom, we want to provide more profound, more real liberties, not less. Socialism can provide the economic base for more complete liberty, without restricting a single aspect of bourgeois liberty." For the time being, it seemed that other members of the opposition had chosen to believe in the good faith of statements like this one, probably because this belief saved them from attacks and criticism from the Communists.

2. With the exception of Arabian sheiks and several presidents from small Latin American republics, no head of state had visited Spain during Franco's reign except two U.S. presidents—Eisenhower and Nixon. It is also worth noting that on December 2, 1975, the Spanish press published the following news item: "The staff of the American base at Rota contributed 99,123 pesetas to the appeal made in behalf of the families of the murdered officers of the police force." It was exactly on the days of the European protests that Washington announced that negotiations to renew the Spanish-American treaty regarding bases had reached a "happy conclusion." The State Department took advantage of the Spanish government's desire that the agreement be signed precisely amidst full world protest in order to obtain concessions. Evidently, no one was worried about the damage that this would inflict on the image of the United States in Spain, which was already quite tarnished.

3. The death certificate, signed by the thirty-two doctors of the team that attended Franco in those last days, a team that had grown proportionately to the discoveries of new complications, listed the following afflictions from which Franco suffered in the last five weeks of his life: Parkinson's disease, severe infarction of the myocardium, severe digestive ulcers with repeated massive hemorrages, peritonitis, severe kidney failure, trombophlebitis of the left leg, bronchial pneumonia, and shock.

# 21

# A King Again

Juan Carlos de Borbón was crowned King Juan Carlos I of Spain on November 22, 1975. He was thirty-seven years old. In the two and a half days that had gone by since Franco's death, the Council of Regents held the power as established by the law of succession. The legislators had been warned to dress for the ceremony in civilian clothes, although some wore the blue shirt of the Falange (among them ex-minister Girón).

According to the formula prepared by the Regency Council of Regents, the king swore to uphold the laws of the kingdom and to see to it that others did so too. He further pledged to uphold "the principles inspired by the National Movement." He then delivered a brief message in which no reference whatsoever was made to the Civil War or the movement. He promised "firmness and prudence" as the king of all citizens, since "a modern society requires the participation of all." He further promised to maintain the efficiency of the armed forces. After expressing his "respect and gratitude" to Franco, he added that "a just order, equal for all, would allow recognition, within the unity of the kingdom, of regional characteristics." He affirmed that Europe should accept Spain, since Spaniards were Europeans. He promised to fight for the integrity of Spanish territory (an allusion to Gibraltar), and pledged that all Spaniards would be heard and that none would be privileged.

The legislators only applauded the references to Franco and Gibraltar, maintaining a frozen silence in rebuttal to the affirmations that seemed to indicate a desire for change. As the ceremony ended, with the king in another room receiving ceremonial demonstrations of obedience and respect from his wife and the ministers, the television cameras, instead of recording this act, focused on Franco's daughter in a gallery. The legislators gave her a much longer ovation than they had given the king. The die had been cast. The king entered his reign not with the support of the institutions but at odds with them. It was foreseeable. Yet it did worry the millions of Spaniards who sat glued to their television sets.[1]

On November 24, Franco was buried in the Basilica of the Valley of the Fallen.[2] Sixty thousand Francoist veterans of the Civil War rushed to this site from all over the country. Although they were old men, they were potentially dangerous, since they were armed. Such a large crowd in Spain could only be armed with the help of government members and the police. After the ceremony ended, the king, accompanied by the government, went out onto the enormous runway facing the basilica. He was met by shouts of "Franco! Franco!" and other openly hostile Falangist battlecries. Aware that some members of the "bunker" had prepared a march on Madrid of these exwarriors and also that the military leaders had warned that they would block the way if they tried to pass, the king moved forward through the ranks of the almost threatening throng that continued to shout with raised arms. Little by little the shouting subsided to the point that the king ended his promenade amidst total silence. Spaniards were not aware of the fact that an attempted coup had actually just been avoided.

Pinochet, Chile's dictator, and several other minor foreign dignitaries were present at the funeral. On November 27, many government leaders witnessed the Mass of the Holy Spirit and the military parade in honor of the king. Among them were the president of the West German Republic, the president of France, the duke of Edinburgh, and many others, including U.S. vice-president Nelson Rockefeller.

During the mass, the cardinal archbishop of Madrid Monsignor Vicente Enrique y Tarancón, delivered a sermon which everyone assumed had been previously screened and approved by the king. In it he said that the church was ready "to speak out and shout if ever necessary in behalf of liberty and human rights." He went on to say that the church would never determine which authorities should govern, but that it would demand that all such authorities act at the service of the community, respect human rights, and protect and promote the exercise of freedom for everyone. As mass was being celebrated, two thousand people, among them several very popular film stars, assembled in front of Carabanchel Prison requesting amnesty. The police detained several dozen of them for a few hours.

The demand for amnesty was not to ease up for months. In the beginning, police allowed demonstrations to take place. The press published many telegrams that asked for amnesty. Professional associations spoke out in favor of it. Everyone thought that this tolerance veiled a desire to grant amnesty, since on November 25, the day after his enthronement, the king announced the pardon traditionally granted in Spain on the inauguration day of each chief of state. This pardon allowed some three thousand political prisoners (together with a number of nonpolitical prisoners) who had been sentenced to less than twenty years in prison for acts other than terrorism. Some fifteen hundred political prisoners remained behind bars. It was for these that amnesty was asked. The people were disappointed to see that the pardon was not amnesty and that it was limited rather than comprehensive. Nonetheless, several formerly imprisoned personalities were now back on the street. One of them was Marcelino Camacho, former leader of the Workers' Commissions who, once he had become a well-known figure, became a Communist. The government began to grant passports to members of the opposition to whom it had formerly refused to do so.

No one knew exactly what constituted the political relationship between Don Juan and his son. The former has not renounced his rights as the dynasty's first in line of succession. In recent years he has made such liberal statements that in the summer of 1975 the government refused to allow him to enter Spain. Many assumed that he would relinquish his rights to the throne when his son was proclaimed king in order to make the latter's task easier and also to provide the still-loyal monarchists with the opportunity to maintain undivided loyalty to the king within the spirit of the dynasty. But Don Juan would have nothing to do with this. Some tried to influence him through the Democratic Junta to which a former advisor of his and a member of Opus Dei belonged. In any event, on November 24, Don Juan issued a statement in Paris affirming that he could not adbicate his duties as son and heir of Alfonso XIII. He added that in order to be of use to Spain, the monarchy must be an arbitrating power which would make it easier to surmount the effects of the Civil War, establish social justice, eliminate corruption, consolidate a pluralistic democracy, integrate Spain into the European community, and to afford the Spanish nation peaceful access to the national sovereignty which would, in turn, give an authentically representative character to the institutions which "until now have emanated from

General Franco." These objectives, he stated, "should be fundamental ones for my son and heir, Juan Carlos." Thus Don Juan's attitude remains unclear.

Nor was anything made clear regarding the new king's intentions until December 16, when his first government assumed power. The history of this government reveals the kind of political difficulties which confront the Spaniards' desire for change. Nearly three weeks had to go by before the first of these obstacles could be overcome.

In order to understand the situation, one must remember that the institutions the king inherited were like a straitjacket tailored by Franco. These institutions were established by the 1966 reforms of the Fundamental Laws. The center of the system was occupied by the caudillo, chief of state, head of government, leader of the National Movement, and generalissimo of the combined air, land, and sea armed forces. Of all these titles, the king had only inherited that of chief of state.

The government (composed of some twenty ministers) was the instrument Franco had used to implement his policies. These policies were supported by Parliament, (Cortes), composed of the 20 ministers; the 95 members of the National Council of the National Movement who were named either directly by Franco as head of the movement, or by institutions whose leaders were chosen by Franco; the president of the Supreme Court and 4 other high officials (of course, named by Franco) and bishops; 25 legislators (*procuradores*) named at large by the chief of state in consultation with the Council of the Realm; 12 university deans and 6 presidents of the royal academies; 30 representatives from professional associations who were elected by members of their respective schools; 150 union legislators (of which 36 were chosen by virtue of the position they held in the union organization, while the rest were designated by union leaders); 115 legislators selected by municipal and provincial authorities; 108 "family" legislators who formed the so-called family third (although they made up less than one-fifth of Parliament), who were elected on the ratio of two per province by heads of families and married women after first having been approved as candidates by provincial authorities.

Thus of the 565 members of Parliament, Franco had named 25 as chief of state, 20 (his ministers) as head of government, 95 (the members of the National Council of the movement) as caudillo, i.e., 140 of them. In addition, all the "elective" positions had been filled by persons named by the government, as much in local and provincial administration as in the unions. University deans were named in the same manner. Therefore, the only legislators chosen by outsiders were the 108 "family" legislators, the 30 from professional associations, and the 6 from the royal academies.

The Council of the Realm acted as the restraining force of both Parliament, which did not seem to need one, and especially, the king. This council was composed of the senior prelate who was a member of Parliament, the senior officer of the armed forces, the head of the general staff of the armed forces, the president of the Supreme Court, the president of the Council of State (the chief of state's consulting body), the president of the Hispanic Institutes, ten members of Parliament elected by the legislators, and the president of Parliament who also presided over the Council of the Realm. Since all the components of this council held their positions by virtue of the head of state's designations, it was indeed the head of state that controlled the council.

The main function of the council was to present the chief of state with a list of three candidates from which to select the president of government and the president of Parliament when these positions became vacant. In addition, it was to advise the chief of state of whether or not he should veto a law approved by Parliament and also with regard to all the measures that affected the functioning of institutions (e.g., reforms of the institutions themselves). For any change in the system to occur legally, the key players were the council of the realm and the Cortes. Both had been named by Franco and were composed of Francoists with a "bunker" mentality.

A few days after the enthronement of the king, the president of the Cortes, an old-school Francoist, came to the end of his term of office. The Council of the Realm presented the king with a list of three candidates for the presidency of Parliament. The most "liberal" name on the list was that of Torcuato Fernández Miranda, an old Falangist who was vice-president of the government when Carrero Blanco was assassinated. Many years earlier he had been the teen-age Juan Carlos' professor of political science. At least the king knew who he was. He then chose him for the position. Parliament ratified the choice. Thus Fernández Miranda, who had always been opposed to permitting political parties, became president of the two key institutions. It was presumed that out of loyalty to the monarch, he would try to help his policies. The situation became precariously balanced. Only with a very strong government or very powerful pressures could the Cortes be forced to commit political suicide.

This political suicide should be instigated by the king's first government while, at the same time, it must try not to commit its own

suicide. Who would preside over the government with such a difficult task at hand? According to the Fundamental Laws, the Council
of the Realm should present a list of three candidates from which the
king would choose. But given what had occurred with the presidency
of Parliament, it was obvious that the king would be forced to choose
from among three Francoists from the "bunker." This would disap-
point the people, exasperate the opposition, and tie the king's hands
and feet. The king decided to ask Arias Navarro to continue in the
post, since he had completed only two years of the five-year term
prescribed by law. He was the lesser evil, although it was this "lesser
evil" who had been forced to order six executions (one in 1974 and
five in 1975) and who had also frustrated the "opening." In 1974 it
was also Arias who, when faced with pressure from the "bunker,"
managed to get Franco to lean toward the "opening." In 1975, it again
was Arias who had managed the transition from Franco to the
monarchy without incident. Nevertheless, the people guessed that
Arias would only be a figurehead. Who would set the tone of the
government?

The king showed a certain amount of courage, since it was he who
had advised Arias of what the general lines of government were to
be. He put men from FEDISA in key positions, that is, men who had
refused to form a political association, mocked the "bunker" by organizing a business corporation to decide policy, and described
themselves as "civilized right-wingers." Manuel Fraga took over the
Ministry of Interior, which meant that he was in charge of disciplin-
ing the insubordinate police force and also of controlling local and
provincial authorities. Thus he was in a position to apply the law of
associations and to propose constitutional changes. His brother-in-
law headed the Ministry of Education, which has always been the
center of conflicts due to the activism of students, teachers, and professors. A friend of his, a diplomat, received the reins of the Ministry
of Information in order to put an end to pressures exerted on the
press and publishing houses. Areilza, count of Motrico, became the
head of Foreign Affairs, so that he was now able to put to good use
the rapport he had gained as Don Juan's advisor and as an active
opponent of Franco, who had previously named him ambassador to
Washington. The rest of the ministers were technicians, almost all of
them FEDISA members except for two Falangists. One of these two
was an old man who had previously been a minister several times—
José Solís. He was named labor minister so that he could deal with
the workers. The other, a young man, Adolfo Suárez was to head the
National Movement, which in light of the spirit of the government,

would slowly disappear. Martín Villa, a "union" man, represented the "unions" in order to guide the transition toward independent unions exclusively for workers, which was also one of the FEDISA's aspirations. This organism, or actually this party, controlled the government. The only error committed was to name a businessman as minister of finance. Fraga was also chosen first vice-president, and thus was in charge of all internal matters.[3] A general considered Francoist was named to the second vice-presidency and assumed power over all military matters (possibly as a step toward fusing all three military ministries into one, the Ministry of Defense).

The government engendered a guarded hope in the masses and also in a large segment of the opposition. After very long meetings lasting for several hours, which were held to name the high officials (which indicates that there had been a lot of give and take with regard to these power positions), the council approved a declaration of principles.

The government, it said, would follow the path delineated by the royal message of the day of the king's investiture. This "implied a constant perfecting of the institutional system [i.e., reform of the fundamental laws], the achievement of pacific coexistence in harmony among all individuals, groups, and tendencies which accept a democratic and just order [i.e., the promise of political parties except for the 'bunker' and the Communists], and the defense of law and public order [i.e., the government and not the opposition, should continue to take the initiative]." After expressing its gratitude to the armed forces (without stating why, although obviously for having supported the king when he faced the "bunker"), it promised to distribute the sacrifices caused by the crisis among all classes, "within the framework of a market economy." In addition, it affirmed that "unity will come to pass through the recognition of regional and local autonomy." It also announced that concrete plans for the application of this program would be revealed in the next few months.

The government enjoyed some immediate success. The police force could be seen dealing less severely with demonstrators to the extent that in some places demonstrators applauded the police. There was no more terrorism from the "bunker," after several of Fraga's pronouncements which threatened to employ police methods to stop it and also after some changes in the local high ranks of the force. Nor was there more terrorism from the group that called themselves leftists (although toward the end of January 1976, ETA kidnapped the son of a Basque industrialist, asking for ransom money, and in February killed two Basque mayors). Areilza visited several European capitals and was well received. The evacuation of the Sahara was achieved with no problems (they emerged in the former colony once the Spanish troops had left, when Algerians and Moroccans confronted each other). Finally a five-year treaty concerning military bases was signed with the United States on January 24, 1976, to be ratified by the U.S. Senate. Kissinger was in Madrid to sign the treaty, that is, to give the new government his vote of confidence. Other European governments were waiting to do so in the hope that such abstention would pressure the Spanish government to accelerate reforms. Washington, then, had declared itself satisfied while Europe still did not seem to be.

The treaty affirmed that cooperation between Madrid and Washington constituted a contribution to the defense of the West, a statement that Madrid had previously requested but never attained. But this did not commit the United States to defend Spain if attacked—something else that Madrid had sought in vain. Yet Kissinger did state that the United States would feel "morally obliged" to aid Spain. The treaty granted the United States the use of the naval base at Rota and the air bases at Torrejón, Morón, and Zaragoza. In exchange, Spain would receive credits and donations of military, technical, and cultural aid valued at 1.22 billion dollars, of which, 700 million dollars were designated for military aid and 450 million for nuclear plants. Although not stated in the agreement, Washington would continue to press for Spain's admission to NATO. Atomic weapons would not be placed in Spain (there have been none since 1966 when a plane carrying an atomic bomb exploded in Palomares on the Mediterranean coast, causing such alarm that the U.S. ambassador and Fraga himself had to go swimming at the site of the accident to calm the people down). Finally, the treaty did not state whether or not Spain could refuse the use of bases as it did in 1973 for transports headed for Israel. Nuclear submarines would be removed from the base at Rota within a period of four years. Naturally the signing of this treaty did not contribute to calming the opposition, whose sentiments toward the United States were on the cautious side.[4]

These early triumphs were soon forgotten amidst more urgent matters. The government decided to postpone elections called for March because it did not wish to see itself constricted for many more years by institutions composed of Francoists. The government wanted the next elections to be held with universal suffrage and political parties, which meant that the Fundamental Laws would have to be modified. The Council of the Realm rejected the government's proposal calling for the postponement of elections. But pressure was exerted, apparently by the king himself, so that finally the Council of the Realm accepted the proposal that elections be held within fifteen months. The government had a little more than a year to achieve the reform of the Fundamental Laws.

This give and take made the country aware of the problems that the government faced. The fact that the king does not attend the meetings of the Council of Ministers continues to give the impression that what Juan Carlos wants is to be a constitutional king who reigns but does not govern. Nevertheless, no one doubts that as long as this type of monarchy is not defined in the laws, the king will have to intervene underhandedly in order to support the pressure that the government exerts upon the inherited institutions.

The arena in which the government erred was in the economy. It has already been mentioned that a businessman, Juan M. Villar Mir, was named minister of finance. This was a bad risk. The economy was in a state of crisis. This was not only due to the repercussions of the world and energy crises, but it was also a consequence of the government's passivity during the last few years and the corruption that had accompanied the growth of the economy. Efficient measures to deal with inflation have not been adopted. In 1975, the annual rate of inflation rose to 20 percent. Wages had been allowed to rise even higher than the rate of inflation in an attempt to keep the workers away from the opposition. The new minister of finance prohibited all salaries from being raised higher than three percentage points above the cost of living increase. Yet he has not controlled either increases in profits or in prices. Nor has he promised rapid fiscal reform, which is indispensable in a country where a national income tax was instituted scarcely several years ago and where the majority of the nation's income is derived from indirect taxation and sales taxes which hit the poor the hardest.[5] The result was immediate discontent among the workers. It also indirectly resulted in a race between the "bunker" (from their union positions), the Communist party, and the "Marxist" groups of the opposition to lead the strikes that broke out everywhere, sometimes instigated by the "bunker" and manipulated by the Communists and other groups. Of course the "bunker" sought to put the squeeze on the government, while the other groups wanted to use the workers' discontent to penetrate the working class.

Fraga, an authoritarian by temperament and a democrat because he sees democracy as the only road possible for the country, became tougher. When the subway workers in Madrid went on strike, he ordered soldiers to man the subways. But there was no repression.

When postal workers, railroad workers, and later Barcelona's municipal workers threatened to strike, he militarized them, thus averting the strikes. Although the police no longer shot at strikers with real bullets, but used rubber balls instead, there were still a great many clashes between strikers and the police force. This has not placated the Francoists, yet it has alienated many people who now feel closer to the opposition and understand the latter's impatience. The use of repressive measures instead of modification of the economic policy always produces such results.

The silent alliance between the "union bunker," afraid of being displaced, and certain segments of the opposition, is possible since the people are growing impatient. For years they believed that when Franco died, things would change. If they have indeed changed to a certain extent, it has been less than what was expected.

For thirty-eight years the "union bunker" had specialized in keeping the workers resigned to their lot. Suddenly it defended them, not out of interest for the workers, but to throw a monkey wrench into the government's operations. The opposition did not dare denounce the collusion between the "bunker" and the Communists for fear that the latter would accuse them of playing into the hands of the government.

There must have been profound differences in the heart of the government. On January 27, Arias Navarro delivered to Parliament the speech which outlined his program. Parliament, according to law, did not have to approve or debate the program, but merely take note of it. It was a speech which watered down the declaration given a month earlier. Fraga listened to it with a frowning face, which the television cameras (now in the hands of Fraga's friends) took great pains to make visible to the eyes of millions of Spaniards. If Fraga temperamentally desired to come face to face with the institutions that he wanted to transform, Arias tried to placate them and gain their collaboration. He said that the reforms the government would propose were "those that Franco would have wanted," and that the government would act "without haste and without pause." The reforms that he announced were: a Parliament with two chambers, one elected by the people and both with equal powers (supposedly the second chamber would be controlled by the Francoists and could block whatever the other chamber approved; actually it would be the present-day National Council of the Movement); revision of electoral laws to permit the participation of moderate groups, but not totalitarian (Communist) groups or subversive or separatist groups (the so-called extreme Left and ETA); reform of laws dealing with illegal association and the right to assembly; unification of the judicial systems (possible suppression of the special jurisdictions of public order and military for civilian crimes, etc.); reform of the fiscal system (most likely imposed to appease the workers' protests). Finally it was announced that the present Parliament would continue its mandate until June 30, 1977. Thus this was the deadline for the reforms.

As for amnesty, Arias promised only a broadened pardon and accused those who sought amnesty of trying to "make legal what is illegal." He stated that there could be no political participation for terrorists, separatists, anarchists, and "totalitarian Communists." He did not speak of independence for unions, but he did indicate that the next Congress of the Union Organization (official "unions") would study its own reforms. In this way he allowed the "union bunker" the possibility of continuing its control.

Arias' speech gave the impression that either the "bunker" had recovered part of its power or Arias was trying to placate it—which for the moment would mean the same thing. Opposition activities increased as soon as they began to see that the hope of relatively rapid changes was slipping further away. In the face of the stolid pressure from the "bunker," which seemed successful, there had to be pressure from the opposition.

ETA renewed its terrorist activity. The other small terrorist groups will probably do the same. The police have dissolved proamnesty demonstrations whose participants now numbered in the tens of thousands, compared to the hundreds who demonstrated before Franco's death. In Barcelona, there was one demonstration on January 31 in which more than 25,000 people participated. The Christian Democrats met in a Madrid theater without asking permission (limiting themselves to notifying the police of the meeting). Delegates from the Christian Democratic parties of Europe were present and were received afterwards by Arias and the king. The Socialists prepared for a similar meeting, and received delegations from the Swedish, Dutch, and German parties.

Aside from the dogmatic groups who want to start an immediate revolution, although they do not know how to do this, the leftist opposition (there is also a right-wing opposition of "pure" Francoists) has demanded a rupture with the past, i.e., the beginning of a constitutional process which will allow the people to decide if they want a monarchy or a republic and, in the latter case, whether a unitarian or a federal one. The Communist party was the first to adopt this position, but many democratic groups have also tended to adopt it when it has been obvious that changes were being delayed. For the democratic groups, it is more of an emotional reaction than a political one. This position is evidently in agreement with the fundamental principles of democracy. But it has no relationship whatsoever with reality. It is logical that the Communists would support it since they believe that no government will afford them the opportunity in the near future to act legally. But it is less logical that the rest of the opposition should support it, since they know that the army would not tolerate this type of process, and that even if it were possible to impose it, it would probably mean a military coup. Their position can be attributed to the fear of being classified as "collaborators" with the survivors of Francoism and to the lack of political experience of the leaders and militants of the opposition groups. In the same way that the brutal reaction of the masses in 1936 can be attributed to the fact that the monarchy prevented the political education of the masses for generations, the unrealistic "purism" of the opposition today and the consequences it can have should also be blamed on the fact that for thirty-eight years Francoism prevented the masses from acquiring any type of political education.

The fact that during these critical months the Spanish masses have displayed a great deal of political sensitivity, does not mean that it can be maintained indefinitely if disappointments continue. Nor does the fact that Spaniards have kept alive their desire for liberty for almost four decades of living without it mean they can improvise the knowledge of the mechanics needed to make this liberty operative. What the government should do is encourage the political education of the masses, which can only be realized via the legalization of political parties and by accepting the risk of allowing freedom of expression to the masses. This risk is an obvious one, since the opposition is led by people who have never been able to act freely in a democracy. These leaders tend to confuse democracy with simple majority rule, with little thought given to minorities. Yet this risk is not as great as the risk the country would face in the long run if Francoism remains.[6]

There are obstacles to the government's fulfillment of this fundamental function. One is opposition from the "bunker." This group is not dangerous for its strength, which does not amount to much, but rather because those who govern form part of the same "establishment" as the "bunker," so that the opinions of the latter will necessarily dampen their spirits. Those who govern have never acted in freedom or in democracy either. For decades they have been accustomed to considering as "wicked" not only the concepts themselves, but also the terms used to express them—*political party, universal suffrage, independence of the unions*. What is required is a considerable effort on their part to suppress this indoctrination. Perhaps the greatest effort they have to make is that which is necessary to free them from the habit of not having to answer to anyone for orders issued. This is prevalent at all levels, even among the opposition. A policeman with whom one argues regarding an order is likely to whip out his pistol. A mayor of a town where the people differ with his opinion is likely to ask the police for help. A minister who is not obeyed often resorts to having the "guilty one" punished. Within the opposition, discrepancy becomes scission, discord, and even accusations of treason. Everyone is used to look at the political life as a conspiracy, nobody trusts the capacity of the common man to decide, and thus the "liberalizers" as well as the opposition see themselves as guardians of the people instead of as their servants. The potential for liberty and democratic stability exists in the country. Lacking at all levels is the development of awareness of both the acceptable and unacceptable methods for governing, deciding, and debating.

The 1974 government of Arias proved that in a total dictatorship it is impossible to show a relative amount of tolerance if one is not ready to quickly broaden the area of what is tolerated. In this sense, the "bunker" was right—dictatorship should remain a dictatorship, the more severe, the better. What cannot be maintained is a velvet-glove dictatorship. General Berenguer had already proven this at the end of Primo de Rivera's regime. Apparently, the components of Arias' second government did not learn this lesson, or if they did, pressure from the institutions the king inherited did not allow them to take advantage of it. Or perhaps they hoped that as they broadened their tolerance base, forces would form that would allow them to counteract the "bunker" without running the risk of being overrun by these forces. It would be a matter of balancing out tolerance with repression, of pressing the accelerator and the brake at the same time. But everyone knows that if this is done, you ruin the engine. The government gives the impression of a swimmer with one foot in the sand and the other in the water, trying to win the gold medal in swimming.

What really happened was that Arias Navarro and his team of old ex-Francoists went under. There was no opposition party registered as a "political association." Consequently, there was no possibility of holding acceptable elections. In the Basque Country terrorism continued both by ETA and the extreme Right groups. The situation was at a standstill until the king intervened upon his return from his first trip abroad to the Dominican Republic and the United States, where he had openly expressed to Congress his desire to democratize

Spanish life. He asked for Arias Navarro's resignation, and then filled his slot as government head with one of the few young ministers who had not lived through the Civil War, a member of Juan Carlos' own generation, and a personal friend of his, Alfonso Suárez.

Suárez, a short time prior to his "promotion," had delivered the best prodemocratization speech in Parliament. As a man, he can best be described as rather cool, with no Spanish Emotionalism—a man with his whole career ahead of him, being forty-four years old. One can expect him not to defend past positions, but rather to create positions for the future, for himself and for the monarchy.

The people greeted his government, composed of young ex-Francoists and technocrats, with skepticism. None of his ministers was outstanding, with the exception of Martín Villa of the Department of Interior, a "union" man who favored a move toward freedom for the unions. Within six months, Suárez had won the confidence of the country. Even the opposition respected him. Perhaps the best way to illustrate the action this government has taken is to present a chronological perspective which will show the accelerating pace of reform and the simultaneous efforts to create a base for the Center in a country polarized between the present and the past, and the need to pacify the Francoists and the opposition alike.

*July 1976.* Suárez formed his government on July 3. In Rome a conference of the Spanish Communist party (PC) was held. The Spanish press was kept well informed of the proceedings. Santiago Carrillo continued as secretary general and Dolores Ibarruri as president. The PC abandoned the doctrine of dictatorship of the proletariat. The head of the Workers' Commissions, Marcelino Camacho, who had tried to conceal his membership in the PC, was elected a member of the Central Committee; thus he could no longer keep under wraps the communist tendencies of the Workers' Commissions.

*August-September.* The king granted political amnesty to all except those sentenced for crimes of terrorism. This exception made the amnesty more palatable to the extreme Right, the police, and the army, although since the majority of those who were not pardoned were Basques, it made the situation in the Basque Country even more tense, with new assassination attempts, entire areas terrorized by the extreme Right, and constant demonstrations. Several mayors and other city officials resigned (in spite of having been appointed by the Franco regime, hoping to open up a new political future for themselves) because the Basque *fueros* (traditional local civil liberties) had not been reestablished. Despite several trips made by the Minister of Interior and the shifting around of Francoist members of the police force, the latter continued to take matters into its own hands.

The opposition continued to be fragmented into more than a hundred groups, but efforts were made to coordinate them by negotiations between the Democratic Junta and the Democratic Platform, establishing the Platajunta. The latter was losing influence as it became apparent that the slogan of "breaking down the regime" or "rupture with the past" had been an error. The opposition did not take the initiative, which remained in the hands of the government. Thus it paid the price for having confused the defense of the right of the Communists to act legally with the assumed duty to ally itself with them. It also persisted in the mistake of wanting to present the fiction of a single opposition. The politically clever procedure would have been to present two: (1) the moderate bourgeoisie in order to capture the Right and negotiate with the government; and (2) a Left composed of the middle and working classes to support the bourgeoisie, organize the workers, and exert pressure as much on the government as on the bourgeois opposition. But, with unity at any price, there emerged the possibility that the ex-Francoists, and even the unrepentant ones, would form the Right of the future, with the government, which should have been the Right, remaining in the Center, leaving the opposition to form the Left. That is, the door was opened to members of the old regime to continue playing a political role which would not have been possible had there been a two-pronged opposition.

Although he had been denied a passport, Carrillo was back in Madrid, his presence tolerated by the government. The Communists acted with greater dynamism (since they had many more resources at their command) than the other components of the opposition, which wasted their time and energy seeking an amnesty which they knew would come anyway. There were numerous strikes, tourism decreased, many workers returned from abroad, and the economic crisis grew worse. Spain owed more than 12 billion dollars to other countries. The index of economic growth dropped from 5 percent in 1974 to 2.5 percent in 1975. Monetary reserves fell to half of what they had been in 1973. No one dared seek austerity measures to deal with the energy crisis. Spaniards were still enthralled with the automobile. The government dared not undertake an energy conservation policy since it needed to neutralize both the bourgeoisie and the proletariat for its policy of democratization. It did not suit their purpose for there to be a great deal of pressure exerted by the workers, so as not to alarm the capitalists and drive them to the waiting arms of the Francoists. Therefore, no effective antiinflation measures could be adopted. Nor could workable wage controls be established, although the government did announce, shortly after it was formed, that it would not allow any salary increases higher than the increase in the cost of living. The government was also powerless to wage battle with unemployment, since it would be very expensive due to the government's reluctance to undertake a tax reform. Unemployment grew, reaching 6 percent by the end of the summer, as did the debit side of the balance of payments ledger. On the world market, the peseta fluctuated on a downward spiral.

But no one paid much attention to the economy, since the people were caught up in the fervor of political evolution. This made the opposition parties refrain from presenting detailed programs which would constitute their platforms, should they be in the government. Thus once again the initiative was left to Suárez and his ministers.

This initiative was evident in a series of energetic measures, adopted without resorting to sensationalism, but rather as mere steps in a process, enacted at the end of the summer vacation period when everyone flees the cities.

*October.*  Civil and military members from the "bunker" continued to exert pressure. Only the military worried the government since they were the only ones who could create a dangerous situation despite the fact that the failure of the military in Portugal had discouraged many interventionists. General Fernando de Santiago—a Francoist and the first vice-president of the government, in charge of defense matters—was replaced by General Manuel Gutiérrez Mellado, considered a liberal.

Salaries were frozen and a law passed by Arias' government to make it virtually impossible to fire a worker without giving him a high severance pay, was repealed. This pacified the wealthy classes without adding to the workers' restlessness, since rivalries among the four illegal but tolerated union federations—Socialist, Anarchist, Communist, and Christian—paralyzed the workers' pressure. The king traveled to France and then to Venezuela and Colombia, another public relations success.

The government suppressed the so-called sociopolitical brigade of the police force which had "taken care of" political matters since much before and even during the Republic. The brigade was hated by members of the opposition for its brutal methods and torture techniques. At the same time, the high command of the police (as has already been explained, in Spain the police force depends exclusively on the Ministry of Interior) was reorganized. There was a general strike in the Basque Country protesting terrorism from the "Bunker" and demanding amnesty for the members of the ETA who were still in prison.

*November.*   In September, the government had presented to Parliament a proposed reform of the Fundamental Laws, which would establish a bicameral system with deputies and senators elected by universal suffrage (except for one-fifth of the senators, to be appointed by the king). A simple majority of the members of Parliament would be sufficient for any constitutional reform. A constitutional parliament was in the making. This proposal would have to be approved by the existing Parliament, that is, the Francoist one. While the government exerted pressure on members of the legislative assembly (many of whom had positions in the administration or in state bodies), several groups from the extreme Left came up with the idea of declaring a general strike on November 12 to demand amnesty and to protest the salary freeze. The PC, afraid of being outdone by the Left, took over the idea. The rest of the opposition did not dare reject the plan. On November 12, from a base of 10 million workers, some 300,000 went on strike. It was a disaster. A teachers' strike and a postal strike also failed since they were manipulated by political groups.

The failures helped the government to convince many undecided legislators, since they were presented with the hope that in the future Parliament to be elected the opposition would not hold the majority. Other members were convinced by more sophisticated means; many of the legislators were not only politicians but also businessmen, and Spanish businessmen seldom make impeccable tax returns. Finally, on November 19, after two days of open debate and 49 speeches, the Cortes voted. There were 425 votes in favor, 59 against, and 13 abstentions. The government announced that on December 15 the reform would be submitted to a referendum as prescribed by law.

*December.*   The opposition scored quite a disaster, which modified election perspectives. After much debate, the opposition decided to advise abstention on the referendum. This seemed completely illogical. To call for elections for years and then to abstain when it came time to support the law which would make elections possible was a subtlety that the Spaniards did not understand. The opposition argued that they were not given equal time in the media to present their points of view and that the reform was not as broad as was desired. The final say, once again, was that of the PC, which viewed abstention as a means of pressuring the government to accept the party. Actually, the government was now in a better position to accept the PC. This was due to Ford's defeat in the U.S. presidential election, which meant that Kissinger would disappear from the scene, and likewise, the pressure the United States was exerting not to legalize the PC. But pressure from the extreme Right still continued. On the one hand, it came from some generals and the police, who found a new support when, on December 11, a group of armed men kidnapped the president of the Council of State, Antonio María de Oriol, an old Basque Francoist banker. The kidnapping was carried out by—or blamed on—a group called GRAPO (the First of October Antifascist Revolutionary Group). On October 1, 1975, this group made its debut by killing four policemen walking the beat. Many people suspected in 1975 and continued to suspect in 1976 that GRAPO was either an invention of the extreme Right or was manipulated by agents of the extreme Right, since its actions in 1975 served to reinforce Francoism in its last months and could now serve to reinforce those who opposed constitutional reform. The Francoists could say: "As soon as democracy is even mentioned, look what happens—terrorists are rampant." Undoubtedly, this would lead many voters to oppose reform. In exchange for Oriol, the terrorists demanded the release of fifteen men who had been sentenced. It seemed that the government was preparing to grant amnesty to the terrorists after the referendum. But the kidnapping made this a political impossibility, since it would have been viewed as a concession to the terrorists.

At the beginning of December the Socialist party (PSOE) held its congress. It had previously been scheduled for November, but it was postponed due to a secret agreement with the government so as not to give a pretext to the enemies of reform while it was being debated in the Cortes. This proves that the Socialists, who advocated abstention, actually wanted the reform, which in turn makes its abstentionist position even more incongruous. In an attempt to explain this position, it has even been suggested that the government encouraged it since it was feared that if the opposition voted in favor of reform, many who would have approved it would vote against it so as not to vote with the opposition. The PSOE Congress was a spectacular success with Mitterrand, Willy Brandt, Olaf Palme, and other Socialist leaders in attendance. It decided to seek the elimination of U.S. military bases in Spain (while Carrillo, leader of the PC, stated that he was not opposed to the existence of the bases).

The referendum took place on the 15th. Ninety-four percent of the votes were in favor of reform, 2.6 percent against, and 3.4 percent were blank. The abstention campaign gleaned 25 percent of the votes, of which at least 10 percent should be discounted as normal abstentions due to apathy, illness, absence, or other reasons. The people— as one Catalonian member of the opposition put it—defeated the opposition and the Francoists. In those areas with the greatest number of "no" votes, these did not exceed 6 percent. Abstentions were especially strong in the Basque Country (40 percent) and in Catalonia (25 percent). Outside of these regions, no more than 10 percent of the voters abstained.

Reinforced by the success of the referendum, the government maneuvered in order to strengthen the centrist and reforming position and undermine the forces that were more dangerous than the opposition: the extreme Right. On December 22, PC leader Santiago Carrillo was arrested. The arrest was carried out by policemen who had tried to put the squeeze on the government after Carrillo had provoked it by holding a press conference in Madrid. It was no longer possible to look the other way. Immediately there were protest demonstrations against the arrest. The government used the occasion to its advantage to change the high command of the police force, replacing these high officials with others who were not such staunch Francoists. In addition, General Campano, the Francoist head of the Civil Guard, was replaced by General Antonio Ibáñez. Several dozen policemen were also arrested for organizing antigovernment demonstrations. The problem of the police force continued to be the largest thorn in the side of the government, since it was the police force on which the "bunker" relied.

On the 26th, the government recognized Catalan as the coofficial language (with Spanish) of Catalonia. Three days later, a street which had been named in honor of one of the generals involved in the 1936 uprising was renamed for Pau Casals, the famous Catalonian musician who had systematically opposed Franco and had died in exile.

On December 30, Carrillo was released on bail and was indicted for illegal entry into the country, a crime which carries a meaningless sentence. At the same time, the government eliminated the Public Order Tribunal, which had been responsible for political repression since 1960. Political crimes and even terrorist activities thus fell under civil jurisdiction, no longer tried by military authorities. Although this irritated the extreme Right, it also satisfied many younger military men who viewed the police role played by the army as distasteful.

*January 1977.* This should mark the year in which Spain recovered a democratic system and ceased to be a people under tutelage. But the "bunker" still did not accept the change. On January 24, a group from GRAPO kidnapped General Emilio Villaescusa, president of the Military Supreme Court. Next, five Communist labor lawyers were murdered in their offices by terrorists from the Right. Three policemen were killed on the street by GRAPO. For the first time, several members of the "bunker" were arrested as well as members of extreme leftist groups. The government suspended constitutional rights. Suárez, in a television broadcast, pleaded for tranquility, assuring the people that terrorism would not prevent the democratization of the political system.

*February.* A new step toward the elections was taken on February 8. A legal decree established a registry of political parties, open to all parties wishing to register. All of these would have the right to participate in the elections. If the government wished to prevent the registration of a given party, it had to appeal against it to the Supreme Court, which had to deliver its decision within thirty days. Three days later, the PSOE was the first party of the opposition to register. At the same time, by another legal decree, military men were forbidden to actively intervene in politics and "to publicly express their political preferences."

The measure was a clever one, in that it allowed the government to oppose registration of the PC, thus pacifying the "bunker," while allowing the Supreme Court to rule that the PC had the right to register. This was possible since, after the many statements by Communist leaders, it could not be said that the party obeyed any foreign discipline nor that it sought to install a totalitarian system—the two conditions set by the law of political associations of Arias' government to refuse registration. The legal situation was confusing—there were laws which cancelled each other out. Yet, in the country's situation, this was of little importance. Everyone knew that it was simply a matter of preserving form, of saving face for the Francoists.

On February 9, while the king was in Rome being received by the pope, the government established diplomatic relations with the U.S.S.R. and with all "peoples' democracies." Franco had already established relations with East Germany and China, and had maintained commercial relations with all the Communist countries. Recognition of the U.S.S.R. was at odds with the "gold problem," since

Madrid had demanded the return of the gold from the Bank of Spain which had been sent to Moscow during the war to pay in advance for the weapons that Stalin sold to the Republic. But apparently this demand had been cast aside. At some other point in time, recognition of the U.S.S.R. would have meant submission of the PC to the desires of the government in Moscow. But now, with the PC in the Eurocommunist mainstream, there would be no important political repercussions. In order to emphasize its distance from Moscow, the PC began to organize a conference of Eurocommunist parties "in defense of civil rights in the U.S.S.R." No criticism of the U.S.S.R. came out of this meeting. Nevertheless, these Communist gestures of pacification toward Washington, the government, and the army did not inspire a great deal of confidence within the opposition, since they coincided with a reinforcement of PC activities which, by employing Stalinist methods (defamation, underhanded threats, voting by a show of hands, manipulation of strikes, etc.), tried to undermine its allied parties. Carrillo spoke like Berlinguer and acted like Cunhal; the party had achieved independence, replacing the old loyalty to the U.S.S.R.

On the 12th, the police found out where Oriol and Villaescusa had been held and freed them. They had not been harmed. This reinforced the popular belief that the whole episode had been a maneuver by the extreme Right. No one knew whether the PC would be able to participate in the elections, although it was taken for granted that Communists would figure in the candidate lists of some of the smaller parties that had played into the PC's hands. In this way, the emotional pledge of the opposition toward the PC would finally disappear. It would be possible to form electoral alliances with related groups, leaving aside the myth of the opposition's united front. Such was the view as seen from the vantage point of March 1977, when without a word being spoken, the election campaign had, in fact, already begun.

*March.*   Once the road was open to the legalization of political parties, it became necessary to open the road to freely organized unions. The right to strike was recognized on March 5. A month later, on April 2, the Francoist CNS was suspended and its resources, including some 30,000 bureaucrats, reverted to the state.

March 11 marked a new amnesty decree which freed 170 prisoners, including 15 sentenced to life imprisonment. Yet that still left some 50 Basque prisoners accused of terrorism. A campaign to free them began in the Basque Country. It was to continue for months, and was marked by demonstrations, confrontations with the police, city government protests, kidnappings, assassination attempts against police officers (carried out by ETA, which resumed its terrorist activities), and general strikes. Total cost, some 20 lives.

At the end of the month, the king and queen visited Jordan and Egypt. Suárez, the head of government, fearful of the advances made by the Popular Alliance—a coalition of Francoist groups led by ex-minister Fraga Iribarne—maneuvered to take in tow the Center groups of ex-Francoists who were in favor of reform, and formed the UCD (Union of Democratic Center). In this way he sought to block a victory of the Francoist Right. The fact that the rivalry was not between Suárez and the opposition, but rather between Suárez and the Francoists, demonstrates the extent of the ineptness of the opposition and the little contact it had with reality.

Finally, on March 28, diplomatic relations with Mexico, which had been "interrupted" in 1939, were resumed. Mexico automatically dropped its recognition of the Republican government in exile, which became little more than symbolic.

*April.*   A month of decisions. The initiative continued with the government. The first move was the suppression of Article 2 of the 1966 Press Law, which limited freedom of the press, although strong measures against defamation and attacks on the monarchy and the army were left intact. The government could no longer suspend newspapers. The same day, a decree suppressing the National Movement—the Falange's successor—was approved, with the movement's patrimony and bureaucrats reverting to the state. On the 9th, after the Supreme Court handed down the opinion that it was not its role to decide on the matter of legalization of political parties that the government dared not legalize, the government gave the green light to the PC. In response to this, the minister of the navy resigned. The High Military Council convened, stating that it accepted the legalization of the PC "as a duty in service to the fatherland," adding that this was done reluctantly. Since there was no admiral prepared to accept the position of minister of the navy, a retired admiral was named. On the 15th, the date of the elections was set for June 15. Civil servants who sought candidacy began to resign, since the law did not allow anyone holding an official position to be a candidate.

The monarchs made their fourth trip, this time to Germany. April 22 signaled the legalization of employer and employee unions without previous authorization. Eleven union federations were registered, but the only ones of any importance were the two traditional unions (the anarcho-unionist CNT and the socialist UGT) and a new one, the (communist) Confederation of Workers Commissions (CCOO).

On the 28th, President Suárez became the first Spanish politician in forty years to go to Mexico without first declaring himself in exile. He also visited the United States and held an interview with President Carter. Everyone believed that he tried to change Washington's position which, until then, had favored Fraga. It seems he was successful. Then, Vice-President Walter Mondale and Secretary of State Cyrus Vance included Madrid on their European itinerary.

*May.* The government prohibited the workers' demonstrations of May 1, apparently due to pressure exerted by the police and the old generals. There were some clashes and other incidents, but nothing serious. The situation in the Basque Country steadily grew worse during the entire month of May. There were further kidnappings and assassinations, confrontations with the police, barricades, and demonstrations. No politician emerged on the scene who was able to convince the Basques not to risk the elections and the democratization process for twenty-three prisoners who most likely would be granted amnesty by the future Parliament. ETA, GRAPO, and the extreme Right groups, who continued to receive aid from Italian and Argentine fascists, seemed intent on rocking the boat to prevent the elections and instigate a military coup.

Although a coup was frequently mentioned, it did not materialize. The closest it came to actuality was the moment in which the PC was legalized. It has even been suggested that the king had warned the generals that if they were to interfere in the decisions of the government, he would depart, leaving them responsible for the country. Faced with this alternative, the old generals backed off. In any event, the government was always forced to take into account the reactions of the survivors of the Civil War who held high positions of command and those in the police force, who, in the Basque Country, seemed to take matters into their own hands. For this reason, instead of allowing demonstrations and protests which would have been peaceful, the government forbade them, which inevitably led to confrontations with the police which in turn provoked an even more heartless response from the forces of order. A National Union of Police was secretly organized within these forces. Its main intention was to depoliticize the police and to try to isolate the more Francoist elements. Spain has one police officer for each 138 inhabitants, as compared to one officer per 275 Italians, 413 West Germans, 481 Frenchmen, and 500 Britishers.

In order to placate the Basque Country, where three of the four civil wars which Spain has had in the last century and a half originated, the government, on the 20th of the month, offered political prisoners who had not been granted amnesty the right to seek expatriation.

Suárez, in a television address, announced that he would be a candidate. In the same speech he defended legalization of the PC (although he did not explain why many minor parties to the Left of the Communists were not legalized) and appealed for stability.

As for the king, he visited military camps, reviewed the Civil Guard military exercises, and attended the launching of a navy ship. With these gestures he continued to appease those military men who were most inclined to resist reform. The king's position was fortified in the eyes of the monarchists when his father, Juan de Borbón, who considered the monarchy to be consolidated, conceded to his son his rights as head of the royal family. To abdicate was not feasible since he had never come to reign. For those who place importance on these things, the monarchy thus won dynastic legitimacy. It was no longer a monarchy established by Franco, but one restored by the head of the dynasty.

All parties condemned the terrorism, while the PC went to the extreme of accepting the monarchy. It even went so far as to display the royal flag at all its public functions. But this moderate policy of Carrillo's was threatened by the return of the old "La Pasionaria," Dolores Ibarruria, a legendary figure from the Civil War. She was viewed with hatred by the workers' movement for her defamations against the Communists' adversaries. "La Pasionaria," the president of the PC, returned to Madrid against her party's orders. She made statements praising the U.S.S.R. Some say that she was sent by Brezhnev to try to regain the PC's loyalty to the Soviet Union.

While the radical youth, some progressive priests, the Basques, and the "bunker" spoke as if Franco were still alive, the masses thought only of the elections. Even soccer, the national sport, lost its attraction as the number of spectators who filed through the turnstiles to view the championship games was much lower than usual. The elections were not far off. The electoral campaign officially began on May 24. At that time, no one was willing to bet on the results of the elections or even on whether or not they would take place. "The people" were still an element of surprise. And the people also suspected that the Francoist forces perhaps had a surprise of their own in store.

The Spanish economy was faltering. The annual rate of inflation had risen to 20 percent. The foreign debt rose to 14 billion dollars. Reserves were diminishing. Rains and storms had devastated extensive agricultural regions. Energy consumption did not taper off sufficiently. Workers went on strike to obtain salaries that would keep up with the cost of living increases. Printing presses were turning out pesetas at full speed. Exports declined, since the rate of exchange for pesetas was much too high. The worldwide extension of the fishing limit to 200 miles placed the Spanish fishing industry in a dangerous position. Restrictions on credit had semiparalyzed the construction industry, triggering an increase in rental costs. Unemployment increased, the ranks swelled by Spanish workers returning from Western Europe. All of these occurrences were a consequence of the interaction of world recession, a policy of runaway development based on tourism, corruption, ill-planned state investments, and unplanned foreign investments—all results of Francoism.

But neither the Spaniards nor the government were very worried about the economic crisis. The solution—if there were one—would come after the elections. At the moment, it was a matter of applying first aid to keep going from day to day. It was the electoral campaign that stirred the people. In the campaign not a word was mentioned about the crisis.

The university was in a state of chaos, between student strikes and those of their professors, attendance was no more than one hundred class days per year. Thus students left the university with very little training. Elementary schools were insufficient, with instruction carried out exclusively in Spanish. Health care was pure fiction. Social security was a joke. Urban politics were a sham for dirty deals. But neither was any of this mentioned in the campaigns. Everything would be taken care of by the future Parliament.

The life of the country is controlled by an oligarchy of bankers—ex-aristocrats who had been "promoted" from latifundists to usurers with official sanction (interest on bank loans can be as high as 18 percent). The banks form a tightly knit web which snared every Spaniard. Even the newly-created political parties had sought—and obtained—bank loans to foot the bill for the electoral campaign. This did not leave out the PC or a Popular Socialist party of university professors which openly received subsidies from Ghadaffi of Libya, therefore declaring itself an anti-Zionist party. The Socialists also received help from the West German SDP, the Christian Democrats from the German Christian Democracy, the Right and Center from banks and industries, the Communists from banks and from Yugoslavia, Rumania, and Italy's PC. This went on despite a decree that each candidate for deputy chosen by his or her party would receive, if elected, a subsidy of one million pesetas from the government and another which declared that each party make its accounts public. Popular contributions were insufficient. Even so, there were no less than eight hundred political rallies a day, which entailed some two thousand speakers, most of them boring, since no one had ever before spoken in public. Now they were only beginning to learn. But the public hardly noticed, since the only voice heard in the country had been Franco's—flute-like, faltering, and completely uncharismatic.

What did this swarm of speakers talk about? Those from the Right, of the dangers of communism. Those from the Left, of the dangers of Francoism. Those from the Center, of the need for equilibrium, order, and progress. Those from the Right and the Left accused the Center of manipulating the elections (since Suárez, the head of government, was a candidate from the Center). There were no concrete programs; at most, only vague proposals such as "with order there will be prosperity and we are order," or "with socialism there will be no unemployment."

No party had a program of government, but merely declarations of abstract principles. This is easily explained when one remembers that only 15 percent of the country's population had any first-hand experience of what political life had been like before Franco's victory. Furthermore, those who made up the political parties, mostly young people, only knew how a party operated in secrecy. The parties were badly organized. There was improvisation as much in practice as in theoretical concepts. Except for the Right and the Center, no one believed that the elections would carry their party to power. The political life of the country resembled a new car being broken in. Forty years with the engine out of commission made it inevitable that it would run badly and that the driver would not know how to operate it. What is truly amazing is exactly what inspired confidence in the people—despite the odds, the motor *was* running and it was off to the races.

The proliferation of political parties was incredible. In clandestinity, only small groups revolving around a single personality could exist. Now few of those parties had consented to consolidation forming larger parties, except for the traditional ones: the Socialists and the Communists (aside from the main group in the case of the latter, there were five different factions, forming as many distinct parties). The explosion of nationalist sentiments was not limited to Catalonia,

Galicia, and the Basque Country, but also affected Andalusia, Valencia, Mallorca, Asturias, and the Canary Islands. Thus besides the national parties, there were also regional parties. In total, some 161 parties had been legalized. That left some 50 unlegalized parties and a half dozen terrorist and antipolitical groups (from the Right and Left) and the anarchists. To simplify matters somewhat, nine electoral coalitions had been formed which presented some 6,000 candidates for 350 deputy positions and 207 senatorial slots (in addition, the Senate would include 41 senators named by the king). The voters were confused. Thus it is not strange that the bombardment of candidates left some 40 percent of the electorate undecided in their choice of candidates.

The audiences at the political rallies were composed of youth and senior citizens. The Franco generation, those between the ages of thirty-five and sixty, was absent. Either they were still afraid or indifferent. The highest percentage of nonvoters or undecided ones came from this age group. Yet as the campaign advanced, the percentage of voters who intended not to exercise their franchise decreased. On the eve of the elections, this percentage had been reduced to a normal 20 percent. But 30 percent had still not decided for which of the coalitions or parties they would cast their ballot (only the Socialist, Communist, and Christian Democratic parties had presented their slates with no coalignment).

The campaign was intense yet unheated. The speakers were unaware of ways to trigger the audience's applause. Neither did the audience know how to applaud. Yet the audience did lend its undivided attention to the interminable monotonous speeches. It was such an uncharacteristically Spanish spectacle, that one wonders if Franco, in addition to making corruption a feature of Spain, had also made political frigidity a characteristic of present-day Spaniards.

Yet there was no lack of interest. The people did not understand the intricacies of the proceedings—a very complicated proportional electoral system called d'Hondt. Yet the audience asked questions, listened patiently to the explanations and persisted. In a country where there had never been a dialogue between student and professor, priest and laity, the ruled and the rulers, the questions poured forth at the political rallies. The people wanted to be heard, but they were unschooled in how to make themselves heard. This was a breath of fresh air, since it showed that the political "virus" was not dead, although it could be dangerous if it were to lead to collective disappointment or frustration. All this was most likely inevitable after forty apolitical years.

The walls of the cities and towns plastered with election posters exuded an air of exhiliration which the great majority of Spaniards had never before seen. The posters made many anxious and even worried some, but they stimulated almost everyone. In the local bars, soccer was discussed very little while politics dominated the conversations. People had begun to lose their fear of saying what was on their minds.

Terrorism continued with new kidnappings and sabotage. The government, not wanting to appear to make concessions, expatriated the remaining political prisoners. On May 31, Torcuato Fernández Miranda, the ex-Francoist who had deftly maneuvered to attain approval of the reform by the Francoist Cortes, resigned as president of the Cortes. The king, who was one of his followers, made him duke, granting him the Golden Fleece (Toison d'Or).

*June 15.* Election day. Twenty-two million voters went to the polls. Of these, only some three million had ever voted, that is, prior to 1936. Complete order. While the people were still voting, the king named the forty-one senators which, according to the law of reform, he was to designate. They were moderate people, some intellectuals, some military men, some ministers, some former Republicans. He also named an apolitical jurist, Antonio Hernández Gil, as president of Parliament (a different position from those of chairperson of the Chamber of Deputies and chairperson of the Senate, who would be elected by these bodies).

Every possible ideological option had been presented in the elections, from Falangists, Francoists, and anti-Francoist Fascists, to Trotskyites and Maoists, through Conservatives, Liberals, Christian Democrats, Socialists, and Communists, or Catalonians, Basques, Galicians, and other nationalists.

Voting took place with some stumbling blocks. People were unfamiliar with the mechanical aspects of the voting act. Some asked for advice. Tabulating the votes was a lengthy process. All the parties concurred that on the whole, the elections had come off without a hitch and had been clean and free. The results showed that once again the people of Spain were more perceptive than their leaders who had formed hundreds of parties. The people had sent to Parliament half a dozen of them, and only two in an appreciable number. It appears that Spain has begun an evolution toward a predominantly two-party system; one, conservative centrist; the other, socialist.

The coalition organized by Suárez (UCD) won 6 million votes (47 percent and 165 seats in the Chamber of Deputies, 10 short of half of the 350 slots. The Socialists of the PSOE gained 5 million votes (33 percent and 119 seats (15 of which went to Catalonians with their own party). The Communists gleaned 1.5 million votes (5.71 percent) and 20 seats, half of which went to Catalonians. Francoists of the Popular Alliance gathered 1.4 million votes (4.85 percent) and 17 seats. Dissident Socialists won 760,000 votes (1.61 percent) and six seats. The Basque Nationalist party (Christian Democrats) took 274,000 votes (2.2 percent) and 8 seats. The Catalonian Liberal Conservatives won 10 seats. Two (Catalonian) Christian Democrats were also elected.[7] Thus Parliament will be essentially composed of almost half of the representatives from the Center with a strong Socialist minority, and small Communist, Basque, and Catalonian Nationalist minorities.

The big winners were Suárez and the Socialists. The big losers were the Francoists (many of whose leading personalities, among them ex-president Carlos Arias Navarro, were not elected) and the Christian Democrats who, with the exception of Catalonia, did not win a single deputy's seat. This was the price they paid for not wanting to participate in Suárez' coalition which would have given it a less ex-Francoist character. The minority groups of dissident Communists, Falangists, extreme Right Fascists, Trotskyites, did not win a single seat. Consequently the chamber will not turn out to be as fragmented as expected. The Senate has a similar composition, with a greater representation from the Center, which gained nearly half the seats, and with a strong block of all the Catalonian senators who share the same Nationalist affiliation.

Suárez offered his resignation to the king, who confirmed him as head of government. The government was to be reorganized with the addition of several ministries (health, culture, minus the Ministry of Information, and a Ministry of Defense consolidating the three previous military ministries) and a few changes of faces. Parliament was to convene at the end of July to draft its own rules and to begin its tasks. The latter consist of the preparation of a new constitution (which once approved by Parliament, will be submitted to a public referendum), the confrontation with Basque and Catalonian pressures for the reestablishment of their pre-Franco statutes of autonomy, and the adoption of economic measures to deal with recession and inflation, which have grown worse.

The politicians must find a way to avoid the disappointment of the masses when they realize that the elections, by themselves, have not solved their problems. In addition, Suárez must maintain the cohesion of his coalition and, if he can, reinforce it to gain the majority and transform it into a stable party. Felipe González, leader of the Socialist party, will have to forestall the impatience of its partisans, exert pressure so that the constitution be as acceptable to the workers as possible, and prepare the party to become a viable alternative. The party had stated that it had no desire to participate in the first government of the new phase, but rather to prepare itself as its possible successor. After so many years, there will finally be municipal elections which will emphasize the extent of the Francoist administrative corruption. These elections will also permit many minority political groups which are only influential in certain regions or cities to gain local victories.

Spain has entered a new phase. Spaniards, by voting en masse (78 percent and in the larger cities 85 percent), by giving victory to two large factions, by not supporting the extremists (Communists and Francoists), and by not letting terrorism from the Left and Right make them nervous, have buried Francoism. In so doing, they have demonstrated that they no longer need the guardianship imposed by Franco which constituted the "justification" of his dictatorship. They were fortunate to find, at precisely the right moment, a handful of men who quickly learned how to measure the pulse of the masses: the king, Suárez, and González. Yet all this is little more than the beginning of a new period in which the Spanish people have freed themselves from tutelage. There still remains much to be done.

The reform of the political system has been carried out by the young ex-Francoists who had not invested anything in the Civil War and whose future lies in front of them, and by the king. Yet the opposition, despite all its mistakes, has played an essential role. Without it, there would have been no democratization, or at best, it would have been slow-moving and incomplete. If it had not been for the opposition, the only pressure to democratize would have come from the desire to enter the European Common Market, a desire which waned to a large extent with the economic crisis experienced in Western Europe.

Democratization is only political change. It is not a change in the social structure. Spanish society continues to be a mixture of feudal leftovers, a young capitalism which capitalizes by means of over-exploitation and dubious efficiency. Democratization has strengthened Spanish capitalism; it has rescued it from continuing to be manipulated by the banking and agricultural oligarchy; and it offers capitalism the possibility of grasping the power reins. One segment of the opposition (Communists, Catalonian and Basque Nationalists) will become the Left of this capitalism. The other part (Socialists, anarcho-syndicalists) will be in a position to pressure for social reforms, for the democratization of society. This is where the monarchy will find itself in a bind. Given the world situation, the monarchy had to be democratized, making an effort toward a metamorphosis from a monarchy installed by Franco to a monarchy supported by the people (achieved indirectly with the referendum). But the monarchy represents forces which, if they are dynamic on the political field, appear almost immobile on the social level.

It is impossible to predict if the monarchy will be able to stop playing the role of defender of the "social order." If it achieves this, there can be social change without a change in regime. But if it fails, thus becoming an instrument of capitalism, the moment will come when the monarchy and social change will be incompatible.

In Spain, the Bourbon dynasty was both. In the era of enlightened despotism, it attempted to encourage the development of the bourgeoisie against feudal forces. Then, in the 1876 Restoration, it supported the feudal forces against the bourgeoisie. Finally, the bourgeoisie, in alliance with the middle and working classes, got rid of the monarchy in 1931. The king, in the not too distant future, will be forced to choose. His decisions can make social change less difficult or, on the other hand, set up an obstacle to it. What is certain is that with the end of Francoism and the beginning of political democratization, Spain is entering a period in which the problems which led to the Civil War must be resolved. Despite the changes that occurred in the last forty years, Francoism did not solve these problems, but rather kept them in hibernation through terror and deceit. In other words, the democratic-bourgeois revolution being carried out will be followed by a socialist revolution—without violence or drama.

## NOTES

1. The behavior of the television people, controlled by the Francoists, was so bad in those days that in consideration of the anticipated ceremonies scheduled for four days later, the king's Civil House ordered that Italian experts be contracted to transmit the ceremony using their own cameras.

2. A few days after the burial, Franco's widow returned to various convents the relics that had been sent to surround the caudillo's bed. Among them was a hand of Saint Theresa of Avila which Franco had kept by his side since the Civil War. The following week the government gave Franco's widow the Señorío de Meirás, the Galician estate that had been Franco's vacation spot. Franco's daughter was given a title of nobility. A special pension for the dictator's widow was also proposed to Parliament.

3. Fraga was the minister who had suppressed censorship and had pressured for reforms of the Fundamental Laws in 1966. In 1969, allied with Solís, he had tried to put an end to the Opus Dei's favored position. Although he

failed in this endeavor, in 1974 he accepted the position of ambassador to London. In 1975, when political associations were allowed, he made several statements in Barcelona proposing to form one with a program for political democratization and independence of the unions. Arias read this program to Franco who reportedly limited his comments to "For which country is it intended?" This sufficed for the government to indicate to Fraga that no political association with such a program would be authorized. It was then that Fraga and those "purged" in November 1974 formed FEDISA.

4. In 1975 USIA invited for the first time several members of the moderate opposition to visit the United States. Until then, the opposition had only existed for Washington during the Kennedy era. On the other hand, several U.S. universities have granted professorships to Spanish intellectuals (such as Tierno Galvan and Aranguren) who were unemployed or living in exile to avoid persecution by the Franco regime.

5. Here are some concrete data: the GNP for 1975 for 35 million inhabitants was 75 billion dollars, that is, less than one quarter of the U.S. federal budget. Per capita annual income reached 2,000 dollars in 1974, yet the distribution range is quite unbalanced. Exports for 1975 amounted to 6.7 billion dollars, while imports accounted for 14.3 billion. Reserves held in foreign currency and gold reached 6.2 billion, nearly 20 percent lower than the previous year. One out of every ten Spanish wage earners works in other European countries, where jobs are getting scarce. The official unemployment figure in the country is 2.4 percent, although economists believe that it is really closer to 5 percent and will increase as the foreign job market closes its doors to unskilled Spanish workers. This reserve of unskilled labor has kept salaries low—one-third of U.S. salaries and one-half of those in France. In the last ten years the rate for economic growth has been between 7 and 8 percent annually. Today Spain produces more steel than Sweden, more cement than Great Britain, and 750,000 cars annually. The only income that has not decreased has been that derived from tourism, which brings into the country some 5 billion dollars per year.

6. It would seem that Juan Carlos I has understood this situation. By March 1976 there were so many strikes—even of municipal police—that more man-hours had been lost in two months than in all 1975. The restlessness of the Francoist generals and the "bunker" was so visible that on March 2 the king called together the Council of the Realm for a highly unusual meeting, to make a long statement singling out two powers he has and that he termed "particularly significant": the power to take exceptional authority in grave internal or external crises, and the power to submit laws to popular referendum. "In moments of crisis" he said, with a clear reference to the "bunker," "certain minorities may pose as the expression of the popular will." The thrust of this statement was clear: either the "bunker" stops opposing changes or the king will go over the head of the institutions and appeal directly to the people.

7. The Hondt system helped form the large blocs that perhaps will permit Spain to go the way of a two-party system, but at the same time gave an obvious advantage to the Center. For instance, the 165 deputies of the Center were elected by an average of 36,490 votes each, while the 119 Socialists got an average of 42,006 votes, the 20 Communists an average of 79,101 votes, and the 17 Francoists, 85,240 votes. It is possible that the next Cortes will

change the system and make it less unfair to small parties without atomizing Parliament.

# 22

# *The Future is Now*

For almost twenty years, the question asked most frequently of the Spaniard abroad was: What will happen after Franco? It was not a frivolous question, since the answer would affect millions of Spaniards and could possibly have international repercussions. Things being the way they were, the answer was grey: General Franco would be succeeded by a monarchist regime, conditioned by the army. In light of the history outlined in this book, a deeper question would be: When will Spain come of age? Or, expressed in different terms, when will the Spaniards be allowed to decide for themselves, and to govern themselves?

It has already been shown that Spain could have been born at the end of the fifteenth century, but this birth was postponed until the eighteenth century. Then the reader watched as Spain stumbled through a tottering infancy, on to an agitated adolescence, which led to a long period of tutelage from which Spain has still not freed itself, save for brief periods of fantastic fireworks, such as those displayed during the First Republic and the Civil War. Has the moment not yet arrived for Spain to escape from this tutelage, which has been offered at times by its oligarchy and at others by its elite? Has not the moment come for Spaniards to govern themselves?

In order to answer these questions, it is necessary to understand what the Spaniard of today is like. The basic character traits of the Spaniard, his boastful arrogance, his dignity, his stubborn *no hay derecho* (that's not right), his envy, his familiarity with death—all of these have more than likely remained unchanged. Yet anyone who has lived in Spain since 1936 until the present can prove that other characteristics, perhaps less peculiar and not as basic, ones which are more related to one's daily life, have suffered deep transformations. The metaphysical Spaniard remains intact, but the physical and social Spaniard has changed. The Spaniard is not a "new man," but rather a man who differs from what he had been for centuries.

This fact should not be so surprising in an era which has seen the Russians change radically with Stalinism, the Germans with nazism, and even the English with the loss of their empire. Possibly the Slavic mystique, the Hegelian metaphysics, and the puritan moralism have continued as the basis of the character of these peoples; yet they are different from what they had been a half century ago with regard to the practical objectives in life, namely, power, wealth, and action. In a like way, the Spaniard is also different.

Spain offers an impressive example of how deeply and extensively a people can be changed by the action of an authoritarian regime. The isolation, imposed by the censorship and lack of participation in power, the fear of the police and the need to survive, instead of altering the structure of the Spaniard's character, has clothed it in new flesh. Those who perceive dictatorship as transitory phenomena, should examine the Spanish case. The Franco regime was transitory, but will the changes that this regime has made in the Spaniard's personality likewise be transitory? Although this question cannot be answered in advance, anyone who knows Spain and has lived in the country both before 1936 and today, will not hesitate to prognosticate that what will probably happen is that the changes will survive their cause, and that, when all is said and done, these changes will decide when the moment of Spain's coming of age will occur.

Perhaps the best way of getting acquainted with today's Spaniards is to look at their behavior during the crucial last weeks of 1975 and the first weeks of 1976. In three months Spain experienced five executions and a wave of chauvinism disguised as national pride as a reaction to foreign protests triggered by the executions together with a feeling of being orphaned during Franco's long illness and death. There was also a moment of hope, although somewhat skeptical, at the proclamation of the king, and a moment of panic at the passing but real perspective of a coup from the extreme Right, followed by a period of expectation before the first government of the new king. All these events tumbled out, understandably so, amidst growing social and political tension caused by the simultaneity of the new government's announcement that it proposed to lead the country to a democratic regime and the impatience of many who sought a more rapid evolution of democracy.

Once again the old political proverb rang true: It is more difficult to leave a dictatorship than it is to establish one (although Franco's dictatorship was not exactly established with ease, since it required thirty-three months of civil war and hundreds of thousands of deaths). Around the corner Portugal offers further proof of the proverb's truth. Certainly Portugal was on many minds during those three months. During the days of Franco's illness and the king's proclamation, many wondered if the new chief of state would be capable of avoiding in Madrid a repetition of what had happened in Lisbon.

Franco's death gave rise to some apparently contradictory reactions. Intense emotion, in many homes, no so much due to political causes than to Franco's dramatic struggle against death; in many other homes, champagne was drunk, not so much to celebrate the death of a hated enemy than the physical destruction of the main obstacle to change. The opposition and the extreme Right felt equally disconcerted and, in some way, orphaned. The former would no longer have its scapegoat to blame for everything, while the latter no longer had a guide to whom to run when they lost strength in the country.

At the same time, there was a rapid politicization. In the month of Franco's illness, the people became interested in politics via the dramatic news releases concerning the operations that Franco endured. Politics no longer were the privilege of small urban groups. Rather, attention to politics was awakened in people from all corners of the country who previously only viewed politics as a source of disturbance and fear. All the provincial newspapers published two or three editions daily, even as many as eight on the day of Franco's death. People had to stand in line to buy a newspaper. More money was spent on magazines than people normally spent to celebrate the Christmas holidays. Towns which normally only received magazines for women and sports enthusiasts now saw political and informative weeklies appear on magazine stands.

This sudden politicization frightened the extreme Right and upset the opposition. Both sides were accustomed to everything happening in restaurant meetings and private homes with no real participation from the masses. Suddenly, people ran out into the streets spontaneously, not as they had previously (for example, in October to protest the five executions), when they had been mobilized by the government.

Hundreds of thousands of people filed by Franco's coffin. Day and night they stood in lines that covered miles of icy streets. For the majority, it was not a political demonstration but an emotional one. "They are bidding farewell to being under legal age," remarked a professor from the University of Madrid who watched the procession on television. "They know that from now on there will be no one to decide for them. They are afraid and, at the same time, somewhat proud."

Several days later these same hundreds of thousands of people filled the enormous plaza in front of the Oriente Palace. One disappointed leader of the opposition commented: "These are the same people who, six weeks ago, filled this same plaza shouting out against Germany, France and England for their protest against the executions. Now they feel proud because the duke of Edinburgh, Giscard d'Estaing, and President Schell have come to the mass in honor of the new king."

They were not the same people although physically they had not changed. In that month and a half they had been politicized. They had discovered that they could no longer leave decisions in Franco's hands since Franco was not around anymore nor could anyone play Franco's role.

The will to decide emerged with the possibility to decide. Those who had rushed to praise Franco and insult Europe had been mobilized. Those who went to see the king did so spontaneously, since the king still did not have his own organization and the state organization did not want the king to receive popular support. The more favor the king stimulated, the fewer possibilities would the "establishment" have to manipulate him.

A French newspaper reporter, fond of clichés, asked one of the women standing in line to pay her respects to Franco's remains, how much money they had given her. The woman was insulted. The narrow-minded reporter who simply could not understand that it is impossible to "buy" hundreds of thousands of people, was almost lynched. But these same people standing in line told each other jokes and rumors (those rumors which replace news items in a dictatorship).

Jokes about Franco, even on the tongues of his most loyal admirers, numbered in the hundreds during those days. Two merit mention. One tells of how shouts from the street reached the bedside of the dying leader, who asked what they meant. He was told, "Your people have come to say good-bye," to which he replied, "Where are they going?" Another suggested that "Franco had already died, but no one dared tell him." There is no better synthesis of the role Franco played for almost forty years and his relationship with his followers and partisans.

There is no doubt that Franco had charisma. Yet no one could define the characteristics of this quality. Short, chubby, with a flute-like voice, he did not have the martial bearing of a military man (although he was one to the core) nor the oratorical bearing of a demagogue (although he never scorned social demagogy). Neither Franco's words nor his physical appearance had anything to do with his charisma, which was a result of the circumstances and not the man.

Perhaps no other contemporary politician knew how to separate reality from official fiction as he did. The Spanish people lived through almost four decades on two different planes: the first, that of everyday facts—fifteen years of terror and hunger, followed by a quarter of a century of corruption and insidious fear; the second, that of official declarations. But up until five years ago, Franco represented on both planes the image of a father-policeman who maintained order when everything in the world seemed to be disorder. Perhaps his charisma can be attributed to the fact that the people knew that he would not vacillate before anything in order to keep himself in power. Five years ago, when he began to vacillate due to his age and poor health, his charisma vanished. It reappeared briefly during his long deathwatch.

It is indicative of the Spanish character that during these weeks before his death, as rumors circulated that Franco was suffering terribly, many resentments and hatreds were dissolved. I have heard from the lips of people who spent twenty years in jail or who had parents or spouses executed, statements like this one: "That slow death has been my revenge. Now I no longer hate anyone."

Perhaps the people understood even better than the leaders that Franco was a great politician (although his politics were hateful), very competent and very perceptive. Hard-hearted, introverted, calculating, capable of playing one faction against the other—in none of these characteristics was he a typical Spaniard. To a certain extent the people felt for him the type of sentiments they reserve for foreigners.

Franco had been the absolute master for thirty-eight years. Sociologists may speak of his representing such a given group, but in the people's eyes he was the arbitrator between all groups and it was he who had the last word (which really was the way it was). One proof of his political perception is the fact that as he prepared for his succession for ten years, he foresaw that there would be no possible successor for his absolute power ("Franco is only responsible before God and History," reads the law that played the role of constitution in the Franco regime). For this reason he continued to create mechanisms that provided greater participation in government to the "establishment" of his regime, not to the people. These mechanisms would thus insure the continuation of the regime and the limitation of his successor's power to change the regime.

From this comes a new ambivalence, a new ambiguity—that of the relationship between the people and the king. No one, outside of a few intimates, knows what Juan Carlos, the new king, is like or what he thinks. The people have a favorable image of him as young, strong, serious, and plain. His wife attends classes at the university and has never been absent except on the day of her husband's coronation. The couple and their three children continue to live at the small Zarzuela Palace instead of moving in to the Oriente Palace, the traditional residence of Spanish monarchs. Several statements made by the king to foreign newspapers express a moderately liberal democratic flavor. But these statements were known only to those initiated into politics. The masses have only seen him on television, for example, when he swore to his duties as prince before Franco, promising to defend the "principles of the National Movement," that is, the Franco regime. The people also listened to the speech he delivered before the Cortes after he was proclaimed king. In this speech he stated that Spain is part of Europe and that no one should be privileged before the crown.

The people had not taken the prince seriously while Franco was still alive: he was used to inaugurate highways and open veterinarians' conventions. Even so, little by little his tongue became looser. But his lips did not pronounce any political declaration. Spaniards became aware of the impossible role that was his to play. He kept silent in 1974 when Franco became ill, handed power over to the prince, then recovered and took it back as chief of state. But the people also noticed his serenity and detachment as he lived through those difficult years.

The king had no power base. There was no important monarchist party. The monarchic tradition had been short-circuited in 1931. There existed no respected nobility. The people had hoped that when he was enthroned he would grant amnesty. They were disappointed when all he granted was a pardon which did not touch the majority of political prisoners—those sentenced to more than twenty years imprisonment. But they also understood that they would have to wait some time for amnesty since there were powerful forces that opposed it—the Francoists.

A logical conclusion is that the king has been favorably received by the people, but they have done so without illusions. He enjoys a margin of confidence, although no one will venture a guess as to how long it will last. Apparently the king himself knows that if he loses this margin, it will mark the beginning of a period in which the republic will again become the immediate objective of the opposition, which will attract many more people than did the opposition to Franco.

The king is advised principally by several friends from his military and university days who neither have positions in the government nor are involved in politics. In addition, some of his former teachers form a part of his circle of intimates.

As a boy, Juan Carlos received a strictly Francoist education, supervised by Franco himself. Although certainly not a leftist, Juan Carlos is a young man of thirty-seven. Even as a personal reaction, he should try to separate himself from Francoism in order to create his own personality. In fact, almost spontaneously, the demythification of Franco has already begun. With time, the same thing will happen to him that happened to Stalin. It is especially the man on the street in Spain, who knows little of politics but who does have common sense, who hopes that this will happen. Until now, the king has demonstrated a certain ability to maneuver. From the beginning he has adopted the attitude of a constitutional king: he named the head of government and since then has not attended the ministers' meetings. From the beginning he has wanted the Spaniards to realize that the king reigns but does not govern. It remains to be seen if he will manage to maintain this position when tensions increase.

He has no authority over the old Francoists and the extreme Right, which considers him to be short of a revolutionary, despite the gestures of respect and obedience they make. His authority with the Left will depend on the rapidity with which reforms are put into effect. The old republicanism has passed away. If the reforms are a long time coming, it may revive.

What the king does have in his favor is the army, although not completely, since the old generals of the Civil War would prefer the continuation of Francoism, which gave them benefits, influence, and prestige, although not real power. But the young officers who are in the majority did not partake in the Civil War. They seem to want an unpolitical army and they seem to accept with pleasure a constitutional monarch. As long as there are no serious disorders, the army will support the king. Even the few officers who belong to the illegal UMD (Democratic Military Union)[1] are ready to accept him, but it is doubtful that the king views them favorably. Neither does most of the opposition see them in a favorable light since, after the Portuguese experience, it fears an army politicized to the Left as much as one politicized to the Right. The Communists are the ones who encourage these officers. Despite their protests of democratic pluralism, the Spanish Communists would do the same thing as the Portuguese— and more, if the opportunity arose. For many years the opposition believed in the army to unseat Franco, but this belief was in vain. When it seemed cured of this typically Spanish vice, this group of military men surfaced. This put in jeopardy the depoliticization of the army that Franco had obtained, for personal reasons, of course. Such a depoliticized army is indispensable to carry out reforms and install a democratic system. The crown still does not rest easy. Juan Carlos inherited Franco's throne. Now he has to earn it on his own. This observation—from a cabdriver in Madrid—summarizes the situation.

The fact that the situation seems to revolve around personalities, reveals an aspect of the circumstances which will have considerable influence in the near future. Suffice to note that Franco was not toppled, nor was Francoism displaced from its power base, and that Francoism still strives for preservation, in order to understand the tremendous weight of the figure that was Franco—and still is, even after his death. Two weeks after the caudillo's burial, no one spoke anymore of him. His name barely appeared in the press. His portrait in official offices had taken a back seat to make room for the king's. But Franco still loomed over the country since he looms in the Spaniards' subconscious. In thirty-eight years of absolute personal power the people have become accustomed to personalizing politics. This is dangerous for the king, because it will take the people a long time to get used to seeing him as a symbol rather than the supreme ruler. What is not done will be blamed on him. It is possible that this will move him at times to intervene in the government and thus lose the quality of constitutional monarch that he seeks.

The king has a problem of equilibrium which is not easy to resolve if he does not want to break with the past. He has to placate the opposition with tolerance but without giving cause for alarm to the extreme Right which could move Francoist groups in the army and outside of it.

The workers' agitation is growing rapidly, not only due to the workers' desire to not be affected by inflation and to oppose salary controls, but also because the old trade-union tradition of the country was just waiting for the chance to be revived. This presents problems for the government, but above all for the companies, which under Franco had become accustomed to firing striking workers en masse (which made them lose seniority, pensions, etc.). They still do it, since it is legal, but now such actions provoke more strikes, which is not what the government wants. (The companies which most systematically fire strikers are those with foreign capital, especially from the United States. There are Spanish companies, whose executives share a good rapport with the moderate opposition, which do not exercise reprisals, which is not the case with foreign companies. This naturally provokes even worse anti-U.S. feelings than Eisenhower and Nixon engendered.)

The situation is also dangerous for the workers' movement. The first danger is fragmentation—there are dozens of groups of middle-class intellectuals and students who declare themselves to be very revolutionary. Before Franco's death, when one of these groups intervened in a strike, the workers returned to work because they did not want their strike manipulated. Now these groups have more opportunities to act and attract a segment of the workers. The Communists form the main of these groups. Divided into three parties, the one headed by Santiago Carrillo is the strongest. Thanks to subsidies from the Italian, Rumanian, and Yugoslavian Communist parties, it now counts on paid militants and good propaganda and legal defense machinery. Although Carrillo declares himself a pluralist and a democrat, and that he has split off from Moscow and criticizes Cunhal, his party continues to employ the same methods of yesteryear in their daily actions: maneuvers, accusations against their adversaries, blackmail, and even physical terror.

The Socialists and the old anarchists have penetrated the working class at this point to a lesser extent than the Communists. Yet everything seems to indicate that they are quickly advancing. In spite of this, the Socialists as much as other opposition groups, affirm that if there is freedom in the future to organize parties, neither the Communists nor any other group which promises to accept the rules of the game should be excluded. The question rests on deciding if it is possible to believe the democratic promises of the Communists.

Another danger of the workers' movement is monolithism. The CNS, organized by the government and controlled by old-time Francoists, has technicians, employers, and workers in its ranks. It also possesses a good deal of wealth and controls the pension system. It could possibly happen that the government will convert the CNS into workers' union organization but use the lure of these holdings to keep the unions reduced to fighting for immediate claims (something unknown in Spanish workers' traditions). These unions would be indirectly controlled by the government, although the latter affirms that future unions must be independent. In the event this happens, ideological battles in the unions will result. There will be severe and bitter struggles for the "spoils of war" that managing the unions represents. The party or ideology to achieve control of the unions will have in its possession an instrument capable of exerting a great deal of pressure, greater than that of union movements in any other Western European country (due precisely to the wealth the "unions" now hold). Yet (due precisely to the desire to preserve this wealth), the group that prevails in the union will find itself converted into a movement with no interest in opposing the government, no matter what its economic policy may be.

These two dangers, although somewhat disguised, also face the political opposition. On the one hand is the danger of fragmentation. Besides the three parties which will certainly prevail (Christian Democratic, Socialist, and Communist), and in addition to their equivalent groups in the Basque Country, Catalonia, and Valencia, there are a great many small leftist groups (as many as twenty-seven) and several small groups of the extreme Right (as many as five).[2] The difficulty of uniting these groups is apparent. Those that do not manage to attract the masses might very well turn their attention to terrorist activities (as some of the left-wing and extreme right-wing groups have already done). On the other hand, there is the danger of monolithism in two areas: first, the danger that the important parties will not want to be confederated with their counterparts in the regions seeking autonomy (this would strongly debilitate them); second, the danger that one of these parties, namely, the Communists, will try to achieve absolute dominance.

The ideological terrorism of the Communists is quite strong in Spain. Newsmen, politicians, and intellectuals fear that they will be accused of being moderates by the Communists, who enjoy considerable influence in many publishing houses and newspapers if they oppose them. The result can be that the Communists may silence the activities of non-Communist opposition groups. In spite of their cries of democratic spirit, the people do not trust them. One anecdote illustrates the extreme this mistrust and fear of the Communists has reached. In 1970, an Assembly of Catalonia was organized in Barcelona. It brought together almost all the opposition and was manipulated by the Communists. In 1974, when the Democratic Junta was formed by the Communist party, a secret meeting of that assembly was held to decide whether it should join the junta. It soon became evident that the majority was against joining. The meeting was then discovered by the police who arrested those present. Many people from the opposition assumed that the meeting had been denounced to the police by the Communists in order to avoid the vote against the junta. This was possibly not the case, but it does reveal that the people would consider Communist betrayal for political motives before attributing the event to police efficacy. In spite of this, they continue to collaborate with the Communists.

As for the terrorist groups, they were weakened by the 1975 repression and found themselves isolated. Another anecdote will illustrate how much more perceptive is the man on the street compared to these groups composed of young boys from the middle class. In Bilbao the ETA had always counted on the favor of the populace to distribute manifestos. On the day of the king's coronation, a group from ETA wanted to place a poster in a plaza in Bilbao. The same passersby who days earlier had protected and applauded the group now hooted at them and dispersed the group with boos. The people simply wanted to open a possible road for the partisans to change and they were opposed to being thrown into the arms of the extreme Right as a result of terrorism.[3]

What makes the situation difficult for the opposition is not knowing how far its pressure can go without causing a shift to the Right and without trying to force the pace of change if the opposition itself is not in a situation to take over the power. It is evident to everyone that it is not now, nor will it be, as long as there is no freedom of organization.[4]

As for the opposition, then, the tactic is to pressure for tolerance to achieve freedom and for concessions to achieve recognized rights. Only then can it begin its journey on the long road that will lead it to become an alternative to the opposition within Francoism, which has been transformed into the government by the king, or to the king himself, if he is not ready to allow the present opposition to govern. All of this will take time.

There will also be a need for flexibility and ability, which can only be acquired in a legal, organized opposition—since these characteristics are not necessary in secret, illegal struggle—which requires more tenacity and more of a spirit of sacrifice than ability to maneuver.

There is one more danger which can leave the opposition reduced to the workers and condemn them to fight for their immediate demands and nothing else. This danger is the ability of the new government body, acquired in the Francoist "establishment." It is possible that Suárez is counting on the fact that by granting freedom to the press, eliminating the censorship of books, allowing peaceful demonstrations and economic strikes, that is, by making concessions to the intellectuals and the middle class, he will achieve the division of the opposition into those who are ready to be satisfied with this and await political rights and those who are not satisfied with freedom of expression and want freedom of action. If the government is clever, and it is, it can cause the weakening of the opposition, satisfying its nonworker element and those who do not have economic problems, but only political ones. Then it will not be difficult for it to manipulate the workers and please them for a time with some economic concessions. In this way, the government will find itself free from pressures to accelerate its reforms and would be able to apply its programs at its own pace, to assure ex-Francoists control of the future political system and limit the changes to politics without carrying them out in the social structure.

The fantastic political instability of Spain reflects an overwhelming social stability. Spanish society began to change only because of the last civil war which was unleased precisely in order to maintain a social structure which was not satisfying the needs and aspirations of the country, a social structure that was an anachronism and totally oppose to the grain of events in the rest of the world. But Spain has still not made what a Leninist would call a democratic bourgeois revolution. Francoism, in its last form (1965-75), instigated the development of an authoritarian Spanish capitalism without destroying the feudal remains.

The country, no matter how authoritarian the regime, will not achieve political stability as long as its society does not change. This was demonstrated with Francoism, under which there erupted guerrillas, terrorism, strikes, conspiracies, street disorders, and executions. Social change implies not only the establishment of a democratic political system, but also the creation of forces which can serve it as its base and defense. That is, the formation of a rural middle class via agrarian reform, the satisfaction of the aspirations of the oppressed nationalities via a federal system of government, a more just distribution of wealth via some form of democratic planning.

Under Franco, the bourgeoisie has grown and its character has changed. Today it is composed of the new rich, with a moderately democratic and European ideology and the mentality of American executives. The working class has also changed: it is composed mainly of rural workers who have emigrated to the cities, with no tradition of organization or ideological formation. The middle class has greatly increased, it has been politically radicalized, and is beginning to adopt European and American lifestyles. The old dominant class of large aristocratic landholders still preserves a great deal of strength, but it is evidently declining. These changes in the social classes mean that there will also have to be changes in the distribution of power and wealth.

For almost forty years, Spaniards have lived subjected to fear—fear of war, fear of official terror, fear of the police, fear of poverty, fear of the Communists, fear of remaining outside the favor of the government for some, fear of seeming to be moderates for others. With Franco's death, the man on the street, who before had been very cautious, has lost his fear and has discovered his impatience. This is a new factor in the country's politics. No one has governed in the last forty years without counting on the fear of those governed. It remains to be seen who—if anyone—will be able to learn to do so. To return to intimidating the Spaniards massive doses of terror would be necessary. There is probably no political force, neither the Francoists of the past, the "establishment" of the present, nor the Communists, who could use so much terror without falling off the tightrope on which all Spaniards, from the king to the terrorists, are trying to walk at the present time.

If one looks at Spain as it has been presented in this book, that is, as an ensemble of peoples that have always lived against the grain of history, outside the era, at times preceding it, at others lagging behind, these Spaniards of today with all their impatience, fears, and mistakes, seem, in a certain way, to be a consolation. At last, several generations of Spaniards have ceased to be basically different from their contemporaries in Europe. What the personal contact with the Spaniards of today reveals is exactly that: the contemporary Spaniard is much more like the contemporary Frenchman, Italian, and German, whereas the Spaniard of other times never seemed to be a European at all. This could mean the loss of the picturesque, yet in the long run it will be of enormous benefit to the country. To a certain extent, it could affirm the fact that serendipity has come about, that is, that the regime, while seeking one result, has instead reached another. Since the social structure of Spain differs greatly from that of Western Europe, and since the human type is at odds with this social structure of Spain, the Spaniard has been "Europeanized." That is, he has become more European as an evasion from his social structure, as an individual solution to the collective problems over which he had no influence. With time, when this disparity becomes unbearable to him, he will have to seek and find the way to change the social structure, to adjust it to his own "new" personality. And this will come, whether swiftly or through a lengthy process. No one can now foresee when or how it will come about, but it is inevitable.

For centuries, the Spaniards lived without a present, escaping into a utopia; at times, running back to the past, and at others, living in the future, always waiting for something, always trying—often with violence—to find a place in the present. But their eyes did not see the present because it was distasteful to them, both within the context of the past and the future. It is noteworthy that the Spanish language has very complicated verb forms to describe any future or past action. All the language's nuances of time, especially in its conditional forms, prove a reef which shipwrecks most who never learn the language in the context of this constant evasion of today that has been the life of the Spaniard and which is reflected in his language.

For him, the present did not merit respect or defense. No one could feel satisfied with the present. The present was substituted by the rhetoric concerning destiny and Spain's mission. As the country became immobilized, it began to boast of its past, to live at its history's expense, and to take refuge in this history. The country, now impotent, consoled itself with the memory of past loves to compensate for the lack of present adventures. A poet of the turn of the century said it this way:

> Don't ask for heroism of a nation
> that lives in misfortune so agreeably,
> and sleeps in the laurels of its history,
> draped in full-dress uniform.

But the past could only be sufficient for those who had inherited it. Those who inherited nothing were attracted to the future. From the latter ranks rose the anarchists, the Republican dreamers, the "Europeanizing" intellectuals, those who awaited the "great night" to build a new society.

This flight from an inhospitable present adopted different forms, all of which shared this romantic base, which bridged the heroic and the rhetoric, the brutal and the tender, the cynical and the believing which characterized the search for absolute solutions surpassing the limits of politics and economics. It is precisely because the present had imposed so many limitations that the reaction against the present comes with excessive gestures and a total rupture. If land ownership is a limiting factor, the property registers are burned. If it is the church that limits, convents are set aflame. If it is industry that limits, bombs are planted and employers murdered. A French anarchist lives just as a French wage earner does; an American populist lives as an American who belongs to the lower middle class; but a Spanish liberal, Republican, anarchist, or Traditionalist does not live as a Spaniard from the middle class, nor as a wage earner, but rather as a liberal, as a Republican, as an anarchist, or as a Traditionalist. It is a matter of living the present as one would wish to live in the future or in the past.

Antonio Machado, the poet who died at the end of the most feverish and emotional attack of utopianism that Spain has suffered, indicated this lack of a valid present in Spanish life in his poetry, almost without realizing he was doing so: *"El vano ayer engendrará un mañana"* (an empty yesterday will engender a tomorrow), he said. In another work, he insisted:

> Mas otra España nace,
> la España del cincel y de la maza,
> con esa eterna juventud que se hace
> del pasado macizo de la raza.
> Una España implacable y redentora,
> España que alborea,
> con un hacha en la mano vengadora,
> España de la rabia y de la idea. [5]

Machado also spoke of the "Spain which has passed, but has never been."

It is a breath of fresh air to meet now Spaniards who have discovered that the present exists, Spaniards who live in the present, and who try to make Western Europe their individual present. Years may pass, perhaps, before the institutional forms change. But the important fact remains that the magic circle that had separated Spain from the world has been broken. The present, with all its defects, at last exists for Spaniards. And this present, at least in desire, is the present of the rest of the world. Thus it is a plausible hope that Spain will at long last march in step, although possibly wavering and limping, with the rest of the world. Taken in this light, however slow the change which can be seen may be, one can be optimistic. Because the future of yesterday is now.

## NOTES

1. Less than 1,000 among 21,000 officers.
2. A poll taken in February 1976 by the popular magazine *Cambio 16* showed that if elections were held at that moment, the Socialists would have received 25 percent of the votes, the Christian Democrats 24 percent, the

Francoists and extreme Right 15 percent, the Communists 5 percent, and several groups of extreme Left and Center, 30 percent.

3. Of all the terrorist groups, ETA was the first to become active again after Franco's death. At the end of January 1976, the group kidnapped the son of a Basque industrialist, asking 300,000 dollars ransom. Immediately, many opposition groups criticized this action, as did the Basque Nationalist party, which had survived the Civil War and represented the nonviolent partisans of Basque Nationalism. There were even popular demonstrations against ETA by the same people who up until several months earlier had sympathized with it. Reliable witnesses report that these demonstrations were not organized, but rather truly spontaneous.

4. This is exactly what the "bunker" sees. Since the Communists do not represent a danger for the regime, because they are not an alternative—no one believes that they can take over the power—the staunch Francoists play the game of helping the Communists indirectly, knowing that the government would resign itself to holding back or paralyzing the evolution if there is the danger that the Communist will control the opposition. Thus, the large strikes of January and February 1976 could be held not only because the workers wanted to better their lot, so they took advantage of the temporary tolerance and the fact that the opposition supported them, but also because the members of the "bunker," from their positions in the official "unions" aided and abetted these strikes. For thirty-eight years, these members of the "bunker" had used the unions to prevent workers' protests. Now they instigated them, not due to their concern for the workers but rather with the desire to cause the failure of the government. The non-Communist opposition knows this, but it does not dare denounce it for fear that the communists will accuse it of being moderate or an accomplice of the government. If this is not understood, the situation itself will not be understood. It must also be remembered that for many years many Francoists—especially in the universities, the press, the educational system, the publishing business, and even radio and television—had their own "good communist," as an insurance for the future (in the same way that under the nazi occupation many Vichy people had their own "good Jew"). This has given the Communists key positions in the universities and other places, which they now use to promote their party.

5. *But another Spain is born,*
  *The Spain of the chisel and the mace,*
  *With that eternal youth which forms*
  *From the past, a solid block of race.*
  *An implacable and redeeming Spain is born.*
  *With an axe in its vengeful hand,*
  *A Spain of fury and intent.*

# Bibliography

Alba, Víctor. *Catalonia: A Profile*. New York, 1975.
———. *Cataluña de tamaño natural*. Barcelona, 1975.
———. *Histoire du POUM*. Paris, 1975.
———. *Historia de la segunda república española*. Mexico, D.F., 1961.
———. *Histoire des républiques espagnoles*. Paris, 1948.
Alcofar Nassaes, J.L. *Los asesores soviéticos en la guerra civil*. Barcelona, 1971.
Alonso, Bruno. *Los últimos momentos de la guerra civil de España*. Mexico, D.F., 1943.
Altamira, Rafael. *A History of Spain*. New York, 1949.
———. *La civilización española en los siglos XVI, XVII y XVIII*. Buenos Aires, 1937.
———. *A History of Spanish Civilization*. New York, 1966.
Alvarez del Vayo, Julio. *The Last Optimist*. New York, 1950.
———. *Freedom's Battle*. New York, 1940.
Alzina, Jaume. *L'economia de la Catalunya autónoma*. Barcelona, 1933.
Amo, Julián, and Shelby, C. *La obra impresa de los intelectuales españoles en América*. Stanford, Calif., 1945.
Amsden, Jon. *Collective Bargaining and Class Conflict in Spain*. London, 1972.
Anderson, Charles W. *The Political Economy of Modern Spain*. Madison, Wis., 1970.
Andrade, Juan. *La burocracia reformista en el movimiento obrero*. Madrid, 1935.
Anllo, Juan. *Estructura y problemas del campo español*. Madrid, 1967.
Ansaldo, Juan Antonio. *¿Para qué? De Alfonso XIII a Juan III*. Buenos Aires, 1942.
Antistato, L. *Un trentenio di attivitá anarchica*. Cesserra, 1955.
Aranda, Antonio. *La guerra de Asturias, Aragón, y Levante*. Madrid, 1949.
Aranguren, José Luis L. *El problema universitario*. Barcelona, 1968.
Arauz, Alvaro. *La Wilhelmstrasse y el Pardo*. Mexico, D.F., 1949.
*Archives secrètes de la Wilhelmstrasse*, vol. 3. Paris, 1952.
Areilza, José M. *Embajadores sobre España*. Mexico, D.F., 1947.
Areilza, José M., and Castiella, Fernando M. *Reivindicaciones de España*. Madrid, 1941.
Arnheim, Rudolf. *Picasso's Guernica: The Genesis of a Painting*. Los Angeles, 1962.

Arquer, Jordi. *Salvador Seguí*. Barcelona, n.d. (1932).
Arrarás, Joaquín. *Historia de la segunda república española*. Madrid, 1956.
————. *Memorias íntimas de Azaña*. Madrid, 1939.
Arribas, Antonio. *The Iberians*. New York, 1964.
Artigues, Daniel. *El Opus Dei en España*. Paris, 1971.
Atkinson, William C. *A History of Spain and Portugal*. London, 1967.
Aubier, Dominique. *Spain*. New York, 1960.
*Authors Take Sides*. London, 1937.
Autrán, Eduardo de. *El riel asfixia a España*. Madrid, 1936.
Azaña, Manuel. *Obras completas*. Mexico, D.F., 1968.
Aznar, Manuel. *Historia militar de la guerra de España*. Madrid, 1940.
Balcells, A. *Crisis económica y agitación social en Cataluña, 1930-1936*. Barcelona, 1971.
Barangó Solís, Fernando. *Un movimiento revolucionario*. Barcelona, 1929.
Barea, Arturo. *La forja de un rebelde*. Buenos Aires, 1951.
Barón, E., and García Delgado, J.L. *Salarios y conflictos en la España del desarrollo*. Madrid, 1957.
Baer, Yitzahak. *A History of the Jews in Christian Spain*. Philadelphia, 1961.
Bartolí, Josep, and Molins i Fábrega, Narcis. *Campos de concentración*. Mexico, D.F., 1944.
Bastos Ansart, Francisco. *El desastre de Annual*. Barcelona, 1923.
Bates, Ralph. *The Olive Field*. New York, 1966.
Benavides, Manuel D. *El último pirata del Mediterráneo*. Barcelona, 1934.
Benson, F.R. *Writers in Arms*. New York, 1967.
Bertran y Güell, F. *Caudillos, profetas, y soldados*. Madrid, 1939.
Bertrand, Louis, and Petrie, Charles. *The History of Spain*. New York, 1945.
Blanshard, P. *Freedom and Catholic Power in Spain and Portugal*. Boston, 1962.
Bolin, Luis. *Spain: The Vital Years*. Philadelphia, 1967.
Bolloten, Burnett. *The Grand Camouflage*. London, 1961.
Bonamusa, F. *El Bloc Obrer i Camperol, 1930-1932*. Barcelona, 1974.
Borchsenius, Paul. *The Three Rings: The History of the Spanish Jews*. London, 1963.
Borkenau, Franz. *The Spanish Cockpit*. Ann Arbor, Mich., 1963.
Borrow, George. *The Bible in Spain*. London, 1906.
Bowers, Claude. *My Mission to Spain*. New York, 1954.
Brasillach, Robert, and Bardèche, Michel. *Histoire de la guerre d'Espagne*. Paris, 1939.
Brenan, Gerald. *The Face of Spain*. London, 1943.
————. *The Literature of the Spanish People*, Cambridge, 1951.
————. *South from Granada*. London, 1957.
————. *The Spanish Labyrinth*. Cambridge, 1943.
Brockway, Fenner. *The Truth about Barcelona*. London, 1937.
Brome, Vincent. *The International Brigades*. New York, 1966.
Brossard, Chandler. *The Spanish Scene*. New York, 1968.
Broué, Pierre, and Temime, Emile. *La revolución y la guerra de España*. Mexico, D.F., 1962.
Buckle, Enrique. *Bosquejo de una historia del intelecto español*. Valencia, n.d.
Buenacasa, M. *El movimiento obrero español*. Barcelona, 1928.
Bullejos, José. *Europa entre dos guerras*. Mexico, D.F., 1945.

——. *La Comintern en España*. Mexico, D.F., 1972.

Burnes, Emilio. *La conspiración nazi en España*. Mexico, D.F., 1938.

Busquets Bragulat, Emilio. *El militar de carrera en España*. Madrid, 1967.

Calvo Serer, Rafael. *La literatura universal sobre la guerra de España*. Madrid, 1962.

——. *Franco frente al rey*. Paris, 1973.

Cambó, Francisco. *La valoración de la peseta*. Madrid, 1928.

——. *Las dictaduras*. Madrid, 1929.

Campoamor, Clara. *La révolution espagnole vue par une républicaine*. Paris, 1937.

Canals, Salvador. *Los sucesos de España*. Barcelona, 1910.

Caravaca, Francisco. *La iglesia contra el poder civil*. Barcelona, 1932.

Cardó, Carles. *Histoire spirituelle des Espagnes*. Paris, 1946.

Carpandi, Armando. *Ensayo bibliográfico de las obras y folletos publicados con motivo del Movimiento Nacional*. Bermeo, 1940.

Carr, Raymond. *Spain, 1808-1939*. Oxford, 1966.

——, (ed.). *The Republic and the Civil War in Spain*. New York, 1971.

Carretero y Nieva, Luis. *Las nacionalidades españolas*. Mexico, D.F., 1952.

Carrillo, Santiago. *Demain, l'Espagne*. Paris, 1974.

——. *Después de Franco, ¿qué?* Paris, 1965.

Carrillo, Wenceslao. *A propósito del Consejo Nacional de Defensa*. Mexico, D.F., 1943.

Carrión, Pascual. *La reforma agraria*. Madrid, 1931.

Casasnovas, L., et al. *¿Concilio o rebeldía? Los latifundios clericales en Lérida*. Barcelona, 1966.

Castelar, Emilio. *Discursos*. Madrid, 1881.

Castillejo, José. *Education and Revolution in Spain*. London, 1937.

Castro, Américo. *The Structure of Spanish History*. Princeton, 1954.

——. *La realidad histórica de España*. Mexico, D.F., 1950.

Castro, Cristóbal de. *Al servicio de los campesinos*. Madrid, 1929.

Castro Delgado, Enrique. *Mi fe se perdió en Moscú*. Mexico, D.F. 1951.

——. *Hombres made in Moscú*. Mexico, D.F., 1960.

Cattell, D.T. *Communism and the Spanish Civil War*. Berkeley, Calif., 1956.

——. *Soviet Diplomacy and the Spanish Civil War*. Berkeley, Calif., 1957.

*Causa General*. Madrid, 1943.

Chapman, C.E. *A History of Spain*. New York, 1965.

Chase, A. *Falange: The Axis Secret Army in the Americas*. New York, 1943.

Chejne, Anwar G. *Muslim Spain*. Minneapolis, Minn., 1974.

Ciano, Galeazzo. *Ciano's Diary, 1939-1943*. London, 1949.

Claudín, F. *La crisis del movimiento comunista*. Paris, 1970.

Claugh, James. *Spain in the Modern World*. New York, 1953.

——. *Spanish Fury*. New York, 1964.

Colodny, Robert C. *The Struggle for Madrid*. New York, 1958.

Comín, Alfonso C. *España, país de misión*. Barcelona, 1966.

Comin, Colomer E. *Historia del Partido Comunista de España*. Madrid, 1962.

Conze, Edward. *Spain Today*. London, 1938.

Cosa, Juan de la (Luis Carrero Blanco). *España ante el mundo*. Madrid, 1950.

Costa i Deu, Josep. *La veritat del 6 d'octubre*. Barcelona, 1935.

Creach, Jean. *Le coeur et l'epée*. Paris, 1958.

Crockett, Lucy. *Kings without Castles*. New York, 1957.

Crow, John A. *Spain: The Root and the Flowers*. New York, 1963.

Crozier, Brian. *Franco*. Boston, 1967.

Cruzado, Clemente. *La España política de 1930*. Madrid, 1931.

Cruells, Manuel. *Els fets de maig de 1937*. Barcelona, 1970.

———. *El 6 d'octubre a Catalunya*. Barcelona, 1970.

Cuadrado, M.M. *Elecciones y partidos políticos en España, 1868-1931*. Madrid, 1969.

Davies, R. Trevor. *The Golden Century of Spain, 1501-1621*. New York, 1954.

Deakin, F.B. *Spain To-day*. London, 1924.

Descola, Jean. *A History of Spain*. New York, 1963.

Devlin, John. *Spanish Anticlericalism*. New York, 1966.

Díaz Plaja, Fernando. *La guerra, 1936-39*. Madrid, 1963.

———. *The Spaniards and the Seven Deadly Sins*. New York, 1969.

Dixon, Pierson. *The Iberians of Spain*. London, 1940.

Dolgoff, Sam (ed.). *The Anarchist Collectives*. New York, 1974.

*Documenti diplomatici italiani I, 1935-1939*. Rome, 1952.

*(Un) documento histórico: la sentencia contra el presidente de la Generalitat de Cataluña*. Bogota, 1949.

Domingo, Marcelino: *¿A dónde va España?* Madrid, 1969.

Dos Passos, John. *Rocinante to the Road Again*. New York, 1922.

Doussinage, J.M. *España tenía razón*. Madrid, 1950.

Dueñas, F. *La ley de prensa de Fraga*. Paris, 1969.

Dwelshauvers, Georges. *La Catalogne et le problème catalan*. Paris, 1926.

Ebenstein, William. *Church and State in Franco Spain*. Princeton, 1960.

*Economic and Social Development Program for Spain, 1964-1967*. Baltimore, 1965.

Elliot, John Huxtable. *Imperial Spain, 1469-1719*. London, 1963.

———. *The Revolt of the Catalans*. Cambridge, 1963.

Ellis, Havelock. *The Soul of Spain*. New York, 1926.

Epton, Nina. *Love and the Spanish*. London, 1961.

Eremburg, Ilia. *España: república de trabajadores*. Madrid, 1932.

Esch, Patricia A.M. van der. *Prelude to War: The International Repercussions of the Spanish Civil War*. The Hague, 1951.

Escrivá de Balaguer, J.M. *Camino*. Madrid, 1957.

Estivill, Angel. *El sis d'octubre: l'ensulciada dels jacobins*. Barcelona, 1935.

Feis, Herbert. *The Spanish Story: Franco and the Nation at War*. New York, 1966.

Fernández Almagro, Melchor. *Historia del reinado de Alfonso XIII*. Barcelona, 1933.

———. *Historia política de la España contemporánea*. Madrid, 1956.

Fernández Carvajal, Rodrigo. *La Constitución española*. Madrid, 1969.

Fernández Campos, José Luis. *El apremio de la enseñanza en España*. Bilbao, 1968.

Fernsworth, L. *Spain's Struggle for Freedom*. Boston, 1957.

Ferrándiz Albors, Francisco. *La bestia contra España*. Montevideo, 1951.

Fisher, B.W., and Bowen-Jones, H. *Spain: An Introductory Geography*. New York, 1958.

Foix, Pedro. *Los archivos del terrorismo blanco*. Barcelona, 1932.

Foltz, Charles. *The Masquerade in Spain*. Boston, 1948.

Franco, Francisco. *Discursos y mensajes del jefe del Estado*. Madrid, 1955, 1960, 1964, 1968.

Franco Salgado, F. *Mis conversaciones privadas con Franco*. Barcelona, 1976.

Francos Rodriguez, José. *El año de la derrota*. Madrid, 1930.
Frank, Waldo. *Virgin Spain*. New York, 1926.
Fresco, Mauricio. *La emigración republicana española*. Mexico, D.F., 1950.
Gallop, Rodney. *A Book of the Basques*. London, 1930.
Ganivet, Angel. *Idearium Espanol*. Buenos Aires, n.d.
Garate Córdoba, J.N. *Espíritu y milicia de la España medieval*. Madrid, 1967.
García Alonso, Francisco. *Mis dos meses de prisión en Málaga*. Seville, 1936.
García Durán, J. *Bibliography of the Spanish Civil War*. Montevideo, 1964.
García Martí, Victoriano. *De la zona atlántica*. Madrid, n.d.
García Morente, Manuel. *Idea de la hispanidad*. Buenos Aires, 1938.
García Palacios, L. *El segundo bienio*. Madrid, 1936.
García Valiño, Rafael. *La campaña del Norte*. Madrid, 1949.
García Venero, Maximiano. *Historia del nacionalismo catalán*. Madrid, 1944.
———. *Historia del nacionalismo vasco*. Madrid, 1945.
Garosci, Aldo. *Gli intelletuali e la guerra di Spagna*. Turin, 1959.
Gescher, B.H. *L'Espagne dans le monde*. Paris, 1937.
Gil Casado, Pablo. *La novela social en España*. Madrid, 1968.
Giménez Caballero, E. *Trabalenguas sobre España*. Madrid, 1931.
Goldeston, Robert. *Spain*. New York, 1967.
Gómez Hidalgo, Francisco. *Cataluña-Companys*. Madrid, 1936.
González Moralejo, Rafael. *El momento social de España*. Madrid, 1959.
———. *Las hermandades de trabajo*. Madrid, 1959.
González, Valentín ("El Campesino"). *La vie et la mort en URSS*. Paris, 1950.
González Blanco, Edmundo. *Costa y el problema de la educación nacional*. Barcelona, 1920.
Gorkín, Julián. *Caníbales políticos*. Mexico, D.F., 1941.
———. *Revolucionario profesional*. Barcelona, 1975.
———. *Un proceso de Moscú en Barcelona*. Barcelona, 1974.
Green, Otis H. *Spain and the Western Tradition*. Madison, Wisc., 1963.
Grossi, Manuel. *La insurrección de Asturias*. Barcelona, 1935.
Gutkind, E.A. *Urban Development in Southern Europe: Spain and Portugal*, vol. 3. New York, 1967.
Guttman, Allen. *The Wound in the Heart: America and the Spanish Civil War*. New York, 1962.
Halimi, F. *Le procès de Burgos*. Paris, 1971.
Halsey, F.W. (ed.). *Seeing Europe with Famous Authors: Spain and Portugal*, vol. 9. New York, 1914.
Hamilton, Bernice. *Political Thought in Sixteenth-Century Spain*. London, 1963.
Hamilton, E.J. *War and Prices in Spain, 1651-1800*. Cambridge, Mass., 1947.
Hamilton, F.J. *Appeasement's Child*. London, 1963.
Hanichen, F.C. *Nothing but Danger*. London, 1943.
Hayes, Carlton J.H. *Wartime Mission in Spain*. New York, 1945.
———. *The United States and Spain*. New York, 1951.
Helli, André. *Esta guerra empezó en España*. Buenos Aires, 1942.
Hemingway, E. *The Fifth Column and Four Unpublished Stories of the Spanish Civil War*. New York, 1969.
Hennesy, C.A.M. *The Federal Republic of Spain*. Oxford, 1962.
Hermet, Guy. *Les communistes en Espagne*. Paris, 1971.
Hernández, Jesús. *Negro y Rojo*. Mexico, D.F., 1946.
———. *Yo fui un ministro de Stalin*. Mexico, D.F., 1953.

Hernández Mir, F. *La dictadura ante la historia*. Madrid, n.d.
Herr, Richard. *The Eighteenth-Century Revolution in Spain*. Princeton, 1958.
Hidalgo de Cisneros, F. *Cambio de rumbo*. Bucharest, 1964.
Hills, George. *Franco: The Man and His Nation*. New York, 1967.
————. *Spain*. London, 1970.
*Historia del Partido Comunista de España*. Paris, 1965.
Hoare, Samuel. *Complacent Dictator*. New York, 1957.
————. *Ambassador on Special Mission*. London, 1946.
Hodgson, Robert. *Spain Resurgent*. London, 1953.
Holt, Edgar. *The Carlist Wars in Spain*. London, 1967.
*Huit-cent-quatre-vingt-neuf jours de lutte*. Paris, 1963.
Hume, M. *Philip II of Spain*. New York, 1969.
Ibarruri, Dolores. *Memoires*. Paris, 1963.
Iglesias, Ignacio. *El proceso contra el POUM*. Paris, 1975.
————. *Trotsky et la révolution espagnole*. Lausanne, 1974.
Ilie, Paul. *The Surrealist Mode in Spanish Literature*. Ann Arbor, Mich., 1968.
International Bank for Reconstruction and Development. *The Economic Development of Spain*. Baltimore, 1963.
International Commission of Jurists. *Spain and the Rule of Law*. Geneva, 1962.
Irizarry, Carmen. *The Thirty Thousand: Modern Spain and Protestantism*. New York, 1966.
Irving, Washington. *The Conquest of Granada*. London, 1930.
Jackson, Gabriel (ed.). *The Spanish Civil War*. Boston, 1967.
————. *The Spanish Republic and the Civil War, 1931-1939*. Princeton, 1965.
Jaume, Alejandro. *La insurrección de octubre*. Felanitx, 1935.
Jean, André. *Economic Transformation of Catalonia*. Barcelona, 1938.
Jelineck, Frank. *The Civil War in Spain*. New York, 1938.
Jiménez de Asúa, Luis. *Al servicio de la nueva generación*. Madrid, 1930.
Johnson, Verle B. *Legions of Babel*. London, 1967.
Johnson, W.F. *The Changing Face of 20th Century Spain*. New York, 1963.
Karl, Mauricio. *El comunismo en España*. Madrid, 1935.
Kazantzakis, Nikos. *Spain*. New York, 1963.
Kenny, M. *Spanish Tapestry: Town and Country in Castile*. Bloomington, Ind., 1961.
Kindelan, Alfredo. *Mis cuadernos de guerra*. Madrid, 1945.
Klein, Julien. *The Mesta: A Study of Spanish Economic History*. Cambridge, Mass., 1920.
Koestler, Arthur. *Spanish Testament*. London, 1937.
Koltzov, Mikhail. *Diario de la guerra de España*. Paris, 1963.
Krivitsky, Walter. *I Was Stalin's Agent*. London, 1939.
La Cierva, Ricardo de. *Historia del franquismo*. Barcelona, 1975.
Lain Entralgo, Pedro. *El problema de la universidad*. Madrid, 1968.
Lambert, Renée. *Mouvements ouvriers et socialistes: chronologie et bibliographie, Espagne*. Paris, 1953.
Landau, Katia. *Les staliniens en Espagne*. Paris, 1938.
Lane-Pool, S. *The Moors in Spain*. Beirut, 1967.
Langdon-Davies, John. *Gatherings from Catalonia*. London, 1953.
Largo Caballero, Francisco. *Mis recuerdos*. Mexico, D.F., 1954.
Larios, José. *Combat over Spain*. New York, 1966.
La Souchère, Elena de. *An Explanation of Spain*. New York, 1964.

Lea, H.C. *A Religious History of Spain*. Philadelphia, 1890.
Lerma, Marqués de. *De la Revolución a la Restauración*. Madrid, 1928.
Lerroux, Alejandro. *La pequeña historia*. Buenos Aires, 1945.
Lewis, Flora. *One of Our H Bombs Is Missing*. New York, 1967.
Lewis, Norman. *Spanish Adventure*. New York, 1935.
*Libro Blanco. Cataluña–White Book. Catalonia*. Buenos Aires, 1956.
Líster, Enrique. *¡Basta!* Paris, n.d. (1969).
————. *Nuestra guerra*. Paris, 1966.
Livermore, Harold. *A History of Spain*. London, 1958.
Llorente, J.A. *A Critical History of the Inquisition of Spain*. Cambridge, Mass., 1967.
Lloyd, Alan. *The Spanish Centuries*. New York, 1968.
London, Arthur. *Espagne*. Paris, 1966.
Llorens, Vicente. *Liberales y románticos*. Mexico, D.F., 1954.
Lluhí Vallescá, Joan. *Lluis Companys Jover*. Mexico, D.F., 1944.
Longo, Luigi. *Le Brigate Internazionale in Spagna*. Rome, 1956.
López Muñoz, A., and García Delgado, S.L. *Crecimiento y crisis del capitalismo español*. Madrid, 1968.
López Ochoa, E. *Campaña militar de Asturias, en octubre de 1934*. Madrid, 1936.
Loredo Aparicio, S. *La piedad de Franco*. Mexico, D.F., 1946.
Lorenzo, Anselmo. *El proletariado militante*. Madrid, 1974.
Lynch, John. *Spain under the Habsburgs*. London, 1964.
MacGuigan, D.S. *The Habsburgs*. New York, 1966.
MacKendrick, Paul. *The Iberian Stones Speak*. New York, 1969.
Madariaga, Salvador de. *Spain: A Modern History*. New York, 1958.
————. *Englishmen, Frenchmen, and Spaniards*. London, 1939.
Madrid, Francisco. *Film de la república comunista libertaria*. Barcelona, 1932.
————. *La Guinea incógnita*. Madrid, 1933.
Maeztu, Ramiro de. *Hacia otra España*. Madrid, 1942.
Maiski, A. *Spanish Notebooks*. London, 1966.
Malagón, Javier. *Historiografía de la guerra española*. Mexico, D.F., 1965.
Marañón, Gregorio. *Antonio Pérez*. Madrid, 1954.
————. *Españoles fuera de España*. Buenos Aires, 1947.
Maravell, J.M. *Trabajo y conflicto social*. Madrid, 1967.
Marbá, Palmiro. *El movimiento sindicalista obrero español*. Madrid, 1921.
Marías, Julián. *Miguel de Unamuno*. Cambridge, Mass., 1966.
Mariepol, Jean H. *The Spain of Ferdinand and Isabella*. New Brunswick, N.J., 1967.
Marrero, Vicente. *La guerra española y el trust de cerebros*. Madrid, 1961.
Martin, J.G. *Political and Social Changes in Catalonia during the Revolution, July 19-December 31, 1936*. Barcelona, 1937.
Martín Alonso, A. *Dieciseis años de regencia*. Barcelona, 1914.
Martín Artajo, Alberto. *El primer lustro de los convenios hispano-americanos*. Madrid, 1958.
Martín Blázquez, J. *Guerre civile totale*. Paris, 1938.
Marx, Karl. *La revolución española*. Madrid, 1929.
Matthews, Herbert L. *A World in Revolution*. New York, 1973.
————. *The Yoke and the Arrows*. London, 1957.
Maura, Miguel. *Cómo cayó Alfonso XIII*. Mexico, D.F., 1962.
Maura Gamazo, Gabriel. *Bosquejo histórico de la dictadura*. Madrid, 1930.

————. *Historia crítica del reinado de Alfonso XIII en su minoridad*. Madrid, 1925.
————. *Recuerdos de mi vida*. Madrid, 1934.
Maurín, Joaquín. *Los hombres de la dictadura*. Madrid, 1930.
————. *La revolución española*. Madrid, 1932.
————. *Hacia la segunda revolución*. Barcelona, 1935.
————. *Intervenciones parlamentarias*. Barcelona, 1937.
Máximo. *El anticlericalismo y las órdenes religiosas en España*. Madrid, 1908.
Medina Sidonia, Duquesa de. *La huelga*. Paris, 1970.
————. *La base*. Paris, 1971.
Medlicott, W.N., and Toynbee, A.J. (eds.). *Survey of International Affairs: The War and the Neutrals*. London, 1956.
Menéndez Pidal, Ramón. *The Cid and His Spain*. London, 1934.
Merkes, Manfred. *Die Politikgenuber des Spanische Burgerkrieg*. Bonn, 1961.
Michener, James. *Iberia*. New York, 1968.
Milany, Joan de. *Un aviador de la República*. Barcelona, 1970.
Miravitlles, Jaume. *De Jaca a Sallent*. Barcelona, 1932.
————. *Episodis de la guerra civil espanyola*. Barcelona, 1972.
Mogui. *La révolte des basques*. Paris, 1970.
Molas, Isidre. *Lliga Catalana*. Barcelona, 1972.
Molins i Fábrega, Narcis. *U.H.P.* Barcelona, 1935.
Monroe, James T. *Islam and the Arabs in Spanish Scholarship*. Leiden, 1970.
Mora, Constancia de la. *Fière Espagne*. Paris, 1946.
Morón, Gabriel. *El Partido Socialista ante la realidad política española*. Madrid, 1929.
Moronte, Luis. *La moral de la derrota*. Madrid, 1932.
Morris, James. *The Presence of Spain*. New York, 1964.
Morrow, Felix. *Revolution and Counter-revolution in Spain*. New York, 1939.
Mousset, Albert. *La política exterior de España*. Madrid, 1918.
Munnis, G. *Jalones de derrota, promesa de victoria*. Mexico, D.F., 1948.
Muñoz, Máximo. *Tragedia y derroteros de España*. Mexico, D.F., 1952.
Muste, John M. (ed.). *Say We Saw Spain Die*. Seattle, Wash. 1966.
Myhill, H. *The Spanish Pyrenees*. London, 1966.
*Negotiations on Gibraltar: A Spanish Red Book*. Madrid, 1968.
Negrín, Juan, and Prieto, Indalecio. *Epistolario*. Paris, 1939.
Nelken, Margarita. *La condición social de la mujer en España*. Barcelona, n.d.
Newmark, M. *Dictionary of Spanish Literature*. New York, 1956.
Nin, Andrés. *Les dictadures dels nostres dies*. Barcelona, 1930.
————. *Els moviments d'emancipació nacional*. Barcelona, 1935.
————. *Los problemas de la revolución española*. Paris, 1971.
Oliveira Martins, J. *La civilización ibérica*. Madrid, 1935.
Ollivier, Marcel. *La Guépéou en Espagne*. Paris, 1937.
Organization for Economic Cooperation and Development (OECD). *The Mediterranean Regional Project*. Paris, 1965; *Technical Assistance and the Economic Development of Spain*. Paris, 1968; *Science and Development: Spain*. Paris, 1968.
Ortega y Gasset, José. *Invertebrate Spain*. New York, 1937.
Ortzi. *Historia de Euzkadi*. Paris, 1972.
Orwell, George. *Homage to Catalonia*. London, 1938.
Ossorio y Gallardo, Angel. *Vida y sacrificio de Companys*. Buenos Aires, 1943.
Oteyza, Luis de. *Abd-el-Krim*. Madrid, n.d.

Padefood, Norman S. *International Law and Diplomacy: The Spanish Civil Strife*. New York, 1939.
Pagés, Pelai. *Andreu Nin*. Madrid, 1975.
Paget, M. *La integración del trabajador en la empresa*. Barcelona, 1967.
Palencia, Isabel de. *Smouldering Freedom*. New York, 1945.
Pámies, Teresa. *Quan érem capitans*. Barcelona, 1974.
Pascazio, Nicola. *La rivoluzione di Spagna*. Rome, 1934.
Paul, Elliot. *The Life and Death of a Spanish Town*. New York, 1942.
Payne, Robert. *The Civil War in Spain*. New York, 1962.
Payne, Stanley G. *Falange: A History of Spanish Fascism*. Stanford, Calif., 1961.
———. *A History of Spain and Portugal*. Madison, Wisc., 1973.
——— (ed.). *Franco's Spain*. New York, 1967.
———. *Politics and the Military in Modern Spain*. Stanford, Calif., 1967.
———. *The Spanish Revolution*. New York, 1970.
Peers, E. Allison. *Spain in Eclipse, 1937-1943*. New York, 1943.
———. *The Spanish Tragedy*. London, 1936.
———. *Catalonia Infelix*. London, 1938.
Peirats, José. *La CNT en la revolución española*. Toulouse, 1951-52.
Pemartín, José. *Los valores históricos de la dictadura española*. Madrid, 1928.
Pérez Baró, Albert. *Trenta mesos de collectivitzacions a Catalunya*. Barcelona, 1969.
Pérez Madrigal, A. *Tipos y sombras de la tragedia*. Avila, 1938.
Pérez Salas, Jesús. *Guerra en España*. Mexico, D.F., 1947.
Pi i Margall, Francisco. *Las nacionalidades*. Barcelona, 1917.
———. *Historia de España en el siglo XIX*. Barcelona, 1914.
Pi i Sunyer, Carles. *La República y la guerra civil*. Mexico, D.F., 1975.
Pike, David Wingate, *Vae victis!* Paris, 1969.
Pilapil, Vincent R. *Alfonso XIII*. New York, 1969.
Pinilla de las Heras, Esteban. *Los empresarios y el desarrollo capitalista*. Madrid, 1968.
Pitt-Rivers, J.A. *The People of the Sierra*. Chicago, 1961.
Pla, José. *Historia de la segunda república española*. Barcelona, 1941.
Plenn, Abel. *Viento en los olivares*. Mexico, D.F., 1947.
Prados Arrarte, M. *El plan de desarrollo de España*. Madrid, 1964.
Prescott, William H. *History of the Reign of Philip the Second of Spain*. Philadelphia, 1890.
Prieto, Indalecio. *Cómo y por qué salí del Ministerio de Defensa Nacional*. Mexico, D.F., 1940.
———. *Epistolario*. Paris, 1939.
———. *De mi vida*. Mexico, D.F., 1965.
Primo de Rivera, José Antonio. *Obras completas*. Madrid, 1943.
Pritchett, V.S. *The Spanish Temper*. New York, 1954.
Prudhommeaux, A. *Catalogne libertaire*. Paris, 1937.
Puzzo, Dante A. *Spain and the Great Powers, 1936-1941*. New York, 1962.
Quintanilla, Luis. *Los rehenes del Alcázar de Toledo*. Paris, 1968.
Ramírez, Luis. *Francisco Franco*. Paris, 1965.
———. *Nuestros primeros veinticinco años*. Paris, 1964.
Ramos Oliveira, Antonio. *Politics, Economics, and Men of Modern Spain*. London, 1964.
———. *El capitalismo español al desnudo*. Madrid, 1935.

Ratcliff, Dillwyn. *Prelude to Franco*. New York, 1957.
*The Red Domination in Spain*. Madrid, 1953.
Regler, Gustav. *The Great Crusade*. New York, 1940.
*Regulación del ejercicio del derecho civil a la libertad religiosa*. Madrid, 1968.
Reparaz, Gonzalo de. *Lo que pudo hacer España en Marruecos y lo que ha hecho*. Barcelona, 1937.
Reventlow, R. *Spanien in diesem Jahrundret*. Frankfurt, 1970.
Rico, José Antonio. *En los dominios del Kremlin*. Mexico, D.F., 1950.
Ridruejo, Dionisio. *Escrito en España*. Buenos Aires, 1962.
Rocker, Rudolf. *Extranjeros en España*. Buenos Aires, 1938.
Rodríguez Castillo, E. *Communist World Offensive against Spain*. Madrid, 1949.
Rodrígues Revilla, Vincente. *El agro español y sus moradores*. Madrid, 1931.
Rojo, Vincente. *Alerta a los pueblos*. Buenos Aires, 1939.
Rolfe, Edwin. *The Lincoln Battalion*. London, 1939.
*Romancero libertario*. Paris, 1971.
Romanones, conde de. *El ejército y la política*. Madrid, 1920.
———. *Notas de una vida*. Madrid, 1946.
Romeo G, José de J. *La hidra roja y España*. Mexico, D.F., 1946.
Romero Solano, L. *Vísperas de guerra en España*. Mexico, D.F., 1947.
Rosal, Amaro del. *Nuestra banca*. Madrid, 1935.
Rovira i Virgili, A. *História del catalanisme*. Barcelona, 1933.
Sala, A., and Duran, E. *Crítica de la izquierda autoritaria en Cataluña*. Paris, 1975.
Salaberri, Kepa. *El proceso de Euzkadi en Burgos*. Paris, 1971.
Sánchez, José M. *Reform and Reaction*. Chapel Hill, N.C., 1964.
Sánchez Albornoz, Claudio. *De mi anecdotario político*. Buenos Aires, 1972.
———. *Estudios sobre las instituciones medievales españolas*. Mexico, D.F., 1965.
Sanders, Roger S. *Spain and the United Nations, 1945-1950*. New York, 1966.
Santillán, Diego Abad de. *Por qué perdimos la guerra*. Buenos Aires, 1940.
———. *After the Revolution*. New York, 1937.
———. *La revolución y la guerra de España*. Barcelona, 1938.
Sanz Oller, Julio. *Entre el fraude y la esperanza*. Paris, 1972.
Saña, Heleno. *España sin equilibrio*. Madrid, 1975.
Sastre, Miguel. *Las huelgas de Barcelona, 1902-1914*. Barcelona, 1903-1915.
Savory, H.N. *The Prehistory of the Iberian Peninsula*. New York, 1968.
Schulte, Henry F. *The Spanish Press*. Urbana, Ill., 1967.
Sedwick, F. *The Tragedy of Manuel Azaña and the Fate of the Spanish Republic*. Columbus, Ohio, 1963.
Semprún Guerrea, J.M. de. *España en la encrucijada*. New York, 1956.
Semprún Maura, Carlos. *Revolución y contrarrevolución en Cataluña*. Barcelona, 1974.
———. *L'an prochain à Madrid*. Paris, 1974.
Senador, Julio. *La ciudad castellana*. Barcelona, 1917.
Sencourt, Robert. *Spanish Ordeal*. New York, 1940.
Sender, Ramón J. *Seven Red Sundays*. New York, 1945.
Serrano Suñer, Ramón. *Entre Hendaya y Gibraltar*. Madrid, 1947.
Servicio Histórico Militar. *Documentos para la historia*. Madrid, 1945.
Shafer, R.J. *The Economic Societies in the Spanish World*. Syracuse, N.Y., 1958.
Sieberer, A. *España frente a Cataluña*. Mexico, D.F., 1944.

Smith, B. *Spain: A History in Art*. New York, 1966.
Smith, L.E. *Mexico and the Spanish Republicans*. Berkeley, 1955.
Smith Rea, Marsh. *Spain: A Modern History*. Ann Arbor, Mich. 1965.
Somoza Silva, Lázaro. *El general Miaja*. Mexico, D.F., 1944.
Sordo, Enrique. *Moorish Spain*. New York, 1963.
Southworth, Herbert T. *El mito de la cruzada de Franco*. Paris, 1963.
————. *La destruction de Guernica*. Paris, 1972.
Stewart, John D. *Gibraltar. The Keystone*. Boston, 1967.
Suárez, Andrés. *El proceso contra el POUM*. Paris, 1974.
Szulc, Tad. *Portrait of Spain*. New York, 1972.
————. *Bombs at Palomares*. New York, 1967.
Tamames, Ramón. *La estructura económica de España*. Madrid, 1969.
————. *Los monopolios en España*. Madrid, 1967.
Taylor, F. *The Diplomatic Relations between the United States and Spain during the Civil War*. New York, 1956.
Temime, Emile, and Broué, Pierre. *Guerre et révolution en Espagne*. Paris, 1961.
Templewood, Lord (Samuel Hoare). *Ambassador on Special Mission*. London, 1946.
Thomas, G., Witts, M.M. *Guernica*. New York, 1976.
Thomas, Hugh. *The Spanish Civil War*. London, 1961.
Torrente Ballester, G. *Panorama de la literatura española contemporánea*. Madrid, 1965.
Torres Campañá, Manuel. *El gran fraude franquista*. Mexico, D.F., 1957.
Torhyo, Jacinto. *La independencia de España*. Barcelona, 1938.
Touberville, A.S. *The Spanish Inquisition*. London, 1932.
Tovar, Antonio. *Universidad y educación de masas*. Madrid, 1968.
Tracy, Honor. *Spanish Leaves*. New York, 1964.
Traina, Richard. *American Diplomacy and the Spanish War*. Bloomington, Ind., 1968.
Trend, J.B. *The Origin of Modern Spain*. Cambridge, 1934.
Trotsky, Leon. *Leçon d'Espagne*. Paris, 1938.
————. *Escritos sobre España*. Paris, 1971.
Trueta, Josep. *The Spirit of Catalonia*. London, 1945.
Tuñón de Lara, Manuel. *La España del siglo XIX*. Paris, 1966.
————. *La España del siglo XX*. Paris, 1968.
Ubieto, A., Reglá, J., and Jover, J. *Introducción a la historia de España*. Barcelona, 1963.
Ullman, Joan Connely. *The Tragic Week*. Cambridge, Mass., 1968.
Ullman, Pierre L. *Mariano de Larra and Spanish Political Rhetoric*. Madison, Wisc., 1974.
Unamuno, Miguel de. *En Torno al casticismo*. Madrid, 1930.
————, and Ganivet, Angel. *En torno al porvenir de España*. Madrid, 1931.
United Kingdom (Government of the). *Documents on German Foreign Policy, 1918-1948: Germany and the Spanish Civil War*, series D., vol. 3. London, 1951.
United States (Government of the). *Foreign Relations of the U.S., 1936-1939*. Washington, D.C., 1952-54.
Valdeavellano, Luis G. de. *Historia de España*. Madrid, 1952.
Vanni, Ettore. *Yo, comunista en Rusia*. Barcelona, 1950.

Velarde Fuentes, Juan. *España ante la socialización económica*. Madrid, 1970.
Vicens Vives, Jaume. *Historia social y económica de España y América*. Barcelona, 1957-59.
————. *Aproximación a la historia de España*. Barcelona, 1952.
Vidarte, Juan Simeón. *Todos fuimos culpables*. Mexico, D.F., 1973.
Vigón Suero, Jorge. *El espíritu militar español*. Madrid, 1950.
Vilar, Pierre. *Spain: A Brief History*. Paris, 1967.
Voros, S. *American Commissar*. Philadelphia, 1961.
Watkins, K.W. *Britain Divided*. London, 1963.
Weintraub, S. *The Last Great Cause*. New York, 1968.
Welles, Benjamin. *Spain: The Gentle Anarchy*. New York, 1965.
Whitaker, Arthur P. *Spain and the Defense of the West*. New York, 1961.
*White Paper. Gibraltar: Recent Differences with Spain*. London, 1965.
*White Paper. Gibraltar Talks with Spain*. London, 1966.
Whitney, Fred. *Labor Policy and Practice in Spain*. New York, 1965.
Wiseman, F.S. *Roman Spain*. New York, 1956.
Wolfe, Bertram D. *Civil War in Spain*. New York, 1938.
Wolgesinger, M. *Spain: 23 Photographs*. New York, 1957.
Woolman, David. *Rebels in the Rift*. Stanford, Calif., 1968.
Wright, Richard. *Pagan Spain*. New York, 1957.
Xuriguerra, Ramón. *La repressió contra els obrers a Catalunya*. Barcelona, 1937.
Yanguas Messía, J. de. *Beligerancia, no intervención y reconocimiento*. Burgos, 1938.
Ynfante, Jesús. *La prodigiosa aventura del Opus Dei*. Paris, 1970.
————. *Las sagradas familias de Barcelona*. Toulouse, 1975.
Young, George. *The New Spain*. London, 1933.
Zancada, Práxedes. *El obrero español*. Barcelona, 1902.
Zugazagoitia, Julián. *Pablo Iglesias*. Madrid, 1927.
————. *Guerra y vicisitudes de los españoles*. Paris, 1968.

# Index

Abad de Santillán, Diego, 70
*ABC*, 71, 218
Abd-el-Krim, 57, 58, 59
Abderraman I, 23
Abderraman III, 24
Abramovich, Rafael, 167
Adrian, 22
Action Française (*see* France)
Africa, 2, 21, 23, 29, 32, 34, 42, 67,
 82, 91, 134, 184;
 population 13, 96;
 North Africa 183, 209, 210, 219;
 and Spanish Civil War 153
Agrarian Party, 76, 85, 86, 94, 100,
 101, 102, 129
Agrarian Reform, 79;
 Institute of 78
(The) Agricultural Institute of San
 Isidro, 92
Aguirre, José Antonio, 126, 169,
 212
Air Foreign Legion, 139
Alans, 23

Alba, Duke of, 131, 191
Alba, Santiago, 61, 90
Albacete, 119, 137
Albornoz, Alvaro de, 69, 94, 212
Alcalá de Henares, 167
Alcalá Zamora, Niceto, 61, 66, 67,
 68, 76, 77, 80, 82, 91, 93, 94, 97,
 100, 103, 106, 113, 211
Alfonsians, 128–29
Alfonso XII, 43, 46, 50
Alfonso XIII, 53, 61, 82, 131, 191,
 253
Alfonso of Bourbon (*see* Alfonso
 XII)
Alfonsonians, 46
Algeciras, 118;
 Convention of, 181;
 Pact of, 219
Algiers (Algeria), 238;
 Nationalists, 219;
 Sahara conflict, 258
Alicante, 119, 129, 140, 144, 159,
 160, 166

Allied Committee of Control, 193
Allies, 180, 181, 182, 183, 184, 185,
    186, 187, 190, 191, 193, 194, 210
Almadén, 32
Almería, 120, 150
Altamira, 21
Alvarez del Vayo, Julio, 150, 154,
    166
Alvarez Mendizábal, Juan, 40
Amadeo I, 43, 44
Amadeo, Jorge, 217
Amado, Jorge, 217
America, 9, 13, 16, 28, 29, 31, 32
    33, 34, 36, 42;
    colonies of, 39;
    conquest of, 26–28, 30
Amnesty: Arias, 261;
    Juan Carlos I, 290;
    Suarez, 264, 268, 271
Ampurias, 21
Amsterdam, 32, 234
Anarchism, 50, 53, 60, 63, 85, 298,
    299;
    anarchist groups, 237;
    post-Franco, 277, 293;
    pseudo-anarchist groups, 240
Anarcho-Syndicalists, 214, 218,
    229, 280
Andalusia, 3, 15, 16, 21, 22, 35,
    37, 39, 41, 42, 45, 50, 76, 82, 85,
    92, 120, 135, 136, 224;
    post-Franco nationalism, 277
Annual, 57, 111
Añoveros, Antonio (Monsignor),
    241
Anton, David, 210
Antonov-Ovseenko, Vladimir,
    165, 167
Aosta, Duke of, 163
Apertura, 236, 238, 242, 245, 246
    256;
    aperturistas 237, 238, 239, 243,
    246;
    antiaperturistas, 237, 238
Arabs, 7, 12, 13, 23, 24, 25, 26, 27,
    29, 30, 33, 118, 153, 158, 159,
    165, 179, 193, 201, 220
Aragon, 3, 24, 25, 31, 40, 120, 124,
    143, 153, 155, 164;
    Council of 143

Aran Valley, 190
Aranda, Antonio (Colonel), 119
Aranjuez, 37
Araquistain, Luis, 111
Areilza, J. M. (Count of Motrico),
    228, 243, 256, 257
Argentina, 4, 53, 187, 193, 201;
    fascist aid to Francoist, 273
Argüelles (Sergeant), 97
Arias Navarro, Carlos, 236, 237,
    238, 239, 241, 243, 246, 248, 256,
    260, 261, 263, 264, 266, 270, 279
Arias Salgado, Gabriel, 224
Arnedo, 82
Arrese, José Luis, 174, 216
Arriba, 221
Artois, 33
Association for Service to the
    Republic, 62, 76
Asturias, 16, 24, 82, 96, 97, 119,
    120, 126, 144, 153, 179, 217, 224,
    227, 228;
    post-Franco nationalism, 279
Athens, 2
Atlantic Ocean, 2, 17, 36, 149
Atholl, Duchess of, 148
Attlee, Clement, 138, 150
Australia, 139;
    U.N. delegate, 202
Austria, 32, 33, 92
Avila, 118
Axis, 179, 180, 181, 183, 184, 185,
    192, 202, 205
Azaña, Manuel, 65, 69, 75, 76, 80,
    82, 83, 85, 86, 87, 91, 93, 94, 97,
    98, 99, 101, 103, 105, 107, 112,
    113, 124, 145, 158, 208
Aznar, Juan Bautista, 62, 65

Badajoz, 135
Bakunin, M., 43, 55
Balbo, Italo, 94
Balearic Islands, 16, 17, 25, 107,
    116, 184
Balkan (countries), 137, 157
Bank of Spain, 271
Barcarena, 140
Barcelona, 2, 5, 17, 18, 31, 40, 41,
    43, 45, 50, 54, 55, 56, 58, 59, 61,
    63, 65, 66, 70, 82, 95, 97, 99,

105, 108, 116, 119, 124, 125, 134,
137, 139, 140, 148, 150, 151, 153,
155, 157, 158, 164, 165, 168, 184,
187, 190, 195, 199, 210, 212, 216,
224, 225, 228, 235, 237, 241, 260,
294;
    Count of, 25
Barrera de Irimo, Antonio, 239
Basque country (*see* Euskadi)
Basque Nationalist Party, 93, 102,
126, 128;
    post-Franco, 279, 300
Basque Workers' Solidarity, 195
Bata, 82
Batet, Domingo (General), 95, 118
Bavaria, 2
Bayo, Alberto (Captain), 134
Bayonne, 38, 153, 237
Begoña, 183
Beimbler, Hans, 137
Belchite, 153
Belgium, 112, 157, 193, 220;
    investments 187;
    U.N. delegate 203
Beneyto, Ricardo (Lt. Col.), 219
Benicarló, 145
Benton Amendment, 205
Berard, Léon, 157
Berbers, 23
Berenguer, Damaso (General), 58,
61, 62, 263
Berlin, 116, 162, 164, 167;
    East Berlin, 195
Bernanos, Georges, 130
Bernieri, Camilo, 145, 167
Berzin (General) (a.k.a. Goniev),
163
Besteiro, Julián, 70, 80, 91, 155,
159, 160, 169, 173
Betica, 22
Bevin, Ernest, 212
Bidault, Georges, 153
Bilbao, 2, 3, 16, 18, 36, 82, 119,
124, 141, 144, 150, 153, 162, 195,
212, 217, 224, 228, 235, 241, 295
Bir-Hakeim, 210
Bismarck, 12
Bizertia, 159, 185
Black Hand, 50
Blasco Ibañez, Vicente, 60

Bloque Obrero y Campesino (*see*
BOC)
Blue Division, 182, 183, 193, 202,
216
Blum, Leon, 19, 148, 149
BOC, 60, 61, 71, 91, 93, 94, 167
*Bohemia*, 216
Bonaparte, Joseph, 38
Bonnard, Abel, 193
Bordighera, 181
Bourbon dynasty, 33, 35, 36, 41,
42, 46, 194, 281
Bourgeoisie, 296
Borrow, George Henry, 7, 8
Brandt, Willy, 268
Brezhnev, Leonid, 274
Brockway, Fenner, 168
Brouckère, Louis de, 168
Brunete, 153, 158
Brussels, 195, 234
Buenos Aires, 201
Buero River, 24
"Bunker," 237, 238, 239, 241, 242,
243, 245, 246, 247, 248, 249, 252,
255, 256, 257, 258, 262, 263, 266,
267, 269, 270, 274, 300;
    vertical unions, 260, 261
Bujaraloz, 5
Bulgaria, 211
Burgos, 31, 118, 129, 151, 153, 156,
159, 170, 234; Junta de, 130, 131,
140, 142, 144, 149, 150, 153, 154,
157, 162, 174, 183
Burgundy, 32

Cabanellas, Virgilio (General), 82,
116, 119, 129
Cabanillas, Pío, 237, 239, 243
Cáceres, 218
Cádiz, 2, 27, 36, 38, 119, 140;
    Constitution of, 39;
    Cortes of, 40
Caetano, Marcello, 238
Cairo, 201
Calcutta, 235
Calderón de la Barca, Pedro, 6
Calvo Serer, Rafael, 240
Calvo Sotelo, José, 59, 86, 106,
108, 116, 117, 129
Camacho, Marcelino, 253, 264

*Cambio 16,* 299
Cambó, Francesc, 57, 61, 63, 76
Campano, Angel (General), 269
(El) Campesino, 143, 164
Canada, 112
Canalejas, José, 57
Canary Islands, 2, 107, 116, 117;
   post-Franco nationalism, 277
Cánovas del Castillo, Antonio, 46,
   49, 50, 54
Cantabrían Sea, 16, 23, 149, 194
Cantalupo, Randolfo, 169
Capitalism (Francoist), 296;
   (post-Franco), 280
Carabanchel, 136;
   prison of, 253
Caracalla, 22
Carbonari, 39
Carlists, 40, 43, 44, 45, 46, 49, 71,
   87, 101, 102, 107, 116, 129, 179,
   192, 218, 299
Carner, Jaume, 82
Carrasco i Formiguera, Manuel,
   153
Carrero Blanco, Luis (Admiral),
   227, 233, 234, 236, 238, 255
Carrillo, Santiago, 229, 240, 264,
   265, 269, 271, 274, 293
Cartagena, 65, 67, 152, 159, 166
Carter, Jimmy, 273
Carthaginians, 13, 22
Casa de Campo, 137
Casado, Segismundo (Colonel),
   158, 160
Casals, Pau, 269
Casares Quiroga, Santiago, 107,
   108
Casa del Pueblo, 91, 92, 118
Casas Viejas, 85
Castelar, Emilio, 45
Castellón, 140, 155
Castellanos, Pablo, 239
Castiella, Fernando María, 219
Castile, 3, 15, 16, 24, 25, 26, 27,
   28, 31, 32, 33, 34, 35, 38, 120,
   190, 224;
   population, 16, 24, 25;
   language, 16, 247
Castillblanco, 82
Castillo, José (Lieutenant), 108

Castro, Fidel, 134, 208, 225;
   Castroists, 229
Castro Delgado, Enrique, 210
Catalonia, 3, 14, 16, 17, 24, 26, 27,
   28, 29, 31, 32, 33, 35, 36, 40, 41,
   42, 45, 50, 51, 52, 54, 58, 60, 62,
   68, 71, 87, 90, 91, 92, 94, 95, 98,
   99, 101, 120, 123, 124, 125, 126,
   134, 136, 142, 143, 145, 147, 153,
   155, 156, 157, 162, 174, 190, 194,
   210, 227, 241, 269, 279;
   Assembly of, 294;
   autonomy of, 279;
   church of, 227;
   culture, 194;
   language, 16, 59, 79, 158, 174,
      194, 215, 224, 247, 269;
   nationalism, 54, 55, 56, 57, 58,
      60, 62, 68, 70, 119, 153, 154,
      208, 229, 230, 276, 278, 280;
   political parties, 191, 294;
   population, 17, 24, 44;
   post-Franco opposition, 265,
      269;
   priests, 225, 241;
   Statute of, 78, 79, 85, 110, 174
Catalonian Action Party, 61, 70
Catalonian-Aragonese Federation,
   25
Catalonian Christian Democrats,
   279
Catalonian Communist Party, 60,
   124
Catalonian Federation of the
   Communist Party, 60
Catalonian Federation of Unions,
   54
Catalonian League (Lliga), 57, 58,
   61, 62, 70, 76, 85, 87, 92, 100,
   101, 102, 129
Catalonian Liberal Conservatives,
   279
Catalonian Parliament, 79, 85, 90,
   92, 93, 94, 212
Catalonian Republic, 66
Catalonian Socialist Party, 279
Catalonian State, 95
Catalonism (*see* Catalonia:
   Nationalism)
Cathars, 25

Catholic Action, 192, 216, 241;
  Workers' Brotherhood, 216, 224, 241
Catholic kings (see Ferdinand, Isabella I)
Catholic unionists (see Basque Workers's Solidarity)
Catholic Working Youth, 216, 241
Cavalleti, Count Franco, 169
CCOO, 273
CEDA, 85, 86, 90, 91, 92, 93, 94, 95, 97, 98, 99, 100, 101, 102, 191
Celtiberians (see Celts)
Celts, 13, 21, 22
Censorship, 177, 239
Centeno, Tomás, 219
Center (political groups), 264, 265, 272, 275, 279, 300
Central Powers, 56
Centrist Party, 102
Ce Soir, 166
Ceuta, 140, 219, 220
Chamber of Deputies (see Cortes)
Chamberlain, Neville, 157, 160
Chapaprieta, Joaquín, 99, 100
Charlemagne, 24
Charles of Austria (Archduke), 33
Charles (Ferdinand VII's Brother), 40
Charles I (see Charles V)
Charles II, 31, 33
Charles III, 35, 36, 37, 40, 176
Charles IV, 35, 37, 38
Charles V, 29, 31, 32, 33
Chile, 154, 173, 252
China, 240;
  China-Spanish diplomatic relations, 270
Christian Democrat Party, 224, 228, 239, 241, 261, 275, 277, 278, 294, 299
Christianity (see Church)
Church (Catholic), 12, 22, 24, 71, 75, 79, 80, 126, 177, 181, 191, 192, 197, 198, 199, 200, 201, 215, 216, 217, 218, 225, 227, 234, 235, 241, 242, 252;
  Progressive Catholics, 226, 229, 241, 274
Churchill, Winston, 183

Ciano, Count Galeazzo, 181
Círculo de Labradores, 83
Ciudad Real, 60
Ciudad Universitaria, 136, 137
Civil Aviation Agency, 193
Civil Directorate, 59
Civil Guard, 42, 51, 67, 68, 82, 83, 96, 97, 107, 119, 133, 173, 190, 269, 274
Civil Wars (Carlist), 44;
  (1936–1939) 5, 12, 14, 15, 38, 121, 133, 137, 138, 139, 140, 141, 148, 151, 152, 161, 163, 168, 169, 172, 179, 180, 181, 184, 187, 189, 191, 193, 196, 197, 207, 210, 213, 214, 215, 216, 221, 223, 226, 229, 230, 231, 237, 241, 243, 245, 251, 252, 253, 264, 271, 273, 280, 281, 285, 287, 291, 300
Claudín, Fernando, 229
CNS, 157, 176, 182, 190, 195, 228, 241, 271, 293, 294, 300;
  wealth of, 293, 294;
  successor to, 294
CNT, 54, 56, 57, 58, 61, 62, 70, 73, 74, 76, 79, 81, 83, 84, 89, 90, 94, 96, 98, 101, 118, 120, 124, 125, 127, 138, 142, 143, 145, 146, 151, 154, 155, 159, 164, 165, 167, 190, 241, 266;
  in exile, 210, 211, 214;
  legalized, 273
Coca Cola Co., 220
Codovila, Vitorio (a.k.a. Medina), 163
Colonial League, 44
Colombia, 266
Columbus, Christopher, 26
Committee of Militias, 124
Communism, 12, 131, 163, 276
Communist groups, 237, 276, 278, 279
Communist Party, 71, 83, 87, 94, 101, 102, 108, 126, 128, 138, 143, 145, 146, 147, 148, 151, 152, 154, 155, 156, 158, 159, 163, 164, 165, 166, 167, 168, 169, 171, 190, 195, 215, 216, 217, 224, 226, 229, 240, 245, 253, 257, 259, 260, 275, 277,

278, 279, 280, 292, 293, 294, 295, 297, 300;
ideological terrorism, 272, 273, 274;
in exile, 208, 210, 211, 213;
legalized, 272, 273, 274;
opposition, 229, 240, 241, 249, 259, 261, 262, 264, 265, 267, 268, 269, 270, 271, 295
Communist Party (factions) 293;
pro-Italian, 217;
pro-Soviet, 217;
pro-Chinese, 217–229
Communist Left Party, 101, 167
Communist Youth, 106
Comorera, Juan, 210
Companys, Lluis, 58, 66, 90, 95, 105, 119, 123, 124, 135, 155, 158, 189, 212
Compostela, 22, 24
Concordat, 195
Confederation of Autonomous Right-Wing Groups (see CEDA)
Confederación Nacional del Trabajo (see CNT)
Congress of the Union Organization, 261
Confederation of Workers Commissions (see CCOO)
Conservative Party, 87, 102, 129
Conservatives, 133;
post-Franco legislators, 278
Constituent Assemblies (1873), 45; (1931), 76
Constitutional Reform, 267
Constitutions:
of Cadiz, 39;
of 1837, 40;
of 1876, 61;
of 1931, 76, 77, 78, 79, 80, 93, 106, 115, 117, 158, 211;
of Franco, 157, 214
Cordova, 24, 44, 119, 130, 134, 198;
Caliphate of, 24
Corpo di Truppe Volontari (see Italy)
Corporations, 293;
foreign capital, 293
Corsica, 25

Cortes, 73, 74, 77, 78, 80, 82, 84, 86, 87, 90, 91, 93, 96, 97, 98, 99, 100, 101, 102, 105, 106, 107, 108, 116, 126, 150, 158, 212;
Franco's, 176, 199, 219, 224, 226, 227, 234, 236, 243, 254, 255, 256, 260, 261, 264, 267, 268, 275, 277, 278, 281, 290;
in exile, 208, 211;
Permanent Deputation, 208;
post-Franco, 277, 279, 283
Corts, 25
Costa, Joaquín, 52, 76
Cot, Pierre, 139
Council of Ministers, 239, 247, 259
Council of Regency, 194, 251
Council of the Realm, 234, 236, 254, 255, 256, 258, 259
Council of State, 255, 268
Counterreformation, 12, 30
Court of Constitutional Guarantees, 77, 86, 92, 93, 94, 99
Crimea (war of), 41
Crocker, John, 8
Cro-Magnons, 21
Cromwell, 145
CTV (see Italy)
Cuadernos para el Diálogo, 225, 228
Cuba, 32, 43, 44, 50, 51, 53, 208, 211, 216, 225
Cunhal, Alvaro, 240, 271, 293
Czechoslovakia, 106, 141, 149, 174, 201, 211, 221, 229, 240

Dacia 13
Daily Telegraph, 130
Daladier, Edouard, 157
Dato, Eduardo, 57
El Debate, 71
Degrelle, Léon, 193, 203
DeGaulle, Charles, 213, 225
Delbos, Yvon, 148
Democratic Alliance, 43
Democratic Conference, 248
Democratic Junta, 240, 248, 253, 294, 295
Democratic Military Union, 241, 292
Democratic Platform, 239, 240

Democratic Union of Students, 226
Democrats, 44
Dencàs, Josep, 95
Department of the Interior, 236, 256, 264, 267
Deutsch, Julius, 137
D'Hondt electoral system, 277
Díaz, José, 210
Díaz Alegría, Manuel (General), 236
Dollfuss, Engelbert, 92
Dominican Republic, 263
Domingo, Marcelino, 69, 174
Dos Passos, John, 5
Doval, Luis, 97
Duclos, Jacques, 163, 164
Durruti, Buenaventura, 70, 143

Ebro River, 155, 157; Battle of, 156, 157, 162, 164
Echeverría, J., 112
Economic Society of Friends of the Country, 36
Economy 275;
  inflation, 238, 275, 292;
  Planning Commission, 235;
  unemployment, 275
Eden, Anthony, 155, 157, 205, 210
Edinburgh, Prince Philip of, 252, 288
Egypt, 272
Ehrenburg, Ilya, 165
Eibar, 66
Eisenhower, Dwight (General), 293
Elcano, Sebastian, 32
El Ferrol, 130, 140
Elizabeth II, 205
El Pardo, 180
Emigration, 275
Employers' Association, 83
Emporion (see Ampurias)
England, 1, 12, 13, 29, 32, 33, 34, 37, 38, 53, 112, 128, 137, 139, 141, 157, 158, 163, 164, 165, 174, 180, 181, 182, 183, 184, 185, 187, 193, 201, 202, 203, 204, 205, 208, 209, 223, 225, 235, 288;
  British companies, 163;

Conservative Party, 149;
  population, 286;
  House of Commons, 210;
  investments, 228;
  Labor government, 12, 102, 220;
  police, 274;
  trade unions, 212
Enrique y Tarancón, Vicente (Archbishop), 252
Episcopal Conference, 241
Escarré, Aureli (Abbot), 225
Escorial, 31, 178
Escriba de Balaguer, José María (Reverend), 217, 218
Espartero, Baldomero (General), 40, 41
Esquerra Republicana de Catalunya, 63, 66, 71, 85, 86, 87, 90, 91, 95, 101, 102, 124, 128, 190;
  in exile, 211
Estoril, 218, 240
ETA, 226, 234, 235, 236, 241, 242, 244, 257, 260, 261, 263, 267, 272, 273, 295, 300;
  Nationalist Marxist faction, 240;
  Trotskyite faction, 240, 243
Ethiopia, 110;
  War of, 162
Eucharistic Congress, 198
Eurocommunism, 271
Europe, 4, 8, 11, 12, 19, 24, 26, 27, 28, 29, 30, 33, 39, 69, 130, 137, 161, 179, 181, 188, 193, 203, 207, 225, 228, 251, 290, 297;
  anti-Francoist protests, 244, 245;
  population, 24;
  union movements, 294;
  Western Europe, 215, 222, 231, 244, 245, 253, 258, 275, 280, 288, 297, 299
European Christian Democratic Parties, 261
European Common Market, 225, 228, 232, 280
European Economic Community, 236, 244
European Institutions, 224
European Parliament, 204
Euskadi, 15, 16, 18, 40, 42, 50, 52,

92, 120, 124, 150, 169, 190, 195,
217, 226, 243, 263, 264, 267, 269,
271, 272, 273, 274, 294;
church, 227;
Fueros, 264, 265;
Government, 153, 169 [in exile,
212];
language, 16, 247;
nationalism, 70, 76, 93, 144, 146,
153, 154, 208, 230, 277, 278,
280, 300 [in exile, 211];
police, 253, 265, 273;
political parties, 191, 294;
Population, 2, 17, 80;
Priests, 225, 241;
Statute of autonomy, 110, 126,
174, 279;
Terrorism, 263, 264, 271, 272,
273 [extreme right, 264, 267]
Euskaro (see Euskadi)
Eximbank, 204
Extremadura, 15, 82, 92, 120,
134, 158, 224

FAI, 60, 61, 70, 74, 81, 190
Falange Española, 85, 91, 105,
115, 116, 129, 131, 136, 157, 171,
173, 174, 175, 176, 180, 183, 187,
192, 196, 199, 205, 214, 215, 216,
217, 218, 219, 226, 228, 251, 252,
272;
Brotherhood of Peasants, 176;
Congress, 204, 205;
Education and Rest for
Recreation, 176;
Falangists, 116, 118, 136, 176,
178, 179, 182, 184, 186, 187,
189, 191, 192, 193, 194, 195,
204, 214, 215, 216, 218, 219,
228, 233, 235, 238, 249, 255,
256, 278, 279;
Flechas, 175;
National Council of the, 157;
National Unionist Center (see
CNS);
Pelayos, 175;
social assistance, 176;
Spanish University Union (see
SEU);
vertical unions, 176, 238, 241,
242, 257;

Womens' Section, 175;
Youth Front, 175, 199
Fanelli, Giuseppe, 43
Fanjul, Joaquín (General), 116,
118, 127
Faraudo, Carlos (Captain), 108
Farinacci, Roberto, 163
Farley, James A., 220
Fascism, 12, 129, 148, 163, 175,
242
anti-Francoist, 278
Federal Party, 190
La Federación, 43
Federalists, 76
FEDISA, 243, 256, 257
Ferdinand V, 26, 27, 28, 29, 31, 33
Ferdinand VI, 35
Ferdinand VII, 37, 38, 39, 47, 115,
123
Fernandez Miranda, Torcuato,
236, 255, 278
Fernando Poo, 51
Ferrer Guardia, Francisco, 55
Fiat Co., 19
Fifth column, 143, 155, 156, 159
Fígols, 82, 84
Figueras, Estanislau, 44, 45
Figueres, 158
Finances (banking system), 275
Financial Times, 201
Finland, 106;
Finnish legation, 221
Flanders, 29, 32, 33
Flórez Estrada, Alvaro, 78
Ford, Gerald, 268
For Whom the Bell Tolls, 163
Foreign Legion, 96, 97, 118, 134,
135, 136, 153, 179, 193
Foreign Legion (French), 210
Foster Dulles, John, 220
Fraga Iribarne, Manuel, 224, 227,
228, 243, 256, 257, 258, 259, 260,
272, 273, 296
France, 12, 13, 21, 23, 25, 29, 32,
33, 36, 37, 45, 53, 57, 60, 68, 69,
84, 106, 111, 112, 116, 120, 124,
128, 137, 139, 141, 153, 155, 156,
158, 164, 165, 181, 182, 184, 185,
189, 190, 193, 194, 208, 209, 210,
212, 219, 220, 222, 226, 237, 243,
288;

Action Française, 149;
Cartel of the Left, 12;
CGT, 213;
Communist Party, 166;
companies, 187;
Free French Forces, 210;
German occupation, 208, 209, 300;
government, 134, 139, 148, 149, 193, 209, 211, 252;
investments, 228;
OAS, 213;
police, 274;
resistance, 184, 190, 193, 209, 210;
revolution, 37;
Third Republic, 12
France-Navigation Co., 166
Franche-Comté, 33
Francis I, 29
Franco, Francisco Bahamonte, 105, 107, 116, 117, 129, 130, 131, 134, 136, 139, 140, 145, 149, 150, 157, 158, 159, 161, 162, 163, 165, 166, 168, 169, 170, 171, 172, 173, 175, 176, 178, 179, 180, 181, 182, 183, 184, 185, 186, 187, 189, 190, 191, 192, 193, 194, 195, 196, 198, 199, 201, 202, 203, 204, 205, 210, 211, 212, 213, 214, 215, 218, 219, 220, 221, 224, 225, 226, 227, 230, 233, 234, 235, 236, 237, 239, 240, 242, 243, 244, 245, 246, 248, 249, 251, 252, 254, 255, 256, 260, 261, 264, 269, 270, 274, 276, 277, 279, 280, 281, 285, 286, 287, 288, 289, 290, 291, 292, 293, 296, 297, 300;
family, 252;
funerals, 252, 292;
illnesses, 235, 238, 247, 287, 288, 290
Franco, Nicolas B., 131, 192
Franco, Ramón, 62
Franco Martínez, Francisco, 219
Francoism, 233, 234, 236, 237, 242, 243, 244, 246, 248, 252, 255, 256, 257, 258, 260, 262, 263, 266, 267, 268, 269, 270, 271, 272, 273, 274, 275, 276, 278, 279, 280, 281, 291, 292, 293, 295, 296, 297, 300;
post-Francoism, 246

Frankfurt, 234
Franks, 24
FRAP, 240, 243, 244, 245
Free Basque Fatherland (see ETA)
Free Institution of Learning, 52
Freemasonry, 39, 82, 99, 131, 144, 148, 173, 244
*Front de la Llibertad*, 190
Funck-Brentano, Frantz, 177

*Gaceta*, 92
Galán Fermín, 62
Galicia, 16, 18, 24, 51, 119, 120, 239;
language, 247;
nationalism, 70, 230, 277, 278;
Statute of Autonomy, 108, 110
Gallo, Max, 137
Gamazo, Count of, 112
Gambara, Gastone (General), 160
Gandía, 160
García, Cristino, 193, 212
García Hernández, Angel, 62
García Lorca, Federico, 130
García Oliver, Juan, 143
García Ruíz, 239
GAS, 242
Gandesa, 156
Gaul, 13
General Union of Workers (see UGT)
Generalitat de Catalunya, 68, 79, 85, 90, 91, 93, 95, 97, 99, 105, 108, 119, 123, 124, 142, 143, 145, 155, 158;
in exile, 212
Generation of '98, 52
Geneva, 150, 191, 234
Genoa, 2, 17, 25, 28
George VI, 155
German Holy Roman Empire, 32
Germanics, 13, 22, 23
Germany, 29, 50, 53, 56, 108, 111, 112, 116, 129, 131, 140, 141, 149, 151, 158, 161, 162, 163, 164, 166, 167, 170, 174, 175, 180, 181, 182, 183, 184, 193, 209, 286;
Condor Legion, 162;
Gestapo, 167, 189;
German forces, 135, 139, 144, 150, 159, 173;

peasants, 36
(East) Germany, 221;
  German-Spanish diplomatic
    relations, 270
(West) Germany, 4, 222, 252, 272,
  288;
  Christian Democracy, 275;
  investments, 222, 228;
  police, 274;
  SPD (Social Democrat Party),
    261, 275;
  Western Occupation Forces of,
    221
Gerö, Enro (a.k.a. Pedro), 163
Gestapo (see Germany)
Ghadaffi, Mohammed el,
  (Colonel), 275
Gibraltar, 2, 57, 140, 181, 182, 184,
  185, 205, 225, 228, 251;
  autonomy, 225;
  Strait of, 118, 134, 135, 185
Gijón, 119, 141, 153
Gil Robles, José María, 85, 90, 92,
  94, 98, 99, 100, 101, 131, 134,
  179, 191, 194, 225, 239
Giner de los Ríos, Francisco, 52
Giolitti, Giovanni, 87
Giral, José, 124, 128, 211
Girón, José Antonio, 233, 243, 251
Giscard d'Estaing, Valéry, 252, 288
Goded, Manuel (General), 105,
  107, 116, 119, 127
Godoy, Manuel, 37
Goicoechea, Antonio, 93, 98
Golden Fleece Order, 278
Gomá, Isidro (Cardinal Primat),
  130
Goniev (see Berzin)
González, Valentín (see El
  Campesino)
González, Felipe, 239, 240, 279,
  280
González Peña, Ramón, 97
Gordón Ordás, Felix, 212
Goths (see Visigoths)
Goya, Francisco de, 14, 35
Gramsci, Antonio, 39
Granada, 24, 26, 119, 130, 134,
  191, 228
Grandees, 84

Grandi, Dino, 149, 156
GRAPO, 268, 270, 273
Grau Sanmartín, Ramón, 211
Greece, 1, 4, 17, 25, 184;
  population 13, 21
Grinko, G., 166
Gromyko, Andrei, 202
Groups for Syndicalist Action (see
  GAS)
Guadalajara, 119, 144, 154
Guam, 51
Guardias de Asalto, 82
Guatemala, 211
Guernica, 150, 162
Guerrillas of Christ the King, 242
Guevara, Ché, 226;
  Guevarists, 229
Guillén, Nicolás, 217
Guinea, 51, 153;
  Gulf of, 175
Gutierrez Mellado, Manuel
  (General), 266

Hamburg, 2
Hannibal, 22
Hassan II, 247
Hedilla, Manuel, 129
Hegel, Georg Wilhelm Friedrich,
  286
Helsinki, 222
Hemingway, Ernest, 14, 138, 163
Hendaya, 134, 181
Heraldo de Madrid, 91
Hernández, Jesús, 163, 210
Hernández Gil, Antonio, 278
Herranz, Francisco, 228
Herrera, Emilio (General), 212
Herrera, Ignacio, 112
Herriot, Edouard, 84, 148
Hidalgo, Diego, 96
High Military Council, 272
Himmler, Heinrich, 181
Hispania, 13
Hispanic Institutes, 255
Hispano-Romans, 22, 23
History of Philosophy, 177
Hitler, Adolf, 108, 150, 164, 169,
  170, 173, 174, 180, 181, 183, 184,
  185, 186, 193, 233, 237
HOAC, 216, 266

Hoare, Sir Samuel (Lord Templewood), 181, 184
Holland (*see* Netherlands)
Hollywood, 60
Holy Brotherhood, 31
Holy See, 27, 41, 43
Huesca, 119, 124
Hungary, 131, 211, 215, 221

Ibañez, Antonio (General), 269
Ibarra, Marquis de, 112
Ibarruri, Dolores (La Pasionaria), 159, 210, 264, 274
Iberian Anarchist Federation (*see* FAI)
Iberian Bloc, 181
Iberian Peninsula, 1, 204
Iberians, 13, 22
Ibiza, 134
ICFTU, 217
Ifni, 91, 110, 153, 220
Iglesias, Pablo, 49
"L'Illustration," 68
Independent Monarchist Party, 102
Independents of the Center Party, 87, 90, 100
Independents of the Left, 76
Independent Radical Socialist Party, 87, 91
Indians, 31, 39
*Indice,* 216
Indies, 28, 31;
   Council of, 28
INI, 176
Inquisition, 14, 29, 38
*Insula,* 216
International Association of Workers, 43
International Brigades, 137, 138, 139, 144, 156, 163, 167
International Confederation of Christian Unions, 195
International Confederation of Free Trade Unions (*see* ICFTU)
International Court, 193, 247
International (Third), 124, 163, 165
International (Fourth), 229
International Libertarian Movement (*see* MIL)

International Labor Organization, 109
Interparliamentary Union, 222
Iraq, 201
Ireland, 149
Irla, Josep, 212
Irún, 134, 135
Isabella I, 26, 27, 29, 31
Isabella II, 39, 40, 43, 46
Islam, 23
Israel, 258
Istiqlal, 219, 220
Italy, 11, 26, 29, 53, 58, 90, 108, 110, 112, 129, 131, 141, 149, 151, 155, 156, 159, 161, 162, 163, 166, 174, 181, 182, 185, 201, 213, 225;
   Communist Party, 240, 276, 293;
   CTV, 163;
   exiles, 207;
   investments, 228;
   Italian forces, 134, 135, 139, 140, 144, 150, 153, 158, 160, 163, 174, 184;
   Littorio Division, 169;
   Police, 274;
   Population, 223
ITT Co., 59. 76, 187

Jaca, 62, 66, 91
Jackson, Gabriel, 172
Jaén, 120
Jane the Mad, 29
Japan, 32, 131
Jarama River, 144
JARE, 208
Jérez, 3, 228
Jesuits, 30, 37, 75, 80, 109, 112, 186, 217, 218
Jews, 12, 13, 25, 27, 30, 200, 300
Jímenez de Asúa, Luis, 107, 212
John XXIII (Pope), 225
Jordán, 272
Jordana, Count of, 183, 192
JSU, 106
Juan de Borbon, Count of Barcelona, 67, 131, 191, 192, 194, 218, 227, 240, 253, 254, 256, 274
Juan Carlos de Bourbon, 194, 218;
   Prince of Spain, 227, 238, 239,

240, 244, 247, 290;
King of Spain, 248, 249, 251,
252, 253, 254, 255, 256, 257,
258, 261, 263, 264, 266, 272,
273, 274, 278, 279, 280, 287,
288, 290, 291, 292, 295, 297
Juntas de Ofensiva Nacional
Sindicalista (*see* JONS)

Kagan, 166
Karaganda camp, 211
Kellogg-Briand Pact, 78
Kierkegaard, Sören Aabye, 52
Kindelán, Alfredo (General), 191
Kissinger, Henry A., 258, 268
Kleber, Emilio, 137, 163
Koniev (General), 163
Kropotkin, Pierre, 55
Krupp Co., 112

Laburu, Enrique María (Jesuit),
215
Lafargue, Paul, 43
Laín Entralgo, Pedro, 214
La Línea, 135
La Montaña (military barracks),
119, 120
Landau, Kurt, 145, 167
Landru, 193
Language, 298
Largo Caballero, Francisco, 70, 73,
91, 93, 98, 102, 107, 128, 142,
145, 146, 147, 151, 152, 154, 161,
169, 210
Larra, Mariano, 11
Las Casas, Bartolome de, 27, 28
Latin America, 14, 15, 19, 28, 32,
51, 84, 111, 166, 201, 209, 211,
212
Laurel, José P., 184
Laval, Pierre, 193
La Vega, 96
Law of Defense of the Republic,
82, 85, 86
Layret, Francesc, 57
League of Nations, 110, 150, 157,
162
Lebrun, Albert, 160
Leclerc (Division), 210
Left (political groups), 242, 265,
274, 276, 277, 291, 294;

extreme left, 260, 267, 270, 277,
300
*Le Monde*, 225
Lenin, 92, 226;
Leninists, 296
León, 24, 120;
Kingdom of, 24
Lepanto (battle), 29
Lequerica, José Felix, 192
Lérida, 119, 155
Lerroux, Alejandro, 54, 55, 68, 69,
70, 76, 81, 82, 83, 85, 86, 90, 91,
92, 93, 94, 98, 99, 100, 101, 113
Levante, 136
Liberal Democrat Party, 87, 94,
100, 102
Liberal Union, 41
Liberals, 42, 44, 56, 115, 133, 299;
post-Franco legislators, 278
Libertarian Youth, 190
Libya, 275
Lie, Trygve, 203
Lisbon, 32, 129, 131, 140, 191, 192,
244, 287
Llopis, Rodolfo, 212
London, 43, 118, 131, 139, 140,
141, 144, 149, 150, 153, 157, 158,
164, 169, 181, 182, 191, 201, 202,
211, 234
Longo, Luigi, 137
López Bravo, Gregorio, 228
López Ochoa, Eduardo, 96, 97,
126
López Rodo, Laureano, 222, 228
Lorenzo, Anselmo, 43
Los Ríos, Fernando de, 70, 74
Louis Philippe (French king), 235
Louis XIV, 33
Low Countries (*see* Netherlands)
Lucán, 22
Lusitania, 22
Luther, Martín, 12
*Luther*, 177

Machado, Antonio, 52, 299
Maciá, Francesc, 58, 60, 62, 63, 66,
68, 71, 90
MacNeil, Hector, 202
Madrid, 2, 12, 18, 19, 31, 36, 37,
38, 41, 43, 47, 50, 51, 52, 55, 56,
58, 62, 65, 66, 67, 68, 71, 75, 83,

84, 92, 93, 95, 96, 98, 108, 115,
117, 118, 119, 120, 124, 126, 134,
136, 137, 139, 140, 141, 142, 143,
144, 148, 150, 153, 159, 160, 164,
168, 174, 184, 185, 190, 194, 195,
199, 201, 202, 204, 205, 209, 214,
216, 217, 218, 219, 220, 221, 225,
227, 228, 229, 235, 236, 241, 242,
245, 247, 252, 258, 259, 261, 265,
269, 270, 271, 273, 274, 287, 292;
Defense Junta of, 136
Magdalenians, 21
Magellan, Ferdinand, 32
Málaga, 36, 119, 120, 141, 144, 236
Maldonado, José, 212
Mallorca, 29, 119, 130, 134;
post-Franco nationalism 277
Malraux, André, 138, 139, 142
Mancommunitat de Catalunya, 55,
56, 59
Manresa, 190
Manuilsky, D. Z., 165
Manzini (General), 169
Maoists, 229, 240, 241, 278
Maragall, Joan, 52
Marañón, Gregorio, 65
Marca Hispánica, 24, 25
Marcial, 22
March, Juan, 83, 134
Marguliz, 166
María Cristina (Alfonso XII's
wife), 50
María Cristina (Ferdinand VII's
wife), 39
Marian Archipelago, 51
Mariana, S. J. Juan de, 78
Maritain, Jacques, 148, 153
Marseilles, 2, 208
Marshall Plan, 201, 202, 204
Martín Artajo, Alberto, 192, 203,
214, 216, 220
Martínez Barrio, Diego, 70, 86, 91,
106, 107, 124, 126, 158, 208, 211,
212
Martínez Campos, Arsenio, 46, 50
Marty, André, 163
Marx, Karl, 43, 67, 68, 226;
Marxists, 138
Marxist groups, 237, 259
Matesa Affair, 226
Maura, Antonio, 55, 70

Maura, Miguel, 70, 74, 80, 94, 109,
211
Mauriac, François, 148, 153
Maurín, Joaquín, 60, 71, 101, 167
Mauritania, 238, 247
Maximilian, 29
Maxton, James, 168
Mediterranean coast, 235, 258
Mediterranean Pact, 220
Mediterranean Sea, 22, 25, 134,
141, 149, 163
Melilla, 220
Menéndez, Teodomiro, 97
Menorca, 34, 134, 158
Mera, Cipriano, 143
Mesta, 30, 36
Mexico, 1, 27, 32, 42, 134, 140,
149, 158, 194, 208, 209, 210, 211,
244, 272, 273;
Spanish-Mexican diplomatic
relations, 272
Mexico City, 211
Miaja, José (General), 136, 155,
160
Middle class, 297, 299
Mieres, 96
Mikado, 184
MIL, 240
Military Directorate, 58, 59
Military establishment
(post-Franco), 252, 268, 270,
272, 273, 274, 291, 292
left-leaning, 292;
right-leaning, 292
Military Information Service (see
SIM)
Military Juntas of Defense, 56
Military Supreme Court, 270
Miranda de Ebro (Camp), 184
Mitterand, François, 268
Mohammedans, 200
Mola, Emilio (General), 75, 107,
116, 118, 124, 129, 137, 140, 152
Molero, José (General), 118
Molotov, V., 221
Monarchist Party, 76, 101
Monarchists 191, 194, 214, 218,
227, 290;
Confederation of Monarchist
Forces, 194
Monarchy, post-Franco, 251, 252,

253, 254, 255, 256, 258, 281;
Arias government, 256, 258, 259;
economic crisis, 259, 275, 292,
293;
Elections, 258, 259, 274, 275,
276, 277, 278, 279, 280;
political reform, 280;
Suarez government, 264, 274,
275, 278, 293, 296;
strikes, 259, 260, 271, 275, 293,
300
Mondale, Walter, 273
Mondoñedo, Bishop of, 144
Mont-de-Marsan, 181
Montserrat, Monastery of, 225,
241
Moors (see Arabs)
Moral, Marquis del, 150
Moriscos (see Arabs)
Moroccan Unity (party of), 194
Morocco 42, 43, 51, 53, 55, 57, 58,
59, 83, 84, 96, 116, 117, 140, 150,
169, 179, 184, 194;
French Protectorate, 219;
independence, 220, 238, 247;
nationalism, 165, 219;
Sahara Claim, 246;
Sahara occupation, 247, 258;
Spanish Protectorate, 219, 220;
Sultan of, 182, 219, 220
Morón (Air base), 258
Moscardó, José (Colonel), 134, 157
Moscow, 60, 147, 152, 163, 164,
165, 166, 167, 181, 208, 210, 212,
221, 229, 240, 271, 293;
trials, 167, 168
Mozarabs, 23
Muladíes, 23
Mondo Obrero, 128
Munich, 225;
Conference of, 164;
European Congress, 225
Muñoz Grandes, Agustín
(General), 182, 183, 220, 224,
227, 234
Murat, Joachim, 37
Murcia, 107
Mussolini, Benito, 12, 58, 90, 94,
105, 108, 115, 140, 141, 149, 150,
169, 174, 181, 183, 184, 185, 186,
193, 201, 233

Naples, 17, 25, 29, 31, 140
Napoléon I, 37, 38;
Russian Campaign, 38
Napoléon III, 12
Narváez, Ramón María, 41
Narvick (battle), 210
National Alliance of Democratic
Forces, 190, 191, 211
National Assembly, 60
National Confederation of
Workers (see CNT)
National Council of Defense, 158,
159, 164
National Councils of Democracy,
190
National Council of the Falange,
129
National Ecclesiastical Advisory
Board, 198
National Institute of Industries (see
INI)
National Movement 227, 233, 234,
243, 251, 254, 256, 272, 290;
National Council of, 254, 260
National Union, 190
National Unionist Center (see
CNS)
Nationalist forces, 134, 135, 137,
140, 141, 144, 152, 153, 154, 155,
159, 160, 161, 162, 169, 179
Nationalist zone, 131, 133, 141,
142, 157, 163, 172, 229,
NATO, 204, 220, 258
Navarre, 24, 40, 107, 116, 118, 120
Nazism, 181, 192, 286
Neanderthalians, 21
Negrín, Juan, 146, 147, 148, 150,
151, 154, 155, 158, 159, 164, 165,
166, 167, 168, 169, 170, 201, 208,
210, 221
Neighborhood associations, 240,
241
Nelson, Horatio (Admiral), 27
Nenni, Pietro, 137
Neruda, Pablo, 217
Netherlands, 29, 32, 33, 193, 222;
Socialist Party, 261
"New Force," 242
(The) New State, 175, 178, 184,
188, 189, 190, 201, 234;
Fundamental Laws, 254, 256,

258, 259, 267
New York, 198, 202, 221
*New York Tribune*, 67
Nin, Andreu, 101, 143, 145, 165, 167, 168
Nixon, Richard M., 293
NKVD (*see* Soviet Union)
Nobility, 290
Nod-Baker, Philip John, 150
Nombela, J., 100
Non-Intervention Committee, 141, 149, 153, 156, 162;
Control Committee of the, 156
Normandy, 2, 184, 186, 210
Norway, 220
Núñez de Prado, Miguel (General), 119
Nuremberg (Trials), 185

Odessa, 166
O'Donnell, Leopoldo, 41
Olivares, Count-Duke of, 33
Omeyan Dynasty, 23
Opposition (to Franco's Regime), 228, 239, 240, 241, 243, 248, 287, 288, 291;
Church, 241;
extreme right, 242;
military, 241;
Noncommunist left, 245;
police, 243, 244;
professional organizations, 240, 253;
terrorism, 236, 242, 243, 244, 257
Opposition (post-Franco), 252, 258, 260, 261, 265, 267, 268, 269, 272, 280, 291, 292, 293, 294, 295, 300;
democratic, 262, 264, 265, 267, 271;
falangist, 252;
Francoist, 252, 259, 260, 264, 295;
noncommunist, 294, 295;
rupture, 261, 262, 265, 269
Opposition (Students'), 214, 215, 225, 226, 228, 229, 240;
monarchists, 214;
socialists, 214;
terrorists, 240
Opus Dei, 217, 218, 219, 222, 227,

228, 230, 235, 236, 240, 245, 253
Order of Isabella the Catholic, 220
ORGA (*see also* Galicia's Nationalists), 70, 76, 91
Oriente Palace, 244, 249, 288, 290
Oriol, Antonio María de, 268, 271
Orlov, Alexander, 166, 167
Ortega y Gasset, José, 52, 62, 69, 76, 128, 214
Orthodox Radical Socialist Party, 87, 91
Orwell, George, 138
"Osservatore Romano," 153, 192
Oviedo, 96, 97, 118, 144

Pacts:
Anti-Komintern, 174, 182;
of Laredo, 169;
Russo-German, 180
Palma de Mallorca, 140, 150
Palme, Olaf, 268
Palomares (atomic bomb accident), 258
Pamplona, 195, 217
Panama, 202, 211
Pardo Palace, 246, 249
Paris, 61, 68, 135, 140, 141, 143, 150, 153, 158, 164, 169, 193, 210, 211, 212, 219, 225, 234, 240, 244, 253;
Commune of, 43
*Paris-Soir*, 103, 139
Parliament (*see* Cortes)
Patriotic Antifascist Revolutionary Front (*see* FRAP)
Patriotic Union, 59
Paul VI (Pope), 270
Pavía, Manuel (General), 45, 46
Pecchio, 8
Pearl Harbor, 184
Pedregal, Manuel, 107
Peiró, Joan, 70, 189
Penrith, Lord, 150
PENS, 242
Pérez Farrás, Enrique, 97
Pérez Galdos, Benito, 69
Perón, Eva, 201
Perón, Juan (General), 201
Perpignan, 237
Peru, 27
Pestaña, Angel, 70

Pétain, Philippe (Maréchal), 158, 181
Petiot, Dr., 193
Philip II, 31, 32, 33, 176, 180
Philip III, 31, 33
Philip IV, 33
Philip V, 33, 35, 52, 182
Philip the Fair, 29
Philippines, 32, 34, 43, 46, 50, 184
Phoenicians, 13, 21
Pi i Margall, Francesc, 45
Piñar, Blas, 242
Pinochet, Augusto (General), 252
Pirelli Co., 112
Pius XI (Pope), 84, 86, 184
Pivert, Marceau, 168
Pla, Josep, 188
Pla y Deniel, Enrique (Cardinal Primate), 191
Platajunta, 265
Platt Amendment, 50
Plymouth, Lord, 141
Poitiers, 24
Poland, 202, 211, 221;
   UN delegates 202, 203
Police, 268, 269, 273;
   National Union of, 273;
   Sociopolitical Brigade, 266, 267
Polisario Front, 238
Political parties (post-Franco), 275, 276, 277
Ponaccorsi, Arconovaldo, 134
Popular Alliance, 272, 279
Popular Council, 124
Popular democracies:
   diplomatic relations with Spain, 270
Popular Front, 101, 102, 103, 106, 116, 118, 128, 168
Popular Socialist Party, 240, 275;
   antizionism, 275;
   subsidies, 275
Portela Valladares, Manuel, 100, 103, 105, 116
Portugal, 4, 16, 33, 37, 39, 83, 120, 131, 134, 141, 149, 181, 184, 204, 238, 247, 287;
   African colonies, 238;
   Communist Party, 245, 292;
   Military, 266, 292

Portuguese legion, 149;
   "Revolution," 238, 292
Potsdam, 202;
   Declaration of, 193, 202
POUM, 101, 102, 124, 127, 138, 142, 143, 145, 146, 147, 152, 154, 156, 164, 165, 166, 167, 168, 169, 190, 210
Pradera, Juan José, 199
Prague (trials of), 202
Prat de la Riba, Enric, 55
Prats de Molló, 60
*Pravda,* 221
Press Law:
   Franco's, 272;
   Suarez's, 272
Prieto, Indalecio, 70, 76, 83, 86, 90, 93, 98, 101, 107, 113, 146, 151, 153, 154, 155, 164, 169, 194, 208, 210, 211
Prim, Juan (General), 42, 43, 46
Primo de Rivera, José Antonio, 85, 107, 116, 129, 144, 178
Primo de Rivera, Miguel, 58, 60, 116, 262
Primo de Rivera, Miguel, Jr., 205
Progressive Party, 70, 76, 87, 90, 102
Progressives, 40, 42
Protestants, 130, 198, 214
Provence, 2, 25
PSOE (*see* Socialist Party)
PSUC, 124, 125, 145;
   in exile, 210;
   post-Franco, 279
Puerto Rico, 43, 50
Puig Antich, Josep, 237, 240
Punic War II, 22
Pyrenées, 1, 21, 22, 23, 24, 141, 156, 158, 193, 210

Queipo del Llano, Gonzalo (General), 62, 116, 118, 119, 134, 135, 144
Quintilian, 22

Rabassaires, 97;
   Unión de, 124
Rabat, 220, 247
Radical Party, 69, 70, 76, 81, 82,

85, 86, 87, 90, 91, 94, 98, 99, 100, 101, 102
Radical Socialist Party, 86
Raeder, Erich (Admiral), 185
Rebel Zone (*see also* Nationalist Zone), 129, 130, 138
Reconquest, 11, 24
Referendum (1976), 267, 281
Reformation, 12
Regionalist League, 52, 55
Regulars (Moorish troops), 134, 135, 136
Reich (*see* Germany)
Renaissance, 12, 26
Republic (First), 44, 46, 49, 133, 285;
  (Second), 12, 15, 42, 62, 66, 67, 71, 73, 74, 76, 77, 79, 80, 81, 83, 84, 86, 89, 90, 92, 93, 94, 95, 98, 102, 103, 105, 107, 108, 109, 110, 111, 113, 115, 117, 118, 119, 120, 124, 128, 133, 134, 136, 141, 145, 147, 148, 149, 151, 152, 155, 161, 165, 169, 170, 171, 177, 179, 196, 214, 221, 222, 226, 271 [in exile 208, 211, 212]
Republican Action Party, 76, 87, 91
Republican Alliance Party, 69
Republican Conservative Party, 211
Republican forces, 134, 140, 141, 144, 147, 151, 152, 153, 155, 156, 157, 162, 164, 172, 185, 208
Republican government, 131, 135, 145, 153, 156, 157, 165, 181, 199, 221;
  in exile, 195, 211, 212, 272
Republican Left, 190
Republican Leftist Party, 69, 101, 102, 124, 190
Republican Military Union (*see* UMR)
Republican Union, 91, 101, 102, 190
Republican zone, 124, 126, 129, 130, 131, 133, 136, 141, 142, 144, 145, 147, 148, 150, 151, 172, 186, 197, 229

Republicanism, 291
Republicans, 42, 44, 45, 46, 49, 56, 58, 62, 63, 65, 77, 80, 81, 82, 84, 86, 94, 95, 96, 98, 101, 102, 103, 107, 113, 116, 120, 126, 130, 131, 146, 152, 159, 161, 164, 168, 173, 189, 191, 194, 298, 299;
  in exile, 202, 203, 206, 208, 210, 211, 218, 221
Requetés, 116
Restoration, 49, 50, 53, 63, 281
Revolutionary Committee, 62, 63, 65, 66, 67, 68;
  Asturian, 96
Reus, 158
Rhein, Mark, 167
Richthofen, Wolfam von (Colonel), 162
Ridruejo, Dionisio, 216, 239, 240
Right (political groups), 265, 272, 275, 276, 277;
  extreme, 242, 263, 264, 268, 269, 270, 271, 273, 277, 279, 286, 291, 292, 294, 295, 300
Right-Wing Independent Party, 87, 103
Rioja, 3, 85
Riotinto Co., 43, 119, 144
Rockefeller, Nelson, 252
Rodríguez del Barrio (General), 108
Rojo, Vicente (General), 155, 219
Rogers, William, 229
Rokossovski (General), 163
Romanones (Alvaro Figueroa, Count of), 65, 66, 71, 76
Rome, 13, 23, 29, 30, 94, 116, 199, 200, 201, 264, 270;
  Roman Empire, 13, 31;
  Romans, 13, 22
Roosevelt, Franklin D., 141, 181, 183
Rosenberg, Marcel, 149, 165
Rossi, "Count" (*see* Ponaccorsi, Arconovaldo)
Rota (Naval Base), 258;
  atomic submarines, 258
Roussillon, 33
Ruíz Jimenez, Joaquin, 225, 239
Ruíz Senén, V., 112

Rumanía, 106, 211, 240, 276;
  aid to Spanish Communist
    Party, 276, 293
Russia (Campaign of), 38;
  Revolution, 139

Sacred Heart of Jesus, 58
Sagasta, Práxedes Mateo, 49, 54
Sagunto, 3, 155
Sahara, 51, 83, 220;
  Moroccan invasion, 247;
  nationalism, 238, 246, 247;
  self-determination, 247;
  Spanish, 238, 246;
  Spanish evacuation, 258
Saint James, 22, 24
Saint Paul, 22
Sala, Victorio, 168
Salamanca, 130, 163, 167
Salas, Francisco (Admiral), 116
Salazar Alonso, Rafael, 100
Salazar, Antonio de Oliveira, 135,
  184, 238
Saliquet, Antonio (General), 118
Salmerón, Nicolás, 45
Salvochea, Fermín, 50
Samper, Ricardo, 92, 93
Sánchez Albornoz, Claudio, 212
Sánchez Guerra, José, 60, 61, 62
Sánchez Guerra, Rafael, 211
Sandhurst (Military School), 46
San Fernando, 130
San Francisco, 202
Sanjurjo, José (General), 67, 82,
  83, 116, 129, 179
San Sebastián, 61, 119, 134, 135,
  136
Santa María de la Cabeza, 134
Santander, 36, 141, 153
Santiago, Fernando de (General),
  266
Sardinia, 17, 25
Savoy Dynasty, 43
Scandinavia, 137
Schell, Walter, 252, 288
Seat Co., 19
Segre River, 155, 157
Seguí, Salvador, 56, 57
Segura, Pedro (Cardinal
  Archbishop), 74, 198, 200

Senate, 277, 278, 279;
  king's appointed senators, 278
Seneca, 22
SERE, 208
Serrano, Francisco (Duke de la
  Torre), 46
Serrano Suñer, Ramón, 157, 180,
  182, 192
SEU, 175, 178, 205, 214, 215, 225,
  226
Seville, 18, 25, 27, 28, 31, 32, 33,
  59, 82, 83, 118, 119, 130, 134,
  135, 140, 151, 183, 191, 198
Sicily, 17, 25
SIM, 143, 152, 155, 171
Sirval, Luis de, 97
Skorzeny, Otto, 193
Slavs, 286
Social Democratic Party, 239
Social Security, 196, 275
Socialist clubs (see also Casas del
  Pueblo), 92
Socialist groups, 276, 278;
  dissident socialists, 279
Socialist International, 212
Socialist Party, 49, 50, 57, 58, 60,
  61, 62, 63, 70, 73, 74, 76, 77, 79,
  81, 82, 83, 86, 87, 90, 91, 92, 93,
  96, 98, 101, 102, 107, 118, 126,
  127, 128, 138, 146, 151, 154, 159,
  190, 239, 270, 275, 276, 277, 278,
  279, 280, 293, 294, 299;
  Congress, 268;
  in exile, 194, 210, 211, 214, 218,
    239;
  in the opposition, 229, 239, 241,
    261, 268;
  legalized, 270
Socialist Youth, 91, 98, 99, 106,
  190
Society of Jesus (see Jesuits)
Sofia (Queen of Spain), 252, 272
La Solidaridad, 43
Solis, José, 227, 228, 243, 247, 256
Soria, 192
Sormenti, Eneas (see Vidale,
  Vittorio)
Sota, J., 112
Soviet bloc, 228
Soviet Union, 59, 84, 96, 138, 140,

141, 144, 147, 149, 151, 152, 156, 158, 161, 162, 164, 165, 166, 167, 171, 180, 182, 183, 193, 201, 202, 209, 210, 211, 215, 221, 228, 271, 274;
Czechoslovakia occupation, 229;
NKVD, 166, 167, 168;
Soviet arms, 161, 164;
Soviet technicians, 155 [Trade Agreement, 201; Mission 201]
Soviet-Spanish diplomatic relations, 270;
Stalinist Activities, 163, 167, 168;
UN Delegates, 202, 222
Spaak, Paul Henri, 203
Spain: Exile, 208, 209, 213, 234;
Psychology, 286, 289
Spanish Federation of Deported Persons, 211
Spanish Junta of Liberation, 211
Spanish Military Unión (*see* UME)
Spanish National Syndicalist Party (*see* PENS)
Spanish Renovation, 85, 87, 102
Spellman, Francis (Cardinal), 198
Sperrle, Hugo von (General), 162
Stalin, 12, 164, 170, 202, 271, 291;
Stalinists, 138, 156, 271, 286
Stashevsky, Artur, 165, 166
Stendhal, 7
Stepanov, 163
Stern, Lazar (*see* Kleber, E.)
Stockholm, 234
Straperlo, 100, 177
Strauss, M., 99, 100
Suárez, Adolfo, 256, 264, 270, 272, 273, 274, 276, 279, 280;
economic crisis, 265;
government of, 264, 265, 274, 276;
referendum, 267
Suez Canal, 220
Superior Junta of Cinematographic Orientation, 191
Supreme Court, 99;
of new state, 254, 255, 270, 272
Supreme Junta, 38
Sweden, 139, 141, 222;
Socialist Party, 261
Switzerland, 106, 112, 130, 169, 193, 208, 222;
investments, 187
Syndicalists, 102;
syndicalism, 293

Tablada, 76
Tajo River, 134
Talavera, 135
Tangiers, 135, 181, 182, 183, 184, 192, 193
Tarraconensis, 22
Tarragona, 158;
Archbishop of, 130
Technical Junta, 129
Tedeschini, Monsignor, 84
Tenerife, 117
Tercio (*see* Foreign Legion)
Terrorism, 261, 263, 264, 269, 270, 273, 274, 277, 278, 280, 294, 295, 297, 300;
antiterrorist law, 243
Teruel, 154, 164, 169
Teuán, 117, 162
Tharshis, 21
The Hague, 193, 247
Thomas, Norman, 138, 168
Tierno Galván, Enrique, 224, 228, 240
Tito, Josip Broz, 137;
Titoism, 210
Togliatti, Palmiro (a.k.a. Ercole and Alfredo), 163
Tokyo, 184
Toledo, 25, 134, 135;
Alcázar, 107, 134, 135;
Seat of the Archbishop-primate, 75
Tomás, Belarmino, 97
Torrejón (Air Base), 258
Torrent, Martín (Reverend), 177
Torres, Abdelkader, 165
Tourism, 275
Traditionalists (*see* Carlists)
Trafalgar (battle), 37
Trajan, 22
Transjordania, 201
Treaties:
French-Spanish, 219;
of Paris, 50;
Spanish-American, 258

Tribunals:
of Political Responsibilities, 173;
of Public Order, 235, 269;
popular, 127
Trilla, Gabriel Léon, 193
Trotsky, Léon, 167;
Trotskyites, 138, 165, 167, 168,
229, 240, 241, 278, 279
Trubia, 96
Truman, Harry, 201
Turks, 29, 32

UCD, 272, 275, 276;
elections, 278
UGT, 50, 56, 57, 61, 70, 73, 81, 91,
92, 96, 118, 124, 125, 151, 159,
210, 266;
Legalized, 273;
National Federation of
Landworkers of the, 92
UHP, 95
UME, 116
UMR, 62, 116
Unamuno, Miguel de, 5, 52, 59,
60, 130
UNESCO, 203
Unified Socialist Party of Catalonia
(see PSUC)
Unified Socialist Youth (see JSU)
Union of Proletarian Brothers (see
UHP)
Unió Socialista de Catalunya (see
USC)
Union of Democratic Center (see
UCD)
United Kingdom (see England)
United Nations, 193, 194, 201, 202,
203, 211, 221, 222, 244;
Constitutive Assembly, 202;
First General Assembly, 202,
211;
Sahara's question, 246, 247;
Security Council, 202, 203, 244
United Press, 175
United States, 1, 4, 37, 42, 44, 50,
51, 106, 112, 137, 139, 141, 149,
162, 167, 172, 181, 182, 183, 187,
193, 198, 200, 202, 203, 204, 205,
208, 209, 220, 221, 225, 244, 245,
263, 268, 273, 282;

aid, 222, 258;
anti-American feelings, 293;
American companies, 163, 293;
bases, 204, 228, 249, 258, 268,
269;
Congress, 204, 263;
Department of State, 185, 212,
229;
government, 234, 252;
investments, 222, 228
Navy, 220;
Pentagon, 204;
Senate, 201, 204, 205, 258;
U.N. Delegates, 222
Universities, 226;
Barcelona, 215;
deans of, 254;
Madrid, 214, 288;
post-Franco, 275
Urbanization, 245
Urquijo family, 112
USC, 61
USSR (see Soviet Union)

Valencia, 2, 15, 16, 17, 18, 25, 31,
36, 50, 60, 98, 119, 120, 124, 126,
136, 140, 145, 150, 153, 155, 159,
160, 190, 197, 217, 221;
political parties, 294;
post-Franco nationalism, 277;
post-Franco opposition, 265
Valladolid, 31, 118, 130
Valley of the Fallen, 219, 252
Vallina, Pedro, 76
Van Aster, 177
Vance, Cyrus, 273
Vandals, 23
Vandervelde, Emile, 138
Van Zeeland, Paul, 187
Varela, José Enrique (General),
183, 194
Vatican, 75, 91, 138, 153, 181, 195,
199, 200, 225, 234;
Council, 225;
Vatican II, 227
Vázuez (Sergeant), 97
Velada de Benicarló, 145
Velázquez, 33
Venezuela, 4, 32, 211, 266
Venice, 17

Ventosa Calvell, Joan, 112
Vera del Bidasoa, 60
Vichy, 192, 208, 300
Vickers Co., 112
Vidal i Barraquer, Emili
    (Archbishop), 71
Vidale, Vittorio (a.k.a. Contreras,
    Carlos, Sormenti, Eneas), 167
Vietnam, 32, 38, 172
Vigo, 140
Villa Cisneros, 83
Villa, Martín, 256, 264
Villaescusa, Emilio (General), 270,
    271
Villar Mir, Juan M., 259
Villaverde, Marchioness of, 248,
    252
Villaverde, Marquis of, 219
Visigoths, 23, 24, 26
Vitoria, 195;
    Bishop of, 130
Vitoria, Francisco de, 27
Vives, Lluis, 78
Von Stohrer, 185

Wars:
    independence, 39;
    Franco-Russian, 43;
    World War I, 55, 106, 111, 137;
    World War II, 12, 137, 161, 162,
        174, 178, 180, 191, 202, 209,
        219
Washington, 140, 184, 201, 211,
    220, 228, 249, 256, 258, 271, 273;
    Capitol, 184
Weimar:
    constitution of, 76;
    Republic of, 69
Welcher (House of), 32
White Book, 185
White Russians, 207
Wolf, Erwin, 167
Workers' Alliance, 91, 94, 95, 96
Workers' and Peasants's Bloc (see
    BOC)
Workers's Brotherhood of Catholic
    Action (see HOAC)
Workers' commissions, 226, 227,
    253, 264, 266
Workers' Congress, 43

Workers' Federation, 44, 50
Workers' movement, 293;
    agitation, 292, 293
Working class, 293, 296, 297;
    anarchist penetration, 293;
    CNS penetration, 293;
    Communist penetration, 293;
    Socialist penetration, 293
World Trade-Union Federation,
    212

Yagüe, Juan (General), 135, 144,
    157
Yeste, 107
Youth attitudes, 231;
    post-Franco, 274
Yugoslavia, 161, 211, 240, 275,
    276;
    aid to Spanish Communist
    Party, 276, 293

Zaragoza, 18, 98, 119, 124, 130,
    151, 153, 179, 217;
    American air base, 258
    Archbishop of, 57
Zarzuela Palace, 290
Zugazagoitia, Julían, 154, 189
Zurich, 169